Foundations of
ENGLISH

Executive Editor: Katherine Cleveland

Editors: Laura Brown, Caitlin Clark, Caitlin Edahl

Designers: Bryan Mitchell, James Smalls, Patrick Thompson, Tee Jay Zajac

Cover Design: James Smalls

VP Research & Development: Marcel Prevuznak

VP Sales & Marketing: Emily Cook

A division of Quant Systems, Inc.

546 Long Point Road

Mount Pleasant, SC 29464

Printed in the United States of America 🇺🇸

10 9 8 7 6 5 4 3 2

ISBN: 978-1-941552-59-9

Table of Contents

Table of Contents

Chapter 1
Study Skills

Understanding Different Learning Styles

Think about the last time you gave a friend directions to your house. How did you do it?

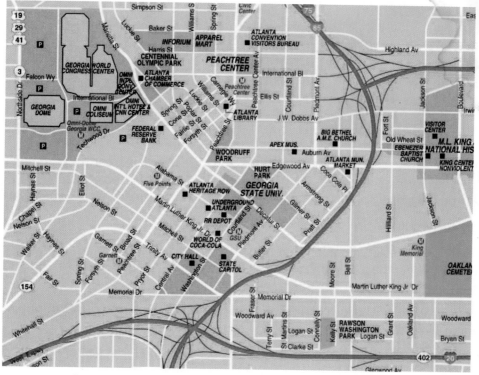

One person may find this map helpful while another may find it confusing.

Most likely, the way you gave those directions affected how easily your friend found the destination. You thought printing out a map would be the best choice, but your friend had a hard time following all of the turns. After arriving at your house, he or she told you that a list of street names would have worked better.

In this example, the map that you gave your friend wasn't *wrong*; it just wasn't the most *helpful*. This is because different people understand information in different ways. While you would have been lost without a map, your friend found it confusing.

The different ways that people learn new information are often called **learning styles**. You've probably heard this term used before, and you might even be familiar with some of the commonly discussed types of learning styles.

This lesson is going to focus on the system developed by researchers Richard Felder and Linda K. Silverman. They organize learning styles into four pairs:

Visual and Verbal Learning

Active and Reflective Learning

Sensing and Intuitive Learning

Sequential and Global Learning

Within each pair of learning styles, Felder and Silverman found that most people lean toward one style over the other. However, learning styles aren't clear-cut. You should think about each pair of preferences as a scale. Some people might be closer to one side or the other; some people might be closer to the middle.

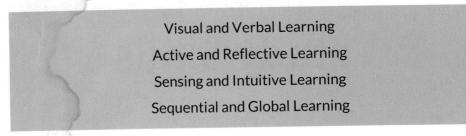

For example, you may feel equally comfortable learning to change the oil in a car by watching a video or reading a manual, but one of your classmates might feel much more comfortable watching a video. This probably means that you fall closer to the middle of the Visual-Verbal scale while your classmate falls closer to the Visual side.

Being familiar with learning styles is valuable in every part of your life. At school, you can use the knowledge of your own preferences to become a better student. Tailoring your study habits to fit your learning styles will help you work more efficiently.

You can also use learning styles on the job or in your personal life by adapting your communication to the specific needs of your audience.

In this lesson, you will learn about the following learning styles:

Visual and Verbal Learning
Active and Reflective Learning
Sensing and Intuitive Learning
Sequential and Global Learning

You will then apply this knowledge in Lesson 1.2 to identify success strategies that fit your own personal learning preferences.

Further Resources
The learning styles described in this lesson are based on the research of Richard Felder and Linda K. Silverman. To read more about learning styles and strategies, visit Richard Felder's website: http://www.ncsu.edu/felder-public/.

Visual and Verbal Learning

When you think of the word *visual*, you probably think of something that you can see with your vision. **Visual learners** use images to learn new concepts. Pictures, shapes, and colors are much more memorable to visual learners than words. Because of this, these learners may feel lost or distracted when they aren't able to see the information.

In contrast, **verbal learners** understand information from words. While they might find visuals helpful or interesting, they learn more from reading or hearing about a concept than from seeing it. These learners are usually good at remembering what people said, but they may struggle to remember what people look like.

Visual and verbal learners usually find different kinds of resources useful.

Visual learners prefer resources like these:

photos	charts	maps	demonstrations
videos	animations	diagrams	color-coding

Verbal learners prefer resources like these:

books	summaries	class notes	podcasts
articles	audiobooks	videos	journals

> **Reflection Questions**
> You've probably heard the phrase, "A picture is worth a thousand words." How does this phrase fit into your understanding of visual and verbal learning styles? What are some situations when a picture would be more effective than words?

Visual and verbal learning are closely related. Usually, both types of information are necessary to understand something fully.

Imagine that you're trying to put together a new desk. Inside the package, you find a stack of boards and a bag of hardware: nails, screws, and nuts. If the instruction manual were just text, you might have a hard time understanding the differences between the types of screws. If the manual were just pictures, you might have a hard time knowing which board to use next. In this example, a mix of both text and pictures is necessary to help you understand the instructions completely.

> **Group Activity**
> As a group, make a list of at least five learning resources you commonly use at school, at work, or in everyday life. Then, discuss the percentage of visual and verbal learning in each. Be prepared to defend your conclusions to the class.

Students can sometimes feel tempted to use their learning styles as an excuse. For example, a visual learner might think, "Since I'm visual, I won't learn anything from a class reading. I'm not going to waste my time doing this assignment."

Remember that people aren't *just* visual or *just* verbal. Almost everyone can benefit from both types of learning. In this case, the student should try reading the assignment first, then looking up a diagram of the topic or drawing a flowchart of the information.

Active and Reflective Learning

"If you always act before reflecting you can jump into things prematurely and get into trouble, while if you spend too much time reflecting you may never get anything done."

- Richard Felder and Barbara Soloman

Active learners like to be active. These are the kinds of people who enjoy lively class discussions or group projects. They are not afraid to try out new ideas and share what they have learned with others.

Because active learners like participating in activities, sitting through a class lecture can be difficult. When active learners are studying on their own, they stay alert by quizzing themselves with flashcards or making up review games.

The following statements best describe an active learner:

> I enjoy getting together with friends to work on projects.
>
> I pace around when I'm thinking about something important.
>
> I don't like wasting time planning out every single detail.
>
> I consider myself more of a hands-on learner.

Reflective learners, on the other hand, generally like to reflect on new information by themselves. Reflecting simply means thinking about something quietly and calmly.

It can take reflective learners a little longer to get used to new ideas, so they generally prefer to study a topic independently before discussing it with anyone else.

The following statements best describe a reflective learner:

> I like listening to music while I'm reading or studying.
>
> I sometimes practice important conversations in my head.
>
> I am good at figuring out things on my own.
>
> I sometimes find myself procrastinating on big projects.

Although everyone falls at different places on the Active-Reflective scale, finding a balance between both learning styles is important.

Active learners need to slow down and think about what they're learning. Otherwise, they might miss the *why* behind their work. Reflective learners need to force themselves to take action so they don't get stuck in the planning stage.

Reflection Questions

Imagine that one of your friends has asked you to tutor her in biology. What are some specific ways that you could use active learning in your tutoring sessions? What are some specific ways that you could use reflective learning?

Sensing and Intuitive Learning

The word *sensing* is related to your five senses. In science, the senses are used to observe nature and establish facts. **Sensing learners**, therefore, like to solve problems through methods that are logical and scientific. They are the most comfortable with objective facts and don't like surprises. Because sensing learners are practical, they like to see how their work connects to real life.

The word *intuitive* comes from the word *intuition*, which means knowing something by instinct or "gut feeling." **Intuitive learners** enjoy exploring all the possibilities in a situation. They often find new and creative ways to solve a problem and feel comfortable working with abstract ideas and topics. Generally, intuitive learners dislike memorizing facts.

If a sensing learner and an intuitive learner were both shown this photo, they would probably ask different types of questions.

Photo courtesy of Wikimedia Commons

Sensing	Intuitive
<ul><li>Who is this girl?</li><li>Who is the photographer who took this photo?</li><li>What was happening in the area when this photo was taken?</li></ul>	<ul><li>What is this girl thinking?</li><li>Why does this photo grab our attention?</li><li>What is the photographer trying to tell us with this photo?</li></ul>

According to Richard Felder and Barbara Soloman, "Everybody is sensing sometimes and intuitive sometimes." If you were a completely sensing person, you would never try new restaurants or enjoy hanging out with friends. If you were a completely intuitive person, you would ignore practical tasks like paying your cell phone bill because your head would always be in the clouds.

Both learning styles are also important in any profession or subject. Think about what this would look like in the medical field. A nurse has to memorize objective facts, like the procedure for taking blood pressure or the potential side effects of a prescription drug. However, all patients are different. Nurses need the ability to find creative solutions in situations that aren't perfect textbook examples.

> **Further Resources**
> Richard Felder and Linda K. Silverman based their idea of sensing and intuitive learning, in part, on an idea proposed by psychologist Carl Jung. One of the most famous applications of Jung's theory is the Myers-Briggs test, a test that divides personalities into sixteen types.
> You can read more about the differences between sensing and intuitive personality types on the Myers-Briggs website: http://www.myersbriggs.org/my-mbti-personality-type/mbti-basics/sensing-or-intuition.htm.

> **Group Activity**
> As a group, choose a fictional character from a book or movie. Decide if this character is a sensing or intuitive learner and make a list of specific pieces of evidence that supports your conclusion.

Sequential and Global Learning

Sequential learners prefer to learn information in a linear sequence. (*Linear* means step-by-step in a straight line.) Once they understand one piece of information, they are ready to move on to the next. These types of learners may feel overwhelmed by a project or task unless it has been broken down into orderly steps. While sequential learners will understand the details, they may not fully understand the big picture.

A sequential learner might make one of the following statements:

> I love checking things off my list.
>
> Tell me what I need to do first.
>
> Some people call me a perfectionist.

In contrast, **global learners** like to understand the big-picture global ideas first. They see the learning process as a web of related information. A global learner will store up knowledge until suddenly everything fits together and makes sense. This process is usually disorganized and random. Even after they've solved a problem, global learners may have a hard time understanding the details or explaining the solution.

A global learner might make one of the following statements:

> Describe the big picture for me.
>
> Just do what I did.
>
> I'll come back to that later.

Both learning styles have their own strengths and weaknesses. Because sequential learners absorb information at a regular pace, they catch on to new topics quickly. They are also able to work on a task without understanding how that task is related to the whole idea. This ability helps sequential learners perform well on tests or evaluations, but it can also prevent them from fully understanding what they're doing.

Global learners are very good at understanding the overall purpose and meaning of a project. They see relationships between ideas and events, which helps them apply their knowledge to new situations. However, global learners can take longer to understand a concept and may feel lost up until they do.

In both cases, understanding the challenges of sequential and global learning styles can help prevent frustration for these types of learners.

Group Activity

As a group, design two posters. One should represent sequential learning, and the other should represent global learning. Present both posters to your class, making sure to explain the reasons behind your design choices.

Learning Style Tip

If you're a **visual** learner and you're having trouble remembering the eight learning styles, try drawing an icon to represent each one. For example, visual learning could be represented by an eye while verbal learning could be represented by a speech bubble. Make a list of learning styles and icons to use while you study.

Lesson Wrap-up

Here's a review of the 4 pairs of learning styles:

- **Visual**: learning information through **pictures, shapes, and colors**
- **Verbal**: learning information through **written and spoken words**

- **Active**: learning information through **participation in activities**
- **Reflective**: learning information through **independent study**

- **Sensing**: learning information through **logical methods and objective facts**
- **Intuitive**: learning information through **creative methods and abstract ideas**

- **Sequential**: learning information through **a step-by-step process**
- **Global**: learning information through **seeing the big picture**

Key Terms

Active Learning: learning information through participation in activities

Global Learning: learning information through seeing the big picture

Intuitive Learning: learning information through creative methods and abstract ideas

Learning Style: the different ways that people learn new information

Reflective Learning: learning information through independent study

Sensing Learning: learning information through logical methods and objective facts

Sequential Learning: learning information through a step-by-step process

Verbal Learning: learning information through written and spoken words

Visual Learning: learning information through pictures, shapes, and colors

Lesson 1.2
Determining Your Personal Learning Styles

In the past, you have probably taken a course that didn't "click" with you. You paid close attention during class time and completed all the homework, but you still felt like your instructor was speaking a foreign language. This situation was even more frustrating because your best friend took the same course and loved it.

At the time, maybe you thought that your teacher didn't know how to teach or that your friend was just smarter than you. But were these thoughts really accurate?

Learning can become frustrating when you don't recognize the source of your confusion.

Part of the problem could have been the way the material was covered. If you're more of an active learner, but your class involved a lot of lectures, you probably had a hard time paying attention to your instructor. On the other hand, if you're a reflective learner, a class made up of group activities might have overwhelmed you.

In these situations, knowing your personal learning styles can help you overcome your frustration. While you can't change the structure of the course itself, you can change your study habits to learn more effectively.

> Reflection Questions
> Do you think it's possible for a person's learning styles to change? Why or why not?

In Lesson 1.1, you learned about the eight different types of **learning styles**:

- **Visual**: learning information through **pictures, shapes, and colors**
- **Verbal**: learning information through **written and spoken words**

- **Active**: learning information through **participation in activities**
- **Reflective**: learning information through **independent study**

- **Sensing**: learning information through **logical methods and objective facts**
- **Intuitive**: learning information through **creative methods and abstract ideas**

- **Sequential**: learning information through **a step-by-step process**
- **Global**: learning information through **seeing the big picture**

In this lesson, you will learn about the following:

Exploring Your Personal Learning Styles
Learning Style Strategies
Learning Styles Outside of School

Further Resources
The learning styles described in this lesson are based on the research of Richard Felder and Barbara Soloman. Richard Felder's website has a short quiz to help you determine your learning styles. The results will also show you which of your learning styles seems to be stronger and which seem to be more balanced. You can take the quiz here: https://www.webtools.ncsu.edu/learningstyles/

Exploring Your Personal Learning Styles

To find your personal learning styles, you need to think about your past learning experiences and study habits. Read through these student profiles carefully. In each pair, circle the profile that seems to describe you best; if both profiles fit you equally, circle both.

Visual Learner	Verbal Learner
You learn best when your instructor uses PowerPoints and charts in class. Even when you pay close attention, you feel like long lectures go right over your head. If a friend tries to describe something, you often ask him or her to draw a picture so that you can visualize the concept or object more clearly. After meeting people for the first time, you can usually picture their faces, but you can't always remember the details of your conversation.	You take thorough notes during class and save them to study later. Although you might think lectures are a bit boring, you can generally follow everything that your instructor is saying. You find written or verbal instructions helpful when you're doing something for the first time. If you think about a trip or vacation that you took in the past, it's difficult for you to picture the places that you visited.
Active Learner	**Reflective Learner**
You enjoy working with classmates on group activities and feel confident sharing your opinions and ideas right away. You're a hands-on learner who doesn't want to waste too much time talking about a problem. In the past, you've had to redo a project at school or work because you didn't fully understand the guidelines before getting started.	You prefer to work in a quiet place on your own. While you're not afraid to join class discussions, you feel most comfortable sharing your thoughts after you've had a chance to study the topics first. You enjoy planning parties and other activities almost as much as you enjoy attending them.

Sensing Learner	Intuitive Learner
Your friends always tell you that you have a lot of common sense. Because of this, your favorite classes involve skills that apply to the real world. You dislike discussing theories or hypothetical questions. When you make a decision, you carefully weigh the options and make the most practical choice. If a solution has worked for you in the past, you feel comfortable using it again.	You are creative and imaginative. In class, you enjoy discussing theories and making predictions. You find new solutions to tough problems by thinking outside the box. If a job is repetitive or routine, you start to feel frustrated. You sometimes rely on your instincts to make big decisions.
Sequential Learner	Global Learner
You learn best in small steps. For papers, you usually write all of the paragraphs in order, starting with the introduction. You're very detail-oriented, but you sometimes struggle to understand the big picture. At home, you always follow recipes or instructions step-by-step.	You like to know the goal of a project before you start working. If an instructor starts with the details, you feel overwhelmed and confused. When you learn something new, you often have a series of sudden "aha!" moments. You are always finding connections between topics you're covering in class or events happening in the news.

Learning Style Strategies

Now that you have a better idea of how you learn new information, you can use your learning styles to become a better student. In some cases, you might be able to ask your instructor to explain the information in a different way. Most instructors would be happy to meet with you during their office hours or recommend online resources you can use to review the material.

You can also brainstorm creative study ideas to use on your own. Remember that learning styles are never an excuse for bad study habits. You won't succeed by skipping classes or missing assignments.

Helpful Hint
Students sometimes find themselves struggling in class no matter how hard they work. This could be a sign of an undiagnosed learning disability. If you feel like this might be you, make an appointment to speak with your school's student disabilities office. They can help you figure out the reasons behind your difficulties and find helpful strategies for managing your work.

Visual and Verbal Learning

If you're a visual learner, you should use more pictures, charts, or graphs during your study time. Try using these strategies to become more successful:

- Create a visual timeline of people or events with photos from Google image search (https://www.google.com/imghp) or Wikimedia Commons. (http://commons.wikimedia.org/). Be sure to include any important names, facts, or dates next to each photo.

- Use highlighters or markers to color-code your class notes. For example, key terms could be highlighted blue while important names could be highlighted pink.
- Watch a YouTube (http://www.youtube.com/) video about the topic. If you find a helpful video, consider sharing it with the rest of your class.

If you're a verbal learner, look for opportunities to study with books or audio recordings. You can use these strategies to become more successful:

- Write or type a summary of class lectures and readings. You can use a notebook to keep hand-written notes organized or Google Docs (https://docs.google.com/) to keep digital documents organized and up-to-date.
- Listen to an audiobook while you're reading. Project Gutenberg (http://www.gutenberg.org/wiki/Gutenberg:The_Audio_Books_Project) has a collection of free classics, and your local library has modern titles to checkout or download.
- With your instructor's permission, record class lectures and listen to them at home. If you don't have an audio recorder, you can usually borrow one from the campus library.

Everyone learns best from a mix of visual and verbal learning. Don't limit yourself to just visuals or just text. Using a balance of both will help you make the most of your study time.

> **Learning Style Tip**
> If you are using the *Foundations of English* courseware, you can view a mini lecture for each lesson by clicking "Watch" in Learn mode. These videos contain audio for verbal learners and visuals for visual learners.

Active and Reflective Learning

If you're an active learner, you like to turn ideas into actions. To become more successful, try these strategies:

- Meet with a group of classmates for a study group. Assign a section of information to each group member and take turns teaching your topics to the rest of the group.
- Make your own practice quizzes or review games. You can use index cards or a website like Quizlet (http://quizlet.com/) to test yourself.
- Take short breaks while you're studying. Stretching your legs and getting a breath of fresh air can help you stay focused on less active tasks.

> **Helpful Hint**
> To create your own practice tests in Hawkes, click on the Tests tab, then Practice Tests, and then the Create Practice Test button. After taking the practice test, you can see a summary of your score and review the correct answers. Use your results to focus your study time on any specific lessons or topics you're struggling to master.

If you're a reflective learner, you usually spend time thinking about an idea before acting on it. Try using these strategies to become a more successful learner:

- Find a quiet **workspace** that's free from distractions. You can try using a white noise website like RainyMood (www.rainymood.com/) to block out noisy family members or roommates.
- Use a folder to save class notes and returned tests to review later. If you review them during class, don't be afraid to write down any corrected answers or notes.
- Use a notebook or note-taking app like Evernote (https://evernote.com/) to journal your thoughts about what you learned in class and how you can apply this to the world around you. Read back through your journal entries while you're preparing for class.

To learn more about workspaces, see Lesson 1.4.

Only acting or only reflecting can get you into trouble. If you act too quickly, you might not fully understand the information. On the other hand, if you spend too much time reflecting, you might put a task off until the last minute. Knowing your own tendencies can help you watch out for this kind of behavior. Work to find a balance of both learning styles.

Sensing and Intuitive Learning

If you're a sensing learner, you feel the most comfortable learning objective facts and applying those facts to the real world. You can use these strategies to become more successful:

- Research how a topic is used in real-life situations. Don't be afraid to talk with your instructor about how the information could apply to different professions.
- Use a site like Pinterest (http://www.pinterest.com) to start a collection of helpful study tips or project ideas. Just don't let yourself get distracted by double-chocolate caramel brownie recipes!
- Meet with a study group to discuss the *why* behind facts. Talking to people with different points of view can help you understand all sides of a topic.

If you're an intuitive learner, you enjoy thinking creatively. To become more successful, try these strategies:

- Use a variety of study locations. Sometimes a new location can help inspire you with new ideas.
- Listen to music while studying "boring" subjects. You can use an app like Spotify (https://www.spotify.com/) to make yourself a custom study playlist.
- Use a **planner** to keep assignments organized. An online resource like Google Calendar allows you to plan your schedule and set reminders for important tasks.

To learn more about planners, see Lesson 1.4.

Knowing your personal learning styles can help you recognize your own limitations. For example, if you know that you're a sensing learner, you may have to schedule yourself extra time to study abstract or theoretical ideas. If you know that you're an intuitive learner, you may need to spend extra time quizzing yourself over key terms or definitions.

Sequential and Global Learning

If you're a sequential learner, you learn information in small, linear steps. Try using these strategies to become more successful:

- Write down a list of key ideas from class readings. Then, arrange this information into an outline or bullet list that you can use to study later.
- Find a step-by-step tutorial on a site like WikiHow (http://www.wikihow.com/). You could even consider writing your own step-by-step directions to help you think through the entire process.
- Use checklists or to-do lists for large projects. You can print paper checklists or use an app like Wunderlist to keep a digital list (https://www.wunderlist.com/).

If you're a global learner, you learn information in random bursts of understanding and like to look at the big picture first. To become more successful:

- Skim through the table of contents or section headings before starting a reading. Use this information to get a better idea of how the different chapters or sections fit together.
- Draw a diagram to show how smaller ideas are connected to the main idea. Programs like Microsoft Word or PowerPoint have built-in tools to create flowcharts, cluster diagrams, and idea trees.
- Research a topic before starting a new reading or project. Even though it's not a reliable source for academic papers or presentations, Wikipedia (http://wikipedia.org) can be a great place to read an overview of a topic.

> **Learning Style Tip**
> If you're a **global** learner, take the time to read through the objectives at the beginning of each lesson. These will give you a general overview of the information that the lesson is going to cover.

When you feel lost or overwhelmed, it's frustrating. Use your knowledge of learning styles to help you find the source of this frustration and overcome it.

Sequential learners who are overwhelmed can break up a project or topic into smaller, more manageable tasks. Global learners who are lost or discouraged can use their knowledge of the big picture to help them understand the smaller details.

> **Reflection Questions**
> Every learning style has unique strengths and weaknesses. What are some of the strengths and weaknesses of your personal learning styles?

Learning Styles Outside of School

When you think about learning styles, you probably automatically think about school. However, your learning doesn't stop outside of the classroom. You can use the same learning styles strategies to help you find success at work or in your personal life.

Understanding your personal learning styles can help you succeed in the workplace.

At any job, you receive training. Sometimes, you complete a few weeks of formal training, and sometimes you have to learn on the job. Depending on the amount of training that's available, you may need to spend extra time studying and working on your own. Using your personal learning styles will help you work more efficiently and avoid potential frustrations.

> **Learning Style Tip**
> If you are an **active** learner, you may find it difficult to sit through long training sessions. Taking notes will keep you engaged in the material.

To learn more about taking good notes, see Lesson 1.6.

In your personal life, you're probably always learning new things whether you realize it or not. Just online, you can find tutorials teaching you to do anything from making a paper airplane to styling your hair like a celebrity. Now think about the books, recipes, magazines, manuals, brochures, and videos you encounter every day.

Knowing your learning styles can help you determine exactly which resource or technique is going to make the most sense to you. For a simple task, it may not make a big difference; however, for a more difficult task, like filing a tax return or changing a flat tire, you will be much more successful if your approach fits your personal learning styles.

> **Reflection Questions**
> How have you seen your learning styles affect the way you work at school, at your job, or in your personal life? Try to think of one specific example for each.

You will also have plenty of opportunities to use your knowledge of learning styles to improve your own communication. Whether you're with coworkers or family members, you can become a more effective communicator by using a variety of approaches.

Imagine that you're training a coworker to complete a task. While you've explained the steps multiple times and even given a short demonstration, he doesn't seem to be catching on. In this situation, your coworker could be a more active learner. Giving him a hands-on training might help him understand the process better.

Lesson Wrap-up

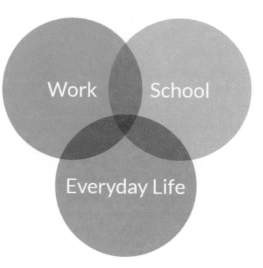

In this lesson, you learned that all eight learning styles not only have unique characteristics, but they also work best with different types of work and study strategies.

Take time to think about the ways that you learn best. Then, make a list of specific strategies that you can use to be successful in school, at work, and in everyday life. Having a solid understanding of your own strengths and weaknesses will help you build confidence in your own abilities.

> **Group Activity**
> Take ten to fifteen minutes to discuss everyone's personal learning styles. Then, come up with specific strategies that each group member could use to be more successful in class.

Key Terms

Active Learning: learning information through participation in activities

Global Learning: learning information through seeing the big picture

Intuitive Learning: learning information through creative methods and abstract ideas

Learning Style: the different ways that people learn new information

Planner: a place for you to organize your schedule and record any important tasks or responsibilities

Reflective Learning: learning information through independent study

Sensing Learning: learning information through logical methods and objective facts

Sequential Learning: learning information through a step-by-step process

Visual Learning: learning information through pictures, shapes, and colors

Verbal Learning: learning information through written and spoken words

Workspace: a location free from distractions and clutter for working and studying

Lesson 1.3

Understanding and Reducing Stress

Stress is part of life. At some point, everyone has experienced stress in school, at work, or in everyday life. A healthy amount can help you stay focused and motivated. Too much, however, will leave you feeling overwhelmed, exhausted, or physically sick.

School can be an especially stressful commitment whether you're returning for the first time in many years or starting right after high school. Not only are you trying to balance a full schedule, but you are also managing a large amount of work and learning new, challenging concepts. If you don't already have a strategy for dealing with this stress, you may find yourself feeling more and more overwhelmed.

> **Reflection Questions**
> Think about the last time you experienced stress. What was the situation? How did you deal with it?

While you'll never be able to avoid stress completely, you can learn ways to keep it under control. This lesson will help you understand the causes of stress and give you practical strategies for reducing it.

In this lesson, you will learn three ways to manage your stress more effectively:

Determine Causes of Stress

Put Everything into Perspective

Make a Plan to Move Forward

Determine Causes of Stress

The first step in managing stress is to understand what's causing it. Often, when we think of stress, we think of **external**, or outside, sources like class projects, job responsibilities, or family commitments. While these situations can be overwhelming, stressful situations usually involve an **internal conflict** as well.

For example, if you're feeling stressed out about an upcoming exam, you may also be experiencing fears about your class grade or GPA. Being aware of both external and internal reasons for stress will help you deal with your stress more completely.

External ▶ ◀ Internal

Read through each of the following scenarios. What external and internal factors might be causing stress in these situations?

> Jordan has been working as an administrative assistant for the last eight years. Eventually, he wants to become an office manager, so he decides to return to school to finish a two-year degree in office management. The first two weeks of class are overwhelming, and he is considering dropping out because of the amount of stress he is feeling.

> Kimani can't believe he missed marching band practice yesterday. Usually, he's very reliable, but this week he has struggled to juggle all of his commitments. It's pledge week at his fraternity, and auditions for the spring play start tomorrow. He is stressed out and worried about getting through the semester.

> Layla is having a difficult time managing her schedule. October is always the busiest month at work, so she's been working overtime for the last few weeks. She has two sons, which makes juggling work and school difficult. Her sister usually helps babysit the kids, but Layla hasn't spoken to her sister since their big fight last week. She's feeling overwhelmed by stress.

To start managing your stress, try making a list of external and internal causes. Be as specific as possible. You might end up with something that looks like this:

External Causes	Internal Causes
Class registration deadline	I'm worried about balancing my work and school schedules this semester.
Research paper for Economics	I'm nervous because it's 30% of my final grade, and there are so many steps.
Missed call from my brother	He's failing his classes, and I'm upset with him.
Speech class	I hate public speaking.
Asked to plan fundraiser booth	I'm feeling annoyed because I planned the last one.

Once you make a list of the situations and responsibilities causing your stress, you will be able to start managing them more effectively. You may even find that your list doesn't look quite as long as it feels.

Further Resources
A 2015 study (http://www.cbsnews.com/news/the-biggest-cause-of-stress-in-america-today/) found that money is the biggest cause of stress in America. This can be especially true in college, when you have tuition expenses, as well as transportation costs, textbooks, and more.
If you need help with your finances, the U.S. government has a helpful website (https://www.usa.gov/) with information about jobs, housing, and health care. You can also contact your school's financial aid office for more information about paying for college.

On Your Own

Think through the causes of your own stress and add them to the table below. Make sure to consider both external and internal sources.

External Causes	Internal Causes

Put Everything into Perspective

The next way to manage stress is to put it into perspective. Sometimes, when you're feeling stressed, every task seems equally huge and unmanageable. If you step back and re-evaluate, however, you'll probably find that not everything is as big as you thought. Dealing with five things can be overwhelming, but dealing with one big thing and four small things is much more manageable.

Factors like deadlines or time commitments can affect an item's importance. An assignment that's due tomorrow is probably more important than an assignment due next week. Similarly, a large project is generally more time-consuming than a small one. This means that you may need to start working on the larger assignment as soon as possible.

Helpful Hint
Be careful not to fall into the trap of procrastination! Even if an assignment isn't due immediately, getting a head start will help prevent stress later.

Regardless of deadlines and time commitments, some situations or responsibilities are simply more important than others. For example, registering for classes or resolving an argument with a family member is probably more important than getting a haircut.

Take the time to think through each situation honestly and ask yourself some of the following questions:

Is this a special circumstance that should take priority over other responsibilities?

Does this item have a deadline that makes it a priority?

Will I be able to focus on another item as long as this item is incomplete?

To start putting your stress into perspective, review the list of items causing you stress. Then, determine where each one would rank on a scale of 1-3, with 1 being the least important and 3 being the most important.

Stress	Rank	Reason
Class registration deadline	2	I'm worried about balancing my work and school schedules this semester.
Research paper for Economics	2	I'm nervous because it's 30% of my final grade, and there are so many steps.
Missed call from my brother	3	He's failing his classes, and I'm upset with him.
Speech class	I	I hate public speaking.
Asked to plan fundraiser booth	I	I'm feeling annoyed because I planned the last one.

On Your Own

Prioritize your own stress in the table below.

Stress	Rank	Reason

Gaining perspective on your stress will help you prioritize your time and energy. You can then focus on managing your stress and moving forward.

Learning Style Tip
If you're a **visual** learner, try converting your list into a cluster of shapes. Instead of a number, use shape size to indicate the importance of each item. The most important items should be largest while the least important items should be smallest.

Make a Plan to Move Forward

When you're stressed, you feel stuck, unsure how or where to make changes. It's easy to feel overwhelmed. However, once you've identified the causes of your stress and put them into perspective, you can begin finding ways to deal with them. To manage your stress more effectively, try some of these strategies:

- **Take action.** Now that you've identified the causes of your stress and decided which tasks and responsibilities are the most important, take action on them. Start at the top of your to-do list and check off each item as you complete it. If situations outside of your control are causing stress, consider asking a trusted friend or counselor for support and advice.

- **Keep yourself organized.** One way to manage stress is staying organized. This is especially important for assignments like research papers or presentations. Searching for important documents or files will waste time and add to your stress level. You also need to organize your schedule by setting aside time to complete the most important tasks first, especially if there is a deadline looming.

- **Don't be afraid to ask for help.** Asking for help can be difficult. You may feel embarrassed about needing help or unsure where to find it. While you're in school, you have a number of resources available. Most colleges and universities provide a **Student Services** office that can help you find counseling or tutoring services. For other types of stress, reach out to a trusted friend or a professional counselor.

- **Relax and recharge.** Your physical and mental health play a big role in how you respond to stress. If you're exhausted, even small situations or responsibilities can seem overwhelming. Getting enough sleep is one of the best ways to prepare yourself to handle stress. You can also try relaxation techniques or yoga to clear your mind and prepare you for the day ahead.

- **Prevent stress before it starts.** One of the best ways to prevent stress is to avoid procrastination. The longer you put off a task, the more stressful it will become. If you're a person who works better under pressure, try setting mini-deadlines to keep yourself on track.

Further Resources

Many studies show that dietary habits can impact a person's mental well-being. To learn more, listen to this discussion (http://www.npr.org/sections/thesalt/2014/07/14/329529110/food-mood-connection-how-you-eat-can-amp-up-or-tamp-down-stress) of a study conducted by National Public Radio with the Robert Wood Johnson Foundation and the Harvard School of Public Health.

Lesson Wrap-up

Key Terms

External Stress: outside sources of stress like class projects, job responsibilities, or family commitments

Internal Conflict: fears and anxieties that are not easily recognized as sources of stress

Student Services: the office responsible for academic advising and career services

---

Lesson 1.4

Keeping Yourself Organized

Balancing your different roles as a student, employee, parent, sibling, or volunteer can be difficult. Perhaps you're taking fifteen class hours this semester, working twenty-eight hours a week, and caring for an elderly family member.

In the past, you've been able to keep a mental to-do list, but recently, you've found yourself struggling to stay on top of your schedule and responsibilities. Not only did you miss an appointment with your advisor, but you also forgot to pay an electric bill and arrived two hours late for your shift at work. What happened?

No one has a perfect memory. The more responsibilities you have, the more likely you are to forget one or two of them. Missing one class or one bill payment may not seem like a big deal, but these situations can quickly snowball into a huge mess. If you're not careful, you could even end up with a failing grade or an expensive fine.

Reflection Questions
Make a list of your different roles in school, at work, and in your everyday life. What responsibilities have you taken on as part of these roles? Have you ever felt overwhelmed by these responsibilities?

Staying on top of your responsibilities is much easier when you have a solid plan for keeping everything organized. Some people are natural organizers. They love having a place for everything, and they love keeping everything in its place. Most of us, however, have to work a little harder to stay organized. Even though organization may not come naturally to you, it is an important skill that will prove useful in every aspect of your life.

Learning Style Tip
People with certain **learning styles** tend to stay more organized than others. If you lean toward **active** or **global** learning, you may have to work harder to keep yourself organized. Don't be discouraged! Anyone can learn better organization skills with the right amount of practice.

This lesson will discuss three helpful ways to keep yourself organized and on track:

Keep a Planner
Use a File System
Create a Workspace

Keep a Planner

A **planner** is a place for you to organize your schedule and record any important tasks or responsibilities. Keeping all of this information in one place will help make sure that you don't forget something important.

Helpful Hint
Most stores sell two types of planners: those organized around the calendar year (January-December) and those organized around the academic year (August-July). While you're in school, it will probably make the most sense to use a planner that covers the academic year.

Most planners include pages for both monthly and weekly calendars. Because monthly planner pages don't have a lot of space for each individual day, they work best as a broad overview of your schedule. You should use these pages to record important events like work shifts, upcoming due dates, or appointments.

In contrast, weekly planner pages include plenty of space for each day. You can use this extra room to record the details of homework assignments and daily to-do items.

Monthly planners are perfect for keeping track of work shifts, important due dates, or appointments.

Weekly planners are perfect for keeping track of homework assignments and daily to-do items.

Before filling out your planner, gather everything with important dates and deadlines, including any course **syllabi**. These documents include class policies, major project deadlines, and assignment due dates. You should also gather the following items:

- Your work schedule
- Your class schedule
- Your school's academic calendar
- Billing statements for bank accounts, electricity, utilities, etc.
- Itineraries for any trips you have planned

Use a top-down strategy to fill in your planner. This simply means adding the most important commitments before scheduling any non-essential events or tasks.

Checklist: Filling in a Student Planner

☐ Start by adding the most important items to your schedule: work shifts, medical appointments, family commitments, homework due dates, or monthly bill payment deadlines.

☐ Next, schedule any items that are important, but flexible, like study sessions or grocery trips.

☐ Finally, reward yourself for a productive week by planning fun, relaxing activities with friends and family.

Learning Style Tip
As an **active** learner, you prefer learning in a collaborative atmosphere. Since you are building your planner, this is a good time to reach out to some of your classmates and schedule regular study group sessions.

Once you've filled out your planner, you need to stay up-to-date by recording any changes or additions. If your instructor pushes back a due date or if you switch shifts with a coworker, record the change as soon as possible. To avoid accidentally over-scheduling yourself, check your planner before making any new commitments.

Helpful Hint
Be sure to use consistent strategies for updating your planner. Choose a specific day and time when you'll review and update your schedule for the week.

Learning Style Tip
Reflective learners need time to reflect on new material in order to understand it. When you review/update your weekly planner, try to schedule time for summarizing class notes or creating a list of questions about new concepts.

If you have a laptop or smartphone, you can use a **digital planner** to keep yourself organized. An app like Google Calendar allows you to record your schedule, color-code different types of events, and set email or text alerts for upcoming to-do items.

Some people prefer to use digital planners, while others prefer to use hand-written planners. Some people even use both. Based on your own preferences and tendencies, take time to determine what type of planner would fit you best.

Digital planners allow you to keep track of important dates on a computer or phone.

Reflection Questions
Think about the differences between a paper and a digital planner. What are some of the benefits and drawbacks of each?

Use a File System

Saving class papers is a good idea for a variety of reasons. For example, one of the best ways to make the most of your study time is to use quizzes and worksheets from class. You can review the topics and look up answers for the questions you got wrong.

If you don't have a system for filing your important documents, they will end up in a disorganized pile.

Keeping track of class handouts is also beneficial for reviewing class policies and assignment guidelines. Many instructors include overall guidelines for all major assignments in the course syllabus. Before turning in an assignment, you'll want to have these guidelines handy so that you can make sure you have followed the directions exactly.

It's important not only to save your papers, but also to keep them organized; otherwise, they may end up in a crumpled mess at the bottom of a backpack or lost in a junk drawer. Use the following suggestions to create a system for organizing your papers.

The first step in staying organized is knowing *what* to save. If you save everything, the sheer amount of documents or files can be overwhelming.

While you're in school, a good rule of thumb is to save any papers from your current classes. Once the semester is over, you can throw away any old tests or handouts you won't need anymore. You should consider keeping copies of important papers or projects to include in your portfolio. These documents may be helpful for future classes or jobs.

> **Helpful Hint**
> One way to reduce clutter is to save electronic copies of important items and recycle old paper copies.

The second step in staying organized is deciding *where* to save everything. File folders or notebooks hold groups of documents or papers together. You should keep a separate folder for each of your classes and responsibilities. Labeling and color-coding the items in your folders will help you quickly find the information you need. For example, in your *Math 098* folder, you might group the documents into *Handouts, Returned Tests,* and *Class Notes.*

At home, you can use a similar system for bills, receipts, or other important papers. Keeping a copy of these documents can be helpful in case of a lost check or misunderstanding. Even bills you pay online will send you a confirmation number. You should print or save this number in case a company ever loses track of your payment. Bills older than one year can be thrown away.

Electronic documents should also be organized into files. Keeping everything saved on your desktop is overwhelming and confusing. Follow the same guidelines on your computer or flash drive and create a folder for each class or responsibility. Put any documents or emails into the correct folder. If you have multiple papers or projects for the same class, you should create subfolders for each one.

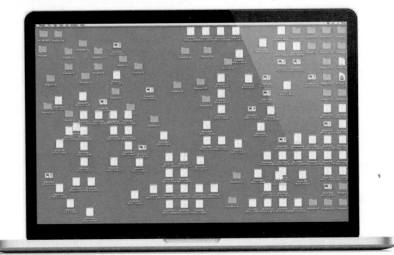

A disorganized computer is overwhelming and confusing.

> Reflection Questions
> Think about the way you usually organize important papers. Do you have a system? Are there any aspects of your current system that could be improved?

Create a Workspace

An organized **workspace** is essential for working efficiently. You should find a place that is comfortable and free from clutter. Some potential workspaces could be a desk or a kitchen table. You also need space for any tools such as textbooks, calculators, or computers. It's much easier to work when you have plenty of space to spread out.

Finding a good workspace often requires planning, especially if your assignment involves special equipment or collaboration with classmates. Even when working on your own, planning ahead can ensure that you are able to find the ideal workspace to fit your needs.

A good workspace should have plenty of space for your computer, textbooks, and supplies.

On Your Own

To think through your own study preferences and habits, check the box in each pair that best fits your studying preferences.

Do you prefer studying in the morning or evening?

- ☐ Morning
- ☐ Evening

When you study, do you prefer silence or noise?

- ☐ Silence
- ☐ Noise

Would you rather study inside or outside?

☐ Inside
☐ Outside

Do you prefer studying alone or in a group?

☐ Alone
☐ Group

Depending on the way you study and the type of work you need to do, you may need to wake up at an earlier time or reserve a room in the library. Taking the time to plan a good workspace will help you be as productive during your study and work times as possible.

In a crowded house or dorm room, finding a workspace can be tricky. You may need to get a little creative. It might not be practical for you to work at the table while everyone else is talking/eating. Consider setting up a quiet space for yourself in your bedroom.

If you don't have a room to yourself, ask your roommates if you can establish a "quiet hour" when you all agree to dedicate the room to studying only. If this doesn't work, you may have to get really creative by hanging up a curtain around your bed and buying a pair of cheap earplugs.

> **Reflection Questions**
> Think about your personal learning styles. How are your workspace preferences related to the way you learn? What types of environments should certain types of learners use or avoid?

If you don't have space to work at home, you can consider creating a mobile workspace at a local library or coffee shop. Use a pencil pouch to hold all the pens, calculators, and smaller items that you will need, and use a backpack for books and other heavy items. Making a checklist will help you remember everything you need.

Many campus buildings have study rooms available. Take advantage of these spaces and don't be afraid to get creative. You may even find that you're more productive in a new kind of environment.

Regardless of where you work, a workspace should be free from distractions. Some people find complete silence distracting, while others can't work without it. If you're easily sidetracked by the television, don't sit near one. If you get caught up talking to friends or family, stay away from a local hangout. On the other hand, if music or noise help you concentrate, make sure to have access to those in your workspace.

> **Helpful Hint**
> A website or app like Google Play Music (https://play.google.com/music/listen?szsbn=1) can help you find the perfect study soundtrack. In addition to music, you can also listen to background sounds like ocean waves or white noise.

You need to create a clear computer workspace as well. If you've been keeping your documents organized, you should already be halfway there. Because an important aspect of a workspace is removing distractions, make sure you don't have social media sites like Facebook or Twitter open while working.

Group Activity
Draw a picture of your ideal workspace. As a group, share your drawings and discuss similarities and differences.

Lesson Wrap-up

Key Terms

Active Learning: learning information through participation in activities

Digital Planner: an online calendar or organizer

Global Learning: learning information through seeing the big picture

Learning Style: the different ways that people learn new information

Planner: a tool for organizing your daily schedule and recording important tasks or responsibilities

Reflective Learning: learning information through independent study

Syllabus: a course overview with information about instructor office hours, class policies, major projects, and assignment due dates

Workspace: a location free from distractions and clutter for working and studying

Lesson 1.5

Managing Your Time Effectively

Have you ever made it to the end of a day and wondered where all your time went? Sometimes, it feels like there aren't enough hours in the day. When you think back through your schedule, though, you realize that you spent a couple hours on Twitter and an hour or so watching TV, and by the time you sat down to work on your homework, you were already exhausted.

It's easy to lose track of time when you're watching TV or playing video games.

Finding time to work can be difficult. Some interruptions, like unexpected traffic or family emergencies, are simply outside of your control. Other distractions, however, are inside your control: hanging out with friends, watching TV, spending time on hobbies, etc. While you should allow time for these activities, you need to make sure that they don't fill up all of your time, especially if you have an upcoming deadline for a school project or a work assignment.

Managing your time is important because you can never get that time back. Once it's gone, you either have to rush yourself or cram the work into your schedule. Not only will you start feeling stressed out, but you may also find yourself turning in late or incomplete work.

This lesson will discuss three strategies for managing your time more effectively:

Use a Time Budget
Take Breaks
Avoid Multitasking

Reflection Questions
How well do you think you manage your time? Do you have specific strategies that you use to keep yourself on track?

Use a Time Budget

Time budgets help you find the time you need to complete necessary projects and tasks. Just like a financial budget shows you how you spend your money, a **time budget** shows you how you spend your time. You can then identify "wasted" time that could be used more productively.

To begin budgeting your time, you first need to get an idea of how you usually spend it. For one week, keep track of everything you do in fifteen-minute time blocks. To be as accurate as possible, you should write everything down as it happens. Don't wait until the end of the week to add your activities as you probably won't remember everything accurately.

Here's an example of what your record of activities might look like:

Time	Activity
12:00am – 7:30am	Sleeping
7:30am – 8:15am	Getting ready for class
8:15am – 8:45am	Driving
8:45am – 9:00am	Walking to class
9:00am – 10:30am	Speech class
10:30am – 10:45am	Getting to next class
10:45am – 11:30am	English class

Once you've recorded your entire week in fifteen-minute time blocks, you can calculate how much time you spend on different types of activities. First, review the activities you entered and assign each of them to one of the following categories:

- **Sleep** – Time spent sleeping
- **Meal** – Time spent preparing food and eating meals
- **Work** – Time spent at work and any travel time to work
- **Class** – Time spent in class and any travel time to class
- **Study** – Time spent studying and working on class assignments
- **Extracurricular** – Time spent on activities like club meetings, volunteer work, and sports practice

- **Exercise** – Time spent exercising
- **Personal** – Time spent on personal care, laundry, appointments, etc.
- **Family** – Time spent on family commitments
- **Entertainment** – Time spent on hobbies, TV, movies, and the internet
- **Social** – Time spent at parties or with friends
- **Other** – Time that doesn't fit into another category

On Your Own

Now, use the table below to add up how many hours you spent on each category. These calculations will help you determine what changes you need to make to budget your time more effectively.

Time Budget Calculator			
Hour	**Minutes**	**Activity**	**Category**
Total:	**Total:**		

Look back at your week of activities and think through the following questions:

- Do you feel like you had enough time to fulfill all your responsibilities?
- Were you surprised by how much time was spent on any particular activity?
- What are some important activities you should have spent more time doing?

- What are some activities you'd like to spend more time doing in the future?
- What are some activities you'd like to spend less time doing in the future?

Based on your answers to the previous questions, create a new weekly time budget. One week contains only 168 hours. If you want to spend more time on a particular activity, you'll need to find that time somewhere. Be sure to include an appropriate length of time for each of your activities, including sleep and travel time.

> **Further Resources**
> Insufficient sleep can keep you from doing your best in school and at work. This page (http://www.cdc.gov/Features/Sleep/) on the Centers for Disease Control and Prevention (CDC) website explains how to improve your chances of getting quality rest and how many hours of sleep you should be getting based on your age.

Try using your time budget to help you plan out all 168 hours in the upcoming week. Your **planner** should already include important items like classes, work shifts, and appointments. Use the same top-down strategy you used for your planner to add study sessions, meals, travel times, and morning/evening routines to your schedule. Finally, add any remaining activities, making sure to stay within your budgeted hours.

> **Helpful Hint**
> As a general rule, you should set aside at least two hours of study time for every one hour of class time. That means that a three-credit course would require at least six hours of outside work per week.

Once you have the week completely scheduled, compare it with last week's time blocks. How different do they look?

While you probably won't plan all 168 hours every week, you can use your time budget to keep yourself focused and on track. Keep a copy of your budget in your planner and use it to prioritize the time you spend on important tasks, like school work, and limit the time you spend on extra activities, like checking Instagram.

Take Breaks

When you are working on an important project or studying for a big exam, you may feel tempted to go as long as possible without taking a break. This is especially true when you're working or studying at the last minute. While staying focused is important, working yourself until you're mentally drained will lower the quality of your work and force you to take even more time recovering.

Working without any breaks can lead to exhaustion and even injury.

Think about the way that overworking can affect your body physically. If you're weight-training, you have to take frequent breaks both between individual sets and entire workout sessions. If you don't let your muscles recover, you will feel exhausted, start using bad form, and possibly injure yourself. A pulled muscle or back sprain could leave you laid up for weeks.

Just like taking breaks helps your physical body recover, it will also help your brain reenergize and refocus. During study sessions, you should plan to take a **study break** at least once an hour. If you usually work indoors, take this time to get a breath of fresh air and clear your head.

Study and work breaks should usually last around five minutes. The longer the break, the harder it is to start working again. Instead of stopping for half an hour, take a five-minute break and reward yourself with some downtime when the task is complete.

> Helpful Hint
> If you find your breaks getting longer and longer, try setting a phone alarm or kitchen timer to remind yourself when it's time to start working again. You can also use an online timer like Timer-Tab (http://www.timer-tab.com/).

Some courses have a built-in break during the middle of the class period. Stand up and move around even if you don't feel tired. Even this little bit of physical movement can help you think more clearly.

> Further Resources
> Whether you're writing a paper or working on a home project, taking regular breaks can help you work better. To learn more, read this article (http://www.nytimes.com/2012/06/17/jobs/take-breaks-regularly-to-stay-on-schedule-workstation.html) from *The New York Times*.

Avoid Multitasking

Multitasking is working on more than one task at a time. When you have multiple assignments to complete, you may be tempted to work on two or three of them at once. While this strategy might seem like a time-saver, you will probably end up using more time than if you had done each task individually. Not only will you have to switch your focus from one task to the next, but you will also make more mistakes that will need to be corrected later.

Multitasking usually ends up wasting time instead of saving it.

Multitasking can often become an excuse for distractions, especially electronic ones. Have you ever tried to write a paper, watch TV, and Snapchat friends all at the same time? You probably did one of these things well and two of these things badly. That's because your brain can't give its full attention to three tasks at once. To stay focused in class or while studying, try stashing your phone in your backpack or purse and staying logged out of your computer until you need it.

> **Group Activity**
> As a group, come up with ten to fifteen potential distractions. Then, have each group member rank the items as high, medium, or low depending on how distracting they are. Compare your answers.

People don't multitask nearly as well as they think they do. One of the most dangerous examples of this is texting while driving. Research studies have shown that multitasking while driving is similar to or even worse than driving while drunk.

While multitasking on a project for school or work may not be dangerous, it can lead to wasted time and silly mistakes. Instead of trying to do two things at once, schedule yourself time to work on one task at a time. To-do lists can be helpful tools for keeping yourself focused on finishing one item before moving on to another. You'll do better work and save yourself time.

> **Further Resources**
> To learn more about why multitasking doesn't work at school or at work, check out this brief video (http://youtu.be/p-20BrxIb80) that summarizes some of the recent research on multitasking.

Lesson Wrap-up

Key Terms

Multitasking: working on more than one task at a time

Planner: a place for you to organize your schedule and record any important tasks or responsibilities

Study Break: a time, usually about five minutes long, to help you reenergize and refocus

Time Budget: a tool to plan the amount of time you want to spend on certain activities

Lesson 1.6
Taking Notes and Annotating Texts

Have you ever found yourself in one of these situations?

> You're sitting in class, keeping detailed notes about the lecture. As your instructor continues, you find yourself falling further behind. You just can't write fast enough to keep up with the discussion. Later that night, you try reviewing your notes and realize that you missed most of the material from the second half of class.

> According to your class syllabus, you have a three-page personal reflection paper due tomorrow. You completely forgot to work on your paper earlier this week, so you stay up all night finishing it. When you get to class the next day, you find out that your instructor had postponed the due date until next week.

> At the beginning of class, your instructor announces a quiz over last night's reading assignment. You feel confident because you know that you spent extra time carefully reading the assignment. As you

take the quiz, however, you struggle to remember the details of the reading. When your class grades the quizzes together, you can't believe that you failed.

If you've ever experienced a similar situation, you know how frustrating it felt. You fulfilled all the requirements of the course, yet you continued to struggle.

While attending class and doing your homework are important, your work doesn't stop there. Good listening and note-taking skills are essential for getting the most out of your class and study times. Developing these abilities takes a bit of practice, but as you continue getting better, you will find yourself becoming more and more successful.

Skills in listening and note-taking are important for getting the most out of class time.

Listening and note-taking are important both inside and outside of the classroom. Throughout your week, you participate in training demonstrations, job interviews, medical appointments, and personal conversations. Just like in class, your success in these activities relies on your ability to pay close attention and keep track of key details.

In this lesson, you will learn about the following:

Building Skills in Active Listening
Effective Note-Taking Methods
Annotating Texts for Active Reading

You can then use these strategies to find success in school, at work, and in everyday life.

Listening Skills

During class, you are presented with a large amount of information in a short amount of time. To make sure that you don't miss important concepts or instructions, you need to practice active listening. **Active listening** involves actively paying attention to the speaker, asking questions about confusing concepts, and making connections to your prior knowledge.

Preparation is a key step in active listening. Without any background knowledge, you will have a hard time following the class lecture. Be sure to complete any reading assignments even if you won't be quizzed on the information. You will learn more in class if you are already familiar with the major topics.

Come to class prepared with all your materials: paper, pens, highlighters, and textbooks. If you are required to bring a laptop or tablet, make sure you have a charger as well. Electronic devices can easily be a source of distractions. To keep yourself focused, keep your phone stored in your backpack and your laptop closed until you need it.

> **Further Resources**
> While computers can be useful tools, they can also become major distractions. Companies have started developing apps to keep you focused while you study or work. To learn more, check out this article (http://www.npr.org/sections/alltechconsidered/2013/07/23/204848805/distractions-in-the-digital-age-call-for-apps-to-block-sites) from National Public Radio's technology blog, *All Tech Considered.*

Before class starts, think about the best place to sit. You'll want to stay away from potential distractions like noisy equipment, open windows, or talkative classmates. Generally, sitting near the front of the room is a better idea than sitting in the back. Not only will you be able to see any visual aids better, but you will also be less distracted by the movements of other people.

As you listen to your instructor, write down any questions that come to mind so that you don't forget them later. If you have a question about a topic, chances are some of your classmates are probably wondering the same thing. Don't be afraid to ask, but be sure to wait for an appropriate time to bring up your questions. You don't want to interrupt your instructor in the middle of an important example or explanation.

Active listening also involves making connections to your prior knowledge. **Prior knowledge** is what you already know about a topic from previous class discussions or reading assignments. As you learn new material, think about how this information fits into what you've already learned as a class. If you are having a hard time making connections, ask your instructor for help.

Note-Taking

Note-taking is a skill that goes hand-in-hand with active listening. When you are listening in class, writing down important information will help you pay attention to the lecture and understand the material more effectively.

> **Learning Style Tip**
> If you are an **active** learner, organize a weekly study group with your classmates to review and discuss your notes.

Regardless of the type of notes you take, you should follow a few important guidelines:

- **Use neat handwriting.** You can't study from notes that you can't read. If you know that you make a lot of mistakes when writing, consider using a pencil instead of a pen.
- **Use abbreviations and phrases.** If you take word-for-word notes, you won't be able to keep up with the information being presented.
- **Use your own words.** Remember that class notes are your own personal study resources. You must be able to understand the information when you review it later.

There are several well-known ways to structure class notes. Some of the most popular are outlines, the Cornell Method, and graphic organizers like mind maps. Don't be afraid to try all three until you find a system that works the best for you.

> Reflection Questions
> What has been your process for taking notes in the past? How do you think you could improve in your note-taking abilities?

Outlines

Outlining class lectures helps you understand the way a topic is structured by grouping all the information into topics and subtopics. Look at the following example:

Floor Support

    I.   Joists: beams that support a floor
        a.   Potential problems
            i.   Rotten beams: water damage
            ii.   Squeaking boards: boards rubbing together
        b.   Types
            i.   Solid lumber: cheaper, but limited size
            ii.   Open: less wood, can't be changed on-site
    2.   Subflooring: support floor covering, even surface
        a.   Potential problems
            i.   Sinking floors: water damage, wrong installation
            ii.   Creaking floors: wrong thickness?
        b.   Types
            i.   Plywood: cheap, common
            ii.   Concrete slab: must be completely dry

In an **outline**, subtopics are indented under main topics. For example, plywood and concrete slab are both types of subflooring. Joists and subflooring are both floor supports. Seeing this information clearly laid out in an outline helps you quickly identify the relationships between each topic.

Outlines also make good study resources because you can easily read through all the topics rather than trying to scan an entire page of notes.

If you have a hard time following the organization of a topic during class, try writing down all of your notes during class and rewriting them in outline form later. The more you practice making outlines, the better you will get at it.

> Learning Style Tip
> Outlines are useful tools for **global** learners. If you are a global learner, you can use an outline to see the relationships between ideas and understand how those ideas connect to the big picture.

Cornell Notes

Another method for taking notes is the **Cornell Method**, a strategy first created by Dr. Walter Pauk at Cornell University.

To take Cornell notes, divide your paper into four sections:

- Section 1 is the top of the page. Use this space to list the class information, date, and lecture topic.
- Section 2 is for taking notes during class. Instead of complete sentences, use lists or clusters of words, phrases, or even abbreviations. Feel free to color-code your notes or highlight important terms.

- Section 3 is for after class. Make a list of new or important terms from the session. Then, come up with questions. Some of these questions can be reflective, helping you think more about what you learned in class. Others should be questions that you still have about what was covered. Consider these action items for preparing for your next class or your next test.
- Finally, when you finish reviewing your notes, write a brief summary of the topic in Section 4. This summary should boil down the main point of the lecture in fewer than five sentences.

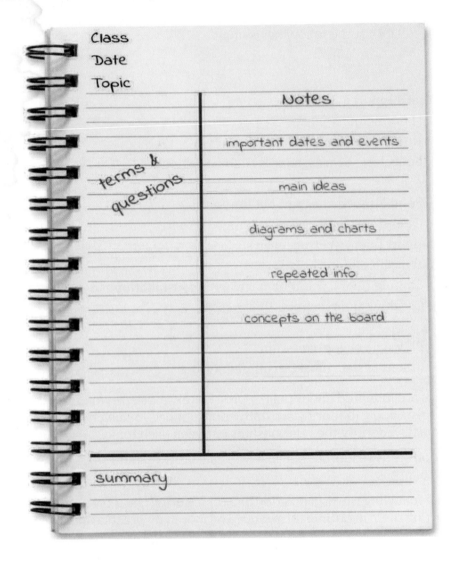

Here are some questions you might want to include in Section 3 of your notes:

How is this related to other topics?

Why is this important?

Do I have any follow-up questions about these concepts?

Do I understand what the instructor emphasized most?

What exam questions might I anticipate based on what we learned today?

Graphic Organizers

A **graphic organizer** is a note-taking template for visually demonstrating relationships between ideas. The layout of a graphic organizer could include shapes, charts, timelines, diagrams, or drawings. Filling out a graphic organizer can be a very useful method for not only reviewing notes, but also summarizing texts and brainstorming for writing assignments.

One popular type of graphic organizer is a mind map. **Mind maps** organize the main points of a topic visually. They are similar to outlining because all of the related ideas are grouped together.

Mind maps make it easy to visualize information.

The main concept goes in the center of the mind map. Any important topics are connected to the main concept by lines. These topics can then be connected to subtopics that are even more specific.

This format is a visual representation of the material that allows you to quickly see connections between ideas. Just like with outlining, you may not be able to group everything together perfectly the first time. Don't be afraid to take down regular notes during class and create a graphic organizer when you review your notes later.

Further Resources
If you're looking for resources for creating your own graphic organizer, try out Coggle (https://coggle.it/), Mindmeister (https://www.mindmeister.com/), or drawing tools in PowerPoint.

On Your Own

In addition to mind mapping, try out some other types of graphic organizers to prepare for an upcoming class or assignment. Use the following examples as worksheets or as ideas for your own creations.

Timeline of Events

Topic/Text:

Timeline of Events		
Topic/Text:		
Big Idea:		
Detail:	Detail:	Detail:
Big Idea:		
Detail:	Detail:	Detail:

Annotating

Annotating involves marking a text and taking notes in the margin. An annotated reading looks like this:

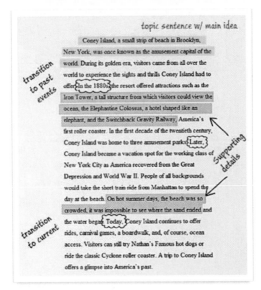

Annotating is a specific type of note-taking that can be used for reading assignments outside of class. As a college student, you read a large amount of information for your classes. Annotating helps you stay focused and remember important details later.

Before annotating a reading assignment, carefully read through the entire text once. This will give you a chance to focus on the information without any extra distractions.

Once you've finished, review the material again, this time adding notes and marking important information:

- **Definitions**: If you come across any difficult words or terms, look them up and write the definition in the margin of the page.
- **Important ideas**: Mark the most important ideas by highlighting, underlining, or circling the important words or phrases. Try to mark only the most important information. If everything is important, nothing is important.
- **Prior knowledge**: Your prior knowledge is what you already know about a topic. If something you read reminds you of another topic you've experienced or discussed, write a short note to yourself in the margin of the page.
- **Questions**: As you read, write down questions you have about unclear or confusing information so that you can look up the answers or ask your instructor later.
- **Summaries**: You may need to re-read a confusing section multiple times before you understand it completely. Once you figure out the meaning, write a short summary in the margin of the page. This will help you understand the passage when you're studying later.

Finally, scan through the text one last time, and add the following information:

- **Answers**: Look for any questions that you wrote down as you read. If you found the answer later in the reading, write it down next to the question. Any information that you still don't know should be marked so that you can ask your instructor later.
- **Connections**: As you read, you probably noticed that certain ideas in the text were connected to other ideas. Write down a brief note about this relationship next to both ideas.
- **Structure**: Go back through and mark the structure of the text by labelling the introduction, each of the main points, and the conclusion. Use large brackets or a highlighter to show which **paragraphs** belong to which section.

You can use sticky notes, pens, and highlighters to annotate a text. Try adding special colors or symbols for different types of information. For example, questions could be in blue with a question mark, and important ideas could be in red with a star.

The process of annotating a text will help you read an assignment more thoroughly. Just like note-taking keeps you focused in class, annotating keeps you focused while reading.

Additionally, an annotated text is a valuable study resource. When you are reviewing the information for a test or a project, you can use your notes to quickly locate and understand important information.

Lesson Wrap-up

Key Terms

Active Learning: learning information through participation in activities

Active Listening: listening that involves paying attention, asking questions, and making connections

Annotating: a strategy for taking notes while reading

The Cornell Method: a strategy that divides a page of notes into four sections

Global Learning: learning information through seeing the big picture

Graphic Organizer: a note-taking template for visually demonstrating relationships between ideas

Mind-Mapping: a method for making visual connections between topics

Outlining: grouping information into topics and subtopics

Paragraph: a short piece of writing that focuses on one main idea

Prior Knowledge: what you already know about a topic

Lesson 1.7
Using Effective Study Strategies

Your life is busier than ever before. You have work commitments, family responsibilities, and extracurricular activities in addition to all your classes and projects. Without good study habits, you will find yourself falling behind.

You may have been able to get through some of your previous classes without studying. As you continue working on your degree, however, your courses will become more and more difficult. Practicing good study habits now will help you develop the skills you need to excel in later courses.

This lesson will teach you three ways to improve your study habits:

Make Studying Part of Your Routine
Use Creative Study Strategies
Avoid Procrastination

Make Studying Part of Your Routine

To get the most out of your classes, add daily study times to your routine. This will keep your mind active and ready to receive new information. Learning is like caring for a houseplant. The best way to keep a plant healthy is to water it a little bit each day. You can't just dump in a gallon of water once a month and expect it to thrive.

You're more likely to absorb information when you study a little bit every day.

In a similar way, cramming for a test dumps gallons of information into your memory. Your brain isn't ready to learn that much material at once, so some of it is lost. By studying daily, you will absorb a greater amount of information over time than you would in one emergency study session.

To make studying part of your daily routine, try using the following strategies:

- **Find a study time that works for you.** Everyone feels alert and focused at different times of day. If you're a morning person, wake up early for a brief study session each morning. If you struggle to stay awake after eating lunch, don't plan to study in the early afternoon.
- **Schedule study times in your planner.** Adding study sessions to your **planner** makes them harder to skip. It's all too easy to put off studying until later. Unfortunately, *later* can quickly turn into tomorrow or the next day. Make studying a required event, just like work shifts or family commitments.
- **Be flexible when necessary.** Unexpected events are bound to happen once in a while. Don't feel guilty about rescheduling your study time around these disruptions. If you know that you'll have some downtime during your other commitments, you might also consider bringing your notes to study when possible.
- **Keep study times separate.** When you have multiple assignments due for class, you may find yourself spending all your study time working on projects. Even if you only have fifteen minutes to spare, reserve time for studying your class notes.

Use Creative Study Strategies

An important part of studying is reading back through your class notes and handouts. Some students, however, limit all their study time to these activities. While reviewing class materials is important, it's not enough. You need to use additional strategies to identify and remember important concepts. Everyone has different **learning styles** and study preferences. Using a variety of creative study strategies will help you find the ones that work best for you. To make the most of your study time, try some of the following ideas:

Checklist: Utilizing Creative Study Strategies

☐ **Meet with your instructor.** At the beginning of the semester, schedule a short meeting with your instructor to discuss the course material and class expectations. This is the perfect opportunity to ask for tips on how to be successful in the course.

☐ **Read your notes out loud.** When you read silently, you may start skimming through the material without even realizing it. Reading out loud forces you to slow down and carefully read through every word.

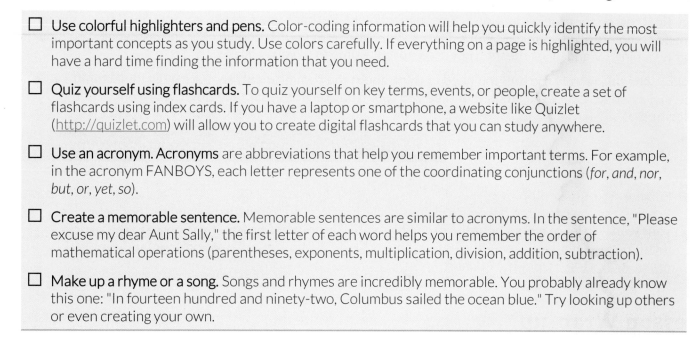

- ☐ **Use colorful highlighters and pens.** Color-coding information will help you quickly identify the most important concepts as you study. Use colors carefully. If everything on a page is highlighted, you will have a hard time finding the information that you need.

- ☐ **Quiz yourself using flashcards.** To quiz yourself on key terms, events, or people, create a set of flashcards using index cards. If you have a laptop or smartphone, a website like Quizlet (http://quizlet.com) will allow you to create digital flashcards that you can study anywhere.

- ☐ **Use an acronym. Acronyms** are abbreviations that help you remember important terms. For example, in the acronym FANBOYS, each letter represents one of the coordinating conjunctions (*for, and, nor, but, or, yet, so*).

- ☐ **Create a memorable sentence.** Memorable sentences are similar to acronyms. In the sentence, "Please excuse my dear Aunt Sally," the first letter of each word helps you remember the order of mathematical operations (parentheses, exponents, multiplication, division, addition, subtraction).

- ☐ **Make up a rhyme or a song.** Songs and rhymes are incredibly memorable. You probably already know this one: "In fourteen hundred and ninety-two, Columbus sailed the ocean blue." Try looking up others or even creating your own.

Avoid Procrastination

The most common study pitfall that causes students to struggle is **procrastination**: putting work off until the last minute. Procrastination is a bad idea. Not only will you feel overwhelmed by the amount of information you need to learn, but you may also find yourself with more work than you can handle.

Procrastination is caused by multiple factors. In some cases, you may feel overwhelmed by the size of a project. Maybe you've never written a paper with that many pages or sources. To help yourself get started, break up the assignment into smaller chunks. Instead of working on a ten-page paper for two weeks, set yourself a goal of finishing one page a day. This strategy will prevent you from putting off the entire paper until the night before.

Studying consistently will prevent you from feeling overwhelmed by assignments.

Procrastination can also stem from fear or self-confidence issues. If this is the case, you might feel like your work will never live up to your expectations. In these situations, remind yourself that your identity is much more than your GPA. Even if you don't score as highly as you'd like on an assignment, you can take the opportunity to learn from your mistakes and perform better the next time.

One final reason for procrastination is time management. Perhaps you feel like you just don't have enough time to complete all of your class work. Take an honest look at your schedule over the last week. You may find that watching TV and using the internet used up more time than you realized.

If your schedule is truly too full, you need to think about the commitments that are most important to you. You may need to reduce the amount of time you spend on activities that take time away from your top priorities.

To learn more about managing your time effectively, see Lesson 1.5.

Further Resources
Procrastination can often become a vicious cycle, causing you to fall further and further behind on your work. To learn more about the breaking the "doom loop" of procrastination, read this article (http://www.theatlantic.com/business/archive/2014/08/the-procrastination-loop-and-how-to-break-it/379142/) from *The Atlantic*.

Lesson Wrap-up

Key Terms

Acronym: an abbreviation that helps you remember important terms

Learning Style: the different ways that people learn new information

Planner: a place for you to organize your schedule and record any important tasks or responsibilities

Procrastination: putting off work until the last minute

Lesson 1.8
Reducing Test Anxiety

Tests. Assessments. Exams. These words can strike fear into the heart of almost any student.

Tests can be a major source of stress for students.

Everyone gets a little anxious before a big test or exam. This is a completely normal reaction. Feeling nervous can even motivate you to study harder.

In some cases, however, **test anxiety** begins to affect your mental health, leaving you overwhelmed by fear or stress. Learning to overcome this anxiety will improve both your self-confidence and your grades.

Remember that tests aren't a complete picture of your abilities. Many smart and creative people struggle on exams but excel in other ways. While you may never become a great test-taker, you can become more confident in yourself and your abilities.

This lesson will discuss three strategies for reducing test anxiety:

Keep a Positive Attitude
Know What to Expect
Use Test-Taking Strategies

When you think about tests, you probably think about the exams you take in school. However, tests are part of almost every workplace. Training certificates, specialized licenses, and even job interviews all involve either written or oral tests. In these situations, you can use the same strategies to deal with test anxiety that you use for assessments in school.

Keep a Positive Attitude

Your attitude sets the tone for how you react to a situation. If you are constantly thinking negatively about yourself and your abilities, you won't feel confident about taking a test, regardless of how well-prepared you are.

Researchers have found that your attitude has an enormous influence on your actions. Think about the last time you went into a store. What music did they play in the background? Most likely, they played something with an upbeat melody and strong beat. Stores use this type of music because they know that when you feel happy and energized, you purchase more items.

Reflection Questions
In what types of situations do you feel the most and least confident? What about each situation influences these feelings?

Changing the way you think about yourself and your abilities doesn't happen overnight. Just like any skill, however, the more you practice, the easier self-confidence will become.

To start thinking more positively, try these strategies:

- **Be more aware of negative self-talk.** You may not even realize how often you talk about yourself in a negative way. Listen carefully to your own words and stop tearing yourself down.
- **Praise yourself and others.** Instead of dwelling on negative thoughts, focus on the times that you achieved your goals. Positive thinking is contagious. When you notice other people succeeding, don't hesitate to congratulate them.
- **Think of setbacks as opportunities for growth.** If you expect only perfection from yourself, you are bound to be disappointed. When you experience a setback, learn from your mistakes and keep moving forward.
- **Find a ritual that makes you happy.** Some people listen to music, take deep breaths, or imagine future success. Regardless of which strategy you choose, find *something* that calms you down and helps you feel confident.

> **Further Resources**
> To learn more about developing the skill of self-confidence, watch this TED talk (https://youtu.be/w-HYZv6HzAs) by Dr. Ivan Joseph, the Director of Athletics at Ryerson University.

> **Helpful Hint**
> To remind yourself about the power of positive thinking, try writing out encouragement to yourself on sticky notes and leaving these reminders somewhere you'll see them often.

Know What to Expect

One of the most nerve-wracking aspects of taking a test is the unknown. If you've never taken a class with a particular instructor, you may feel unsure about the types of questions to expect or which terms to study. Try using the following strategies:

Pre-Test Checklist

☐ **Meet with your instructor.** If you are feeling nervous about a test, talk to your instructor about what you should expect and how you should study. This is also a good opportunity to ask about classroom testing policies. For example, you may want to find out if you are allowed to drink water during the test.

☐ **Take advantage of study guides.** These documents are invaluable because they tell you exactly what concepts will appear on the test. Use your study guide to make flashcards, identify key terms, and create practice quizzes.

☐ **Review old quizzes or tests.** This should give you a fairly good idea of the types of questions you can expect to see on the test. Some instructors even reuse questions from older assessments.

☐ **Study in the testing room if possible.** Being comfortable with your environment can help you feel more at ease during the test. Additionally, your memory is often sharper when you are in a familiar location.

Use Test-Taking Strategies

Regardless of how well you've prepared, anxiety doesn't magically disappear on test day. In fact, it can sometimes get worse while you are taking the test itself. However, there are strategies that you can use to calm your nerves and recall the information that you studied.

Test-Taking Checklist

☐ When you first receive your test paper, take a moment to write down anything you don't want to forget. This might include helpful **acronyms** or important terms. If you record this information right away, you don't have to worry about forgetting it later.

☐ Next, skim through the entire test, playing close attention to any instructions. This will give you a sense of what the questions look like.

☐ Once you've had a chance to look through the entire test, start writing down any answers that you know. Think through your answers, but don't dwell on a question for more than two or three minutes.

☐ Go through the entire test again, answering any questions that you skipped. If you honestly have no idea, take an educated guess by narrowing down your options as much as possible. Do not leave any answer spaces blank. Even a wild guess has a small chance of being correct.

☐ Finally, review the entire test to make sure that you didn't leave any answer spaces blank or make silly mistakes.

If you start feeling overwhelmed at any point during the test, close your eyes and take ten deep breaths. Giving yourself a short mental break will help you calm down and refocus. If your instructor allows you to move around the room during the test, consider stretching your legs or getting a drink.

> **Helpful Hint**
> If you are taking a test that involves a Scantron form, it's easy to lose your place. Try adding a small pencil dot next to any question number you skip so that you can easily relocate any unanswered questions. Wait until the end of your test to erase these marks.

Lesson Wrap-up

Key Terms

Acronym: an abbreviation that helps you remember important terms

Test Anxiety: strong feelings of stress or fear before a test

Lesson 1.9
Taking Advantage of Campus Resources

Many shopping malls are almost like their own miniature communities. You can get a haircut, see your doctor, buy new clothes, and have dinner with friends, all in the same complex.

This is called one-stop shopping. Mall designers have created a place for you to get everything you need without the hassle of finding a new parking spot or getting on the freeway. They hope this convenience will encourage you to become a frequent, satisfied shopper.

In a similar way, colleges offer a variety of services to their student body. These resources are located on campus to make them as convenient as possible. The college's goal is to make you a more successful student by supporting you both academically and socially.

In this lesson, you will learn the purposes and services of five common campus organizations:

Student Services
The Library
The Academic Success Center
The Writing Center
Disabilities Services

Keep in mind that you have already paid for these on-campus services through your tuition. To get the most value out of your education, don't hesitate to take advantage of them.

Similar to a shopping mall, most school campuses offer multiple resources in one place

Student Services

Student Services is the office responsible for academic advising. Your advisor usually meets with you at least once a semester to discuss your course load and career plans. You can also bring up other concerns you might have about your classes.

Student Services can answer your questions about scheduling classes.

Here are some questions you might want to discuss with your advisor:

- How many credits should I take in one semester?
- What classes do I need for my degree program?
- Which placement tests do I need to take?
- What are the differences between in-person and online courses?

Because academic advisors generally work with hundreds of students at a time, you should always schedule an appointment for your meetings. This will give your advisor a chance to review your information ahead of time.

The Student Services office also offers career resources. Throughout the semester, they may hold workshops to help you write a résumé, practice job interviews, or find internships. Keep track of their calendar to make sure that you don't miss any important events.

> **Learning Style Tip**
> If you're a **sequential** learner, ask your advisor for a semester-by-semester explanation of which classes you need for your major. This will give you a clearer idea of your goals and help you monitor your academic progress.

The Library

> **Reflection Questions**
> As more books, articles, and videos become available online, fewer people are using the library to find information. Do you think the library is still important in today's world? Why or why not?

While you probably feel familiar with the campus library, you may not realize how many services it offers. Here are just a few:

> Borrowing videos cameras or audio recorders
>
> Reserving meeting rooms
>
> Ordering books from other libraries
>
> Learning how to conduct research
>
> Printing and laminating documents

Many libraries also create online **LibGuides**. These are websites that have been customized to a specific major or field of study. They include links to databases, websites, and other resources that you might find helpful for course projects and papers.

Campus libraries provide valuable resources.

If you are having trouble using the library catalog or finding a particular book, the librarians are there to help. Some libraries even have a service that allows you to text a librarian with your questions.

The Academic Success Center

The **Academic Success Center** exists to help you succeed academically. If you are struggling in a course, you can schedule an appointment with a tutor to get extra help. Make sure you know where the tutoring office is located. Sometimes, tutors work in a specific building while other times they meet in the library.

A weekly discussion group can help you in a difficult class.

The Academic Success Center may also hold weekly group discussions to help you get the most out of your courses. This is a good opportunity to study the material in a group and hear the perspectives and thoughts of others.

Don't wait until the week before finals to take advantage of these resources. Often, the Academic Success Center has limited tutoring hours available during the end of the semester because there are so many students using their services.

> Helpful Hint
> Don't feel embarrassed asking for academic help! Everyone has strengths and weaknesses as a student. For example, you may excel in math classes but struggle in history classes.

The Writing Center

During college, you will write a lot of papers. The Writing Center offers specialized tutoring for all stages of the writing process. They can help you brainstorm topic ideas, write a strong thesis statement, organize your paragraphs, or make revisions. Feel free to schedule multiple appointments to get assistance on the same paper.

> Reflection Questions
> Have you ever asked a friend or roommate for a second opinion on a paper? Why was this helpful?

Tutors at the Writing Center can help you strengthen your papers.

To get the most out of your time in the Writing Center, follow these suggestions:

Checklist: Writing Center Visit

☐ Before your appointment, come up with two or three specific ways you want to improve your paper. This will help your tutor focus your meeting on the issues that are most important to you.

☐ At the end of your appointment, ask your tutor to help you identify specific action items that you can complete on your own.

☐ Remember that a visit to the Writing Center doesn't guarantee that you will receive an *A* on your paper. The tutors are there to help you become a better writer, which is a process that could take months or even years. You can't expect instant perfection.

☐ The Writing Center may offer specialized tutoring in different course subjects such as biology, history, or psychology. Contact their office to see if there is a specific tutor you should request when making your appointment.

Disabilities Services

The **Disabilities Services** office assists students who have learning disabilities or physical limitations. One of their main purposes is arranging classroom accommodations for students who require assistance in class.

These **accommodations** might include receiving extra time on projects, receiving the help of a translator or note-taker, or taking tests in a quiet environment.

Colleges are legally required to provide accommodations for students who need them. However, these must be coordinated through Disabilities Services. If you have a learning disability or physical limitation, make an appointment with them as soon as possible.

The Disabilities Services office can also help you find accessible course materials such as braille textbooks or closed-captioned videos.

> **Further Resources**
> Learning disabilities are often misunderstood. To learn more about some of the common myths about learning disabilities, read this article (http://www.pbs.org/newshour/rundown/five-misconceptions-about-learning-disabilities/) from PBS *NewsHour*.

Lesson Wrap-up

> **Helpful Hint**
> Use your **planner** to keep track of appointments with your advisor, tutoring sessions at the Academic Success Center, or important library due dates.

Key Terms

Academic Success Center: the office responsible for on-campus tutoring

Accommodations: personalized classroom assistance such as extra time on projects or a separate testing environment

Disabilities Services: the office responsible for assisting students with learning disabilities or physical limitations

LibGuides: a website that contains helpful resources for a particular major or course

Paragraph: a piece of writing that focuses on one main idea

Planner: a place for you to organize your schedule and record any important tasks or responsibilities

Sequential Learning: learning information through a step-by-step process

Student Services: the office responsible for academic advising and career services

Writing Center: a service that provides writing assistance

Chapter 2
Reading Skills

Lesson 2.1
Preparing Yourself to Read

Everyone reads *something*—a book, a tweet, or a cereal box—on a daily basis. The reading you do in your personal life, however, is often very different from the reading you do at work or school.

Reading assignments for work or school are generally longer. They may use unfamiliar terms or discuss complex topics. In these situations, you may find yourself faced with an assignment that seems boring or overwhelming. Where do you even start?

Think about reading like exercising. Before starting a workout, you should always stretch. One of the purposes of stretching is to ease your body into physical activity by warming up your cold muscles. In reading, this is known as pre-reading. **Pre-reading** prepares your mind to get the most out of the time you spend reading.

Just like stretching prepares your body for running, pre-reading prepares your mind for reading.

In this lesson, you will learn three important strategies for pre-reading:

Scan the Title, Table of Contents, and Major Headings

Make Predictions and Find Connections

Create a Plan to Start Reading

Using these strategies will help you mentally prepare not only to read but to also get the most out of your reading.

> **Reflection Questions**
> What types of reading assignments do you encounter at school and at work? How are they different from the reading you do in your personal life?

Scan the Title, Table of Contents, and Major Headings

Title

Before you begin a reading, you should look for a hint about its contents from the title. Based on that information, what do you think the book or document will discuss? Look up any words that aren't familiar. Because titles often use catchy or symbolic language, you should consider all of the possible meanings of a word.

On Your Own

Read through the following titles. What would you expect to read about in each of the texts?

"Shortcut to Victory: Inside the Iowa Primary"

Nickel and Dimed

"Opposition to the Vietnam War and the Effect of the Arts"

"College Athletics: Perspectives on the Winners and the Losers"

The Bluest Eye

Table of Contents

At the beginning of a book or long document, the **table of contents** will show you how the information is organized. The table of contents might also include a brief overview of the topics inside each chapter or section. Not every reading will contain a table of contents, particularly if it is a shorter reading that isn't broken into multiple sections.

Even if you are only reading a small section of a longer work, reviewing the table of contents will help you understand how your reading assignment fits into the structure of the entire reading.

For example, imagine that your environmental studies instructor has asked you to read a chapter about the negative impacts of natural-gas drilling in your textbook. It might be helpful to know that natural gas is one of several different energy sources. By reviewing the table of contents, you may come across section titles that identify those additional sources.

> **Helpful Hint**
> When reading a **scholarly article**, you may not always find a table of contents. However, scholarly articles often *do* include other helpful information in abstracts and/or lists of keywords. An **abstract** is a concise summary of the main ideas or arguments presented in a scholarly article. **Keywords** are terms—fields of study, trends, topics, etc.—that are relevant to the main ideas of the article.

Table of Contents

The table of contents provides an overview of the information you can find in a text.

Reflection Questions
Websites usually don't include a traditional table of contents. Look at this page on the Purdue Owl website (https://owl.english.purdue.edu/owl/section/6/). How do readers know what topics will be covered in that section of the website?

Headings and Topic Sentences

The next step in pre-reading is to skim through the reading to find bold headings and terms. These will give you clues about what each section in the reading covers. While not every type of book or document includes headings, textbooks almost always do.

1.14 Solving Equations with Integers

Objective A   **Negative Constants, Negative Coefficients, and Negative Solutions**

In Section 1.5, we discussed solving equations of the forms

$$x + b = c, \qquad x - b = c, \qquad \text{and} \qquad ax = c,$$

where x is a variable and a, b, and c represent constants. Each of these equations is called a **first-degree equation in x** because the exponent of the variable is 1 in each case. The equations in Section 1.5 were set up so that the coefficients, constants, and solutions to the equations were whole numbers. Now that we have discussed integers and operations with integers, we can discuss equations that have negative constants, negative coefficients, and negative solutions.

For convenience and easy reference, the following definitions are repeated from Section 1.5.

Equation, Solution, Solution Set

An **equation** is a statement that two expressions are equal.

A **solution** to an equation is a number that gives a true statement when substituted for the variable.

A **solution set** of an equation is the set of all solutions of the equation.

Example 1

Solutions to an Equation

a. Show that -5 **is** a solution to the equation $x - 6 = -11$.

$$x - 6 = -11$$
$$-5 - 6 \overset{?}{=} -11$$
$$-11 = -11$$

Therefore, -5 **is** a solution.

b. Show that 6 **is not** a solution to the equation $x - 6 = -11$.

$$x - 6 = -11$$
$$6 - 6 \overset{?}{=} -11$$
$$0 \neq -11$$

Therefore, 6 **is not** a solution.

Headings stand out from ordinary text.

If your reading assignment doesn't have a table of contents *or* headings, try reading the topic sentences in each paragraph. **Topic sentences** usually appear at the beginning of a **paragraph**, and if they are well-written, they should give you a strong idea of what the paragraph will discuss.

To learn more about topic sentences, see Lesson 2.4.

On Your Own

Consider the following topic sentences. What would you expect to read in the paragraph that each sentence introduces?

Social media is a great way to keep in touch with family and friends.

The researchers soon realized that their original study had major issues.

Despite this opposition, I would argue that the benefits of this business model will outweigh the costs.

> **Learning Style Tip**
> If you're a **global** learner, you like seeing the big picture when you're learning something new. Previewing the major topics will help you understand the overall point of a reading.

Make Predictions and Find Connections

Making predictions will prepare you to think more critically about a reading. Don't feel like you need to be 100% accurate in your predictions. The goal is to prepare yourself for reading by predicting what you *might* learn.

The best way to make predictions is to ask yourself questions. Use research questions that begin with *who, what, when, where, why,* and *how*. Here are some examples:

> **Who** is probably the intended audience?
> **What** will be the author's main argument(s)?
> **Where** does the topic probably take place?
> **When** did the topic probably take place?
> **Why** am I supposed to care about this topic?
> **How** will the author want me to respond?

After coming up with your questions, write down your answers and think through them carefully. Keep this information with you while you read so that you can update your notes.

> **Helpful Hint**
> If you are reading for a school assignment, keep the assignment details in mind. What does your instructor want you to learn from the text?

Reading Application

Before reading the following passage, preview its contents and consider how you can apply predictions and connections to better understand its meaning.

Taking Care of Beth

What does the title suggest about the story?

"She's always doing this," whispered Irving to the store clerk; he looked left and right, moving one foot and then the other until he completely turned himself around.

"I can't see her anywhere," he rasped once more to the attendant, who was studying Irving's wild white hair, which looked particularly frazzled from the sun's reflection.

"The woman with you earlier? Your daughter?" the attendant asked.

"My wife! I can't find her. She's always doing this," he said as he struggled to turn his body in the direction he wanted. After slowly moving forward a foot or two, he peered down aisle four; he saw nothing but teddy bears.

"Gracious," he said, "I just can't tell where she is. Do you know where she is? She's always doing this."

Based on the beginning of the story, what can you already tell about the main characters?

"I'll help you, sir," said a sweet, youthful voice. The voice ricocheted down every aisle: "Lost wife. Anyone seen a lost wife?" The condescension in her announcement was not lost on Irving.

Suddenly, he saw a pair of legs that did not belong to a teddy bear. They were the legs he was looking for: elongated, angular, connected to a slim, upright frame. Beth's head appeared out of the stuffed bear collection. He took a moment to analyze the grey curls softening the bony lines of her rigid face.

The wrinkles in Irving's forehead were deep enough to make any of his comrades from Vietnam remember the deep swamps they marched through during the war.

What does this tell you about Irving's past?

"I was looking for you," he said. "You always do this, and you never wait for me!"

Irving and Beth both stared intently down at the bottle of Tide detergent and the toilet brush in her hand. He reached down and grasped at the detergent.

"I could carry this. You never let me carry anything," he said. He regarded Beth. *Why can't she put that toilet brush on the counter more quickly? She is so sluggish.* "Well? Put it on the counter…"

His voice emerged, shaky and uneven. His whole body quivered sometimes; he just couldn't help himself. The doctor called it a severe case of osteo-arthritis. He was pulled from his thoughts by the thwack of a toilet brush on the counter.

What is the author trying to tell you about the relationship between Beth and Irving?

She does this all the time. Can't she see she's embarrassing me? I don't know what to do with her anymore.

Eyes full of amusement, the store clerk looked at the two of them. That same laughter was in her eyes, but it was worse this time, Irving thought. He hated nothing more than being laughed at.

"$8.47," the clerk said with a wink in Irving's direction. Irving and Beth both reached to their pockets at the same time. Beth's gaze shot up to Irving's. *That's right. I'm paying for this*, he proclaimed to himself, pulling a crumpled wad of ones from his pocket. Just as he managed to grab the bills, he looked up and saw the clerk dispensing the receipt from the machine and handing it to his wife.

Irving had a sinking sensation in the pit of his chest. He had never felt more helpless, more alone, or more old.

At the end, ask yourself: What does the author want me to gain from this story?

Finding connections to your prior knowledge is another important aspect of pre-reading. Your **prior knowledge** is what you already know about a topic.

To make connections between your prior knowledge and what you are about to read, use a KWL chart. A **KWL chart** has three columns for what you know **(K)**, what you want to know **(W)**, and what you learned **(L)**. You will fill out the first two columns before reading and the third column after reading.

What You Know

First, you will add your prior knowledge on the topic. Perhaps you are about to read a lesson about verbs: what they do and how they're used. Write down what you already know about verbs. This information is your prior knowledge. Using your prior knowledge gives you a head start on learning because you don't have to start from the very beginning. You can find what you know and keep building knowledge from there.

What You Want to Know

After you've thought about your prior knowledge on the subject, the next step is to add what you want to know: your purpose for reading. For example, if you're reading a lesson about verbs, you may want to know how to tell the differences between action verbs and linking verbs or how to form the different verb tenses. Once you identify what you want to know, you can read more purposefully and actively.

What You Learned

When you've finished reading, don't forget to return to your KWL chart. Look back over what you knew and what you hoped to learn. Then, add a brief description of what you learned from your reading. Did you learn what you wanted to learn? If not, you probably need to go back and read through the assignment again.

Here's an example of what a KWL chart might look like before reading:

Topic: *Using Drones for Mail Delivery*

What I Know	What I Want to Know	What I Learned
Flying, unmanned devices	Can we be sure about accuracy?	
Drones recently in the news	How do we track them?	
Energy efficient	Faster delivery times?	

> **Helpful Hint**
> KWL charts can also be an effective way to prepare for class. Look at the course syllabus to find the topic of your next class meeting. Before attending class, identify what you know and what you want to know about the lesson. After class, note what you learned.

Reading Application

Before reading the following passage, apply pre-reading strategies to help you interact with the text. Utilize the blank KWL provided to guide your pre-reading process, and return to it after reading to note what you learned.

Ghost in the Machine: Debunking the Paranormal

Most people say they don't believe in ghosts, but humans have always been curious about the afterlife and the spirit world. Ancient cultures like the Vikings, Celts, and Egyptians prepared their dead with weapons and food for the journey to the next life.

Ask yourself: What do I know about these cultures and their practices?

Most cultures have legends of mysterious apparitions and visits from the dead. Even in an age that emphasizes science and logic, TV shows like Ghost Hunters and Paranormal States make it clear that we are still curious about the existence of spirits and their ability to contact the living.

As early as the 1940s, amateur ghost hunters began using electronic technology to "prove" their experiences with ghosts, but most of these experiences are easily debunked. Here are a few examples:

Here, the author specifies the focus of the text.

Notice the signal phrase here are a few examples *is used to introduce two sub-sections organized by headings. What other terms guide your expectations of what's coming next?*

EVP recorders

One popular device is the electronic voice phenomena recorder, or EVP reader. These are reasonably affordable, ranging from $40 to $150, but they are little more than a tool to exercise curiosity. The EVP recorder is a hand-held device that picks up low-frequency, unexplainable sounds that can later be slowed down and interpreted. These unlikely sound waves are thought to be voices of the dead. Back in the 1940s, mediums began recording "spirit voices" on such devices. Unfortunately, most of the sounds picked up by EVP recorders are easily explained as radio wave interference.

EMF sensors

Another electronic ghost hunting tool is the EMF sensor. This hand-held gadget detects unexplained electromagnetic field activity. Like the EVP reader, an EMF sensor is affordable. They can be purchased for around $50 to $75, and several low-end apps are downloadable to your phone. These apps can certainly track electromagnetic fields, but no confirmed spirit activity has been proven. Since we can't be certain spirits generate energy or sound waves, these detection devices are only as accurate as their carriers believe they are.

Some paragraphs like this one conclude with sentences that clue you in on the author's main intent: disproving ghost-finding technology.

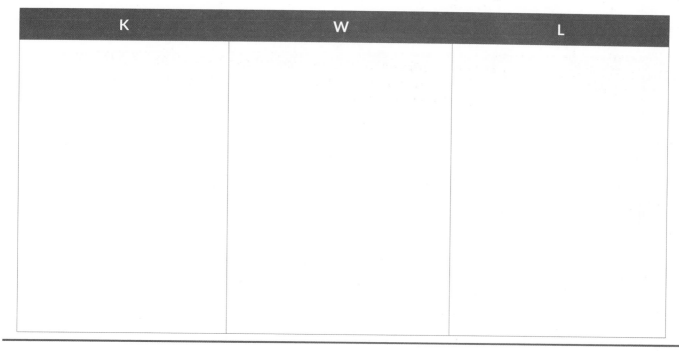

K	W	L

Learning Style Tip
If you are an **active** learner and you're having trouble filling in the "L" column of your KWL chart, try discussing what you read with a friend. This will help you to think about what you learned and put it into words.

Create a Plan to Start Reading

Once you've used pre-reading strategies to prepare mentally, you can map out a plan for completing your assignment. Think through some of the following questions:

> What are the details of the assignment?
> How much time will I need to read?
> What supplies will I need?

For a school or work assignment, think about any specific guidelines from your instructor or manager. He or she may want you to focus on specific aspects of the topic. If so, keep a copy of these instructions handy while you read so that you can take notes on important information.

Depending on the length of the assignment or the difficulty of the topic, you may need to schedule extra time to read. Think about the questions from your KWL chart. How much do you already know, and how much do you need to learn? If the reading is long and covers an unfamiliar topic, you may need to set aside extra time.

Make sure that you gather any supplies you will need before reading. For notes, you may need highlighters or notecards. Computers are useful for taking notes or looking up unfamiliar words. Just make sure you don't open up distractions like Facebook or YouTube. If you read better with background music or a certain type of light, be sure you have those resources available as well.

To learn more about staying organized and on track, see Lessons 1.4 and 1.5.

Lesson Wrap-up

Reading Application

Suppose your instructor has asked you to read the following passage. Using the annotations as a guide, consider how to prepare for this assignment and how you can apply pre-reading strategies to interact with the text.

Considerations for Future Dog Owners

When adopting or buying a dog, there's plenty to consider besides a cute face.

First, think about the size of the dog. While puppies are tiny, they often grow large and quickly. Learn about the breed you're taking home and make sure you have the space to handle it when it's fully grown. If you live in a small house or have a small yard, you may want to consider a small or medium-sized dog.

> The topic sentence provides the focus of this paragraph: dog size considerations.

Next, consider your dog's energy level. Some dogs need exercise daily while others are happily lazy. While all dogs need some exercise and playtime, very active dogs need to run every day. Make sure your activity level matches that of the dog. If dogs don't let out their energy, they can become bored and problematic at home.

> Words like *next* and *another* breaks up paragraphs and signals a change in topic for readers.

Another key factor is the cost involved with a dog breed. While all dogs will need collars, toys, and beds, some breeds have more demanding costs for grooming and feeding. A dog with long hair or fur will need to get washed and groomed regularly. Larger dogs eat more food each day, which can add up. All dogs will require visits to the veterinarian's office once a year for a check-up and shots.

Another thing to consider when choosing a dog is how the dog interacts with children. Some dogs are very protective of their space and toys, which can make it difficult to be in an environment with young kids. If you have children, are planning to have children, or have children visiting your home, make sure you choose a dog that can handle the excitement and unpredictability of small kids.

> This indicates that the intended audience includes parents or people who are often around children.

Finally, think about the amount of time you can spend training your dog. Often, older dogs are already trained to go to the bathroom outside and know simple commands such as *sit, stay,* and *no.* Puppies will need training to learn all the basics, including where to go to the bathroom. If you don't have the time or desire to train a puppy, an older dog is a better choice.

Choosing to adopt or buy a dog can be a rewarding experience. Dogs provide daily affection: they're great furry friends. However, they also require a lot of work. Do some research to find dog breeds that work best with your interests, living situation, and activity level. Doing your homework will ensure that your dog will be a loving, loyal companion for many years to come.

> This concluding sentence supports the topic sentence of the paragraph.

Key Terms

Abstract: a brief summary of the main ideas and arguments presented in a research source

Active Learning: learning information through participation in activities

Global Learning: learning information through seeing the big picture

Keywords: a list of terms—fields of study, trends, or topics—relevant to the main ideas in a research source

KWL Chart: a chart that helps you think about what you know, what you want to know, and what you learned

Paragraph: a short piece of writing that focuses on one main idea

Pre-reading: preparing yourself to learn from your reading

Prior Knowledge: what you already know about a topic

Scholarly Article: a research source written by an expert and published in an academic journal

Table of Contents: a list of chapters or sections and their page numbers within a book or document

Topic Sentence: a sentence that states the main point of a paragraph

Lesson 2.2
Using Visual Clues

Most of the books and documents you read every day contain more than just words. They include pictures, graphs, icons, colors, and shapes. All of these are **visual clues** that add to the meaning of a text just as much as the actual words do.

One type of visual clue that you probably already know is body language. Think about the way people's facial expressions and body movements can add to the meaning of their words. They may tell you that everything is fine, but their body language makes you suspect otherwise. Even if people haven't said anything, you can often guess their moods from the way they cross their arms or the looks on their faces.

One common type of visual clue is body language.

In a similar way, visual clues in a book or document can add to its meaning. You need to read these visuals carefully to make sure that you aren't missing valuable information.

This lesson will help you identify and understand three types of visual clues:

Font Design

Images

Charts and Graphs

Font Design

One way that a book or document calls attention to important information is through the use of **fonts:** the size and style of letters. In your textbooks, you've probably noticed words that are larger or bolder than others. These words are headings that show the organization of the reading or important terms that you need to study.

During **pre-reading,** read through all of the titles and headings to get a better understanding of your assignment. This information will help you see the overall structure and organization of a reading.

To learn more about pre-reading strategies, see Lesson 2.1.

Important terms also appear in a bold font to make them easy to spot in a text. You should pay special attention to these terms and their definitions. If a reading doesn't contain any special fonts, consider adding your own visual clues. Underlining or highlighting important terms or sections will help you study more efficiently later.

> Helpful Hint
> In *Foundations of English*, important terms are displayed in a bold font. These Key Terms are listed with their definitions at the end of each lesson.

The design of the font itself also contains clues about the meaning of a book or document. Think about the different types of fonts you would expect to see in a business letter or a student activities flyer. Most likely, the letter would use a formal font like Times New Roman while the flyer would use something more eye-catching. In both of these situations, the style of the chosen font affects how you interpret the information in the document.

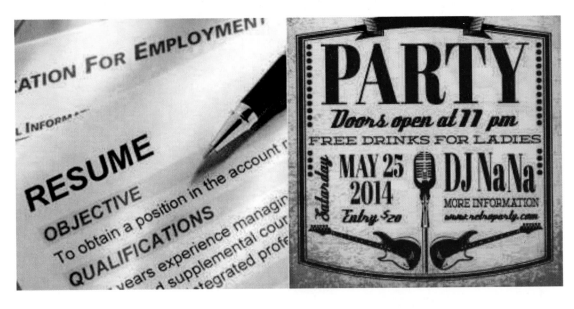

Group Activity
As a group, choose five fonts and discuss how each one could affect the meaning of a text. Create a brief PowerPoint presentation to share your findings with your classmates. Be sure to use clear visual examples of each font to illustrate your conclusions.

Learning Style Tip
Even though **verbal** learners usually prefer words over visuals, they can benefit from both types of learning. Remember that the best resources find a balance of images and words. If you're a verbal learner having a difficult time understanding an image, make sure to read through the image caption or the surrounding explanation.

Reading Application

Review the following résumé, paying attention to the use of font, italics, spacing, and lines. Consider how these decisions impact the overall effectiveness of the résumé.

Tabitha Hawkins

Thawkins808@gmail.com | 843-555-5555 | 661 Limehouse Road, Radnor, PA 19087

Career Objective

I am graduating from high school in May of 2017 and will be attending college to earn a degree in Business with a minor in Recreation Management. I am seeking a position in which I can participate in part time event planning, marketing, and management, so I can further develop my professional skills while earning my degree.

Work Experience

Intern to the Program Coordinator   **2016 - Present**
YMCA
As an intern, I help the program coordinator twice a week after school by responding professionally to emails, updating social media accounts to extend communications efforts, and organizing the office effectively. I also help coordinate and supervise special events when requested.

Part Time Sales Associate   **2014 - Present**
Stonecold Creamery
As a Sales Associate, I am responsible for preparing and serving ice cream, ensuring compliance with health code, and creating an excellent customer experience. I also assist the manager in coordinating parties and private events when requested.

Volunteer Experience

Helping Hands Soup Kitchen   **2014 - 2016**

For the past three years, I have established a tradition to engage in service to others on the holidays. I help prepare and serve a potluck Thanksgiving dinner and Christmas Day breakfast for over fifty people.

Images

Most likely, you're used to seeing images everywhere. *Seeing* images and actually *reading* them, however, are very different. Reading an image takes both time and attention, just like reading a book or a document. You have to pay careful attention to each part of the image and think about how it relates to the overall meaning.

> Learning Style Tip
> If you are an **active** learner, try sketching out a copy of important visuals. Even if you're not a great artist, this practice can help you focus on the meaning of an image.

The first step to reading an image is simply identifying what the image includes. This first step may seem obvious, but skipping over images can be easy, especially if you're in a hurry to complete a reading assignment.

For example, a reading for your anatomy class may include a diagram of the digestive system. Take the time to examine the shape, location, and name of each organ carefully as this is important information you might not be able to find anywhere else.

Once you've examined the contents of an image, you should reflect on your **prior knowledge:** what you already know. Try asking yourself the following questions:

> Have I seen anything similar to this image before?
> Does anything in the image look familiar?
> How does the image relate to what I've already read?
> How does the image relate to other images in this text?

Finding a connection to your knowledge and experiences will make an image easier to understand and remember. Imagine you're in a cultural studies class, learning about holiday customs in other countries. One of your readings describes the Indian celebration of Holi, the Festival of Colors. The textbook includes this photo:

Photo courtesy of Wikimedia Commons

When you reflect on your prior knowledge of Indian holidays, you remember learning about another festival, Diwali, the Festival of Lights. You then quickly think through the differences and similarities between both holidays.

The photo also reminds you of a 5K you did last year, which involved people throwing colorful powder as you ran past them. While this memory doesn't seem to be connected to the reading, it helps you relate to the atmosphere of excitement and celebration taking place in the photo.

> **Learning Style Tip**
> If you are a **sensing** learner, you may find it difficult to make connections between images in your readings and your own personal experiences. Try writing down a few notes about the image first; then, search those notes for familiar words or terms.

Charts and Graphs

Charts and graphs are special types of visuals. They are used to put large amounts of **data**, like numbers or percentages, into a visual format that is easy for readers to understand.

Structure

To start reading a chart or graph, you first need to determine its structure. Structure is important because the way information is arranged in a chart or graph affects its meaning and purpose. There are three common types of charts and graphs: bar graphs, pie charts, and line graphs.

Bar Graphs

Bar graphs are used to compare and contrast groups of information. For example, a graph comparing the average GPA's of students at different colleges might look like this:

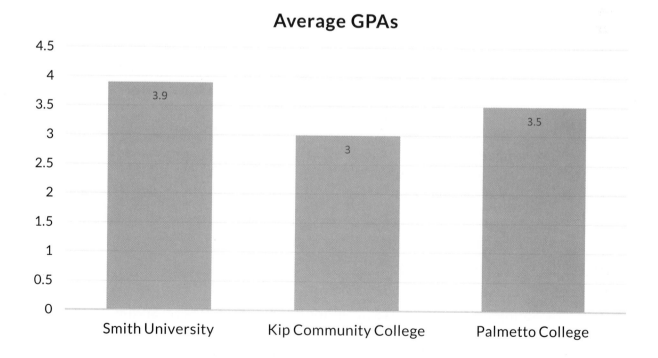

Average GPAs

Pie Charts

Pie charts show percentages of a whole.

A course syllabus usually includes a breakdown of the major grade categories and their weights. This information could be shown in a pie chart:

Assignment Weights

■ Final Exam   ■ Final Project   ■ Homework   ■ Tests   ■ Papers

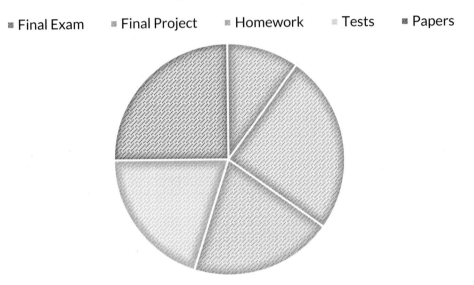

Line Graphs

Line graphs show changes over time. If you wanted to illustrate how much you paid for textbooks over five semesters, you could use a line graph:

Average Textbook Costs

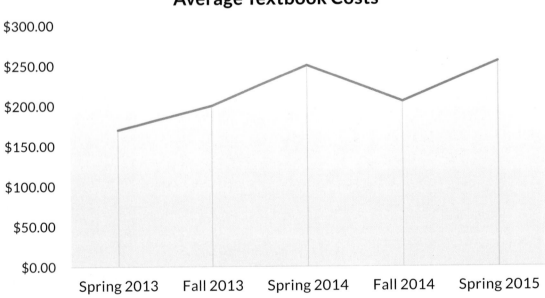

On Your Own

Think about the differences between bar graphs, pie charts, and line graphs. Which of these visuals would fit the following sets of data best?

Data	Visual
A comparison of sales revenue by restaurant location	
The growing number of Pinterest users since 2010	
The heights of your family members	
A comparison of average grocery costs over the last twelve months	
The average cost of rent in three different cities	

Data

Once you've determined the structure of a chart or graph, you need to examine each of its parts. A good place to start is the title. The title will give you a clear idea of the data being illustrated in the chart or graph.

You can then read the **legend,** which shows you the colors or patterns that represent each group of information. Make sure you can match each bar, pie slice, or line to the correct legend item.

Finally, read the numbers and captions on each part of the chart or graph. These will show you how the data is grouped together.

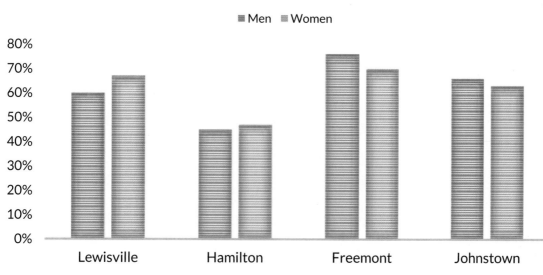

When reading a chart or graph, look for the title, the legend, and the captions.

Charts or graphs usually separate information into groups based on the **purpose** of the study. If the purpose of a graph were to compare the average age of people from different countries, it would probably divide the data into groups based on country. If the purpose of a chart were to show the rise in healthcare costs over the last year, it would probably divide the data into groups based on month.

> **Reflection Questions**
> A good chart or graph will display information as honestly as possible. Some graphs and charts, however, can be accidentally or even purposefully misleading. What are some specific ways that a chart or graph might present data incorrectly?

Lesson Wrap-up

Reading Application

Read the following passage and pay attention to how the visuals enhance the material.

It's a fairly common assumption that the minimum wage has been steadily increasing over the years. It has also become more and more expensive to purchase basic necessities. Once, a bottle of Coke was a nickel, and bread was a dime. What happened? We're still receiving the same goods, so why is the price increasing?

The author uses contractions and informal questions. What does this suggest about the intended audience?

Mostly, it's because of inflation. Inflation is when prices increase because the value of the dollar has decreased. As a result, prices of products increase, and minimum wage is raised to compensate.

Based on the past 100 years, it's not going to stop either. In 1955, the price for bread was 17.7¢ cents. Likewise, the minimum wage was $1. In 1975, the price of bread was 36¢, and the minimum wage rose to $2.10 that same year.

How do the graphs affect your understanding of the information presented?

What is the correlation? Is it raising prices that causes minimum wage to increase, or is it because minimum wage increases, and in response, suppliers charge more for goods? Or is it both?

The world of economics is a dense and complicated one. Understanding the intricacies of supply and demand can take years of study. Still, it's important to know the basics and participate as a wise consumer.

Sources:

https://www.dol.gov/whd/minwage/chart.htm

https://www.bls.gov/opub/mlr/2014/article/one-hundred-years-of-price-change-the-consumer-price-index-and-the-american-inflation-experience.htm#top

Key Terms

Active Learning: learning information through participation in activities

Bar Graph: a graph that compares and contrasts groups of information

Data: technical information, usually numbers or percentages

Font: the size and style of letters

Legend: part of a chart or graph that shows how the groups of information are displayed

Line Graph: a graph that uses a line to show changes over time

Pie Chart: a chart that uses pie slices to show percentages of a whole

Pre-reading: preparing yourself to learn from your reading

Prior Knowledge: what you already know about a topic

Purpose: the goal of a text

Sensing Learning: learning information through logical methods and objective facts

Verbal Learning: learning information through written and spoken words

Visual Clue: a picture, graph, icon, color, or shape that adds to the meaning of a text

Lesson 2.3
Reading Actively and Purposefully

Reading is hard work that requires more than just seeing the words on a page. True reading involves **comprehension:** actually understanding and remembering the information that you have read.

The best way to achieve comprehension is to practice active reading. **Active reading** is a process that focuses your attention on what you are reading, helps you make connections to your own experiences, and asks you to reflect on the information you have learned.

The opposite of active reading is **passive reading.** Passive readers do not fully comprehend the material that they are reading. Instead, they focus on finishing their assignment as quickly as possible. While passive readers may feel like they have saved time, they have actually created more work for themselves in the long run. They will need to spend extra time re-reading and studying the information later.

Reading comprehension is a skill that requires time and practice. Try not to feel discouraged. As you continue to use active reading strategies, you will become a stronger reader.

This lesson will teach you how to use active reading strategies to get the most from your reading.

Make Pre-reading a Priority
Check Your Understanding
Review What You Learned

> **Reflection Questions**
> Are there certain types of texts that you seem to comprehend better than others? Why?

Make Pre-reading a Priority

Pre-reading is an essential part of active reading. This is an opportunity for you to wake up your mind and prepare for learning.

During pre-reading, you should scan the title, table of contents, and major headings. Glancing through this information will give you a general idea of what you are about to read. You will also see how the reading fits into the overall structure of the text.

Next, make predictions and find connections. To make predictions about a reading assignment, ask yourself research questions such as "Who is the intended audience?" and "Why am I supposed to care about this topic?" Write down your answers so that you can review them when you have finished the assignment.

> **Learning Style Tip**
> If you're a **sequential** learner, you may feel strange glancing through a text before reading it. Don't allow yourself to skip this important step.

You can also use a **KWL chart** to outline what you know (K), what you want to know (W), and what you have learned (L). Before you start an assignment, fill out the first two columns by thinking through your **prior knowledge** and recording the information you want to learn.

Once you've had a chance to preview the reading assignment, make plans to get it done. You may need to schedule yourself extra time or gather special supplies.

For more detailed information about pre-reading, review Lesson 2.1.

Reading Application

Read the following essay. Use the annotations to guide you through the pre-reading process.

Rules for Celebrity Ads on Social Media

Celebrities have been a part of advertising since the 1700s, when kings and queens were shown with products in local newspapers. Today, we refer to this as celebrity branding, a type of marketing that uses famous people to advertise a product.

This tactic became popular in the United States in the 1980s, when basketball player Michael Jordan signed an advertising deal with Nike. Today, celebrities are using a new way to advertise and endorse products: Facebook and Instagram.

How can you connect to this idea? Where have you seen celebrities in advertising lately?

However, the problem with social media is that it's not always clear when posts double as paid advertisements. Celebrities often upload photos of their everyday lives, which might include clothing or products. It's sometimes hard to tell if they are actually being paid to promote these items.

In 2009, the United States Federal Trade Commission updated advertising laws to make it clear when a celebrity is being paid to advertise on social media. They now must follow the same advertising rules as celebrity endorsements in newspapers and on television.

For example, the word *ad* or *sponsored* must be present on a social media post if people are being paid to write about a product. Additionally, a paid post on social media must be an honest opinion by the celebrity. A promoter can get into trouble if they get paid to endorse a product that they dislike or have never tried.

Now that you've finished the reading, consider how this information built upon what you already knew.

With the popularity of celebrity social media accounts, it's important to know the difference between an honest review and a paid advertisement. Laws have been updated so that people who follow celebrities on social media know the truth about an endorsement and can make informed consumer decisions.

Check Your Understanding

After pre-reading, you can begin reading the text in small chunks. Don't worry too much about taking detailed notes. Your focus should be on understanding the information as thoroughly as possible. If you are having a difficult time staying on task, try reading out loud to yourself.

Summarize Paragraphs

After each **paragraph**, stop to make sure you understand what you have just read by writing a **summary**: a brief overview of the **main ideas** in a text.

Consider the following excerpt:

> *Franklin D. Roosevelt's "Four Freedoms" speech*
> *Annual Message to Congress on the State of the Union 1/06/1941 (excerpt)*
>
> In the future days, which we seek to make secure, we look forward to a world founded upon four essential human freedoms.
>
> The first is freedom of speech and expression—everywhere in the world.
>
> The second is freedom of every person to worship God in his own way—everywhere in the world.
>
> The third is freedom from want—which, translated into world terms, means economic understandings which will secure to every nation a healthy peacetime life for its inhabitants—everywhere in the world.
>
> The fourth is freedom from fear—which, translated into world terms, means a world-wide reduction of armaments to such a point and in such a thorough fashion that no nation will be in a position to commit an act of physical aggression against any neighbor—anywhere in the world.

Here's a summary:

> **In his "Four Freedoms" speech, Franklin Delano Roosevelt explained that freedom of speech and worship and freedom from want and fear are the four freedoms essential for democracy.**
>
> The excerpt from FDR's nine-page speech is fairly brief itself, so the summary above is even shorter, yet comprehensive.

Summarizing each paragraph will help you identify areas where you did not comprehend the reading. You may need to re-read the passage or look up an unfamiliar word. This is a good time to note any unfamiliar vocabulary so that you can return to it later.

> To learn more about finding meaning in unfamiliar words, see Lessons 2.6 and 2.7.

Once you feel confident in a section, you should think through the predictions you made during pre-reading. If you learned something new, add this information to the last column in your KWL chart. You can then move on to the next few paragraphs in the reading and start the process over again.

Reading Application

Practice checking your understanding as you read the following passage:

While some say "opposites attract," social psychologists suggest we're more likely to be attracted to someone like ourselves. In the best relationships, you enjoy your partner because of who he or she is as an individual, and because of the way you feel when you're together. Trading pieces of yourselves is an ongoing negotiation. You give and they give without asking for something in return. However, a truly mutual exchange usually results in mutual benefit.

Do you agree with these psychologists?

Think of it this way: a happy individual can accomplish a lot. Two people, working together, can accomplish more than twice that. The success of a relationship means bringing your best self but also taking care of yourself. This isn't selfish; it's making sure you're happy, healthy, and fulfilled.

Paragraph summary: If you and your partner bring the best version of yourselves to a relationship, you will both get much more out of it.

As author Ayn Rand pointed out, "Before you say 'I love you,' you must first understand the 'I.'" Without self-knowledge, you can't recognize your strengths and share them honestly with a partner. Healthy self-esteem means knowing who you are and what you bring to a relationship.

Does this idea make sense to you? If so, what does it mean and how can you relate to it?

> **Helpful Hint**
> While reading, you should feel free to take occasional reading breaks. Five minutes of rest between every thirty minutes of reading is usually enough time to clear you mind. Be cautious about taking longer breaks as you may find yourself getting distracted.

On Your Own

Try using this strategy to read the following except from an introductory statistics course. After every paragraph, use the text boxes to write a brief summary of the information.

Cigarettes did not always carry warnings such as "Smoking causes lung cancer, heart disease, and emphysema." In the early 1960s, Congress debated the Surgeon General's plan to label all packages of cigarettes with a warning that smoking could be hazardous to your health. Hearings were held, and testimonies were gathered from interested parties. The tobacco companies did not want a health notice placed on their product, so they sponsored a significant amount of investigation into the health effects of smoking.

On the other side of the issue was a large group of medical researchers who had analyzed the effects of smoking on animals and had collected considerable data on the health of both smoking and nonsmoking populations. The evidence presented seemed unquestionable: heavy smokers had a much higher incidence of lung cancer, about thirty times higher than nonsmokers. Furthermore, researchers found smoking is associated with cancers of the mouth, pharynx, larynx, esophagus, pancreas, uterus, cervix, kidney, and bladder. Even suicide rates were at higher levels for smokers.

The tobacco companies countered with their own experts who pointed out that the underlying cause of both disease and smoking could be attributed to heredity. That is, whatever caused people to have higher rates of lung cancer, heart disease, and so forth, could also cause them to smoke. If this were the case, then the proposed warning on packages of cigarettes would be untruthful. So, the pivotal problem was this: How could someone know whether smoking or heredity caused cancer?

One method of attacking this problem is to perform a controlled experiment. In a controlled experiment, the researcher creates data that will hopefully clarify the relationship between variables. A simple method of accomplishing this task would be to create two groups, smokers and nonsmokers, and compare them. The nonsmokers would be the control group and the smokers the treatment group. Each subject is randomly assigned to one of two groups to avoid bias. The smoking group would be required to smoke a pack of cigarettes per day for 15 years, and at the end of the time period, their health would be compared to the health of the nonsmokers. By randomly choosing members of the population, the hereditary pool of both groups should be similarly mixed; thus, any subsequent differences in health between the two groups could be attributed to the treatment (smoking) that was applied to one group. This method of experimentation has one drawback; it would be impossible to get human beings to volunteer for the experiment. As a result, the experiment has never been done.

However, researchers have performed controlled statistical experiments on many different kinds of animals and have discovered that smoking does cause problems similar to those observed in human beings. In 1964, the Surgeon General produced a historic report linking tobacco smoking to cancer. Since January 1, 1966, all cigarette packages sold in the United States have been required to carry a health warning. Since January 1, 1971, all cigarette television advertising has been banned. The percentage of adults who smoke in the United States has diminished. The prevalence of smoking has fallen in the United States since the exposure of the statistical evidence, from about 40% in 1965 to 29% in 1987, 23% in 2002, and 18% in 2013. However, this is not the case in many parts of the world.

Statistics made a difference. It helped people make informed decisions about their choice to smoke or not. Fortunately, it was not speculation, opinion, or special interest that decided the issue. Research on the effects of smoking continues, and of the 4,000 substances found in tobacco smoke, about 60 are now believed to be associated with cancer or tumor formation.

> So does smoking cause cancer? There is no absolute proof, but the evidence overwhelmingly suggests that it does. In 1998, tobacco companies reached a $206 billion agreement with 46 states to settle a lawsuit on the health damage done by cigarette smoking.

(Excerpt courtesy of *Discovering Statistics* by James S. Hawkes and William H. Marsh)

Review What You Learned

When you have finished reading the entire text and checking your understanding, you need to review what you learned. This will help you remember the material, an important aspect of comprehension. This final stage in the active reading process involves four steps:

1. **Summarize the entire text in your own words.** To test your comprehension of the reading as a whole, try summarizing it. This will help you identify any sections you need to re-read.

2. **Add notes and mark important information.** Review the entire text by adding helpful definitions, writing down questions, and highlighting important ideas. You should also mark the overall structure of the text, including the **introduction**, **conclusion**, and main points.

3. **Record what you learned.** Add anything you learned to the last column in your KWL chart and update the predictions you made during pre-reading. If you have any questions about the material, record them so that you can ask your instructor for help.

4. **Think about your reaction to the text.** After you've finished reading, think about how you feel about the author's main point. Do you agree with the information that was presented?

Even after you have completed the entire reading process, your work is not quite done. Keep all of your notes in a folder so that you can continue reviewing them during your study time. This will keep the material fresh in your mind and prevent you from cramming the night before a test.

For more information about taking notes on a text, see Lesson 1.6.

Lesson Wrap-up

Reading Application

As you read the following passage, consider how you can apply active reading strategies to help you comprehend the author's meaning.

Battle of the Parties: Supreme Court Edition

The Process

The year 2016 was a year of political controversy, and foremost was the search for a new Supreme Court judge. While this process is supposed to be simple, it took over a year to settle.

Active readers ask questions about the text: Why would this be controversial?

The nomination of a Supreme Court judge is a right given to the current President of the United States. The President nominates a candidate to fill the open spot in the nine-seated court, and Congress then conducts an extensive hearing for that judge. Congress decides if the candidate is suitable for the position. During the hearing, they check the judge's background and previous statements made by the candidate. If Congress sees no questionable ethical decisions in the judge's past, then the judge is put on the court. Simple, right?

To practice active reading, summarize each section of the passage.

The Result

Wrong! In 2016, Antonin Scalia, a judge on the Supreme Court, passed away. He left a vacant position for democratic President Barack Obama to fill. However, many Republicans objected to Obama, who had only a few months left in office, selecting a judge who would serve on the Supreme Court for the rest of his or her life. Republican leaders, like the Senate Majority Leader Mitch McConnell, refused to give President Obama's candidate, Merrick Garland, a hearing.

Are you familiar with these names? If not, look them up. Why might these people and their choices be important?

They believed that if they delayed the process, a Republican president would nominate a more conservative candidate. In the end, this plan worked. Donald Trump, a Republican, was voted into office. He nominated Judge Neil Gorsuch, whose hearing began less than six months into Trump's presidency. While Democrats were unhappy with the situation, they did not hesitate in questioning Gorsuch to the fullest extent during his hearing.

Key Terms

Active Reading: a process for reading that focuses your attention, asks you to be reflective, and helps you make connections to your prior knowledge

Conclusion: a paragraph that ties together the ideas in a paper and summarizes the main points, also called a concluding paragraph

Introduction: the paragraph used to introduce the main idea at the beginning of a paper, also called an introductory paragraph

KWL Chart: a chart that helps you think about what you know, what you want to know, and what you learned

Main Idea: the statement or argument that a text communicates about its topic

Paragraph: a short piece of writing that focuses on one main idea

Passive Reading: reading without comprehension

Pre-reading: preparing yourself to learn from your reading

Prior Knowledge: what you already know about a topic

Reading Comprehension: understanding and remembering what you have read

Sequential Learning: learning information through a step-by-step process

Summary: a concise overview of main ideas or events

Lesson 2.4

Deconstructing Topics, Ideas, and Details

Think about the last time someone asked you to catch them up on what they missed in class or tell them about a movie you liked. How did you go about it? Did you give each and every detail of the event?

If you told your classmate only about the little details—the outfit you wore to class, the students who participated, the squirrel you noticed outside the window—you wouldn't be providing very helpful information. Instead, you probably provided some sort of a summary, explaining only the most important and big-picture information.

In a similar way, comprehending and responding to a text requires first understanding the different components of a **paragraph.** Before you can think critically about an argument in a piece of writing, you should be able to locate the main idea(s). Then, you can evaluate the details used to support those ideas.

In this lesson, you will learn how to deconstruct the components of a text using these strategies:

Distinguish Between General and Specific Information

Recognize the General Topic

Locate the Main Idea

Break Down the Supporting Details

Annotate the Paragraph

Distinguish Between General and Specific Information

The first step to finding the main idea of a text is to understand differences between general and specific information.

General information can include a word, phrase, or idea that shapes the scope and overall point of a text. **Specific information** can include a word, phrase, or idea with a narrowed focus on a single piece of a text.

Reflection Questions
Think about how you would describe your personality to someone. What are your general characteristics? What are the specific features that are unique to who you are?

Simply put, general is broad while specific is narrow. Specific words and ideas can fit into general categories.

Here are some examples:

General	Specific
School Supplies	pens notebooks textbooks highlighters
Engineering	Civil Engineering Mechanical Engineering Chemical Engineering Electrical Engineering Geotechnical Engineering
Living Expenses	rent cable water electric

On Your Own

Use the table to fill in your own examples of general and specific information.

General	Specific

Reading Application

Take note of the general and specific information in the following passage:

How to Keep Texting Language from Affecting Our Communication

Most millennials regularly communicate through texting, and it's affecting the way people connect with each other. Texting often involves forming sentences without verbs or without spelling out entire words. Phrases like, "How r u doin?" or "me 2" are sent every day. Though it's a quick, easy way to send information, this form of communication is spilling into academic and professional areas as well as the way we speak. Below are some simple ways to get our language back.

This phrase represents general information that shapes the scope of the entire text.

Have lunch or dinner with friends and without phones. Suggest a place that has a lot of activity going on to avoid any awkward silences. Once you get started, the time will pass easily. I did this a few weeks ago, and it was a great reminder of how these experiences used to be.

Here, the author uses specific information to elaborate on an idea for readers.

Find other ways to communicate! Go back to old-fashioned emails instead of sending a text message. As archaic as it may sound, even sending a letter would be a welcome surprise to your recipient. It's not too often we receive these anymore, so they can be a fun treat.

Pick up the phone and call a friend to address a sticky situation or to say "hello." Often, a phone call will lessen the chances of misunderstanding. When speaking on the phone, you might better express how you feel about a situation and better perceive how your friend feels. Either way, there's nothing like hearing someone's real-life laughter or the smile in their voice.

This is another example of general information, as it points to the overall purpose of the paragraph.

There are certain things we should treasure in life. Our real-life language is one of them.

General and Specific Components of a Text

When you can distinguish between general and specific information, you can more easily locate the major components of a text:

Topic

The **topic**, or subject, of a text is the most general component of a text. It may or may not be explicitly identified. Think of the topic as an umbrella. In a text containing multiple paragraphs, the main idea of each paragraph fits under that umbrella.

Main Idea

The **main idea** is the statement or argument that a text communicates about its topic. Each paragraph in a text should contain a main idea. Texts with multiple paragraphs usually include multiple, related ideas that contribute to a bigger idea about the topic.

Supporting Details

Finally, the **supporting details** in a paragraph serve to support or describe the main idea with more specific information. Supporting details can be broken down into two levels: major details and minor details. Minor details are more specific than major details.

Remember that these components can be listed in order of general to specific information so that you can more easily locate them as you read a text. Recognizing each of these components is key not only for reading comprehension but also for effective writing.

Recognize the General Topic

The **topic** is a general word or phrase that tells you who or what the passage is about. It is very much like a title or heading; in fact, the topic is often used in the title or heading of a piece of writing. The topic is never a sentence and is always a word or phrase.

To determine the topic, ask yourself these questions:

- What words are repeated in this text? (Be sure to note repeated pronouns that refer to repeated subjects.)
- What is the broad subject of this text? What topic could act as an umbrella that houses all of the sentences or paragraphs in this text?

Helpful Hint
Keep in mind that various topics can apply to a text.

Locate the Main Idea

The main idea is a statement or argument that a text communicates about its topic. To determine the main idea of a paragraph, you should consider these questions:

- What big-picture message is the author communicating in this text? What does the author want me to understand?
- What idea or statement is supported by the evidence or details?

The main idea is closely related to the author's **purpose**, or goal, for writing. Consider these examples:

Topic	Purpose	Main Idea
Hurricanes	To inform the audience about what causes hurricanes	Hurricanes are caused by water vapor and warm air.
College Experience	To reflect on the difficulties the author faced when she returned to school	Returning to school was difficult for the author because of financial and emotional reasons.
Smoking	To persuade the audience to quit smoking	Smoking is a dangerous and costly addiction.
Family	To entertain the audience with a funny story about the author's family	The author's family ran into a number of strange situations during their last family vacation.

Reading Application

The following passage is a persuasive introduction written by someone frustrated with the school system. Consider how the author expresses the topic and main idea in the first paragraph.

Building a Safer School Environment

Learning can happen in many environments. In the age of technology, this is truer than ever. So why are we still confining most our nation's children behind four walls each day for eight hours? How can we continue to justify the loss of such a significant time in our children's lives in return for the traditional schooling system? We cannot. We cannot continue to justify forcing families to send their children to schools that are complete with security systems, bullies, and hours-long classes. How can such an atmosphere be considered acceptable and conducive to a learning environment? We are forcing too many kids to go to schools where they feel anxious and afraid, yet we wonder why they are distracted from learning? If this is what traditional schooling has come to, it's time to revolutionize schools one by one and restore them to places of security and growth.

In the title, the author presents the general topic: school safety.

Here, the author presents her main idea: lack of safety in schools promotes student anxiety and learning barriers.

Topic Sentence

The **topic sentence** is the sentence in a paragraph that contains or references the main idea. You can think about the topic sentence as a map pointer, indicating exactly where the main idea is located in a paragraph.

Well-written topic sentences meet these requirements:

- Connect the topic to a more specific (main) idea of a paragraph.
- Express a complete idea, usually in a complete sentence, that the rest of the paragraph will support.
- Serve as the most general statement in a paragraph. The supporting details throughout the rest of the paragraph should be more specific than the topic sentence.

The topic sentence pinpoints the main idea of a paragraph.

Take a look at the topic sentence in the following passage:

In August, I returned to campus for my sophomore year. I had been looking forward to that day since the moment I'd left campus in the previous May. <u>But after everything that had happened that summer, my excitement was met by overwhelming fears and concerns about the challenges ahead.</u>

Notice that the topic sentence in this example is the third sentence in the paragraph. The topic sentence does not always have to be the very first sentence. Based on this topic sentence, we can expect the rest of the paragraph to include specific details about the fears and concerns that the author has.

On Your Own

Locate the topic sentence in the following paragraph.

Successful College Students

Do you ever wonder how to become a successful college student? Some students arrive on campus with no idea or plan for getting good grades or making it to graduation. There are actually several reasons for success in school. The first reason for success in school is simply to be there. That's correct. You must attend classes or you will be unsuccessful. Another reason for success in college is having a good work ethic. For example, a student who keeps up with the work required for a class is almost certain to

> do well, while a student who is not diligent is unlikely to be successful. In fact, college professors generally recommend that you spend two to three hours preparing for class for every hour spent in class.

Some main ideas are not indicated by topic sentences. Instead, they are **implied**. In this case, you should use the rest of the paragraph as context for determining the main idea.

In longer texts, the main idea of each paragraph builds support for a bigger idea. This bigger idea is usually identified in a thesis or purpose statement.

> To learn more about different types of main ideas and details, see Lesson 2.9.

Break Down the Supporting Details

Supporting details make up the body of a paragraph, and they serve to support the main idea. For example, in a paragraph about the importance of budgeting, supporting details might include statistics about how much you could save in a year with proper budgeting tools.

There are two types of supporting details: major and minor. **Major details** support and prove the main idea. **Minor details** support the major details.

One key indicator of supporting details is the use of **signal words** or phrases that introduce evidence. Here are some examples:

There are various ways…	Several factors contribute to…
The first cause is…	The effects are…
One reason this occurs…	The advantages are…

Major Details

When locating major details, look for number words like these:

First, Second…	Last
One, Two…	Another
Next	Several

> **Helpful Hint**
> Keep in mind that signal words aren't *always* specific to major details or to minor details.

Minor Details

Minor details give more specific information about the major details and often include examples and/or explanations.

When locating minor details, look for more specific words like these:

For example	This means	In fact	These include	To clarify
Specifically	For instance	To illustrate	In other words	In particular

Remember that the main idea and major details make up the framework of the writing while the minor details give the reader more information to assist in understanding.

Annotate the Paragraph

Now that you understand each of the components of a paragraph, you can locate and note them using **annotations**:

Kettering is a dynamic neighborhood that has undergone a lot of change over the last four decades, most of which has been negative. Since 1976, the population has decreased from 4,899 to 2,019. The number of vacant or abandoned homes has more than doubled. The average median income has steadily gone down. Major businesses have viewed Kettering as a place that cannot support them. "There just was no longer a viable workforce," said Samuel Horning of Jojo Corp, a manufacturer of kids' toys that recently moved its headquarters to Cleveland, Ohio. "We'd put out a call for jobs and get very few qualified applicants." Meanwhile, "white flight" of the 1960s out of inner city neighborhoods laid the groundwork in Kettering for these failings.

topic sentence

body of the paragraph w/ details

specific details/evidence

Lesson Wrap-up

Reading Application

The following blog post discusses social media etiquette. As you read the passage, note how the author includes several main ideas, supporting details, and both major and minor details.

Pause Before You Post: Social Media Etiquette

While social media is usually a place for fun pictures and updates, you've probably seen posts that spark a lot of action in the comments section. Suddenly, you see your aunt fighting with someone from your fourth-grade class and with terrible grammar, too! Then, you notice your friend posting about how he can't stand his little brother even though his brother will most likely see it. While social media makes it easy and fun to share our lives and keep in touch with one another, there are general guidelines to help maintain polite social media etiquette.

The topic sentence of the first paragraph is located at the end of the paragraph.

If you see a post that you don't like or don't agree with, consider if it's worth getting involved. Some debates can be healthy, and you may even learn something. For example, if you and a friendly acquaintance can hash out who did the best on a recent singing show by comparing video clips back and forth, that was a productive and fun conversation. However, trying to tell someone you don't know very well that her political beliefs are wrong, in a very public space, isn't productive and can lead to further problems.

Phrases like for example *and* overall *often introduce minor details within a paragraph.*

If you think a post might hurt or offend someone, keep it private. Publicly posting hurtful material, whether it's offensive to a group of people or one specific person, is not only poor form but can also result in legal action. Sharing personal information or pictures of someone, especially if it portrays him or her in a negative light, can result in major consequences. Imagine if someone posted that you had failed all your classes and were being asked to leave school. Whether it was true or not, how would you feel? What action would you want to take? While expressing your opinion is generally a good thing, there is a line between sharing an opinion and being offensive. Use your best judgment before sharing things that could be hurtful or degrading to others.

Topic sentences like this one are located at the beginning of the paragraph.

Sometimes, authors present the main idea of a paragraph both in its topic sentence and in its concluding sentence.

Keep it positive! Social media can serve a lot of great purposes like keeping in touch with friends and family, advertising a small business, or sharing information about special events. Share photos of a good thing happening in your life, whether it's a trip across the country, an internship at your favorite magazine, or the funny things that your pets are doing. Focus on how the content you share can benefit yourself and others. For instance, you can share your support for businesses you respect, publications you trust, people you admire, or organizations in which you participate.

The major and minor details in this paragraph discuss ways to keep social media posts positive. Look for examples of signal words here.

Overall, social media is a great tool for keeping in touch personally and networking professionally. However, it's important to keep in mind how many people your posts reach and what effects they may have on others. What may seem like a trivial post to you may greatly impact your relationships with friends, family, and even co-workers. Maintaining a certain level of decorum on social media will ensure that you develop a good rapport with both personal and professional contacts while presenting yourself in the best light.

The main idea is reiterated for emphasis one more time in the concluding sentence.

Key Terms

Annotation: an informal note or comment entered in the margin of a text as a reading strategy

General Information: a word or word group that can be linked to a broad range of specific ideas and details

Implied Main Idea: a main idea that is not directly stated

Main Idea: the statement or argument that an author tries to communicate

Major Detail: a detail that supports and proves the main idea of a paragraph

Minor Detail: a detail with specific information that supports a major detail in a paragraph

Paragraph: a short piece of writing that focuses on one main idea

Purpose: the goal of a text

Signal/Signpost Word: a word or word group that introduces a new idea and/or shows the connection between two ideas

Specific Information: a word or idea with a narrow focus

Supporting Detail: a piece of information, also called evidence, that is used to support a main idea

Topic: the general subject of a text

Topic Sentence: a sentence that states the main idea of a paragraph

Lesson 2.5
Identifying Organizational Patterns

Remodeling a house can be difficult because the changes have to fit into the overall design of the building. You can't tear out a load-bearing wall and expect the house to be structurally sound.

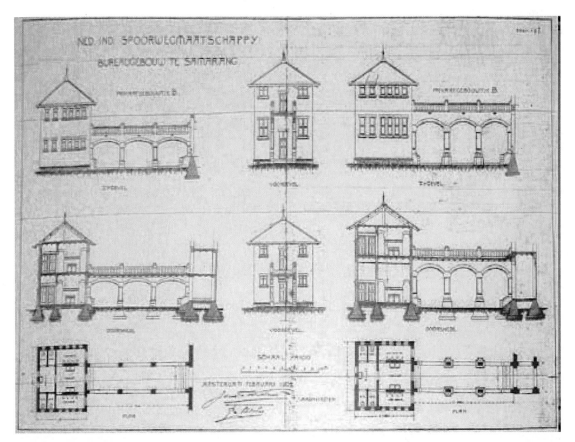

Whenever possible, builders examine the blueprints of a house before starting a remodeling project. This helps them understand the building's structure. Once they know what to expect, they can make decisions about the best way to make their improvements.

The structure of a written text is called an **organizational pattern.** Authors use these structures to arrange their main points more effectively. As a reader, you can use an organizational pattern like a blueprint as you follow the author's train of thought.

This lesson will describe six types of organizational patterns:

Cause and Effect
Chronological
Compare and Contrast
Order of Importance
Spatial
Topical

Cause and Effect

Writing that is organized by **cause and effect** explains the causes or effects of a topic. For example, a research paper about rising healthcare costs in America might discuss why Americans are spending more on healthcare or how healthcare costs are changing American society. Here are two examples of the main points these papers might cover:

Paper 1

1. Effect: Growing healthcare costs

2. Cause: Lack of preventative care

3. Cause: Unhealthy lifestyles

Paper 2

1. Cause: Growing healthcare costs

2. Effect: Rise in insurance premiums

3. Effect: Less access to medications

A book or document organized by cause and effect will use **signal words** that show *why* or *how*:

as a result	due to	reason
because	growth	result
benefits	impact	since
consequently	reaction	therefore

A cause and effect organizational pattern is commonly used in informative or persuasive essays or articles. To determine if a text is organized by cause and effect, try fitting the main points into one of these statements:

The causes of [topic] are [main points].

The effects of [topic] are [main points].

Reading Application

As you read the following example, think about how the organization and word choice indicate cause and effect.

In 1793, revolutionary France's National Convention established a new calendar that expanded weeks to last ten days, celebrated new festivals, and changed the year from 1793 to Year I of the Revolution. The new calendar was meant to replace the Gregorian calendar used by the Roman Catholic Church. This dramatic change had a negative effect on the attitudes and lives of non-political citizens and a positive effect on local politicians and the National Convention.

The new calendar had a negative effect on those who did not actively participate in the revolutionary government. Clergyman Abbé Sieyés responded to the proposal arguing that tradition was too strong to be overcome. He claimed that old habits and customs are not easily neglected. Farmers from Étampes, a few miles away from the turbulence of central Paris, wrote to the National Convention in 1794 to state their complaints about the new calendar. They proposed that Catholic practices were good because they encouraged rest from the distractions of everyday life.

The Gregorian calendar being replaced by the revolutionary calendar had a positive effect on local governments. Picardy, a local government official in the town of Steenwerck, wrote to his superiors about the offensive lack of celebration during the new holidays celebrating reason and philosophy. He also complained that instead of symbols representing liberty, equality, and fraternity, traditional Catholic items were still being displayed. Local government officials supported displacing the Gregorian calendar with the new calendar because it reinforced the power they had gained after the fall of the noble ruling class.

Finally, the new calendar also had a positive effect on the National Convention. The head of the calendar reform committee, Gilbert Romme, spoke before the National Convention and declared the Gregorian calendar to be a symbol of ignorance. He also equated the old calendar with the French royalty that the Revolution had sought to eliminate. Attempting to create a new calendar strengthened the National Convention's revolutionary ideals and its temporary control over France.

The French Revolutionary calendar had a negative effect on the attitudes and lives of many people in France who were not politically involved, including the clergy and the working class. These groups had close ties to the Catholic Church and the Gregorian calendar. However, it had a positive effect on the power of the local governments and the National Convention. This is because the calendar emphasized the Enlightenment ideals that contributed to the French Revolution.

On Your Own

Think of the last time you tried a new food or activity that you did not enjoy. Using cause and effect organization, write a warning to others about why they should not try this food or activity.

Chronological

When a text is arranged **chronologically,** the author discusses the ideas or events in the order that they occurred. This type of organizational pattern helps the audience see how a topic changes through time. If a textbook chapter on the Boston Tea Party were organized chronologically, it would look something like this:

1. Unrest begins to grow in the colonies because of British tax laws.
2. Colonial activist groups begin to organize and meet in secret.
3. A group of colonists destroy over three hundred chests of tea located in the harbor.
4. The British Parliament demands payment for the destroyed tea.

When you're reading a chronological text, look for signal words that indicate time. These words show the reader when the author is moving to a new event and place in time.

The following are examples of chronological signal words:

after	earlier	next	shortly
as	end	preceding	starting with
before	first	previously	then
beginning	following	second, third…	until
beyond	later	since	

Reading Application

Texts that recount past events, like personal narratives or essays about history or literature, are more likely to be written in chronological order. Chronological order is also used for most fictional stories and novels. The following passage is written in chronological order.

From the late 1800s to the mid-1900s, European perceptions of the role of sports changed over time. The Victorian era emphasized the role of sports in morality and character building. After the Victorian era, during WWI, sports were related to war. As the Second World War began, the role of sports was to build physical strength in both men and women.

From 1863 to approximately 1910, sports were seen not only as physically but also morally beneficial. This was the Victorian era, a time associated with ultra-conservative thinking and practices. It was during this time that Robert Baden-Powell founded the Boy Scouts, known today for teaching survival skills and personal integrity. Baden-Powell wrote about the positive moral effect of participating in sports. He claimed that it trained boys for adult life by teaching unselfishness and "a good temper."

As the Victorian era ended, World War I began in 1914. In the years and months leading up to it, the perception of sports became much more warlike. An article by Mark Berner in the *Berlin Soccer, Track and Field Journal* describes the Olympics as "war, a real war." The article also implies that a country's military rank was directly related to the performance of its athletes. A British military recruitment poster combined images of rowing and cricket with the heading "The Game of War." The poster encouraged young men to enlist in the army and used the idea of war as being the ultimate sport. Paris too adopted the aggressive view of athletic games. *The Paris Encyclopedia of Sports*—published several years after WWI ended—described "the young sportsman" as winning victories on the field and thwarting his opponents.

In the years between the end of the First World War and the beginning of the second, the role of sports changed again. Physical strength became the primary goal of sports and other physical activity. Nikolai Semashko, a doctor and Commissar of Health of Soviet Russia, wrote about the healthful effects of nature and exercise. Additionally, as the women's rights movement gained steam, it became more acceptable for men and women to exercise in the same way. Alice Profe, a German physician, argued that women did not need a different set of physical exercises than men to build up strength. Ingeborg Schhröder, a Swedish gymnast in the early 1900s, recalls in her memoir how important physical strength was to both men and women.

From the Victorian era to the 1940s, the Europeans perceived the role of sports changed over time. In the late 1800s and early 1900s, the role of sports was seen as morally strengthening and character building. During WWI, sports became a type of war. In between the Second and First World War, the role of sports expanded to build physical strength and to include women.

On Your Own

Use chronological organization to write about a day in the perfect life, starting with waking up in the morning and ending at bed time.

Compare and Contrast

The **compare and contrast** organizational pattern is used to show the similarities and differences between two topics. The text could be organized in any of the following ways:

- First, describe one topic; then, describe the other topic.
- Discuss a specific similarity or difference in each **paragraph.**
- Explain all of the similarities first; then, explain all of the differences.

The following outlines are examples of how an essay on the differences between high school and college could be organized:

Essay 1

I. High school
    a. Academics
    b. Social life

2. College
    a. Academics
    b. Social life

Essay 2

I. Academics
    a. Differences
    b. Similarities

2. Social life
    a. Differences
    b. Similarities

Essay 3

I. Ways that high school and college are similar
    a. Academics
    b. Social life

2. Ways that high school and college are different
    a. Academics
    b. Social life

A compare and contrast text will probably use some of the following signal words to show differences and similarities:

although	however	just as	on the other hand
as well as	in contrast	like	

Some descriptive and informative essays use compare and contrast. This organizational pattern is also commonly used in advertisements and commercials.

Reading Application

Here is an example of writing that compares and contrasts:

Have you heard of some people being considered a dog person or a cat person? These are ways to describe people who prefer having a dog as a pet as opposed to a cat or vice versa. What are the similarities and differences between owning a dog and owning a cat? Both cats and dogs need their human to feed them and play with them; however, cats and dogs require different levels of care.

Cats should be fed daily, and some people believe that their cats should always have a full bowl of food that they can visit throughout the day. In contrast, most dog owners will not "free feed" their dogs. This is because dogs tend to eat too much unless their portions are carefully monitored by their owners. Many people will allow their pets to eat "people food," which can lead to unhealthy weight gain. Both cats and dogs can run into serious health problems if they are overweight.

Because cats enjoy climbing and hiding, they don't need much room for exercising. Sometimes, at night or early in the morning, you can catch cats chasing things in the air or chasing each other. You can choose to buy them toys to play with, such as feathers that dangle from a string attached to a stick, small balls that make a jingling sound, or a laser pointer. These will keep them occupied for hours. Unlike cats, dogs need a large space to run around freely in, or you will need to take them for walks once or twice a day. Some breeds require more exercise than others, and no dogs should be crated or locked up all day and night with no exercise or movement. Both cats and dogs need playtime with their owners in order to thrive and get enough exercise.

While cats and dogs are both house pets, they require a different level of care. Cats can be left alone for 1-2 days if they have adequate food and water. They require much less care than dogs. Dogs need an owner who can be active and involved. Depending on which animal you like better, what your job is, and how much time you have for care, one might be a better pet than the other. With both pets, remember that they need regular veterinary checkups and medicine.

Order of Importance

When a text is organized by **order of importance**, the information is arranged from most important to least important or from least important to most important.

A business proposal about the need for a new payroll system might be organized like this:

1. A new payroll system would prevent paycheck errors.
2. A new payroll system would save the company money.
3. A new payroll system would be easier to use.

   In this example, preventing errors in employee paychecks is the most important reason to switch systems, while the ease of use is the least important reason.

Putting the most important reason first grabs the audience's attention quickly. In contrast, putting the most important reason last helps your audience remember it better.

The following signal words are used to show importance:

best of all	key	least
finally	lastly	most important

Documents that persuade the audience to make a decision or take action are often organized by order of importance.

Reading Application

Here's an example essay written in order of importance:

What is the average class size of the courses you are taking right now? Whether in high school or college, it seems that the number of students per class is increasing. However, there is still only one teacher to instruct the students. This can cause a lot of problems for even the most talented teacher. The best solution is to reduce class size. Reducing class size would mean that students could receive more one-on-one time with the teacher, and they would feel more comfortable with participating in activities or discussions.

Most importantly, reducing class sizes would make it easier for the instructor to give individual attention to each student. For example, one assignment may take students twenty minutes to complete, and if there is a class of forty people, the teacher only has time to spend thirty seconds with each student. Studies show that an increase in student-teacher interaction is related to an increase in academic achievement. Having fewer students in the class will allow the teacher more time to visit with each and every student.

A less significant but still important benefit of reducing class size is that the students will be more likely to participate. Students need to feel comfortable in order to speak up in class. Large classes of unfamiliar faces can be intimidating. If students are in small groups and are familiar with their classmates, they are more likely to get involved in activities or discussions.

While some people might argue that it is more cost-effective to have more students in the classroom, does it benefit student learning to focus on money rather than the value of the education they are receiving? Reducing class size should be a priority for all schools. The key benefit for students would be more one-on-one attention from instructors. Also, smaller classes would encourage students to participate in discussions and activities. School administrators and teachers can get together and agree on a maximum class size that makes them both happy.

Spatial

Spatial organization is used to describe a topic by its physical characteristics. These descriptions always follow a logical direction: right to left, top to bottom, or inside to outside. An essay about your ideal **workspace** might be organized this way:

1. The perfect room
2. The perfect desk
3. The perfect chair

A spatial text will use words that show location. The following are examples of spatial signal words:

above	below	inside	outside
across	in front of	next to	to the left/right

Spatial organization would work well for an essay about the perfect workspace.

Descriptive essays and documents that help the reader visualize a topic often use a spatial organization pattern. Some scientific and historical reports may also be arranged spatially.

Group Activity

On your own, take some time between classes to sit down somewhere and describe the room or area where you're sitting. When you meet with your group, take turns reading your descriptions and see if your teammates can guess the place you're describing.

Reading Application

As you read the following passage, look for indicators of space, location, and direction.

Ron shuddered as he walked into the silent room, a feeling of nostalgia and displacement creeping through his veins. He scanned the walls. The old, circular window was still there, clouded with dust. How many days had he spent in the living room peering through that window, watching in awe and frustration as his brothers chased footballs? For a moment, the old surge of jealousy hit him unexpectedly. He laughed aloud. "It's hard being the youngest."

On the right, the doorway to the kitchen loomed in front of Ron, daring him to enter. As he walked through the hallway, passing the rows of framed pictures, his unease turned to fondness, his frown to quiet tears. Walking into the kitchen, he could practically smell the blueberry muffins he'd spent hours baking with his mother. She'd reassured him that one day he and his brothers would become good friends. Ron jumped as the faded red curtains swayed with the breeze, and the wind chimes made the sound of home that he'd heard all of his childhood years.

He moved left, to the table, and picked up the last newspaper his father had ever read, and smiled to see the "Job Ads" section circled with red marker. Even in retirement, his father was never content. The memory of his father stayed with him as he walked through the garage door in the corner, his eyes resting on decaying boxes and rusty car parts. He thought of the afternoons he spent as a teenager working with his father to repair the old Ford pick-up. Though the time was seldom spent exchanging words, it was his father's way, and he could hear the clanking of the tools just as vividly as he could smell his mother's blueberry muffins.

Ron lifted the corrugated metal garage door and walked outside. He surveyed the yard, the driveway, and the fence. "The backdrop of my childhood," he thought. He got in his car in the driveway and stared at the house for a few more minutes. Then, he drove home to his own sons. "Alright," he said, "it's time for a game of football. Even you, Ron." And he winked at his youngest son, who lit up as he ran with his brothers to the backyard.

Topical

Topical organization is a general organizational pattern used for equally important main points. This is one of the most commonly used types of organization because it will fit almost any topic. An article about different types of exam questions might use the following topical organization:

1. Multiple choice
2. Short answer
3. True and false
4. Essay

Because a topical text isn't organized by time, location, or importance, a good author will use plenty of clues to help the audience find the main points. Common signal words for this type of organizational pattern are the following:

first	last	next	to begin
finally	main point	second	

Almost any type of book or document can be arranged topically. When you are trying to determine the organizational pattern, only decide on topical if the text doesn't fit anything else.

Reading Application

Here's an example of a topical essay:

Backyard barbecues, poolside afternoons, and lawn games are just some of the welcome activities that summer brings. Unfortunately, these opportunities for enjoying the outdoors are often accompanied by an uninvited guest: the mosquito. Most active early in the morning and late in the afternoon, the mosquito can ruin a perfect summer day with its annoying buzz and itchy bites. Although DEET-based sprays are perhaps most widely available, they can have negative health and environmental effects. Three ways to repel mosquitos, without using DEET, are natural oils, fans, and bacteria.

Some natural oils, particularly those from lemon-scented plants, have been found to keep mosquitoes at bay. Citronella oil is an essential oil made from lemongrass and can be an effective insect repellant. Eucalyptus oil, made from the leaves of eucalyptus plants, is another popular, natural insecticide. Using a combination of several essential oils will create a stronger bug repellant whether you make it at home or buy it ready-made. One disadvantage of natural oils is that they require more frequent re-application, usually every thirty to sixty minutes.

A second way to repel mosquitos is to use a fan. Mosquitoes are poor fliers, so setting up a large fan on a deck or patio can help keep them away from a small outdoor area. The air flow will disrupt their flying pattern and discourage them from flying in that area. Fans can serve a double purpose of keeping you cool in the summer heat and keeping away pesky bugs. However, two issues could arise from this method of repelling mosquitos. First, you may not have an electrical outlet outdoors, or it may not be in the right location on your house. Second, long extension cords can become a safety hazard.

A third option for repelling mosquitos without using DEET is to use *Bacillus thuringiensis israelensis* (Bti). Bti is a kind of bacteria that is harmless to humans but destroys mosquito eggs, which are laid in water. Floating discs of Bti can be used in pools and birdbaths, and Bti pellets can be sprinkled in gutters and other places where rainwater collects. This method will not keep away mosquitos that are already bothering you, but it will prevent them from multiplying.

Natural oils, fans, and Bti are three ways to repel mosquitos. These methods are safer and more natural than DEET-based products. When the weather gets warm, try one or a combination of these strategies to keep mosquitos from ruining the fun!

Lesson Wrap-up

Key Terms

Cause and Effect: an organizational pattern used to explain the causes or effects of a topic

Chronological: an organizational pattern that arranges ideas or events in the order that they occurred

Compare and Contrast: an organizational pattern used to show the similarities and differences between two topics

Order of Importance: an organizational pattern that arranges information in order of importance

Organizational Pattern: the structure of a written text, used to arrange the main points of a work

Paragraph: a short piece of writing that focuses on one main idea

Signal/Signpost Word: a word or word group that introduces a new idea and/or shows the connection between two ideas

Spatial: an organizational pattern used to describe a topic by its physical characteristics

Topical: a general organizational pattern used for equally important main points

Workspace: a location free from distractions and clutter for working and studying

Lesson 2.6
Using Context for Unfamiliar Words or Phrases

Imagine that you are sitting by yourself at Starbucks. There is a young couple sitting a few tables down from you. They are speaking in hushed tones and making angry hand gestures. When you realize they are having an argument, you shift your gaze to a nearby window. Outside, the sky is turning dark gray, and the leaves are shaking in the wind. You don't want to get caught in the rain without an umbrella, so you gather your things and leave.

Even though you couldn't hear exactly what they were saying, you knew that the couple inside the coffee shop was arguing. You could also tell it was going to rain before any raindrops began to fall. How exactly did you know these things?

Every day, you make decisions based on the context clues around you. In the previous example, the darkening sky and the shaking leaves were clues about the state of the weather. You used this information to figure out that it was probably about to rain.

When you are reading a text, **context clues** are the words and phrases that help you piece together the meanings of unfamiliar words.

You may be wondering, why not just use Google? While looking up the definition of a word is always a good idea, there are times when you do not have access to the internet. In these situations, being able to figure out the meaning of a word on your own will help you get the most out of your study time.

By using context clues, you can make logical guesses that help you learn new words, increase your understanding of a text, and save you time while reading.

Without thinking about it, you use context clues every day.

In this lesson, you will learn how to find the meaning of a word based on context clues:

> **Look for Clues in Nearby Sentences**
> **Use Substitution to Test Possible Meanings**

Look for Clues in Nearby Sentences

The first step in finding the meaning of a word is to read back through the nearby sentences, looking for clues. Start by reading the entire sentence again. If the word is located in the middle of a **paragraph**, read the entire paragraph as well. As you read, look for the following types of context clues:

Definition

Sometimes, the writing will give a definition of the word right in the same sentence. Look at the following example:

> The bakery spent all week preparing for an audit, a process that involves reviewing all of the company's financial records.

> This example includes the definition of the word *audit* in the sentence itself. An audit is *a process that involves reviewing all of the company's financial records.*

Definitions can also appear in a separate sentence, like in the following example:

> The agents made sure that their gathering was clandestine. Because the meeting was secret, they met in an abandoned warehouse.

> The meaning of the word *clandestine*, "done in secret," is provided by the second sentence in this example.

Synonym

A **synonym** is a word that has the same meaning as another word.

Authors sometimes use a word and a synonym to add extra emphasis or explanation to the sentence. Here's an example:

> To clean the machine thoroughly, always use a cleaning solution designed to inhibit, or stop, the growth of mold.
>
> In this sentence, the meaning of the word *inhibit* is the same as the word *stop*. The author includes both words to make sure that the audience understands the meaning of the sentence.

Antonym

An **antonym** is a word that has the opposite meaning of another word. In a text, an author might use an antonym to show contrast. The following sentence is an example of this:

> Although some teachers believed that Anton was lazy, he was actually quite diligent about his schoolwork.
>
> The word *diligent* is the opposite of the word *lazy*. In this sentence, the word *although* is used to show contrast.

The following words are commonly used to signal the use of an antonym:

but	on the other hand
even though	similarly
in contrast	unlike

Reading Application

Look for context clues as you read the following passage:

Should Your PE Grade Factor into Your Overall GPA?

When I was in school, the subject I disliked most was Physical Education (PE). I loathed walking into that rancid locker room, filled with bad smells and unwashed corners. Some days I felt uncomfortable and didn't want to put on those recycled gym shorts.

> Based on the description that follows, you can presume that the word *rancid* means dirty or unappealing.

Our teacher would take attendance and look up after she called each name to see if we were dressed properly. If we weren't, she would deduct points from our grade, deterring us, or preventing us, from not changing. If we missed too many days without our uniform, our grade would drop drastically.

> If you are unfamiliar with the word *deterring*, you can apply the synonym strategy and see that it means the same as *preventing*.

Given the discomfort many people feel toward PE, should this grade count towards a cumulative GPA as opposed to being a separate grade? Should the fact that I was about as athletic as a rock factor into this important number? I never could run the "seven-minute mile" in less than twelve minutes, and I wasn't alone. Many people would prefer to swap PE for an elective that is more beneficial to their overall education or interests.

> The word *cumulative* may be unfamiliar to you. If so, use the antonym phrase that follows as a context clue. This way, you can infer that *cumulative* means overall or collective.

There's a lot of pressure to keep up a high GPA, especially when it comes to applying for college. Fortunately, I was still accepted to several schools, but my PE grade certainly didn't do me any favors. School administrators should reconsider their practices when determining their grade structure, or the way they organize and apply this policy. Students should be encouraged to substitute PE for a course that better suits their individual strengths, interests, or career pursuits.

Here, you can apply the definition strategy to see that the word *structure* refers to the way something is organized and built.

Example

Authors sometimes use **examples** to explain the meaning of a difficult word. These examples often follow the phrase "for example." Look at the following sentence:

> The man's behavior was irrational; for example, he often claimed that aliens were spying on him.

> The meaning of the word *irrational* is "crazy." The example that the author includes helps the audience understand the meaning of the word better.

Reflection Questions
Write or draw a set of examples to illustrate the meanings of the following terms:

    unlucky   curious   skeptical   distracted

Inference

An **inference** is a logical conclusion based on what's happening in the text. This type of context clue isn't stated outright. Instead, you have to think carefully about the meaning of the other words in the text.

> In a closed circuit, energy flows without stopping from a beginning point to a terminal point.

> While you may not know the meaning of the word *terminal*, you know that if something starts at a beginning point, it probably ends at an end point. In this sentence, the word *terminal* means "end."

Use Substitution to Test Possible Meanings

Once you've read through the text carefully and located potential context clues, you should use substitution to check the meaning of the unfamiliar word. First, think of a possible synonym and read the sentence with that word. Look at the following example:

> When she lived at the military base, Harmony bought groceries at the commissary every Saturday.

> Through inference, you probably guessed that a commissary could be a type of store. To check your understanding, try reading the sentence with the word *store* instead. If the sentence makes sense, you've probably guessed correctly. A commissary is a type of store located on a military base.

When in doubt, mark the word so that you can look up the meaning later. You don't want to skip something important that might show up on a test or exam later.

Helpful Hint
Remember that words and their substitutes should always be the same part of speech. For example, *second-in-command* is a good substitute for *deputy* because they are both nouns.

On Your Own

Read the following paragraph and use context clues to determine the meaning of the highlighted words.

Nutrition science is relatively new, effectively a 20th century creation. On the basics of what the human animal ought to eat, as expressed in dietary recommendations around the world, the experts are more or less agreed (Cannon). But on many specific issues there are long-running differences of view, often intense, even polemical, in character. Obesity is one area of conspicuous contention. In part, these disputes reflect the youth of the science, including the practical difficulties of conducting controlled research, lasting many years, on the daily routines of large numbers of free-living subjects. The practical consequence is that the many non-nutritionists working on obesity have difficulty finding agreed, actionable conclusions from nutrition science on what to do about the problem.

(Excerpt courtesy of "Obscurity on Obesity" [http://www.biomedcentral.com/1741-7015/12/114] by Jack Winkler)

Lesson Wrap-up

Key Terms

Antonym: a word that has the opposite meaning of another word

Context Clue: a word or phrase that helps you determine the meaning of an unfamiliar word

Example: a specific instance or illustration that demonstrates a point

Inference: a logical conclusion based on your prior knowledge and the information in a text

Paragraph: a short piece of writing that focuses on one main idea

Synonym: a word whose meaning is similar to that of another word

Reading Application

Read the following blog post. How can you use different context clue strategies to make sense of difficult terms and concepts?

Meatless Mondays

Today, I want to explore the idea of Meatless Mondays! Did you know that raising meat takes a toll on animals and the environment? A lot of meat comes from factory farms, or large-scale farms, where thousands of animals are raised for food. These farms are also called CAFOs, or concentrated animal feeding operations. Because these animals are not in open pastures where they can graze on grass, they consume corn and other grains that take high amounts of energy to grow. For example, it takes 6.7 pounds of feed to create one hamburger patty! Animals also create waste that they end up living in. Being in these concentrated areas that are close and confined, surrounded by waste, can lead to the spread of disease. Cows also produce a lot of methane.

Note how these sentences both contain definitions for the terms they introduce.

Locate these synonymous words: *concentrated, close,* and *confined.*

This gas created during digestion is a greenhouse gas, meaning it contributes to global warming by trapping heat in the atmosphere. If we cut out one day of meat-eating per week, the amount of resources—water, food, land—that we use to raise meat will diminish, and our planet will be healthier.

Sometimes, unfamiliar terms (like *greenhouse gas* in this example) precede their definitions.

The average American consumes 100 pounds of meat per year. Certain meats are linked to health concerns like heart disease and diabetes. Eating more vegetables and cutting back on processed meats, like bacon and ground beef, helps reduce the risk of these diseases. While it's hard for some people to incorporate more plant-based foods into their diet, Meatless Mondays help create a routine for creative problem-solving.

Examples can illustrate the meaning of unfamiliar terms like *processed meats*.

I have been trying Meatless Mondays for three months now, and I've found some great staples that I make regularly. These include zucchini noodles with olive oil and chili flakes, sweet potato with honey and goat cheese, and beet salads with arugula, which is a zesty-tasting salad green. While you may not want to go full vegetarian, cutting meat out once a week still contributes to improved personal health and a cleaner environment.

What context clues help you to infer what *staples* means in this sentence?

What is arugula?

Keep reading my blog for more Meatless Monday recipes!

Lesson 2.7
Using Word Parts for Unfamiliar Words

Have you ever noticed that some words in the English language sound alike? For example, the words *television*, *telephone*, and *telescope* all start with the same letters. These similarities might seem confusing at first; however, they are actually useful clues that you can use to expand your vocabulary and understand unfamiliar words.

Many of the words we use every day share word parts with one another.

Understanding word parts will help you find the meaning of unfamiliar words faster. Many words in the English language are made up of multiple word parts. Because these word parts come from the same Latin or Greek words, they can be used to determine the definition of a word.

For example, the word *telephone* can be broken into *tele* and *phone*. These two word parts come from Greek words that mean "from far away" and "sound." A telephone, therefore, allows you to hear sound from far away.

This lesson will teach you how to use word parts to find the meaning of unfamiliar words.

Reflection Questions
Think of five more words that start with *tele*. What do you think their word parts mean?

Helpful Hint
Because the English language borrows terms from multiple languages, not every word can be broken into word parts. In these cases, use **context clues** instead.

To learn more about context clues, see Lesson 2.6.

Roots

The **root** is the main part of a word. A word made up of Latin or Greek word parts always includes at least one root, and this root contains the basic meaning of the word. For example, the word *vision* contains the root *vis*, which means "to see." Vision is the ability to see, so knowing the root *vis* tells you the overall meaning of the word.

Since roots give the basic meanings of words, think of them like tree roots. Just as roots are the foundation of a tree, roots are also the foundation of a word.

Root words are roots that can stand alone without any other word parts. A good example of this is the word *love*. This root can stand on its own or act as the foundation for other words such as *lovely* or *unlovable*.

Roots serve as the foundation, whether they belong to trees or words.

Combining roots are another type of root. These word parts form the base of a word but cannot stand on their own. They must always be combined with other word parts. For example, the root bio means "life." This root acts as the foundation for words such as *biology* or *biography*.

Root	Meaning	Root	Meaning
auto	self	**mal**	bad
biblio	book	**man**	hand
bio	life	**phil**	love
dict	to say, speak	**phobia**	fear
graph	to write	**phon**	sound
homo	same	**tele**	far off, far away
jud	to judge	**vis**	to see

Once you become familiar with root words and combining roots, you can start to identify **word families.** These are groups of words that share the same root meaning. For instance, *bibliography* and *bibliophile* share the root *biblio*, meaning "book," so they are both part of the same word family. Being able to recognize word families helps you connect the words together, remember how to spell them, and learn their meanings.

Prefixes

Prefixes are a second type of word part that are added to the beginning of roots to create new words. For example, the word *bicycle* includes the prefix *bi-*, which means "two," before the root *cycle*.

Another example of a word containing a prefix is *preview*. The word *view* is a root word that means "to see." Because the prefix *pre-* means "before," adding the two word parts together creates the word *preview*, which means "to see before."

Word Part	pre	+	view	=	preview
Meaning	before	+	to see	=	to see before

Prefixes are usually used to show amount, time, or position. They can also be used to make a word negative.

Prefix	Meaning	Prefix	Meaning
bi-	two	**post-**	after
co-	with, together	**pre-**	before
de-	down, reverse, remove	**re-**	again
mis-	wrong, bad	**semi-**	half
non-, un-	not	**trans-**	across, over

Reading Application

Look for word parts as you read the following blog post:

Going Gluten-Free

If you have been to a supermarket lately, you have probably seen a lot of things labeled "gluten-free." Some people automatically buy gluten-free items because they sound healthier. So, what is gluten, and why is it so bad? Gluten is a natural protein commonly found in wheat and other grains. It is frequently added to baked goods to make them soft and chewy and prevent them from falling apart.

The prefix *pre-* means *before*, so the word *prevent* means to stop something before it happens.

Unfortunately, some people are highly sensitive to wheat products. They can become seriously ill if they eat anything containing gluten.

The prefix *un-* means *not*, so the word *unfortunately* means *not luckily.*

Approximately 1-2% of Americans are wheat-sensitive and should avoid products made with gluten. The rest of us can safely enjoy our chewy cookies without worry.

People with a family history of celiac disease or who think they might be even semi-sensitive to wheat should get tested. For most consumers, though, going gluten-free does not necessarily make them healthier.

The prefix *semi-* means half, so the word *semi-sensitive* means *partially sensitive.*

Scientists argue that re-making old recipes can lead to unhealthy alternatives that lack valuable nutrients like fiber, iron, and zinc. Instead of worrying about gluten, they argue, people should consider the amounts of fat and sugar they are consuming.

The prefix *re* means *again,* so the word *re-making* means *to make again.*

Helpful Hint

To remember that prefixes are added to the beginning of a word, think about similar words like *preview* or *prequel.* All of these *pre-* words come *before* something else.

Suffixes

Suffixes are the final type of word part. These are added after a root to change the meaning of a word. Although not all words have suffixes, some words can have one or even two.

Think about the word *friend.* If you add the suffix *-less,* the word becomes *friendless,* which means "without friends." If you add the suffix *-ship* instead, the word becomes *friendship,* which means "the state of being friends."

Word Part	friend	+	less	=	friendless
Meaning	companion	+	without	=	without companions

Reflection Questions

Suffixes determine if a word is an adjective, an adverb, a noun, or a verb. For example, the word *happy* is an adjective, the word *happily* is an adverb, and the word *happiness* is a noun. Can you think of any similar examples?

Suffix	Meaning	Suffix	Meaning
-able	able, can do	**-less**	without
-ance, -ence	action, state, process	**-ly**	like
-ful	full of	**-ness**	state or quality of
-fy	make, become	**-ology**	study, science of
-ion, -sion, -tion	act of, state of	**-or, -er**	one who/that
-ize	cause, become, make like		

On Your Own

Once you've become familiar with the different types of word parts, you can begin using them to expand your vocabulary. Look at the following words and use the roots, prefixes, and suffixes from this lesson to determine their meanings.

Word	Meaning
judicator	
graphology	
autophobia	
diction	

Group Activity
As a group, try to think of at least one example word for each prefix, suffix, and root.

Lesson Wrap-up

Key Terms

Combining Root: a root that forms the base of a word but cannot stand alone

Context Clue: a word or phrase that helps you determine the meaning of an unfamiliar word

Prefix: a word part added to the beginning of a root in order to create a new word

Root: the main part of a word which contains its basic meaning

Root Word: a root that can stand alone without any other word parts

Suffix: a word part added to the end of a root in order to change the meaning of a word

Word Family: a group of words that share the same root meaning

Reading Application

The following article presents tips for job searching. As you read the passage, take note of how certain words are constructed based on roots, prefixes, and suffixes.

Soft Skills

A recent report shows that businesses consider soft skills an important factor in hiring. Soft skills refer to interpersonal skills. They include how well you communicate, adapt to changes in the workplace, and solve problems without direct supervision. If you want to make yourself more marketable when job searching, consider showcasing your soft skills.

The prefix *inter* means *between*, and the root word here is *person*. Therefore, *interpersonal* refers to people and relationship skills.

The suffix *able* means *capable of*. This means that a person is capable of marketing, or advertising, him or herself to employers.

Businesses want employees to have strong written and verbal communication skills. This helps to minimize miscommunications when employees are interacting with each other. Businesses also want potential managers to have these skills so they can clearly express their expectations to others. A desirable employee can also read nonverbal cues such as tone, facial expressions, and body language. This is especially important when meeting and negotiating with clients in person.

> The prefix *non* means *not*. The root *verbal* means *spoken word*. So, *nonverbal* means something not related to the spoken word.

Since the nature of the business world is always changing, employees should be adaptable. This is especially true for employees in the sciences and technology.

> To *adapt* to something means to change. The suffix *able* means *capable of*. This indicates that a person is capable of change.

Employees must be able to learn new skills easily even if they are experienced in their work. Ideally, they will seek out professional development to adjust to new work requirements.

Effective employees are self-motivated and can think critically about problems when they arise. They can work autonomously without the constant need of a leader to micromanage them. When leaders trust their employees to tackle their responsibilities, this gives them opportunities to focus on bigger goals for the business.

> The prefix *micro* means *small*. Therefore, this indicates management of small things, or the little details of a person's work.

Ultimately, soft skills are vital in the workplace. If you are a job seeker, you should re-evaluate your soft skills to address possible deficiencies that can hurt your chances. If you have strong soft skills, be sure to emphasize them on your résumé and in interviews.

> What might re-evaluate mean?

Lesson 2.8
Making Inferences about a Text

Whenever you watch a movie, you make inferences about the characters: their backgrounds, emotions, relationships, and futures. Even though the story doesn't have time to include all of this information, you can usually fill in the gaps with your imagination and instinct.

For example, think about the last action movie you watched. You could probably identify the "hero" and the "villain" almost right away. Obviously, the movie didn't directly tell the audience, "This is the hero of the story." You had to make inferences about the characters based on their actions, words, and even their appearance.

> **Helpful Hint**
> Reading assignments or tests often ask you to make inferences about a text. These assessments usually use the following keywords:
>
> | | | | | |
> |---|---|---|---|---|
> | assume | conclude | indicate | suggests | most likely |
> | predict | interpret | analyze | imply | probable |

Group Activity
Write a comic strip that includes a hero and a villain. What does each character do and say? What do they wear, and how do they sound? How do they treat others? Your readers should be able to infer who is the hero and who is the villain based on the details you include.

We make inferences about characters based on their actions, words, and even appearances.

An **inference** is a logical conclusion about meaning in a text. When you infer, you make an assumption about what the author is saying or how the author wants you to respond.

Inferences are based on several factors:

- Your prior knowledge
- The details included in the text
- The language used in the text

Here are some examples of the questions you can answer by making inferences:

What is the author's **purpose**?
What is the **main idea** of the text?
How does the author feel about the topic?
How does the author want me to respond?
What will be the future or outcome of the topic?

The ability to make educated guesses based on clues in the text is essential for **reading comprehension**. Many books and documents do not directly state everything that an author wants you to know about a topic. In order to gain full understanding, you will have to fill in the gaps by making inferences about the information.

In this lesson, you will learn how to make inferences about a text using three steps:

Activate Your Prior Knowledge
Look for Clues
Ask Yourself Questions

Activate Your Prior Knowledge

Drawing inferences is all about finding meaning in words and details, and you can utilize pre-reading strategies to prepare for this.

Activating your **prior knowledge**—what you already know about a topic—is an especially helpful way to prepare yourself to find meaning in a text. Even before you're asked to draw inferences about unstated information, you should begin making connections and predictions based on the topic of the reading.

Authors often assume that their audiences will have prior knowledge about a topic when they are making decisions about what they should and shouldn't explain. As a reader, you are expected to supply the missing information by making inferences.

Even prior knowledge of a similar idea or situation can help you make educated guesses about unfamiliar information. Try to think outside of the box as you reflect on what you might already know about a topic.

To help yourself organize your thoughts, consider creating a **KWL chart** to keep track of what you know (K), what you want to know (W), and what you learn (L).

> To learn more about KWL charts, see Lesson 2.1.

Look for Clues

After pre-reading, it's critical that you focus on finding meaning as you read the text. What information is stated outright? What is implied?

Implied information includes unstated ideas or intentions an author conveys using textual clues.

As you read, pay close attention to the following types of information:

Visuals

The visuals inside a text can help you understand the author's purpose and goals. Carefully examine the details of the image and think about why the author decided to include this particular photo or illustration.

Visuals can also help you make connections to your prior knowledge. Even if you don't know anything about a topic, one of the visuals in the text may spark something that seems familiar.

> Reflection Questions
> Think of something you value or a cause you support. Suppose you've been asked to make a flyer to spread awareness about that cause, but it can include only images and no words. How would you get your message across?

> To learn more about analyzing visual clues, see Lesson 3.7.

Tone

Language plays a critical role in the meaning an author conveys. **Tone** is the positive, negative, or neutral attitude that an author expresses about a topic. To determine tone, you must pay close attention to the words and details that the author chooses to include in a text. Look at the following example:

> This charming cottage features all of the little details that make a house a home.

In this sentence, the author uses the words *charming* and *home* to describe the house and express a warm and inviting tone.

> To learn more about tone, see Lesson 3.1.

Organization

The **organizational pattern** of a text often contains clues about the author's purpose and main idea. As you read, look for **signal words** that might indicate what type of organization is being used.

Cause/Effect	Chronological	Compare/Contrast
consequently	after	although
due to	before	however
effect	first	in contrast
therefore	then	just as
since	later	on the other hand

Order of Importance	Spatial	Topical
finally	above	additionally
key	in front of	another
least	inside	moreover
most importantly	next to	next
above all	outside	main point

To learn more about organizational patterns, see Lesson 2.5.

Reading Application

Read the following article about social media tips when job searching. Notice how you can infer information about the author's message because of the deliberate tone and organization.

First Impressions

One-third of employers check applicants' social media sites during the hiring process. The first impression you make may not be your handshake at a job interview but your pictures on Facebook. Photos, jokes, and cartoons that entertain your friends may prompt an employer to take a pass on your application. Your online profile is your public face. Before emailing your résumé, check the way you depict yourself on social media.

This statement reveals the author's purpose through clear word choice and a considerate tone.

Obviously, some spring break and prom pictures might be worth taking down. Innocent jokes and cartoons can make you look unprofessional or immature. In addition to removing negative items, consider adding images that will impress employers.

Here, the author creates a compare/contrast structure in the paragraph. You can infer that he will provide critiques as well as suggestions.

Your friends might laugh at pictures of you getting a debating trophy or wearing a lab coat at a science fair, but they may impress an employer. Photos of you skiing, playing tennis, or working out create the image of an active, health-conscious individual. Pictures of charity events, foreign vacations, award ceremonies, or community service demonstrate that you are well-rounded, mature, and civic-minded. Make sure your first impression is one your future employers will find appealing.

The concluding sentence ends with a positive tone, reminding you about the importance of first impressions.

Ask Yourself Questions

A final key step in making inferences is asking yourself questions. These questions help you connect your prior knowledge to the clues you found inside the text. Don't allow yourself to skip this step. All too often, readers rush through a text to get an assignment done instead of stopping to understand the information that an author is sharing.

To make logical inferences based on the textual clues you've found, ask yourself these questions:

What similar experiences have I had in the past?
What knowledge do I have that might help me understand?
Where have I seen something like this before?
Why did the author tell me this information?
How is this related to the author's previous point?
How does this information connect to the main idea?

Once you've thought through these questions carefully, you can use your prior knowledge and understanding of the text to make educated guesses about the answers. Keep in mind that your conclusions may not be 100% correct. However, learning to make inferences will help you think more critically about a text and its meaning.

Lesson Wrap-up

Learning Style Tip
If you're a **verbal** learner, try journaling your thoughts as you read through a text. Seeing the information on paper may help you think through inferences.

Reading Application

Read the following narrative excerpt and see what you can infer based upon the author's suggestions.

Uncle Ted

Some of my fondest memories come from summer visits to my Uncle Ted's house. Along with his dog Buster, my uncle lived in a modest, one-bedroom house in Arkansas.

He lived in the middle of what seemed like endless acres of corn, his little house like a small white ship in an ocean of green. When we pulled up, my uncle would always be sitting on the rickety steps, relaxing after a day out in the fields. He flashed a smile when he saw me get out of the car, his blue eyes sparkling against his sun-tanned face. Uncle Ted always greeted me with wide, outstretched arms. Even after an exhausting day's work, he still found the strength to lift me off the ground and squeeze me.

Though it's not stated outright, we can infer that the uncle was a farmer.

We can infer that the author likes his uncle and is fond of him since he uses a flattering visual description and a positive tone.

Uncle Ted was a superman in many ways, but his greatest skills were in the kitchen. My favorite dish was fried pork chops with creamy mashed potatoes and skillet cornbread. I remember how he would hum a tune as he stirred the potato gravy on the stovetop, smiling as if he was keeping a great secret. His hands were rough and dirty from his work, but they seemed so delicate when he cooked. Uncle Ted may not have worn a fancy chef's hat or a clean white apron, but to me, he was the best cook in the world.

The author seems to admire his uncle and his work.

Based on the details he includes, the author is likely drawing on the memories of a child.

Key Terms

Cause and Effect: an organizational pattern used to explain the causes or effects of a topic

Chronological: an organizational pattern that arranges ideas or events in the order that they occurred

Compare and Contrast: an organizational pattern used to show the similarities and differences between two topics

Inference: a logical conclusion based on your prior knowledge and the information in a text

KWL Chart: a chart that helps you think about what you know, what you want to know, and what you learned

Main Idea: the statement or argument that an author tries to communicate

Order of Importance: an organizational pattern that arranges information in order of importance

Organizational Pattern: the structure of a written text, used to arrange the main points of a work

Pre-reading: preparing yourself to learn from your reading

Prior Knowledge: what you already know about a topic

Purpose: the goal of a text

Reading Comprehension: understanding and remembering what you have read

Spatial: an organizational pattern used to describe a topic by its physical characteristics

Tone: the positive, negative, or neutral attitude that an author expresses about a topic

Topical: a general organizational pattern used for equally important main points

Verbal Learning: learning information through written and spoken words

Lesson 2.9
Recognizing Types of Main Ideas and Evidence

You just found out your favorite band is playing a secret pop-up concert in town tonight. You want to buy tickets, but you don't want to go alone. When you ask your best friend about joining you, he says that he hasn't heard anything about a concert at that venue. How do you convince him to go?

To reassure your friend that there really is a concert, you need to provide **evidence** to back up your claim. Your word alone is not enough in this situation. You show him the text message you got from your sister who works at the venue. This information gives him the extra proof he needs to believe you.

In this example, the main idea of your argument was that your friend should go with you to the concert. The text message was the evidence that you shared to support this idea.

Authors use the same method when they write. They start with a **main idea**: the point they are trying to communicate. They then support their main point by including **supporting details**. These are pieces of information that the author uses as evidence.

In this lesson, you will learn about the following:

Recognizing the Main Idea(s)
Recognizing Types of Evidence
Analyzing the Supporting Details

You can then decide how this information influences your opinion of the text.

Recognizing the Main Idea(s)

Recall that a topic is the most general characteristic of a text. The main idea is the more specific claim the author makes *about* the topic. When pointing out the main idea, the author answers this question: What do I want my readers to understand or believe after reading this text?

Topic	Claim
Climate Change	I want my readers to speak to their representatives about supporting climate change legislation.
Football & Concussions	I want my readers to support my opinion that contact sports like football should not be banned because there is not enough evidence to conclude that it has long-term effects on the brain.
Standardized Testing	I want my readers to support my opinion that American education should reduce standardized testing.

In a well-structured **paragraph**—a short piece of writing that focuses on one main idea—the main idea is contained in a topic sentence. **Topic sentences** give the reader a clue about what to expect.

Reading Application

Read the following excerpt from an essay on the evolution of technology. Try to locate the main idea.

The twentieth century saw an explosion of information technology. For example, the devices to record sound evolved quickly. Wax cylinders were replaced by metal wires that became obsolete with the invention of magnetic tape. Clumsy tape reels were replaced by compact cassettes. Eventually, these were replaced by CDs and digital recording. Moving images were first captured on film, then videotape, then DVDs. As a result, anyone conducting historical research is faced with an array of wires, eight-track tapes, Dictaphone belts, punch cards, and floppy discs that cannot be played on modern devices. Scholars have had to search shops, warehouses, and eBay to find old-fashioned movie projectors and tape players to watch a newsreel or hear a president's speech.

Based on the topic sentence and the paragraph, can you determine the main idea?

To learn more about the basics of main ideas and topic sentences, see Lesson 2.4.

On Your Own

Read the following paragraph and identify the sentence that contains the author's main idea.

> Even though corporations are an intricate part of the United States economy, they are now an influential part of government as well. According to John J. Macionis, corporations are "big businesses with a legal existence, including rights and liabilities, separate from that of their members" (268). Corporations are not just simply the people that work for them; rather, they are their own separate entities. The number of corporations in our country is staggering. Macionis claims that "six million businesses (of more than 32 million total) are incorporated. Of these, the largest 100 corporations are giants, each with more than $35 billion in assets" (268). These corporations are responsible for the country's huge increase in corporate production over the past few decades. However, in a country where money talks, these organizations hold a frighteningly tremendous amount of power in areas outside of the economy.

Sometimes, the author does not directly state the main idea of the text. In this case, it is implied. The reader must use the details included in the book or document to figure out the author's purpose. Implied main ideas are often used when the author is writing to reflect or entertain.

Thesis and Purpose Statements

In a longer text, the main ideas of each paragraph serve to make claims that support a bigger idea. This bigger idea is usually indicated in a thesis statement or statement of purpose.

A **thesis statement** is a claim that sums up the entire argument of a paper, usually consisting of one to two sentences. A thesis statement almost always appears near the end of the **introduction.**

The main idea of a longer work can also be stated as a purpose statement. **Purpose statements** tell you exactly what main points will be covered in a text. Like thesis statements, they appear in the introduction. Purpose statements are most commonly found in business and research reports.

Thesis Statements

> The current unrest in Afghanistan can be traced back to the invasion of British forces in 1834.

> The life of Mary Todd Lincoln was filled with heartbreak and difficulties.

> Although the National Security Agency plays an important role in protecting America, stricter laws are needed to protect the privacy of American citizens.

> Walking is an excellent source of exercise for people of all ages.

Purpose Statements

> This report will describe the design of the consumer survey, explain the results, and share the recommendations of the research team.

> This document will share tips and tricks for starting a home-based business.

> In this paper, the authors will share their experiences as part of a Red Cross disaster relief team in Haiti.

> The purpose of this report is to outline the timeline and goals of the project.

Locating the Thesis

Since thesis statements aren't stated as directly as purpose statements are, they can be trickier to find.

Try following these steps to locate the thesis statement:

1. Find the main idea of each paragraph.
2. Form the main ideas into a summary paragraph.
3. Determine the main idea of the summary paragraph to find the thesis.

Recognizing Types of Evidence

Supporting details are the specific pieces of information that are used to support a main idea. These details often answer questions that start with *who, what, where, when, why,* and *how.* For example, if an author writes an article arguing that e-cigarettes should be regulated, she needs to support her claim by answering some of the following questions:

> **Who** could be affected if e-cigarettes aren't regulated?
> **What** would be the arguments against regulating e-cigarettes?
> **Why** are e-cigarettes potentially harmful?
> **How** would regulations affect the e-cigarette industry?

Authors can choose from several types of information to support their main ideas.

Anecdotes

Anecdotes are long examples told as a story. Some texts include anecdotes about an author's personal experience to support a claim.

Descriptions

Descriptions are passages that explain the appearance of someone or something using words that appeal to the senses. Here's an example:

> Randolph was a short, stocky man with a permanent scowl on his face. My sister Kezia always called him "the bulldog," and after meeting him for the first time, I immediately saw the resemblance. Despite his intimidating appearance, there was something kind about the corners of his eyes. Every so often, they would crinkle with humor, contradicting the frown below.

Examples

Examples are specific instances or illustrations that demonstrate a point. These details are often introduced by the phrases *for example* or *for instance.*

Expert Analysis

Expert analysis is an opinion or statement shared by someone who is knowledgeable about a topic. In an article about space travel, the author might include quotes from former astronauts and NASA researchers.

Facts

Facts are pieces of information that most people generally agree to be true, such as scientific principles and historical events. The following statements are examples of facts:

> Brazil has won five World Cups in 1958, 1962, 1970, 1994, and 2002.

> Water is made up of hydrogen and oxygen.

Reflections

Reflections are the thoughts and feelings of the author. They are often stated using first-person pronouns such as *I* or *me*.

On Your Own

Reflect on your personal reaction to the following passage:

> Author Ray Bradbury once said, "Video games are a waste of time for men with nothing else to do." While video game sales remain on the rise in many countries, it is important to consider the very real danger that they pose to our citizens and our future. Children and teenagers are being irreparably harmed by overexposure to violence and mind-numbing activity brought on by excessive gaming. This damaging hobby can desensitize individuals to violence, making them less likely to find fault in vicious behavior. It can also lead to apathetic tendencies, lack of physical activity, and isolation.

Statistics

Statistics are numbers or percentages that represent research data. For example, a survey may find that 75% of cable TV users think their service is too expensive. This statistic represents all of the people who participated in the survey.

Analyzing the Supporting Details

The **purpose** and **audience** of the text will influence the types of supporting details that the author uses. In a business report, you would most likely see examples and statistics. In a personal narrative, you would see anecdotes and reflections. A well-supported text will use a variety of supporting details.

After identifying the supporting details in a text, you should determine how well they support the author's main idea. Consider the following questions:

> What questions do these supporting details answer about the main idea?
>
> What questions could the audience still have?
>
> How well do these details support the author's main idea?

The answers to these questions will help you decide if the author has made a convincing claim by using good supporting details.

Think about this example:

> Every year, World Malaria Day forces us to look at where we came from, where we are, and what still needs to be done. Joint action over the past decade has led to an impressive impact: malaria infection rates have been cut in half, and 4.3 million lives have been saved ("World Malaria Report 2014"). Fifty-five countries are on track to reach the World Health Assembly target of a 75 % reduction in their malaria burden by 2015 ("World Malaria Report 2014"). Although these huge gains are impressive, they remain fragile if the momentum of the joint action cannot be maintained. Clearly,

not keeping the momentum leads to the resurgence of malaria, as we have experienced in numerous previous elimination efforts at national or subnational level.

(Excerpt courtesy of "Malaria Eradication and Elimination: Views on How to Translate a Vision into Reality" [http://www.biomedcentral.com/1741-7015/13/167] by Marcel Tanner, et al.)

The main idea of this paragraph is that World Malaria Day is a reminder that further work needs to be done to eliminate malaria completely. The author uses two statistics to support this claim.

Lesson Wrap-up

Reading Application

The following persuasive essay argues for increased arts education. As you read the passage, note how the author clearly addresses her main point and uses various types of supporting evidence.

Arts Programs

Around the nation, many public schools are eliminating or decreasing their arts programs, leaving students without access to arts education. This education consists of music, dance, theater, and the visual arts. Though cutting these programs provides short-term fixes to budget problems, these cuts negatively affect students in the long-term. Schools should invest in arts education because a strong arts program provides numerous benefits to students, including improving overall academic performance, lowering dropout rates, and teaching valuable skills in creative problem-solving.

The author presents the thesis statement at the end of the first paragraph.

A strong arts education helps to improve overall academic performance. Research has shown that students who are highly involved in arts programs are four times more likely to be recognized for accomplishments in school. Additionally, a strong relationship exists between arts instruction and the core skills of reading, writing, and mathematics. Therefore, participation in the arts can strengthen a student's performance in their classes.

The topic sentence of each body paragraph makes a more specific claim linked to the thesis.

According to the U.S. Department of Education, a strong arts program decreases student dropout rates. Research proves that students are five times less likely to drop out of school if they are heavily involved in the arts. It is believed that this involvement helps provide a positive and enjoyable school environment for students. Therefore, they are more satisfied and more motivated to stay in school until graduation.

This topic sentence cites an authority on education as evidence.

Lastly, students learn to be creative problem solvers through art exploration. Art students get the opportunity to solve problems uniquely related to the arts. For instance, when I was involved in a theater program in school, I was responsible for designing and building the set for the school play, but I did not have a lot of money or materials to make it happen. I had to be innovative with the materials available. Ultimately, I built a great set for a play production and learned a lot from that experience. Students in arts programs are often placed in unique situations like this one that encourage them to be creative when solving problems.

Arts programs should not be just extracurricular; schools should view the arts as a vital part of their core curriculum. Arts education helps improve a student's overall academic performance, lowers overall dropout rates, and teaches valuable lessons in creative problem-solving. If these programs are starved of funding or eliminated altogether, students will lose access to a vital part of a well-rounded education. Schools should view arts education as an important investment that benefit both students both now and in the future.

In the third body paragraph, the author recounts a personal experience (in a theater program) as evidence illustrating her claim that students learn problem-solving skills through art programs.

In the conclusion, the author reviews her main supporting points and restates her main idea.

Reading Application

The following essay seeks to persuade readers to recycle. As you read the text, take note of the author's main claims and supporting details.

Our Responsibility to Recycle

A wild duck entangled in six-pack plastic rings; garbage littering the sides of highways; dead fish floating in an oily spill. All three of these images can be traced back to plastic: that non-biodegradable material that takes from one hundred to one thousand years to deteriorate and is filling our landfills and roadsides in ever-increasing amounts. This is a huge global problem with a rather simple solution. In order to prevent harm to wildlife, save landfill space, and preserve our natural resources, the world populace needs to recycle plastic.

This thesis statement states the main idea and the supporting details.

Videos abound on the internet that display the volume of garbage swirling around in the ocean. Eighty percent of that garbage is made up of plastic. Sea life and waterfowl often mistake these items for food, ingest them, and sicken or die. Land animals are also in danger of mistaking plastic for food or trying to eat leftovers from a plastic container. It might look funny to see an animal struggle to remove a peanut butter jar from its muzzle, but the animal could be unable to breathe or defend itself. Endangering animals, especially the ones people rely on as a food source, is irresponsible. Human beings are at the top of a food chain that could collapse if a species on a lower level is eliminated. Saving the earth's wildlife is one important reason to recycle.

This paragraph provides minor details that support the major detail: plastic harms wildlife.

An equally important reason to recycle is to reduce the amount of garbage dumped into our landfills and oceans. One ton of plastic takes up 7.5 cubic yards of space, and hundreds of tons are being disposed of every day. Where is it going? It is going into landfills. While some landfills layer garbage on top of plastic to prevent soil pollution, they still require a huge amount of space. For instance, one landfill in Los Angeles covers 700 acres and is five hundred feet high. According to *How Stuff Works*, a landfill can hold the equivalent length of 82,000 football fields of trash buried thirty feet deep. Consider how many landfills are needed to service all the cities in the United States alone. Landfills take up an enormous amount of land that could otherwise be used for growing crops, building recreational areas, or left natural for humans and wildlife to enjoy. What is even more distressing about landfills is that they can accept garbage for only about fifty years before another one needs to take its place.

The transition phrase for instance indicates a minor detail.

A third reason to recycle plastic is to preserve the earth's natural, non-renewable resources. Plastic is made from petroleum, a fossil fuel that is also used to make gasoline. Recycling plastic saves about two thousand pounds of petroleum. In addition, according to *Plastic-Recyclers*, "recycling one ton of plastic results in saving the energy used by two humans in a year and the water required by a person for two months." Recycled plastic can be sorted according to the Resin Identification Code (RIC) printed on the bottoms of bottles and containers. These plastics can then be ground or shredded, re-melted, and formed into new products. For example, plastic #2 is used to make milk jugs and, when recycled, can be turned into picnic tables and benches. Recycling is a wiser alternative to throwing plastic into a landfill and then pumping more oil to make new plastic. We cannot continue to use the earth's resources irresponsibly. Recycling adds resources rather than exhausting them, and it saves the energy that would otherwise be expended to extract and refine new materials.

The words in addition indicate a transition to another piece of supporting evidence.

Throwing away plastic items is unhealthy for wildlife, uses valuable land, and forces the plastics industry to deplete the earth's natural resources. Society needs to become more aware of the how harmful plastic can be, more conscientious of where it ends up, and more diligent to recycle it. Many people know about recycling, but few understand its importance or the consequences of not recycling. When we think about what can be saved by recycling—wildlife, land, and natural resources—we realize that it does not make sense *not* to recycle.

What is your reaction to the claims in this essay? Do you think the evidence is effective in supporting the author's main idea?

Key Terms

Anecdote: a long example told as a story

Description: a passage that explains the appearance of someone or something using words that appeal to the senses

Evidence: a piece of information, also called a supporting detail, used to support a main idea

Example: a specific instance or illustration that demonstrates a point

Expert Analysis: an opinion or statement shared by someone who is knowledgeable about a topic

Fact: a piece of information that most people generally agree to be true

Implied Main Idea: a main idea that is not directly stated

Introduction: the paragraph used to introduce the main idea at the beginning of a paper, also called an introductory paragraph

Main Idea: the statement or argument that an author tries to communicate

Paragraph: a short piece of writing that focuses on one main idea

Purpose: the goal of a text

Purpose Statement: a sentence that tells the audience exactly what points will be covered in a longer text

Reflection: the thoughts and feelings of the author

Signal/Signpost Word: a word or word group that introduces a new idea and/or shows the connection between two ideas

Statistic: a number or percentage that represents research data

Supporting Detail: a piece of information, also called evidence, used to support a main idea

Thesis Statement: a sentence that expresses the main idea of a longer work

Topic Sentence: a sentence that presents the main idea of a paragraph

Chapter 3
Critical Thinking

Lesson 3.1
Identifying Purpose and Tone

If you've ever seen a TV infomercial, you can probably picture it in your mind pretty clearly: the energetic host is demonstrating a roasting pan, a workout DVD, or a mop that will supposedly change your life. His voice, facial expressions, and gestures all show his excitement and enthusiasm for the product.

Now imagine the same presentation given by a disinterested, monotone host. Would people be as likely to buy the product?

In this example, the host's purpose is to convince the audience to buy a product. He used an enthusiastic tone to make his pitch more persuasive. If he had looked bored during the presentation, he would not have achieved his goal.

The author of a written book or document uses purpose and tone in a similar way. As a reader, you must think critically about the *why* and the *how* behind a text. This will give a more complete understanding of what an author is trying to say.

> In this lesson, you will learn how to identify the following:
> Author's Purpose
> Author's Tone

Author's Purpose

Authors are always attempting to achieve a goal, whether it's helping you understand a topic better or convincing you to take action. As a reader, identifying that goal is the first step in understanding the meaning of a text.

While there are many different **purposes** for writing, four of the most common are to inform, to persuade, to reflect, and to entertain.

To Inform
The author of an **informative** text wants to give the audience information about a topic. Texts that commonly seek to inform include the following:

- Textbooks
- Manuals
- News reports

To Persuade

The author of a **persuasive** text wants to convince the audience to adopt a belief or take an action. Texts that commonly seek to persuade include the following:

- Advertisements
- Editorials
- Commercials

To Reflect

The author of a **reflective** text wants to share and reflect on a personal experience or belief. Texts that commonly seek to reflect include the following:

- Memoirs
- Journals
- Narratives

To Entertain

The author of an **entertaining** text wants to engage the reader by exploring a topic or event in a creative or humorous way. Texts that commonly seek to entertain include the following:

- Short stories
- Novels
- Television shows

Being able to recognize the purpose of a text is necessary to understand it fully. Once you know what the author is trying to communicate, you can decide if the text has achieved that goal.

Never assume that the purpose of a text is straightforward. Sometimes authors do not realize that they are getting off-topic. In other cases, authors might be purposefully dishonest about their purposes for writing. In either case, a careful reader will see the author's true purpose and use this information to understand and interpret the text.

Author's Tone

Tone is the attitude expressed about the **topic** of the text. Authors use words and details carefully to establish a clear tone. Tone is usually described using adjectives that are positive, negative, or neutral.

Positive	Negative	Neutral
excited	angry	objective
encouraging	disapproving	straightforward
confident	critical	direct

In most cases, tone is not stated outright; instead, the reader has to read between the lines to determine how the author feels about the topic.

The best way to determine tone is to pay attention to the words and details the author includes. Keep in mind that writing always involves choices. Whether the author realizes it or not, she is constantly making decisions about what to include and what to exclude. Two authors writing about the exact same topic might end up using completely different tones simply because they include different words and details.

The first indication of tone is **word choice.** All words have positive, negative, or neutral feelings attached to them. For example, think about the words *thin* and *scrawny*. Both of these words have very similar definitions, yet they carry two very different meanings.

Think about how you respond to each of the following **synonyms**:

house	home
cautious	afraid
passionate	extreme
cheap	affordable
relaxed	lazy

As you read, pay close attention to the author's word choice to determine the overall tone of the text. If you notice that many of the words have negative meanings, the tone is likely critical, sarcastic, or skeptical. Likewise, if many of the words have positive meanings, the tone may be optimistic, encouraging, or confident.

Using completely neutral language is difficult, but a text that uses words without any strongly positive or negative meanings is trying to be as objective and unbiased as possible.

Learning Style Tip
If you're a **visual** learner, try marking all of the words in a text that seem to indicate the author's tone. When you're done, create a chart with positive, negative, and neutral columns. Write each of your marked words in the appropriate column.

Reflection Questions
Some words have sparked debate over whether or not their tone is negative or neutral. Think about the following words. How have you heard them used in the past? What type of tone do you think they indicate?

feminist   thug   terrorism   riot

The second way to identify an author's tone is to consider the details that have been included or excluded. Think about these questions:

> What details does the author choose to include?
>
> Why does the author feel it is important to include these details?
>
> What details has the author chosen to ignore or exclude?
>
> Why does the author feel these details are unimportant?

If the author includes mainly negative details about the topic, he may want to achieve a negative tone. Likewise, if he includes mainly positive details about a topic, he probably wants to use a positive tone. A mix of positive and negative details would indicate a neutral tone.

Read through these examples:

Negative

This was the worst tornado to come through the town in over fifty years. Entire neighborhoods were damaged or destroyed, and many of the survivors were struggling to find food and shelter.

Positive

After the tornado swept through the town, the community immediately supported everyone who had suffered losses. Friends, neighbors, and strangers united in a way that transformed the entire area.

Neutral

> The aftermath of the tornado resulted in several million dollars of damage. However, local outreach groups provided free food and supplies to those in need.

Purpose and tone are closely related. An author may use tone to make an argument more persuasive or to help the audience relate to the topic. If the tone doesn't support this purpose, the author's writing will be unsuccessful.

Tone can also indicate that the author's purpose isn't as clear as he wants you to think. For example, an author that claims to be informing, but uses an angry or mocking tone, might be using sarcasm.

Helpful Hint
Thinking critically about an author's purpose and tone can help you enhance your own writing skills.

To explore strategies for using tone in your own writing, see Lesson 5.8.

On Your Own

Read the following online review, paying close attention to the words and details. What is the overall tone of this review? Check the box that contains your answer.

> My husband and I visited Marion Diner on the recommendation of a friend who is also a local food blogger. As we were walking into the restaurant, we were greeted with the delicious scent of sautéed garlic and rosemary. The waiter was friendly and knowledgeable about the menu. She even recommended her personal favorites. The menu itself was not lengthy at all. Clearly, this restaurant focuses on a few key specialties and customer favorites. I was surprised to see the blend of fresh, healthy ingredients incorporated into traditional "diner food."
>
> I ordered the Bleu Ribbon Burger with baked onion straws, and my husband had the Grandstand Salad. My burger was cooked perfectly, although the onion straws were more seasoned than I would have preferred. I'm not a salad fan, but even I had to admit that my husband's meal looked great.
>
> Overall, I would definitely recommend Marion to anyone who's looking for a fresh twist on well-loved diner favorites.

☐ Negative   ☐ Neutral   ☐ Positive

Reflection Questions
In a text message or social media post, it's impossible to see a person's body language or hear his or her voice inflection. This can lead to awkward mix-ups when tone is misunderstood. How do you communicate tone in a text message or tweet? Is this method effective?

Lesson Wrap-up

Reading Application

Review the following blog post. What can you learn about purpose and tone from the author's choice in language?

Yesterday, I went skydiving for the first time. It was incredible, and much less expensive than expected! When we arrived, we got into our jumpsuits and harnesses, but it didn't feel real until we got in that airplane. The closer we got to the clouds, the more real it felt. My palms started to sweat. My heart raced feverishly. When the first diver took her jump, I thought I would bail out! I had volunteered to go last, but I started thinking that was a mistake.

> This descriptive sentence sets an exciting tone for the text by using positive wording.

> These details shift the tone from positive to anxious.

Ultimately, I decided not to overthink it. The next thing I knew, I was flying. Even though I was plummeting toward the ground, I felt still. The ground looked like it was rising to meet me. My face, apparently, was not as still—in the pictures I saw later, it was flapping in the breeze like a bulldog.

> The writer uses both creative and humorous details to reflect on their personal experience.

I'll never forget the landing. It was like abruptly waking up from a dream. But, there *was* something comforting about feeling my feet back on the ground. I took a few deep breaths, scanned the open field around me, and enjoyed the rush of the experience. In all, it was an unforgettable day. I would recommend it if you're feeling adventurous or you want to feel alive!

> Although the writer is recommending the experience, her purpose is not persuasive. Instead, she is entertaining her audience and reflecting on her experience.

I'm ready to go again.

Reading Application

Now, read this letter written by a concerned community member. How do the tone and purpose of this writing compare to the one above? How does the author use similar strategies to achieve a different purpose?

To Whom It May Concern:

Cyberbullying is a growing problem in America and schools should do more to combat the epidemic. According to a 2016 report by the Cyberbullying Research Center, almost one-third of students aged 12-17 have been victims of cyberbullying. As an educator, I am deeply concerned about this issue. I have seen its consequences in the eyes of victimized students tortured by online bullies using online communication like weapons. Schools have a responsibility to teach students how to be good digital citizens, but they can't fight cyberbullying alone. This war needs to start at home.

> This indicates the author's main topic: the rise of cyberbullying.

> The word *war* has strong connotations. It suggests the author feels this is a serious issue.

Many instances of cyberbullying can be prevented by vigilant parents who know the signs and who are willing to address these issues. Parents often point the finger at schools to address cyberbullying. However, by the time schools are notified of a problem, it's often too late. Bullied students have already been victimized, and the digital traces can leave emotional scars. Furthermore, cyberbullying disrupts the learning environment. Schools are forced to divert time and resources away from the educational process to handle problems that take place outside of the classroom. Parents can help with early detection and alleviate this burden from school personnel.

The tone here is sympathetic toward schools, further supporting his purpose.

Another thing parents can do is monitor their teen's online activity. Computers and laptops can be housed in public places in the home to discourage poor online behavior, and kids can be monitored. If parents allow their children to have smartphones and tablets, there should be reasonable limits placed on their use. Kids with unlimited access to these devices have unlimited ways of getting into trouble.

The word *can* indicates the author is making a suggestion instead of a demand.

Teens shouldn't be the only people educated about cyberbullying. Parents should educate themselves on virtual slang that their kids may use. This allows parents to better identify cyberbullying when it starts. Parents can review their teens' profile pages and monitor their activity. Kids might complain about invasion of privacy, but they're also less likely to participate in cyberbullying.

The author is making a persuasive recommendation, again supporting his purpose.

Enacting these measures can prevent cyberbullying. Unfortunately, this harassment takes place both inside and outside the classroom, so schools need help monitoring these behaviors. By adopting common-sense rules for online use, parents can help put an end to this torture.

The author's overall purpose is to get the reader to adopt these recommendations.

Warmly,

Jonathan Campbell

Key Terms

Entertaining Text: a text that explores a topic or event in a creative or humorous way

Informative Text: a text that gives the audience information about a topic

Persuasive Text: a text that convinces its audience to adopt a belief or take an action

Purpose: the goal of a text

Reflective Text: a text that shares a personal experience or belief

Synonym: a word whose meaning is similar to that of another word

Tone: the positive, negative, or neutral attitude that an author expresses about a topic

Topic: the general subject of a text

Visual Learning: learning information through pictures, shapes, and colors

Word Choice: also called diction, the words an author uses to convey a particular message

Lesson 3.2
Analyzing Argumentation Strategies

Every day, you are bombarded with arguments about what to think and how to act. How do you decide what to believe?

Without even realizing it, you analyze the argument and make a decision based on that analysis. For example, read through the following email and think about how you would respond.

> Stop the abuse!
>
> Every day, at least six household pets are victims of animal cruelty! These faithful companions deserve love and respect, not mistreatment. If you agree, complete these two easy steps:
>
> 1. Enter your name, home address, and telephone number.
> 2. Think of five friends who would like to receive our daily newsletter and enter their email addresses.

Of course, you agree that animal cruelty is wrong. However, you probably realized quickly that these "two easy steps" aren't the best way to help abused animals. This email seems more like a scheme to get personal information than anything else. After analyzing the argument of this email, you decided not to participate.

Arguments can be broken into three basic parts:

- *Ethos*, an argument based on a person's credibility
- *Logos*, an argument based on logic
- *Pathos*, an argument based on emotion

It's important that you recognize these strategies so that you can make informed decisions. *Ethos, logos,* and *pathos* can be found in any newspaper, magazine, blog, or tweet. All of these texts are trying to **persuade** you in some way.

Argumentation strategies are used in a variety of contexts outside of academics.

Even food packaging is often driven by marketing strategies. If a bag of chips is green and contains the word "healthy" somewhere in the text, some health-conscious consumers may be more likely to make the purchase. Without digging a little deeper, how do they know that the contents of that bag are any healthier than those of the purple one next to it?

While an advertisement or an opinion article is clearly pushing you to buy a specific product or believe a certain way, other texts use argumentation strategies for **purposes** other than persuading.

Imagine that you are reading an article about the history of the telephone. The author's main purpose is to **inform**. Whether or not the author realizes it, however, he or she is also trying to convince you that the article is true and reliable.

This lesson will teach you how to analyze the *ethos, logos,* and *pathos* in an argument.

You can use this knowledge as you analyze the texts you encounter every day.

Further Resources
Misleading packaging of food products has been recently placed in the spotlight. Read more about it in this interactive article from WebMD: http://www.webmd.com/news/breaking-news/food-additives/rm-quiz-food-label-claims.

Ethos

The first argumentation strategy is *ethos*, an argument based on **credibility:** what makes someone or something believable. An effective text will use the opinions of experts to argue its points.

Reflection Questions
Think about the type of people you would consider experts. What are their credentials?

One type of *ethos* is a person's professional credentials. An article about weight loss is more reliable if it includes information from doctors or medical researchers. Similarly, a manual on construction site safety is more trustworthy if it was written by a construction supervisor.

You should also consider personal experience. For example, a prize-winning home gardener would be considered credible even though he doesn't have formal education in gardening. Instead, he has years of personal experience that make him a knowledgeable and reliable source of information.

Finally, *ethos* can be based on someone's trustworthiness. The way that a person has acted in the past will affect his current credibility. You probably remember the old fable about the boy who cried wolf. Because he had a history of lying, the villagers considered him an unreliable source of information.

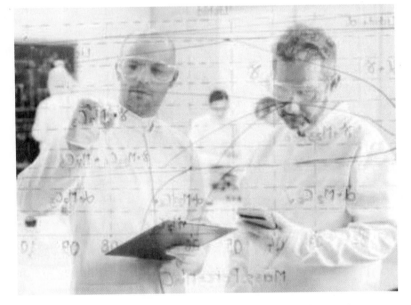

A person's area of expertise affects his or her ethos as an author

When faced with new information, make sure to always check the source of that information. First, look at the author(s) of the text and any sources within it. Are these people credible based on their credentials, experience, or trustworthiness?

You should also look at the arguments that the authors are making. Their credentials, experience, and trustworthiness should fit the purpose of the text. For example, a doctor who specializes in lung disease might not be the best source for information about car maintenance. Likewise, a college athlete would likely know more about college sports than about the NFL.

Keep in mind that *ethos* does not guarantee that an argument is valid. Plenty of experts within the same field disagree or even contradict each other. A good argument will use a balance of *ethos*, *logos*, and *pathos* to prove its point.

Reading Application

Take a look at the following historical excerpt. Note how the author uses *ethos* to support her argument.

As a historian who has specialized in the impacts of WWII my entire career, nothing frustrates me more than America's continued imperial presence on the small island of Okinawa. Following the conclusion of the war in 1945, the United States took over the large island, located on the outskirts of Japan. In 1972, they returned the island to Japan but set up military bases there. US forces remain on the island today, despite vehement protests from its residents. During a 2016 interview with local inhabitant Keita Oshiro, he explained, "I have anger toward your country and its people. We do not feel safe on our own land." Imagine being residents on that small island and feeling as though you have no say in your life or your rights. You would be outraged as well.

The author describes her credentials here, providing credibility, or *ethos*, to her argument.

Including the insight of a local resident from Okinawa establishes further credibility to the argument. This is another example of *ethos*.

Okinawans have valid reasons for objecting to the US presence on their small island: crimes by US soldiers stationed on the island as well as daily intrusions into their lives.

Martin Fackler of *The New York Times* reported that a sexual assault case in 2012 was the "seventh case to result in the arrest of American servicemen since the United States returned Okinawa to Japan in 1972." It's time the US government adjusts their plan in Okinawa—the islanders deserve to feel secure and make their own choices.

Since *The New York Times* is a valid source, this lends the argument credibility, or *ethos*.

Do you feel that this argument is credible? Why or why not?

Fackler, Martin. "Arrests of 2 U.S. Sailors in Rape Case Threaten to Fan Okinawa's Anger." *The New York Times.* The New York Times, 16 Oct. 2012. Web. 17 Apr. 2017.

Logos

The next argumentation strategy is *logos*, an argument based on logic.

A **logical argument** makes a reasonable claim using **supporting details** like facts and statistics. **Facts** can be verified and are accepted by the majority of experts in the field. **Statistics** represent data from research studies, and they are most accurate when gathered from a wide range of research methods and samples. To locate this sort of **evidence,** look for statements like this: "Experts agree that 25% of Americans think cats are better than dogs."

To learn more about types of supporting details, see Lesson 2.9.

Keep in mind that not all facts and statistics are reliable. Always be on the lookout for clues that a source might be untrustworthy or biased, as these factors could impact the validity of the information.

When possible, also investigate how the information was gathered. A survey of only five people would not be as reliable as a survey of over five hundred. The sample size should be large and the research methods should be appropriate for a well-constructed, valid research study.

A logical argument must also be reasonable. The author's **conclusions** should match the types of facts and statistics included in the text. Look at this example:

> Cars are dangerous. Every year, the National Highway Traffic Safety Administration reports that thousands of people have been killed in car accidents. In 2012, over 33,000 people died in the United States alone in traffic accidents ("Traffic Safety Facts" 1). This is 32,980 more fatalities than airline travel, one of the most commonly feared modes of transportation (Locsin). In response to these statistics, state and federal lawmakers have passed legislation to increase driver awareness and vehicle safety. To reduce the number of fatal car accidents, the federal should lower the maximum speed limit on highways to 65 miles per hour.

In this **paragraph,** the author uses good facts and statistics to make her point. The conclusion that she makes at the end of the paragraph, however, doesn't make sense. None of the information she shared would be a logical argument for speed limits.

Pathos

The final argumentation strategy is *pathos,* an appeal to emotion. Human emotions are strong. If an argument makes you feel emotional about a topic, you will probably act on those emotions. An author can use *pathos* by choosing words that appeal to the audience's emotion. Take a look at the following sentences:

> The results of the drought were bad for the town.

> The results of the drought were devastating for the citizens of Claremont Valley.

> Which sentence is the most expressive and powerful? While both sentences suggest that the impact of the drought was negative, using the word *devastating* and sharing the name of the town is more likely to spark an emotional response from the reader.

Emotions can also be communicated through the **anecdotes** or **examples** that an author chooses to include in a text. These stories help the audience personally relate to the logical information being presented. For example, charities often use anecdotes to encourage donations. Once you hear the stories of real people who have been impacted by a charity, you are more likely to donate your time and money.

Finally, one of the most effective ways to communicate emotions is through the use of images. A picture or a video can trigger emotions in mere seconds, even without any words or text. Think about the commercials and advertisements you see every day. Many of them use images of happy families, funny animals, or beautiful scenery to make an emotional impact on their audiences.

While *pathos* can be an effective tool for making an argument, emotions can also be potentially misleading. Have you ever heard of the phrase "don't let emotions cloud your judgement"? This phrase means that you were so caught up in your emotions, you didn't stop to think through the facts. A reliable text will use emotion to support its argument, not to manipulate its audience.

Reading Application

Take a look at the following image and the corresponding paragraph. How does the author use *Pathos* to create her argument?

Unfair Dog Banning Has Permanent Consequences

No other dog breed faces as much discrimination as the American pit bull terrier. Hundreds of cities across the nation have breed-specific laws that ban ownership of pit bulls. <u>All dogs need and deserve love, companionship, and care. To deter this necessary nurturing is to rob these dogs of their basic needs.</u> Additionally, the consequences to those who challenge these bans are cruel and inhumane. Dogs become important parts of our families, regardless of the breed. These laws often rip apart families that include these outlawed breeds. If a family is discovered with a banned pit bull, the dog will often be sent to an animal control facility to be euthanized. <u>This means the family must watch as their loyal pet is put to death for simply being born.</u>

Phrases like *deserve, love,* and *rob these dogs of their basic needs* use *pathos* by appealing to reader's feelings.

The author ends with an image that illustrates cruelty and therefore exemplifies *pathos*.

Reflection Questions
An argument that uses too much *pathos* can quickly become cheesy or melodramatic. When have you experienced this in the past? What was your reaction?

Lesson Wrap-up

On Your Own

Read the following descriptions and check the box that contains the argumentation strategy that is being described.

An argument based on a person's credibility

☐ *Logos*　　　　　　　☐ *Ethos*　　　　　　　☐ *Pathos*

An argument based on emotion

☐ *Logos*　　　　　　　☐ *Ethos*　　　　　　　☐ *Pathos*

An argument based on logic

☐ *Logos*　　　　　　　☐ *Ethos*　　　　　　　☐ *Pathos*

Group Activity
As a group, choose an article from the *New York Times* Opinion website (http://www.nytimes.com/pages/opinion/). Read the article and discuss the use of *ethos*, *logos*, and *pathos* used by the author.

Reading Application

Read the following letter that incorporates all three argumentation strategies. Using the annotations as help, consider how the author deliberately appeals to her audience.

Dear Members of City Council:

It has come to my attention that the city has been gifted a piece of property by a local business and that you are currently deciding what will come of the land. I have lived in Greenville my entire life, and I've seen a lot of changes. What was once open space has been replaced with strip malls, condominiums, and chain stores. When I was young, I had five parks I would regularly visit. Now, there are fewer green spaces for my own children to play. If you're considering selling this land to developers for financial gain, also consider what stands to be lost.

The writer establishes her *ethos*, or credibility, as a life-long resident of the city.

This sentence indicates that this letter is persuasive, asking the reader to adopt a belief or take action.

According to city records, ten new neighborhoods, each with over fifty homes, have been built within city limits in the past seven years. Five big retailers, three new strip malls, and four grocery stores have opened in the past three years. In that time, the city has contributed zero new parks or green spaces. In fact, several commonly used green spaces were sold to allow for construction. Yesterday, I put my dog in the car and drove to our favorite walking trail by the lake. As we got out of the car, we were greeted by a new fence and a "Private Property" sign. Walking back to the car, both of us disappointed, I noticed another sign closer to the road: "Coming Soon: Luxury Condominiums by the Lake!"

Here, the writer is using *logos*, a logical argument based on facts and statistics from a reputable source: the city's own records.

My uncle is a mayor in Pennsylvania. He began an initiative to designate a certain amount of green space per capita, so that as the town grew, the green space would not decrease. While the residents may not have as many shopping options, they have plenty of outdoor opportunities. Furthermore, the city saw better jobs and higher economic growth due to the high quality of living, according to the latest census.

The inherited property is large enough to contain bike and walking trails, a dog park, basketball and tennis courts, and more. There is even enough space for a musical stage. This is a great way to enhance art, entertainment, and culture in the area. The space can also be used for special events like festivals, farmers markets, charity events, birthday parties, and weddings. Having more spaces like this would not only increase the quality of life in our city but also provide potential for generating revenue.

Offering suggestions and solutions is a way to exercise *logos* and to strengthen the persuasiveness of an argument.

It's wonderful that our town is growing and expanding, and we do need places for people to live, work, and shop. But we also need space for play, fun, and exercise. When you imagine yourself having fun as a child, what are you doing? Does the supermarket or department store come to mind? My most cherished memories are riding bikes down dirt trails, lying in the grass playing with my dog, and having family picnics for my birthday. When voting on how this land will be used, please consider not only economic growth but also the growth and happiness of our people. Thank you for your time and consideration in this matter.

Finally, the writer drives home the argument by using *pathos*, or appealing to the reader's emotions.

Sincerely,

Sonia Knope

After reading this letter, do you think Sonia will be successful in her appeal to City Council? Why or why not?

Key Terms

Anecdote: a long example told as a story

Argument: a reason why you should think or act a certain way

Conclusion: the result of a logical argument

Credibility: what makes someone or something believable

Ethos: an argument based on a person's credibility

Evidence: a piece of information, also called a supporting detail, that is used to support a main idea

Example: a specific instance or illustration that demonstrates a point

Fact: a piece of information that most people generally agree to be true

Informative Text: a text that gives the audience information about a topic

Logical Argument: an argument that makes a reasonable claim, usually using facts and statistics

Logos: an argument based on logic

Paragraph: a short piece of writing that focuses on one main idea

Pathos: an argument based on emotion

Persuasive Text: a text that convinces its audience to adopt a belief or take an action

Purpose: the goal of a text

Statistic: a number or percentage that represents research data

Supporting Detail: a piece of information, also called evidence, that is used to support a main idea

Lesson 3.3

Identifying Bias

All authors have personal experiences and beliefs that influence the way they write about specific issues. For instance, someone who rides the train to work every day may have a strong opinion about the importance of public transportation. He would be more likely to write a letter to city hall arguing against a proposal to reduce funding for the train system.

Everyone is influenced by their personal beliefs.

Bias is a term used to describe a person's opinions and preferences. These might be influenced by any of the following factors:

Age	Gender	Occupation
Ethnicity	Hometown	Politics
Experiences	Income	Religion

While everyone is somewhat biased, good authors will work to keep their biases in check. This is because bias can quickly lead to manipulative or dishonest writing. As a reader, you must be able to look for bias in a text and decide how this bias affects the author's overall **argument.**

This lesson will help you evaluate three areas of a text for bias:

Purpose
Tone
Supporting Details

Keep in mind that your own biases can affect the way you interpret or understand a piece of writing. You shouldn't dismiss an author as biased just because she doesn't agree with your own personal views. To help yourself be more aware of your own biases, reflect on the previous list of factors that may influence your thinking.

Purpose

The first step in identifying bias is examining the author's **purpose** for writing. In a biased text, the stated purpose may not be the same as the actual purpose. For example, if the author of a **paragraph** claims that she is **informing** her audience about water conservation methods but spends most of the text **persuading** the audience to volunteer with her organization, the author has a hidden motive or **agenda.** If the author were more straightforward about her purpose to persuade, the text would be more trustworthy.

Thinking about purpose will also help you identify a **conflict of interest.** This happens when an author has a personal stake in a topic. For instance, a report about the health benefits of cheese might be biased if it were written by the president of the American Cheese Society. While the stated purpose of the report is to persuade the audience that cheese is healthy, the actual purpose is probably to sell more cheese.

If authors have personal connections to a topic, their writing could be biased.
Image courtesy of Wikimedia Commons.

Keep in mind that a person's experience in a topic isn't necessarily a sign of bias. In fact, an expert in a particular field is often the best person to write about issues within that field. When a person is connected to a specific group or organization, however, make sure that the purpose of the text is straightforward.

Reflection Questions
What are some topics that might be a conflict of interest for you? Do you think it's possible to write or talk about this topic in a less biased way? Why or why not?

As you evaluate the purpose of a text, ask yourself these questions:

Who is the author?

What is the stated purpose of the text?

What seems to be the actual purpose of the text?

Does the author seem to have a hidden agenda?

Is the author connected to any groups or organizations?

Purpose alone is usually not enough to decide if a text contains bias. Once you've determined the author's actual purpose for writing, use this information to help you evaluate the rest of the text.

Tone

Tone—the positive, negative, or neutral attitude that an author expresses about a topic—can also indicate bias. Selecting extremely negative or positive words often signals that the author is trying to manipulate the audience.

Unbiased   The investigation revealed that the café manager had caused the fire by leaving a pot of boiling water unattended.

Biased   The investigation revealed that the negligent café manager must have thought talking on the phone was more important than monitoring the safety of his kitchen.

Do you notice the difference? The first sentence focuses on giving the reader information, while the second sentence uses negative words to make the manager seem like a villain. Unless the manager is an actual supervillain, the author should make his point using supporting **evidence,** not emotional language.

To learn more about tone, see Lesson 3.1.

Use some of the following questions to evaluate the tone of a text:

Does the author use an extremely negative tone?
Does the author use a positive tone to spin information?
Does the author use stereotypes or exclusive language?

Here are some examples of words that are often considered positive or negative:

Negative	Positive
extremist	visionary
slacker	relaxed
deceitful	brilliant

Authors sometimes use **spin** to put a topic in a more positive light. Here's an example:

> This quarter, profits stayed slightly below average. One possible factor may have been customer satisfaction. While customer complaints were not as low as expected, over 23% of customers stated that they were satisfied with the support they received.
>
> In this example, the author uses an extremely positive tone to describe a situation that is actually negative.

One final way that tone indicates bias is the use of stereotypes or **exclusive language** about a person's age, ethnicity, gender, or religion. This is often an indication that the piece of writing contains bias against certain groups of people.

Look at the following examples:

> The high number of accidents involving female drivers this year gives credibility to the saying that women can't drive.

> The accident was caused when the driver, a woman, grazed the side of the car next to her.

> Both of these sentences show bias by using exclusive language. In the first sentence, the author uses a clear stereotype about women. The bias in the second sentence, however, is a little harder to detect. In this example, the author uses exclusive language by choosing to include the driver's gender, even though this information is unnecessary to the meaning of the sentence.

> To learn more about exclusive language, see Lesson 5.10.

Reading Application

Read the following persuasive letter and consider how language creates a strong tone and clear bias toward one side of the argument.

Dear Mr. Senator,

As an art teacher, I am shocked by your heartless plan to remove national funding for arts programs.

I teach for a program that is partly funded by the National Endowment for the Arts, and I have enjoyed watching my students grow and learn. Millions benefit from having dynamic, free art programs in their communities because these programs promote creativity and inspire the pursuit of inventive careers and new interests.

The tone here is positive and confident, favoring arts programs.

Since my program is partially funded by the endowment, removing it would put the entire program, and its staff members, in jeopardy. It would also rob students of these educational and creative experiences. Art gives students creative freedom to broaden their mind and to try something they haven't done before. It also allows artists to teach others about their craft.

Here, emotionally-charged negative words shows bias and create an adverse tone.

In 2016, The National Endowment paid $149.7 million for arts programs in nearly 16,000 communities across the country. These programs aren't limited to traditional paint and canvas art. They include music, theater, creative writing, dance class, and more. This funding also pays the instructors, who are paying for art supplies, costumes, and even pencils for students.

Mr. Senator, you say your plan to remove the National Endowment for the Arts is to save the country money. You say that private organizations could instead raise money for arts programs in communities and schools. However, putting pressure on organizations to raise tens of thousands of dollars each year will bring their resources and energy away from teaching and creating art, thereby lowering the quality of the programs. Additionally, many arts programs serve low-income areas where communities do not have the finances to run these programs alone.

The author uses clear language to establish a firm and demanding tone.

The National Endowment for the Arts makes up .004 percent of the national budget. That's a nominal cost when you consider that these programs reach millions of Americans in important and meaningful ways.

I am saddened that we have a senator who does not understand the benefit of funding arts programs in schools and neighborhoods. I urge you to reconsider funding this highly important program.

Here, the author recaps the purpose of the text and create a strong, determined tone.

Sincerely,

Jane Woo
Art Educator

Reflection Questions
Cable news networks such as Fox, MSNBC, and CNN are often accused of being biased. Do you agree with this assessment? Why or why not?

Supporting Details

The final way to detect bias in a text is to examine the **supporting details,** or evidence, that the author chooses to include or exclude.

One clue that a text might be biased is inaccurate evidence. An author who uses incorrect **facts** or fake **examples** most likely has a hidden agenda for writing. If you're unsure about a piece of evidence, don't be afraid to double-check its accuracy against other sources.

Another signal of bias is using evidence from unreliable sources. Always investigate the sources mentioned in a text. If the author uses information from a biased person or organization, there is a good chance that the author is blinded by her own beliefs and opinions.

Excluding details also shows bias. A biased text will leave out information that doesn't support its point. Remember that there are almost always two sides to a story. An unbiased author will acknowledge other viewpoints, even if he doesn't spend time discussing each one. If an argument seems one-sided, check other sources to see if important details have been excluded.

Lesson Wrap-up

Reading Application

Let's review another example. Below is an excerpt written in regard to a local policy change. How does the author's use of tone, purpose, and supporting detail suggest bias, even in a short paragraph?

On Monday, the city council voted 8-4 to repeal a set of costly environmental regulations. The mayor backed the standards, but there are some complaints that he over-reached his position. The aim of the rules was to supposedly lower carbon emissions and improve air quality. However, there is little evidence this has had any effect on environmental quality. Instead, many have criticized the regulations as being impractical and costly to small businesses. A recent report estimates that the standards have cost local businesses millions of dollars in expenses and unnecessary upgrades. The report also predicts job losses as many companies delay planned expansions.

The author's purpose seems to be informative. However, the word *costly* indicates a possible bias against the regulations.

In this supporting detail, the author only presents one side of this issue but presents it as a majority opinion.

Reading Application

Take a look at the following blog post written by Cleveland Cable, a national cable provider. What can you determine about the overall purpose and tone of this piece? How are supporting details used to further the company's agenda?

Worried About Your Browsing Privacy? Trust Us!

Many people have come to us with questions about the recent ISP (Internet Service Provider) provisions which were recently repealed by President Trump. If you are not familiar with it, Trump signed a bill allowing us, Cleveland Cable, to access and share your data. This may include your browsing history. Let me guarantee you that there is absolutely nothing to be worried about.

The stated purpose is to provide information about how the new law won't harm consumers.

Our Chief Privacy Officer, Darron Hough, has publicly stated that we do not, and will not, sell our broadband customers' sensitive data, such as banking or health information, without your consent. Furthermore, we will not sell your individual web browsing histories. Cleveland Cable has your best interests at heart, and we are dedicated to providing you with the best possible internet service.

While the Chief Privacy Officer seems like a reliable source, he may have a conflict of interest.

You might be wondering what we plan to do with this information and how can we enhance your internet experiences with these new laws? One benefit of this new law is that we can ensure you are only seeing advertisements related to your interests rather than being exposed to a constant barrage of random ads. However, if you don't care for this service, you can opt-out of these advertisements and go back to your previous preferences.

Note how this supporting detail is included because it benefit's the reader.

Cleveland Cable is dedicated to you, the customer. We value your trust and your business. We do not intend to do anything that will jeopardize the special relationship between us. Rather, we are more equipped than ever to ensure that you are not being taken advantage of by private companies who already have access to your data. Social media platforms, like Facebook, and search engines, such as Google, had no such regulations in place. Now, Facebook and Google must follow the same privacy regulations as all ISPs. We have the power to ensure that your data is protected. Our company signed a voluntary pledge declaring that we will not share or sell any of your data with these private companies. You can always trust us.

This supporting detail is used to strengthen the trust you have in the company.

Key Terms

Agenda: a person's hidden motive

Argument: a reason why you should think or act a certain way

Bias: a person's opinions and preferences

Conflict of Interest: when an author has a personal stake in a topic that affects their purpose

Evidence: a piece of information, also called a supporting detail, that is used to support a main idea

Example: a specific instance or illustration that demonstrates a point

Exclusive Language: disrespectful language that refers to a person's gender, ethnicity or culture, physical or mental ability, or sexual orientation

Fact: a piece of information that most people generally agree to be true

Informative Text: a text that gives the audience information about a topic

Paragraph: a short piece of writing that focuses on one main idea

Persuasive Text: a text that convinces its audience to adopt a belief or take an action

Purpose: the goal of a text

Spin: making a topic seem more positive than it actually is

Supporting Detail: a piece of information, also called evidence, that is used to support a main idea

Tone: the positive, negative, or neutral attitude that an author expresses about a topic

Lesson 3.4
Evaluating Evidence

The Loch Ness Monster is one of the most famous urban legends in the world. According to the stories, this mythical creature has lived in a Scottish lake for hundreds, if not thousands, of years. While some supporters of the Loch Ness legend have produced **evidence** to support their claims, most experts agree that these descriptions, photos, and videos are probably fake.

Sometimes, evidence that seems convincing is actually false.

While you probably don't encounter urban legends in your everyday life, you do come across news reports, product packaging, magazine articles, and junk emails. All of these texts use **supporting details** to strengthen their **conclusions.** You must learn to evaluate this evidence so that you can decide if a text is trustworthy or not.

This lesson will help you evaluate evidence based on three conditions:

Accuracy
Credibility
Relevance

Reflection Questions
How has the internet made it easier to create and share false evidence?

To learn more about the different types of supporting details, see Lesson 2.9.

There are seven commonly used types of supporting details:

Anecdote: a long example told as a story
Description: words that appeal to the senses to explain the appearance of someone or something
Example: a specific instance or illustration that demonstrates a point
Expert Analysis: an opinion or statement shared by someone who is knowledgeable about a topic
Fact: a piece of information that most people generally agree to be true
Reflection: the thoughts and feelings of the author
Statistic: a number or percentage that represents research data

Accuracy

The first step in examining evidence is checking for **accuracy.** If the author uses information that is incorrect, then the text itself is not reliable. Carefully review each supporting detail and ask yourself some of the following questions:

> Does this information seem logical?
> How much detail does the author give?
> Are there any other sources that agree?
> Do the results seem consistent?

In extreme cases, an author makes up a piece of evidence. Even well-known writers and researchers have confessed to using false information. Usually, however, inaccurate evidence isn't completely fake. The author might just be careless or unaware.

Evidence based on research, such as facts and statistics, should be clearly explained by the authors or researchers. Look for information about the research methods and calculations. Be cautious of any facts or statistics that use words like *always, never,* or *every.* Most studies aren't large enough to make those kinds of claims.

When you are evaluating evidence based on personal experience, like anecdotes or reflections, make sure that the author has shared specific details about the story. If the information is vague or generic, the evidence is probably not trustworthy. Also, watch out for evidence that appears overly emotional or manipulative.

> **Helpful Hint**
> If authors are doing ground-breaking research or arguing an unpopular opinion, there may not be other sources who agree with their findings. This doesn't necessarily mean that a source is inaccurate. Make sure that authors give clear explanations for these differences and pay close attention to the way they come to their conclusions.

Credibility

To prove that the evidence in a text is trustworthy, the author must demonstrate that the information comes from a **credible** source.

Credible evidence comes from an expert in the field. In many cases, the authors or researchers have education and professional training that gives them authority on a topic. Of course, the background and credentials of an expert source should match the evidence. A literature professor would not be as knowledgeable about sports-related concussions as a doctor or trainer would be.

Non-expert evidence is acceptable as long as the source has relevant experience in the topic. For example, someone who runs an eBay business out of his home could be an expert in online selling. This person would probably be a good source for a description of the auction process, but not for a statistic about eBay market share.

If the evidence is produced by an organization, that organization should be well-respected and recognizable. Sources that have a personal stake in the information, such as corporations or political parties, are not the best sources of information. Usually, these organizations publish information that upholds their public image and supports their opinions.

Reading Application

Consider the credibility of the article below. Read the provided notes and add some of your own.

Do Vaccines Cause Autism?

Thousands of individuals across the United States believe that vaccines are a cause of autism. Many parents have delayed or prevented their children from receiving vaccines for diseases like measles or Rubella. Sander Van der Linden, a psychologist from Princeton University's Global Health Program, writes that "a recent study found that although outright refusal is still relatively uncommon, in a typical month, over 90% of surveyed US physicians receive requests to delay childhood vaccines" (119). This has sparked a nationwide debate about the ethics of denying these vaccines. Many parents are terrified that their children will acquire illnesses from non-vaccinated children, particularly those too young to be vaccinated or whose immune systems are especially weakened by other illnesses. This leads to two relevant questions: how did this debate begin, and which side does the medical world support?

> Pay attention to the credentials of the person giving the information. Make sure they are credible, like the one described here.

According to Paul Offit and Susan Coffin, researchers at the Children's Hospital of Philadelphia, it began in 1998 when a study in the UK "published a report of eight children …with… autism following receipt of the MMR vaccine. As a consequence of media coverage of this report, MMR-immunization rates in England fell from 94% to 75% and cases of measles increased" (1). These concerns quickly spread to the United States. There are a few items that are significant about this. First, a study made up of only eight participants cannot be considered credible. Most medical studies are completed over many years with hundreds of participants. When there are more participants, the results are more accurate. Secondly, the study does not address whether the vaccines caused autism. It only claims that children with autism were all given this vaccine. It does not mention that many children without autism were also given this vaccine. Even though there are clear problems with this study, the media spread perpetrated this connection.

> When authors include quotes from reliable sources, you can assume the information is accurate and relevant.

> The word *most* shows the author of this essay making a generalization without evidence. Be careful of these types of statements.

"Over 90% of doctors agree that adults and children should receive all recommended vaccines" (Van der Linden 1). Medical experts deserve the nation's trust far beyond the media, who often spread fear-based rumors while researchers use statistics and evidence. Paul Offit agrees when he cites studies by other doctors: "the hypothesis that the MMR vaccine causes autism has been evaluated now in six separate studies … [that] reached the same conclusion—when autism followed receipt of MMR vaccine, it occurred at a rate that would have been predicted by chance alone" (3). So, there is a correlation between the vaccine and autism, but

> Doctors are experts in the medical field. They are credible and reliable sources.

autism is not caused by the vaccine. The connection is purely coincidental.

People need to stop spreading the idea that vaccines cause autism. This false belief is based on an unreliable study that was later disproven, and those who spread it are putting children in danger. When parents do not vaccinate their own child, they also put their child at risk for a deadly illness. It's time to act based off fact, not media frenzy.

> Overall, this reads as a credible source. However, since this essay is trying to convince you of something, there is some bias here.

Offit, Paul A., and Susan E. Coffin. "Communicating science to the public:

MMR vaccine and Autism." *Vaccine* 22.1 (2003): 1-6.

Van der Linden, Sander. "Why doctors should convey the medical consensus

on vaccine safety." *Evidence Based Medicine* 21.3 (2016): 119-119.

Relevance

Finally, the evidence used in a text must be **relevant** to the author's main idea. If an author is writing on the ethics of circuses, she should include facts and statistics that clearly relate to this topic. Using irrelevant or out-of-context information is a sign of an untrustworthy text.

Certain types of evidence are more relevant to some topics than others. A text on a scientific or technical topic should include more expert analysis, statistics, and facts. On the other hand, a text on a personal topic should include anecdotes, reflections, and examples.

Relevant evidence is also current. Usually, research from fifty years ago is no longer the best source of information. This is especially important in the fields of technology, science, and medicine. In these cases, evidence from only one or two years ago may already be outdated. In a field like history or literature, however, dates are much less important.

Helpful Hint
A copyright year is always listed on one of the first few pages in a book. Use this date as you determine the book's relevance.

Lesson Wrap-up

Reading Application

Read this excerpt from an article exploring eyecare in the United States. Note how the author creates an accurate, credible, and relevant argument in a short amount of space.

The Popularity of Glasses

According to a 2016 study from the American Vision Council (AVC), more than 188 million people require some form of vision correction in the United States. *That's over three out of every four adults.*

> The American Vision Council is an expert analysis and credible source for information on vision.

Glasses are the most common type of vision correction that Americans use, the survey states. The eyeglasses business generated more than $39 billion in revenue during the year 2015, according to the survey. This explains why eye doctors' offices are usually busy and difficult to book at the last minute.

Information like this allows you to cite the source directly to check statements for accuracy.

Because of this steady business, today people are buying their prescription eyewear in a new way—online. According to AVC, shoppers spent close to $1.5 billion on prescription eyewear online last year. It was the fourth straight year with more than $1 billion worth of optical products sold online.

This statement provides strong relevance to the overall topic of eyewear popularity.

Key Terms

Accuracy: when information is as correct and unbiased as possible

Anecdote: a long example told as a story

Conclusion: the result of a logical argument

Credibility: what makes someone or something believable

Evidence: a piece of information, also called a supporting detail, which is used to support a main idea

Example: a specific instance or illustration that demonstrates a point

Expert Analysis: an opinion or statement shared by someone who is knowledgeable about a topic

Fact: a piece of information that most people generally agree to be true

Reflection: the thoughts or feelings of the author

Relevance: when information is clearly related to the text around it

Statistic: a number or percentage that represents research data

Supporting Detail: a piece of information, also called evidence, that is used to support a main idea

Lesson 3.5
Understanding the Basics of Logic

Logic is a method for carefully thinking through a topic to find a reasonable **conclusion**. One of the most well-known examples of logic is the fictional detective Sherlock Holmes. Holmes famously solves crimes by considering all of the evidence and deducing the most logical explanation. He notices the tiny details that everyone else overlooks and refuses to let emotion cloud his judgement.

The history of logic, however, goes back much further than Sherlock Holmes. The first person to teach and write about logic and reasoning was the Greek philosopher Aristotle. His ideas have influenced science, technology, and government for thousands of years. Without Aristotle and his teachings on logic, society would look very different than it does today.

Logic is what makes Sherlock Holmes a great detective.

Understanding the basics of logic will help you use critical thinking to become a better reader and writer.

This lesson will focus on three basic elements of logic:

Premises and Conclusions
Inductive Reasoning
Deductive Reasoning

Premises and Conclusions

Aristotle explained logic using statements made up of premises and conclusions. **Premises** are two or more pieces of evidence that support a **logical argument.** These premises should lead to a logical conclusion. To illustrate this, Aristotle came up with the following example:

Premise 1: All men are mortal.
Premise 2: Socrates is a man.
Conclusion: Therefore, Socrates is mortal.

The first premise in this statement is that all men are mortal, a fact that everyone agrees is true. The second premise states that Socrates is a man, another fact that everyone agrees is true. Therefore, if all men are mortal and if Socrates is a man, then the logical conclusion is that Socrates is mortal.

Because both premises in this argument are true, the conclusion is also true. This means that the argument itself is logical.

If one of the premises in an argument is false, then the conclusion will also be false. Think about this example:

Premise 1: All men are American.
Premise 2: Socrates is a man.
Conclusion: Therefore, Socrates is American.

The conclusion of this statement is not logical because one of the premises is false. All men are not American; therefore, the conclusion that Socrates is American is false and illogical.

Reading Application

Read the following paragraph paying close attention to the use of premises and conclusions.

Who Needs Homework?

In the United States, students are often assigned homework on a regular basis. Most teachers believe that homework is helpful to students, and that it extends the learning process outside of the classroom. However, many students receive at least one hour of homework per teacher per night. When this is totaled, students are asked to complete around six hours of homework each night! They often have other responsibilities when they get home like babysitting their siblings, going to after-school jobs, or helping around the house. So, students have a choice: complete hours of homework every night, cheat, or do not do the homework. Some students choose the last two options, using other resources to copy answers or letting their grades slip. In either case, they are not learning much at all. Therefore, it is in the students' best interests for teachers to stop assigning homework.

This is a general premise since it makes a statement about everyone in America.

This premise is more specific because it provides numbers.

A logical conclusion at the end results from knowing that a) students have hours of homework to do each night and b) students have other responsibilities.

On Your Own

Read the following argument and identify the false premise.

All bugs are poisonous.
A frog is not a bug.
Therefore, frogs are not poisonous.

Inductive Reasoning

One specific type of logical argumentation is inductive reasoning. **Inductive reasoning** uses specific premises to reach a general conclusion.

Premise

Premise

Conclusion

A common example of inductive reasoning is political polling. Obviously, interviewing every voter in the United States would be impossible. Instead, polling organizations interview a limited number of people and use those results to predict the behavior of all voters.

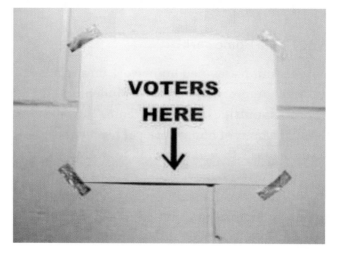

Inductive reasoning is used in many areas, including political polling.

Because inductive arguments use specific examples to make general conclusions, they can never claim that a conclusion is *absolutely* true. Here's an example:

Premise 1: Every tornado I have seen in Kansas has rotated counterclockwise.

Premise 2: The tornado that hit Kansas last night rotated counterclockwise.

Conclusion: Therefore, all tornadoes rotate counterclockwise.

Both of the premises in this statement are true. However, they are based on very specific pieces of information. The general conclusion that all tornadoes rotate counterclockwise cannot be made with such a limited amount of evidence.

An argument that uses inductive reasoning can only claim that a conclusion is *probably* true.

A better conclusion might look something like this:

Conclusion: Therefore, the tornado predicted to hit Kansas tomorrow will probably rotate counterclockwise.

The more evidence included in an inductive argument, the more logical its conclusion. By adding a third premise to the previous example, the inductive reasoning becomes even stronger.

Premise 1: Every tornado I have seen in Kansas has rotated counterclockwise.

Premise 2: The tornado that hit Kansas last night rotated counterclockwise.

Premise 3: The last ten tornadoes in Kansas have rotated counterclockwise.

Conclusion: Therefore, the tornado predicted to hit Kansas tomorrow will probably rotate counterclockwise.

Deductive Reasoning

The second type of logical argumentation is deductive reasoning. **Deductive reasoning** starts with a general premise and argues toward a specific conclusion.

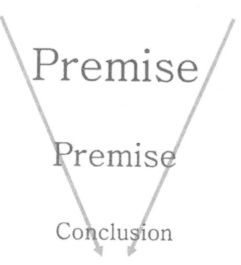

The following is an example of a deductive argument:

Premise 1: All full-time employees at my company receive five paid vacation days.

Premise 2: Kenna is a full-time employee.

Conclusion: Therefore, Kenna has received five paid vacation days.

The argument in this example starts with a general statement about all full-time employees. Since Kenna is part of this group, she receives the benefits of a full-time employee.

The sciences often use deductive reasoning to prove a theory or hypothesis. After conducting experiments, researchers compare their results to known scientific principles and determine if their theory was logical or illogical.

Deductive reasoning is an important part of the scientific method.

Because deductive arguments make claims about very specific examples, their conclusions can be considered true if they follow these guidelines:

Deductive Reasoning Checklist

☐ All of the premises of the argument must be true.

☐ All of the premises must be closely related.

☐ No new ideas can be introduced into the conclusion.

Think about the following example:

Premise 1: Full-time city bus drivers make less than $20,000 a year.

Premise 2: Amanda is a full-time city bus driver.

Conclusion: Therefore, the city should raise the minimum wage to $15 an hour.

In this example, both of the premises are true and closely related; however, the conclusion introduces new information into the statement by introducing minimum wage. To make this argument logical, you must revise either the premises or the conclusion so that no new ideas are introduced in the conclusion.

Reading Application

Read the essay below written in response to a lack of daycare options on a college campus. Note how the author uses both inductive and deductive reasoning to support his claim.

Our College Needs Expanded Daycare

Last month college trustees dedicated $4 million to "improve campus facilities to better serve our changing student body and increase enrollment." Sixty percent of incoming students are working females and half of them have preschool-aged children. The most common complaint from these new students is the lack of daycare options. Therefore, the best way to serve our students and increase enrollment is to provide expanded daycare services.

Premise 1: The college wants to improve services for students.

Premise 2: There is a need for campus daycare.

Conclusion: The best way to serve the college's goals is to provide additional daycare.

The women's dorm was constructed in 1967, when most female students were single teenagers attending college full-time. Today, seventy percent of our students are working adults, and there is less demand for on-campus housing. For example, two floors of the women's dorm are now unoccupied.

Surveys also show that daycare is a major factor when women choose which college to attend. Our current student union daycare center can only handle thirty children, and it is not open on evenings or weekends when demand is the greatest. Transforming the first floor of the women's dorm into a well-equipped daycare center that will be open whenever classes are held will cost less than $2 million. Given complaints from current students and surveys of potential students, the best way to improve our campus is to provide expanded daycare services in the women's dorm.

Premise 1: Potential students seek daycare services in selecting colleges.

Premise 2: The women's dorm has available space.

Conclusion: The best way to serve the college's goals is placing a daycare center in the women's dorm.

> Group Activity
> Write ten statements that use inductive and deductive reasoning. As a group, discuss the strongest examples and your reasons for selecting those.

On Your Own

Read the following **paragraph** and identify the author's conclusion. Is the conclusion logical?

> Studies have shown that advertisements contribute to childhood obesity. In 2007, the Kaiser Family Foundation found that commercials for "high-calorie, low-nutrient snacks, fast foods, and sweetened drinks . . . are a significant risk factor for [childhood] obesity ("The Impact of Food Advertising on Childhood Obesity"). In fact, the more television a child watches, the more calories the child consumes. The same study by Kaiser states that watching three hours of television a day can increase a child's risk of obesity by 50%. This rise in obesity rates is partly due to the advertisements that are bombarding young people every day. One study found that the average child sees over 20,000 ads for high-calorie snacks and cereals a year (Reece et al.). Clearly, the presence of these commercials has contributed to the childhood obesity epidemic.

Lesson Wrap-up

Key Terms

Conclusion: the result of a logical argument

Deductive Reasoning: a type of logical reasoning that starts with a general premise and argues toward a specific conclusion

Inductive Reasoning: a type of logical reasoning that uses specific premises to reach a general conclusion

Logic: a method for carefully thinking through a topic to find a reasonable conclusion

Logical Argument: an argument that makes a reasonable claim, usually using facts and statistics

Paragraph: a short piece of writing that focuses on one main idea

Premise: two or more pieces of evidence used to support a logical argument

Lesson 3.6
Recognizing Logical Fallacies

Have you ever seen a commercial like this?

> An unpopular man walks into a party. He tries to talk to a few people, but no one even notices him. Eventually, he heads into the kitchen and grabs a specific type of drink. The minute he opens it, he becomes the coolest person there. Everyone starts cheering and chanting his name.

Hundreds of other commercials use this same tactic to argue that if you buy a certain type of product, you will become a hipper, smarter person. Obviously, this **argument** doesn't make sense. Simply buying one brand of deodorant or body spray will not make you instantly sexy.

Many commercials use logical fallacies to sell a product.

Companies continue to make these commercials because they are effective. Viewers do not always take the time to look beneath the surface and think critically about what a commercial is claiming.

Group Activity
Choose two commercials to watch on YouTube. As a group, discuss the argument that each commercial is making. How are they different or similar?

A **logical fallacy** is a faulty or incorrect argument. When discovered, fallacies always make a text or presentation weaker. All too often, however, fallacies appear so logical and persuasive that the audience accepts them as fact. This is the goal of a fallacy: to convince a reader or viewer to react before thinking critically.

Personal beliefs can make a person more likely to accept certain fallacies. If you love chocolate, you would be happy to find an article claiming that because dark chocolate has health benefits, you should eat two pounds of chocolate every day. Obviously, this argument sounds questionable. However, your love for chocolate may lead you to accept the claim of the article without any further investigation or research.

Does eating two pounds of chocolate a day really seem like a logical way to be healthier?

Not all fallacies are intentional. Sometimes, a topic is so personal or emotional that authors or speakers do not take the time to think through their arguments fully. The audience may feel the same way, leading them to accept a faulty argument at face value. While these situations are understandable, they are dangerous because fallacies can lead people to make poor decisions.

Reading Application

The following passage is an open letter printed in a local newspaper. As you read, think about how the writing is impacted by the author's personal feelings.

Mayor Wilson Should Resign

Mayor Jane Wilson should resign immediately. She made millions for herself peddling cheap real estate deals all over the state and has no right to run a city. Her latest proposal to build trolleys is impractical and unnecessary. We have been using buses for public transportation for almost one hundred years, which proves there is no need for trolleys. Everybody knows that trolleys are old-fashioned and inefficient. Building trolleys in a modern city makes no sense. This plan reveals she has no clue about running public transportation.

The mayor's real estate career does not necessarily prove she cannot run a city.

Not everyone knows that trolleys are old-fashioned.

Wilson's trolley plan must be stopped. If trolleys are built to replace buses, soon she will want to ban cars. The city will lose thousands of dollars a day in lost parking revenue. We should listen to the people who called into Jerry Lacy's radio show this morning. Five people talked about the trolley plan, and all five were strongly against it. With all this public opposition, Mayor Wilson needs to do the right thing and resign.

Building a new form of public transportation does not automatically mean that cars will be banned.

Five callers do not represent widespread public opposition.

Concerned Citizen,
Oscar Sobo

Reflection Questions
On sites like Facebook and Twitter, people around the world participate in timely and important discussions about current events or social trends. The ability to share these opinions instantly, however, can result in embarrassing or offensive posts. Have you ever seen any examples of this?

While some fallacies are obvious, others are more subtle. Many people are naturally suspicious of advertisements selling a product or service. Recognizing fallacies from a more trustworthy source, however, can be difficult.

News reports, books, and research studies can all contain fallacies, both intentional and accidental. To avoid being manipulated by false information, you must think critically about an argument before accepting it as fact.

This lesson will help you become familiar with the different types of logical fallacies.

Reflection Questions
Think about news websites that you consider trustworthy or untrustworthy. Why do you think of these sources in this way?

Types of Fallacies

To find logical fallacies in an argument, you need to become familiar with what they look like. Don't feel overwhelmed by terms that may seem unfamiliar or complicated. Memorizing the names of the fallacies is not as important as knowing their characteristics.

Ad Hominem

Ad hominem arguments attack a person's character or reputation instead of examining her actual position. Look at this statement:

> This author has admitted to smoking marijuana in the past, so her new book about climate change must be completely unreliable.

> In this example, the author's personal decisions about marijuana do not affect her ability to research and write a book about climate change.

Appeal to Tradition

An **appeal to tradition** argues that something is right simply because it has always been done that way. Think about how this fallacy has been used to argue for injustices like Jim Crow laws. Many people claimed that discrimination was acceptable because different ethnic groups had always been kept separate.

Bandwagon

A **bandwagon** fallacy claims that something is true because many people are doing it. If you ever tried using this fallacy as a child, your parents probably responded by saying, "If everyone were jumping off a cliff, would you jump too?"

Devil Words

Devil words are terms that stir up negative emotions in an audience. You've seen examples of these in political speeches and advertisements. Think about the words *liberal, conservative, socialism*, and *fundamentalism*. Because people often react strongly to these terms, devil words can label someone or something as negative before the audience has had a chance to think it through.

False Authority

False authority claims that a person's fame gives him or her authority on a topic, even if the discussion is completely unrelated to that person's area of expertise. This fallacy is commonly used to sell products that have been endorsed by celebrities. For example, an actor may write a diet book that becomes a best-seller, even though that actor has no medical training or experience.

Hasty Generalization

A **hasty generalization** bases an argument about a large group on evidence from a small group. The more subjects that you include in a study, the stronger your argument becomes. This is why companies spend large amounts money on consumer testing before they release a new product. Conducting a survey of five thousand people will give them more reliable information than a survey of only fifty people.

Post Hoc

The Latin phrase *post hoc ergo propter hoc* means "after this, therefore caused by this." A **post hoc** fallacy assumes that one event caused a second, completely unrelated event. Here's an example:

> I passed an orange cat on my way to school this morning, and then I flunked my biology exam. If I want to do well in class, I should avoid all orange cats.

Straw Man

A **straw man** fallacy changes an opponent's argument to make it easier to attack. If a research study concludes that eating large amounts of sugar can lead to childhood obesity, the food industry may claim that these researchers want to make all sugar consumption illegal. By making the researchers' argument sound more extreme, the food industry can convince the public to ignore the findings of the study.

Further Resources
This lesson focuses on eight common fallacies. To learn more about these fallacies and others, you can check out this infographic from *Information Is Beautiful* (http://www.informationisbeautiful.net/visualizations/rhetological-fallacies/) or this video series from PBS (https://www.youtube.com/playlist?list=PLtHP6qx8VF7dPql3ll1To4i6vEIPt0kV5).

Group Activity
As a group, write a 1-2 minute commercial that uses a fallacy to argue its point. Try to be as convincing as possible. Share your commercial with the class.

Reading Application

Review the following blog post, and ask yourself if the author is a trustworthy source.

Your Food is Killing Me!

Many of us are familiar with Gordon Ramsay, Rachael Ray, and Paula Deen, famous celebrity chefs. Each is on television and has his or her own cooking show. Fans admire these professional chefs and do their best to imitate their cooking. However, these chefs are bad influences on society. Paula Deen has Type 2 Diabetes because she cooks with oily, buttery, and high-fat foods. Should we really be taking cooking advice from someone who is so unhealthy? If we cook like Paula Deen, then we too will someday get Type 2 Diabetes. None of these celebrity chefs cares about the health of the viewers. Rather, they care about their paychecks.

Attacking Paula Deen based on her health rather than her cooking knowledge is an ad hominem *fallacy.*

In addition, celebrity chefs are manipulative and ill-tempered. Just look at Gordon Ramsay! Ramsay does more yelling in the kitchen than cooking. People enjoy watching him bully others more than watching him cook. This is why people voted for a presidential candidate in 2016 who was the most argumentative. They enjoy watching people get upset. Ultimately, celebrity chefs are poor role models for today's youth. They advertise unhealthy eating as well as bullying. America needs to rise against these celebrity chefs by giving them poor ratings and little attention!

Here is an example of devil words which stir up negative emotions in the reader's mind.

These sentences are a post hoc *fallacy. They connect Gordon Ramsay's yelling to the election of Donald Trump. Neither event has anything to do with the other.*

Finding Fallacies

To find potential fallacies in a text or presentation, you must first carefully study the author's argument. Try using the following questions:

> What is the author's main point?
> What evidence does the author use to support the main point?
> What is the author's **purpose**?
> How does the author want me to respond?

Once you've thought through these questions, you can start looking for possible fallacies in the author's argument.

Learning Style Tip

If you're a **global** learner, you learn best when you understand the big picture. When you are analyzing an argument, read through the entire text first to give yourself an idea of the overall structure. Then, go back and re-read the information, looking specifically for fallacies.

On Your Own

Identify any logical fallacies in the following passage:

> The impersonal nature of the internet is one major cause of cyber-bullying. When communicating online, teenagers are more comfortable than they would be in a face-to-face conversation. Research by psychologist Rhonda Peters shows that "typing words on a keyboard feels very different than actually saying them to someone's face" (54). This can lead some young people to write cruel things online that they would never say in person.
>
> Helping teenagers think about the person "behind the screen" can teach them that their words have hurtful, often tragic consequences. According to a survey of thirteen students at McKinley High School, discussing real-life stories of cyber-bullying makes young people less likely to post cruel comments about others online. The results of this survey show that using a similar strategy would greatly reduce cyber-bullying at schools across America.

Further Resources

Choose an opinion article from the *New York Times* website (http://www.nytimes.com/pages/opinion/index.html). Read the article carefully, thinking through the following questions:

- What is the author's main point?
- What evidence does the author use to support the main point?
- What is the author's purpose?
- How does the author want me to respond?
- Does the author's argument contain any fallacies?

Lesson Wrap-up

Key Terms

Ad Hominem: an attack against a person's character

Appeal to Tradition: an argument that something is right because it has always been done that way

Argument: a reason why you should think or act a certain way

Bandwagon: an argument that something is right because everyone is doing it

Devil Words: terms that stir up negative emotions in an audience

False Authority: an argument that claims a person's fame makes him or her an expert on a topic

Global Learning: learning information through seeing the big picture

Hasty Generalization: an argument about a large group based on a small amount of evidence

Logical Fallacy: a faulty, or incorrect, argument that appears logical and persuasive

Post Hoc: the assumption that one event caused a second, unrelated event

Purpose: the goal of a text

Straw Man: changing an opponent's argument to make it easier to attack

Lesson 3.7
Analyzing and Evaluating Visuals

Every day, you encounter hundreds of images on billboards, commercials, websites, and magazines. You see so many that you probably don't even notice half of them.

Images are powerful tools for communicating ideas. They can influence what you buy, how you vote, and even whom you date. Not all images, however, are trustworthy. Just like a book or document can mislead its audience, an image can manipulate or deceive its viewers.

Learning to evaluate images is an essential critical thinking skill. Once you are able to interpret the meaning of a photo or video, you can decide how you want to respond.

In this lesson, you will learn how to evaluate three aspects of images:

Purpose
Composition
Argument

Learning Style Tip
If you're a **verbal** leaner, you may be tempted to ignore images. Remember that both text and images are valuable resources for any type of learner.

It's become normal to see hundreds of images every day.

Purpose

To start analyzing an image, you must first think about its **purpose**. Just like texts, images can **inform**, **persuade**, **reflect**, or **entertain**.

The purpose of some images is easy to determine. Print advertisements and commercials are usually trying to persuade you to purchase a particular brand of product. Finding the purpose of other types of images, however, may be more difficult.

Often, the purpose of an image is made clear through **context**: how and when the image is presented to the viewer. For example, think about the following photograph. How could context help you determine the purpose of this image?

The context of an image provides clues about its purpose.

Depending on the context, this photograph might communicate any of the following purposes:

- To inform the viewer about the physical characteristics of yaks.
- To persuade the viewer that Nepal is an excellent tourist destination.
- To reflect on the photographer's recent trip to Nepal.
- To entertain the audience with a story about drinking yak milk for the first time.

Keep in mind that the actual purpose of an image may be different from the stated purpose. For example, companies sometimes include photos of military veterans on their advertisements. As a viewer, you have to decide if the purpose of these images is to honor veterans or to sell a product.

> Reflection Questions
> Do paintings or sculptures have a specific purpose? Why or why not?

Composition

Once you've determined the purpose of an image, you should carefully consider its **composition:** how the contents of an image have been selected and arranged.

When creating an image, the artist or designer makes decisions about which details to include and which ones to exclude.

Think about the following example:

Composition involves details that are both included in and excluded from an image.

This image includes seven racehorses and their jockeys. Other details, such as the crowd watching the race or the racing facilities, are excluded. Leaving out these details changes the meaning of the image.

In some instances, composition choices are used to manipulate or mislead. For example, a dishonest real estate agent might create a photo slideshow of a house that excludes important details, such as rotting floorboards or a collapsing roof. When you arrive at the house for a showing, you'll see all of the information that was excluded from the photos.

Artists and designers also use composition to emphasize or deemphasize details. When an item is larger or brighter than the rest of the image, your focus stays on that particular item the longest. In contrast, items that are smaller or lighter are easily overlooked.

Emphasizing or including certain details isn't necessarily dishonest. It's important to remember, however, that images are not "photographic truth." Anytime you analyze photos or videos, you need to consider how composition affects the way you interpret their meaning.

Reading Application

Examine the following photograph. Likely, you've seen an image like this before in an ad or online posting. Though it appears ordinary, note how the writer analyzes details, purpose, and composition to better understanding the image's meaning.

The purpose of this photo is to persuade viewers that the organization it represents, Carrier Networking, is professional, accomplished, and creative. The context is established through the office setting and professional clothing of the four figures. It is also important to notice what is not in the picture. The desk surface is clean and without clutter, and there are no coffee cups, snacks, or stacks of paper that would distract viewers or suggest the space is disorganized.

The purpose of the photograph is explained by analyzing its context: the details about the people and office setting.

Notice how the author points out *why* these items are intentionally left out of the photo, and how it adds to the overall meaning.

The position of the participants' hands indicates their role in the meeting. In the background, the woman's hands are folded as she listens to her coworker. The man stretches his left arm toward the computer, his finger pointing to the computer screen. He appears to be commenting on what is being shown. The man and woman in the foreground are focused on the laptop screen. Their heads are turned toward their screen and away from the man and woman in the background. This suggests that they are not a part of the meeting and are working on something else.

Here, the photo's composition is being analyzed as the author includes details about the people's gestures.

Argument

The final step in analyzing an image is reflecting on the argumentation strategies it uses to communicate ideas. All images make some kind of **argument**. Even informative photos and videos must argue for your attention and trust.

Arguments are often divided into three types of strategies: *ethos*, *logos*, and *pathos*.

Ethos

The first argumentation strategy is **Ethos**, an argument based on **credibility**. Images often include experts to build credibility with viewers. For example, a toothpaste commercial might feature a dentist, while a shoe commercial might feature an athlete.

Images can also be used to add credibility to a text. If an author is writing about the time she spent working for the Red Cross, including images of her travels and experiences would strengthen her *ethos*.

Logos

Logos is an argument based on logic. Advertisements often use before-and-after photos to prove that a certain product will result in weight loss or stain removal.

Logos can also be established by showing just the results of an action or event. For example, an educational video on the dangers of drunk driving might include images of car accidents. The logic is that if someone else got into an accident because of drunk driving, the same thing could happen to you.

> **Helpful Hint**
> Most images don't use just one argumentation strategy, so make sure you look for all three: *pathos*, *logos*, and *ethos*. For example, a commercial for face wash that features before-and-after pictures of a celebrity is appealing to both *logos* and *ethos*.

Pathos

Finally, **Pathos** is an argument based on emotion. Images are often the easiest way to touch the emotions of viewers. For example, a documentary might include images of people living in shelters to help you make a human connection to the problem of homelessness.

However, images that use too much *pathos* can become emotionally manipulative.

Once you've thought carefully about the *ethos*, *logos*, and *pathos* in an image, you can evaluate the strength of the argument itself. Try asking yourself some of these questions:

> Does the image use a legitimate expert to establish *ethos*?
>
> Does the *logos* of the image make sense?
>
> Does the image rely too heavily on *pathos*?
>
> Do the argumentation strategies fit the purpose of the image?

> **Group Activity**
> As a group, choose one advertisement or commercial to analyze. Look for the way that *ethos*, *logos*, and *pathos* are used in the image. Present your findings to the class.

Reading Application

Spend a few minutes studying the following image. What can you note about purpose, composition, and argument of the billboard?

Photo Courtesy of Wikimedia Commons

Now, read this visual analysis. Pay attention to how the author analyzes these elements within the billboard.

Across the street from my old middle school, there is a billboard advertising for Apple's iPod. This location is deliberate—a space where young people see it regularly. The color scheme is bright and eye-catching, with shades corresponding to choices for an iPod. While the background of the ad is colorful, the people in the ad are featured in silhouette, leaving them ambiguous in their representation, but also standing out amongst the vibrant background.

> The location of this billboard, *near a local middle school*, provides context.

The people in the ad appear energetic, youthful, and fit: one woman is in a bathing suit while another is wearing schoolbag straps. A shirtless man wears a hat while another sports spiky hair. The ad repeats these same four images, each one in a differently-colored tile. Additionally, they all are dancing while wearing earbuds and holding iPods. While each person is featured in his or her own separate tile, the tiles are placed deliberately to make it appear like they are dancing together.

> This image is composed specifically with a youthful audience in mind. Here, the writer provides details that support that analysis.

When I first saw this billboard, I felt confident knowing that I already had the product that the billboard advertises. It made me feel funky and hip, dancing in my own color tile. It was strange reflecting on billboards like this, part of my everyday visual landscape, and how they could have affected me in the past. Moving forward, I'll be sure to not only see the images around me but also hear what they are saying.

> According to the author, the advertisement uses *pathos* to inspire people like herself to feel young and have fun by owning an iPod.

Lesson Wrap-up

On Your Own

Think about the following photograph. How do purpose, composition, and argument affect the way you understand and interpret this image? Beneath the photo, write your interpretation of the image and which argumentation strategies you think it uses.

Key Terms

Argument: a reason why you should think or act a certain way

Composition: how the contents of an image have been selected and arranged

Context: how and when information is presented

Credibility: what makes someone or something believable

Entertaining Text: a text that explores a topic or event in a creative or humorous way

Ethos: an argument based on a person's credibility

Informative Text: a text that gives the audience information about a topic

Logos: an argument based on logic

Pathos: an argument based on emotion

Persuasive Text: a text that convinces its audience to adopt a belief or take an action

Purpose: the goal of an image

Reflective Text: a text that shares a personal experience or belief

Chapter 4
Grammar & Mechanics

Lesson 4.1
Understanding Nouns

A **noun** is a part of speech that represents a person, place, thing, event, or idea. The English language is full of nouns. Look at the following example:

> Africa has seen many great leaders, but none have been as influential as Nelson Mandela. He fought against Apartheid, a political revolution that violently divided people by race. Mandela is best known for serving time in jail as a result of political protesting. The country mourned his death when he passed in South Africa in 2013.

Now, read the same paragraph again, this time without any nouns:

> has seen a of great, but none have been as influential as. was not only a and, but also the of. He fought against, a political that violently divided by. is best known for serving in as a of political. The mourned his when he passed in in.

Nouns are the *who* and *what* in a sentence. Without them, you wouldn't be able to talk about much.

Nouns come in all shapes and sizes. They can refer to a specific person or a group of people; they can be one thing or multiple things. Regardless of what a noun looks like, it will always be a person, place, thing, event, or idea.

Here are some examples of nouns:

People	Places	Things	Events	Ideas
leader	Charleston	Kleenex	Civil War	frustration
Jack	school	USB drive	baby shower	justice
mom	gym	*Scandal*	election	bravery
friends	Lambeau Field	handshake	meeting	experience
supervisor	libraries	Birchbox	vacation	imagination
Lakshmi	desert	economics	fundraiser	inflation
Harry Potter	Panera Bread	racecar	wedding	luck

This lesson will help you become familiar with a variety of nouns. Because there are so many different types, recognizing them can sometimes be tricky. Being comfortable with their differences will give you the ability to use nouns more effectively as a writer and communicator.

In this lesson, you will learn about the following:

Common and Proper Nouns
Singular and Plural Nouns
Count and Non-Count Nouns
Compound Nouns
The Functions of Nouns

Group Activity
As a group, make a list of all of the nouns you can find in your classroom or computer lab. Try to come up with at least fifty separate nouns. Don't forget nouns that describe invisible things, like *oxygen* or *friendship*.

On Your Own

Identify all the nouns in the following paragraph:

Africa has seen many great leaders, but none have been as influential as Nelson Mandela. He fought against Apartheid, a political revolution that violently divided people by race. Mandela is best known for serving time in jail as a result of political protesting. The country mourned his death when he passed in South Africa in 2013.

Common and Proper Nouns

One way to classify nouns is to divide them into two groups: proper and common. **Proper nouns** are the names of specific people, places, things, events, or ideas.

Common nouns, on the other hand, name non-specific people, places, things, events, or ideas. Because these nouns are general, they do not start with a capital letter unless they are located at the beginning of a sentence.

On Your Own

In the table below, use the list of common nouns to create your own list of proper nouns. For example, for the common noun *city*, you could write *Seattle* or *Budapest*. Write your ideas in the spaces provided.

Common Nouns	Proper Nouns
author	
activist	
friend	
state	

school	
website	
dog	

Singular and Plural Nouns

Nouns can also be singular or plural. **Singular nouns** refer to one person, place, thing, event, or idea; **plural nouns** refer to multiple people, places, things, events, or ideas.

Singular Nouns	Plural Nouns
Paul McCartney	musicians
leader	leaders
friend	friends
Mt. Rushmore	monuments
flock	flocks
Senate	legislators
Taco Bell	restaurants
Cambodian	Cambodians
sympathy	sympathies

> Reflection Questions
> Some nouns, such as *moose*, can be either singular or plural based on the meaning of the sentence. Can you think of any other examples?

Count and Non-Count Nouns

Another way to classify nouns is as count or non-count. Just like the names indicate, **count nouns** are nouns that can be counted while **non-count nouns** are nouns that can't be counted. Here are some examples of non-count nouns:

gravity
milk
soccer
honesty
sand

You can count *glasses* of milk or *grains* of sand, but you can't count the milk or sand itself.

> **Helpful Hint**
> One easy way to test if a noun is count or non-count is to add a number before it. Which of the following examples are count and which are non-count?
>
> three mails   three Targets   three electricities   three concerts

Compound Nouns

Some nouns are made up of more than one word. These nouns are known as **compound nouns**. Some compound nouns are joined together into one word while some are separated by spaces or hyphens. A **hyphen** is a short line that links two words or word parts.

To learn more about hyphens, see Lesson 4.16.

These examples are considered compound nouns because both halves of the word work together as one:

bus stop	softball	sister-in-law
lamp post	sunrise	six-pack

> **Helpful Hint**
> Many compound nouns are words that you use every day. Words like *bedroom* or *mailbox* are so familiar, you probably don't think about the way they are spelled. However, some compound nouns are more difficult. If you're unsure how a compound noun should be spelled, use a resource like *Dictionary.com* (http://www.dictionary.com) to double-check.

> **Reflection Questions**
> Sometimes, compound nouns become so common that they are gradually shortened to one word. One recent example is the word *blog*, which was originally the compound noun *web log*. Over time, this noun became shorter. Can you think of any similar examples?

The Functions of Nouns

Nouns can be used in three basic ways. First, they can act as the **subject** of a sentence. A subject is simply *who* or *what* the sentence is about.

> The shortest road leads to home.

> Braylon and Kat are organizing a get-together next weekend.

On Your Own

Find the noun that is acting as a subject in the following sentence:

> The new software update for my phone is downloading slowly.

Nouns can also be used as objects: direct objects and objects of prepositions. A **direct object** receives the action of a **verb**. An **object of a preposition** completes the meaning of a **prepositional phrase**.

To learn more about prepositions, see Lesson 4.5.

Direct Object

I locked the door behind me.

The ocean waves lapped the sandy shore gently.

On Your Own

Find the noun that is acting as a direct object in the following sentence:

Jem leapt up and caught the Frisbee for the winning point.

Object of a Preposition

The suitcases were packed (in the trunk).

(In the last two years), inflation rates have risen 1.5%.

On Your Own

Read the following sentence and identify the noun that is acting as an object of a preposition.

The lights of the city burned brightly all night.

Finally, nouns can act like **adjectives**, describing other nouns or pronouns.

In the last month, two restaurants and one art gallery have opened in the neighborhood.

The basketball game went into triple overtime.

In some of these cases, nouns act like possessive adjectives, showing ownership over other nouns.

Rob stole Jenny's hat right from the top of her head.

On Your Own

Read the following sentence and identify the noun that is acting as an adjective.

My sister is interested in watching the documentary about barn owls.

Lesson Wrap-up

Key Terms

Adjective: a word that describes a noun or pronoun

Common Noun: a noun that represents a non-specific person, place, thing, event, or idea

Compound Noun: a noun made up of two or more words

Count Noun: a noun that can be counted

Direct Object: a word that receives the action of a verb

Hyphen: a short line that links together two words or word parts

Non-count Noun: a noun that cannot be counted

Noun: a word that represents a person, place, thing, event, or idea

Object of a Preposition: a word that completes the meaning of a prepositional phrase

Plural Noun: a noun that represents multiple people, places, things, events, or ideas

Prepositional Phrase: a group of related words that starts with a preposition and ends with a noun or pronoun

Proper Noun: a capitalized noun that represents a specific person, place, thing, event, or idea

Singular Noun: a noun that represents one person, place, thing, event, or idea

Subject: the person, place, thing, event, or idea a sentence is about

Verb: a word that represents an action, relationship, or state of being

Lesson 4.2
Understanding Pronouns

A **pronoun** is a word that takes the place of a **noun** in a sentence. Just like nouns, pronouns can represent people, places, things, events, or ideas. Using pronouns helps you avoid repeating the same word over and over again in the same piece of writing. Read this example:

Mary Wollstonecraft, however, counters Burke's essay by defending the common person. Mary Wollstonecraft's essay, "A Vindication of the Rights of Men," outlines Mary Wollstonecraft's belief that the English aristocracy unlawfully oppresses the lower classes. Mary Wollstonecraft feels that personal merit, not lineage, should govern one's life. Wollstonecraft's description of the nobility's abuse of the lower class includes harsh gaming laws, slavery, and financially driven marriages. This corruption of authority reflects Mary Wollstonecraft's belief that "all power inebriates weak man," a statement from Mary Wollstonecraft's other well-known essay, "A Vindication of the Rights of Woman" (287). Mary Wollstonecraft argues that if England does not undergo social reform, a revolution will take place as it did in France.

In this paragraph, the same name is repeated multiple times. This level of repetition makes the text choppy and confusing.

Now, look at the same example, this time with pronouns:

Mary Wollstonecraft, however, counters Burke's essay by defending the common person. Her essay, "A Vindication of the Rights of Men," outlines her belief that the English aristocracy unlawfully oppresses the lower classes. She feels that personal merit, not lineage, should govern one's life. Wollstonecraft's description of the nobility's abuse of the lower class includes harsh gaming laws, slavery, and financially driven marriages. This corruption of authority reflects her belief that "all power inebriates weak man," a statement from her other well-known essay, "A Vindication of the Rights of Woman" (287). She argues that if England does not undergo social reform, a revolution will take place as it did in France.

As you can see, adding pronouns made this paragraph much easier to read and understand.

In this lesson, you will learn about three important types of pronouns:

Personal Pronouns
Indefinite Pronouns
Relative Pronouns
Pronouns in Sentences

> To learn more about using pronouns and antecedents correctly, see Lesson 4.10.

Personal Pronouns

Personal pronouns are the most common type of pronoun. They are called personal pronouns because they rename specific people, animals, objects, or places.

> After the interview, I began transcribing the audio recording into a text document.

> Have you seen *The Rocky Horror Picture Show*? It is my favorite movie.

Unlike nouns, personal pronouns change form depending on how they are used in a sentence. To know which form to use, you must consider the four ways that pronouns can be categorized:

- Number
- Person
- Gender
- Case

Number

When pronouns are divided by **number**, they are separated into two groups: singular and plural. Singular pronouns refer to one person or object while plural pronouns refer to multiple people or objects.

SINGULAR	PLURAL
I, me, my, mine, you, your, yours, he, him, his, she, her, hers, it, its	we, us, our, ours, you, your, yours, they, them, their, theirs

On Your Own

Read the following sentence and identify all the singular pronouns.

> Amelia and I were running through the neighborhood when she decided it was a good time to tell me a funny story.

Knowing the difference between singular and plural pronouns is important because pronouns must always have the same number as their **antecedents**, or the word the pronoun renames. In grammar, *number* refers to whether a word is singular or plural. If the antecedent of a pronoun is singular, the pronoun must also be singular. If the antecedent of a pronoun is plural, the pronoun must also be plural.

Person

A second way to categorize pronouns is by **person:** first, second, or third. You use **first-person pronouns** when talking about yourself, **second-person pronouns** when talking directly to someone else, and **third-person pronouns** for everyone else.

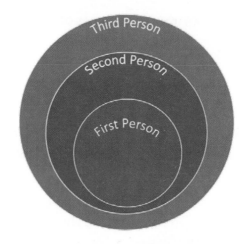

FIRST-PERSON	SECOND-PERSON	THIRD-PERSON
I, me, my, mine, we, us, our, ours	you, your, yours	he, him, his, she, her, hers, it, its, they, them, their, theirs

On Your Own

Read the following sentence and identify all the third-person pronouns.

> A group of robbers tried to steal Abraham Lincoln's corpse from his grave; his body was buried in Illinois, where, in the 1800s, a group of Chicago conmen planned to hold it for ransom.

Gender

The third way to categorize pronouns is by **gender**. There are three genders in the English language: male, female, and neutral. Only third-person pronouns have gender.

MALE	FEMALE	NEUTRAL
he, him, his	she, her, hers	I, me, my, mine, we, us, our, ours , you, your, it, they, them, their, theirs

The gender of a third-person pronoun should always match the gender of its antecedent. If the gender of a person is unknown, you should generally use the term *he or she*.

On Your Own

Read the following sentences and identify all the gender-neutral pronouns.

> You may have heard the story of Bonnie and Clyde, the most famous gangster couple of all time. They started out committing small crimes, but it wasn't long until they were robbing banks.

Case

Finally, pronouns can be categorized by **case**. Subjective-case pronouns are used as the **subject** of a sentence. Objective-case pronouns are used as **objects of prepositions**, **direct objects**, or **indirect objects**. Possessive-case pronouns are used as possessive **adjectives**.

SUBJECTIVE	OBJECTIVE	POSSESSIVE
I, we, you, he, she, it, they	me, us, you, him, her, it, them	my, mine, your, yours, his, her, hers, its, their, theirs

Consider the following examples:

> If not for being sick, I would go to the movies.

> In this sentence, the word *I* is a subjective pronoun because it is being used as the subject of the sentence.

> Steven finally passed the cake around to me.

> In this sentence, the word *me* is an objective case pronoun because it is being used as the object of the prepositional phrase *to me*.

> "My house is your house!" exclaimed Mama.

> In this sentence, the words *my* and *your* are possessive-case pronouns because they both show possession over the word *house*.

Knowing the case of a pronoun helps you determine which one to use in a sentence.

On Your Own

Identify the sentence with an objective-case pronoun.

> I am hungry.

> We ran quickly.

> You gave the shirt to me.

> My leg hurts.

Helpful Hint

In academic writing, authors sometimes use *one* instead of the personal pronoun *you*:

> You should consider the harmful effects of pesticides on the honeybee population.
> One should consider the harmful effects of pesticides on the honeybee population.

Before taking this approach, try substituting a more specific noun when possible.

> Lawmakers should consider the harmful effects of pesticides on the honeybee population.
> Manufacturers should consider the harmful effects of pesticides on the honeybee population.

Indefinite Pronouns

One definition of the term *indefinite* is, "without description or limit." Therefore, **indefinite pronouns** are pronouns that don't rename a specific noun. While they are sometimes appropriate, they can also lead to vagueness in your writing.

> Everyone is required to attend the assembly on Monday at 8:00 a.m.

> Kylie was interested in signing up for most of the special offers.

Unlike personal pronouns, indefinite pronouns do not change based on their function in a sentence. However, they can be divided into three groups: singular, plural, and both.

SINGULAR		PLURAL	BOTH
anybody	nobody	both	all
anyone	no one	few	any
anything	nothing	many	most
each	somebody	several	none
everybody	someone		some
everyone	something		
everything			

When you are writing for school or work, try to avoid using indefinite pronouns. Usually, you can replace the pronoun with a more specific word. Here's an example:

Instead of saying:

> Everyone knows that eating too much sugar leads to health problems.

> Most people know that eating too much sugar leads to health problems.

Try:

> The Federal Food and Drug Administration says that eating too much sugar leads to health problems.

> Consumers know that eating too much sugar leads to health problems.

Relative Pronouns

There are seven relative pronouns:

RELATIVE PRONOUNS			
that	whichever	whoever	whomever
which	who	whom	

Relative pronouns are used to introduce **dependent clauses**, groups of words with a subject and a **verb** that do not express a complete thought.

> During the archaeological dig on Easter Island, the team found two tablets that were covered in Rongorongo, an ancient island language.

> *In this example, the relative pronoun that is being used to introduce the dependent clause that were covered in Rongorongo, an ancient island language.*

To learn more about dependent clauses, see Lesson 4.6.

> **Group Activity**
> Write five sentences that include a relative pronoun, and then switch with a partner. Try to locate these pronouns in your partner's sentences. Pay attention to how they introduce dependent clauses. Use the previous list if you get stuck.

Case

Who and *whom* are the only relative pronouns that have a specific case. *Who* is a subjective-case pronoun, and *whom* is an objective-case pronoun.

When deciding which one to use, you should determine how the pronoun is being used inside the sentence. Try substituting the relative pronoun with a personal pronoun:

Subjective Case

> Who is directing this movie?
> ~~Her is directing this movie.~~
> *She* is directing this movie.

Objective Case

> Callie went to the store with whom?
> ~~Callie went to the store with he.~~
> Callie went to the store with *him*.

You may need to rearrange the word order of the sentence or dependent clause:

Subjective Case

> Harper Lee is an author who has influenced generations with just one book.

> She has influenced generations with just one book.

Objective Case

> Whom are you meeting at the park?

> You are meeting him at the park.

Pronouns in Sentences

Pronoun Reference

When used in sentences, pronouns *refer* to nouns or other pronouns. This **reference** should be clear. Otherwise, your readers might get confused about who is doing what in a sentence.

Here's an example of **unclear** reference:

> They have been graded, and they can review them online.

> *Who* can review *what* online?

Here are some ways to edit this sentence for clearer pronoun reference:

> The papers have been graded, and students can review them online.

Your papers have been graded, and you can review them online.
The papers have been graded, and they can be reviewed online.

Pronouns and Antecedents

An antecedent is a referent that indicates the specific person, place, thing, event, or idea a pronoun renames. Pronouns must agree with their antecedents in person, number, and gender.

After taking the Spanish 104 final, Killian felt like a huge weight had been lifted from his shoulders.

In this sentence, the antecedent of the pronoun his is the noun Killian.

On Your Own

Read the following sentences and identify the antecedents.

The photographer left her camera bag on the train.

A white heron stood on the bank of the pond with a fish in its beak.

Lesson Wrap-up

Key Terms

Adjective: a word that describes a noun or pronoun

Antecedent: the word that a pronoun renames in a sentence

Dependent Clause: a word group that contains a subject and a verb but does not express a complete thought

Direct Object: a word that receives the action of a verb

First-person Pronoun: a pronoun used to refer to the speaker of the sentence

Gender: a basis for classifying feminine, masculine, and neutral words

Indefinite Pronoun: a pronoun that does not rename a specific noun

Indirect Object: a word that receives the direct object

Noun: a word that represents a person, place, thing, event, or idea

Number: a basis for agreement between singular or plural words

Object of a Preposition: a word that completes the meaning of a preposition

Person: the point of view—first-, second-, or third-person—indicated by the form a word takes on in a sentence

Personal Pronoun: a pronoun that renames a specific person, animal, object, or place

Pronoun: a word that takes the place of a noun in a sentence

Pronoun-Antecedent Agreement: the consistency in gender and number between a pronoun and the person, place, thing, idea, or event it renames in a sentence

Pronoun Case: the form a pronoun takes based on its function—subjective, objective, or possessive—in a sentence

Pronoun Reference: the connection between a pronoun and the noun it renames

Relative Pronoun: a pronoun used to introduce a dependent clause

Second-person Pronoun: a pronoun that directly addresses the audience: *you*

Subject: the person, place, thing, event, or idea a sentence is about

Third-person Pronoun: a pronoun that refers to the person, people, or thing(s) being talked about in a sentence

Verb: a word that represents an action, relationship, or state of being

Lesson 4.3
Understanding Verbs

Verbs are an essential part of every sentence. You use verbs every day to describe what's going on in the world around you. Imagine trying to talk to your friends without words like *went*, *saw*, *talked*, or *texted*. You probably wouldn't be able to say much. That's because communication would be impossible without verbs holding everything together.

Look at these examples:

> My sister and my cousin at the same university, Texas State.

> The popular website's article.

> An old bridge on the edge of town.

> In these groups of words, nothing happens. This is because **verbs** are words that represent actions, relationships, or states of being.

In this lesson, you will learn about verb types and tenses:

Verb Types
Simple Verb Tenses
Verb Forms & Functions
Perfect & Progressive Tenses

Verb Types

Action Verbs

When you think about verbs, you probably think of **action verbs**. These verbs show physical or mental action, and they're are often the easiest to identify. Here are a few examples:

> After the race, Jordan guzzled a liter of water.

> My mother bakes the most delicious apple pie in the world.

> During the final exam, most of the students struggled with the essay question.

> In all of these examples, the **subject** of the sentence is doing some kind of action.

On Your Own

Read the following paragraph and identify the action verbs.

> Before playing a violin, there are several steps to complete. First, pluck each string to make sure it is in tune. If a string's note sounds sharp or flat, carefully adjust the tuning pegs. Next, tighten the strings of the bow. After that, apply rosin to the bowstrings in slow strokes. The amount of rosin on the strings affects how the notes will sound. After these steps, your violin is ready.

Direct & Indirect Objects

Sometimes, an action verb is followed by a **direct object**, a word that receives the action of the verb.

> Harmony accidentally threw the ball over the fence.

> The action verb in this sentence is *threw*. The direct object is the object being thrown: *ball*.

Some verbs that have direct objects also have indirect objects. An **indirect object** is a word that receives the direct object.

> This morning, my children brought me breakfast in bed.

> The direct object in this sentence is *breakfast* because it is the object being *brought*. *Me* is the indirect object because it is receiving the direct object, *breakfast*.

> The audience gave Chef Franke a standing ovation after the demonstration.

> Similarly, the indirect object *Chef Franke* is receiving the direct object, *ovation*.

Helpful Hint

Action verbs, direct objects, and indirect objects will never appear inside a **prepositional phrase**, a group of related words that starts with a preposition and ends with a noun or pronoun.

> Volunteers threw t-shirts [to the excited crowd] [during half-time].

In this example, the word *crowd* might seem like it's receiving the direct object *t-shirts*, but since it appears inside the prepositional phrase *to the excited crowd*, it cannot be an indirect object.

Linking Verbs

Linking verbs are the second type of verb. These verbs link the subject to a description. For example, look at this sentence:

> My best friend Laura is a talented musician.

> In this sentence, the subject, *Laura*, is being linked to the description, *musician*.

Some linking verbs are forms of the verb *be*:

TO BE VERB FORMS			
am	be	been	was
are	being	is	were

Linking Verbs vs Action Verbs

Other linking verbs, however, can function as both linking and action verbs. To determine which way they are being used, you should consider the meaning of the sentence.

Think about these examples:

> The hikers smelled the campfire from over two miles away.

> In this example, the verb *smelled* is an action because *the hikers* physically used their noses to smell something.

> The hikers smelled terrible after their two-day trip.

> In this example, the description *terrible* is being linked to the hikers with the linking verb *smelled*.

Here is a list of words that commonly function as both action and linking verbs:

appear	feel	look	seem	stay
become	grow	remain	sound	taste

> **Helpful Hint**
> Notice that many of the words that function as both action and linking verbs are related to the five senses. One way to figure out if a verb is functioning as a linking verb or an action verb is to replace the verb with an equal sign. If the sentence still makes sense, it is a linking verb.
>
> My hair was tangled.
> My hair = tangled
> The expression here still makes sense because it is the *hair* that is being described as *tangled*.
>
> I smelled the wet dog from across the room.
> I = wet dog
> Here, the expression doesn't make sense and changes what the sentence is trying to say.
> Therefore, *smelled* is functioning as an action verb.

On Your Own

Identify the linking verbs in the following paragraph:

Cheetahs are some of the fastest land mammals on earth. Many people don't know that there are several subspecies of the cheetah, including Sudan cheetahs and South African cheetahs. Most cats retract their claws completely. However, cheetahs' claws are always extended. This is because a cheetah's claws, like the spikes on soccer cleats, give the cat better traction. Cheetahs are also different from other big cats because they purr.

Helping Verbs

You've probably noticed that some sentences use verbs made up of more than one word. This is because many verbs include both a main verb and a helping verb.

The group of volunteers sorted the box of donations.

The group of volunteers has sorted the box of donations.

The group of volunteers is sorting the box of donations.

All of these sentences use different forms of the same verb: *sort*. The second and third sentences, however, use two verbs: a main verb and a helping verb.

The **main verb** is the verb that expresses the primary action or state of being in a complete sentence. **Helping verbs** are added to a main verb to create a new verb that grammatically fits the sentence.

As an experienced pediatrician, Holly has treated strep throat hundreds of times.

In this sentence, the helping verb *has* is helping the main verb *treated*.

You were dancing for hours last night.

In this sentence, the helping verb *were* is helping the main verb *dancing*.

> **Helpful Hint**
> Helping verbs are sometimes called "auxiliary verbs."

HELPING VERBS					
am	being	do	have	shall	will
are	can	does	is	should	would
be	could	had	may	was	
been	did	has	must	were	

Helping Verbs vs Linking Verbs

Some helping verbs can also be used as both helping verbs and linking verbs.

> The groundskeeper was mowing the lawn all day.
>
> In this sentence, the verb *was* is helping the main verb *mowing*.

> The groundskeeper was tired from a long day of mowing.
>
> In this sentence, the verb *was* is linking the description *tired* to the subject.

> **Helpful Hint**
> The words *not* and *never* are **adverbs**. Adverbs are *not* part of the verb, even if they appear between a helping verb and a main verb.

On Your Own

Read the following paragraph and identify any helping verbs.

> The marketing company was using both online and offline strategies to reach its audience. Usually, this audience is unified by a common interest or goal, not by the corporation itself. Because the company was planning events, promotions, and contests, the audience was more trusting. This type of marketing is often wildly successful; in many instances, the company even encourages new product development for the corporation.

Simple Verb Tenses

Verbs also have tenses that let the reader know *when* an action is taking place. The most common tenses are past tense, present tense, and future tense.

Past Tense

The **past tense** is used to report an event or reflect on a past experience. The writer uses past tense to let the reader know that the action is over.

> Kayla cooked three chili casseroles for the party last night.
>
> In this sentence, the past tense of the action verb *cook* indicates what the subject, Kayla, did last night.

Jared **was** a talented basketball player before the accident.

In this sentence, the past tense of the linking verb *is (was)* connects *Jared* with the noun *player* to indicate that *Jared* used to be a talented basketball player.

Casey **was using** that chair.

In this sentence, the past-tense helping verb *was* joins the action verb *using* to form the main verb.

Regular vs Irregular Verbs

With regular verbs, the past tense is formed by adding –ed (or –d if the verb ends in e) to the end of the base form of the verb.

Here's an example:

I **watched** the dog play with his ball yesterday.

The past tense of the verb *watch* is formed by adding –ed to the end of the base form of the verb, making it *watched*.

With irregular verbs, however, the past tense is formed differently. Irregular verbs have unique patterns and can completely change form in the past tense.

This is an example of a sentence with an irregular verb in the past tense:

Shelby **wrote** her mom a letter for every day she was at camp last month.

The past tense of the verb *write* is formed here by replacing the *i* with an *o*.

Keep in mind that irregular verbs do not follow one consistent pattern; their past tenses are formed in different ways. Here are some common irregular verbs and their past-tense forms:

VERB	PRESENT TENSE	PAST TENSE
be	am/are/is	was/were
become	become/becomes	became
begin	begin/begins	began
break	break/breaks	broke
catch	catch/catches	caught
choose	choose/chooses	chose
do	do/does	did
deal	deal/deals	dealt
drink	drink/drinks	drank
eat	eat/eats	ate
give	give/gives	gave
go	go/goes	went
keep	keep/keeps	kept
lose	lose/loses	lost
say	say/says	said
see	see/sees	saw
take	take/takes	took
think	think/thinks	thought

> **Helpful Hint**
> If you are unsure about the past tense of an irregular verb, consult a dictionary. Most dictionaries include the past-tense form of a verb before the definition.

> **Helpful Hint**
> Additionally, signal phrases and time expressions—like *yesterday*, *last week*, and *a long time ago*—can tell the reader specifically when in the past an action took place.

On Your Own

Identify any past-tense verbs in the following paragraph:

> Cheryl was going to go to the store after work, but the storm stopped her. Before she knew it, all kinds of debris went flying past her office window. Hail rained down on her car parked just ten feet away, and garbage from the nearby trashcan stuck to its window. She was glad Jennifer had stopped her to discuss the meeting next week, or she would have been caught in that storm!

Present Tense

When writing about events or actions that are happening now, you should use the **present tense.**

> Jerry watches his coworkers celebrate the merger.

> **Helpful Hint**
> Most academic essays, especially literary essays, are written in the present tense even if the author of the examined work has since died. Check with your instructor for the proper verb tense to use for your essay assignments.

The present tense can also be used to describe habits, general truths, or any other action that does not change.

> Gravity causes objects to fall toward the center of the earth.

Here are some more examples:

> The house is strong and sturdy.

> In this sentence, *house* is linked to the description *strong and sturdy* with the present-tense linking verb *is*, which lets the reader know that the house is currently strong and sturdy.

> The dog is hoping he receives a treat for his good behavior.

> This sentence uses the present-tense helping verb *is* to show that the dog is at this moment hoping for a treat.

On Your Own

Read the following paragraph and identify the present-tense verbs.

> The air is frigid, and my hands are numb. I think even the snow foxes are huddled together for warmth. This morning was warmer, but now I am sure the temperature has dropped at least fifteen degrees. My dog stays close to my side and whines to find warmth and shelter. The sun is starting to break through the clouds, but somehow it seems colder than it was before.

Future Tense

The **future tense** is used to describe events or actions that have not yet taken place or to describe plans or instructions.

> Karen will sweep the porch tomorrow after school.

> **Helpful Hint**
> Future tense will sometimes be accompanied by signal words and phrases like *tomorrow*, *next week*, and *the following year*. These kinds of words and phrases let the reader know specifically when a future event or action will occur.

Here's an example of a linking verb being used in the future tense:

> The soup will taste delicious when it is finished.

> The future linking verb *will taste* connects the soup to the description *delicious* and lets the reader know that the soup is not currently delicious but will be when it is finished.

On Your Own

Read the following paragraph and identify the future-tense verbs.

> One day, she will look up and see just how far she has come. She will realize that everything has been building to this moment. She will gaze out over the crowd of people cheering her name, and the weight of ten years' hard work will disappear.

Verb Forms & Functions

Verb forms affect how verbs function in sentences. The **base form** is the simplest form of a verb. Recall that the base form can be altered to create the past form of a verb, used to express the past tense:

BASE	PAST
jump	jumped
succeed	succeeded
forget	forgot

Additionally, the base form can be altered or expanded to create **verbals**: verb forms that function as other parts of speech (adjectives, adverbs, nouns) in a sentence.

There are three types of verbals: infinitives, gerunds, and participles.

Infinitives

The word *to* + the base form creates the **infinitive**: a verbal that can function as a noun, adjective, or adverb in a sentence. Infinitives are often used to reference expectations or intentions.

> Her dream is to succeed as a ballerina.
>
> In this example, *to succeed* acts as a noun receiving the verb *is*.

BASE FORM	INFINITIVE
jump	to jump
succeed	to succeed
forget	to forget

Gerunds

Gerunds are verbals that function as nouns in a sentence. They are formed by adding *–ing* to the base form of a verb. Here's an example:

> Writing is Scarlett's special talent.
>
> Here, the verb *write* has dropped the *e* and added *–ing* to become a gerund and the subject of the sentence.

Past Participles

The **past participle** is a verb form used to show completed mental or physical action. Depending on the function it takes on in a sentence, a past participle can end in *-ed, -en, -d, -t, -n,* or *-ne*. Past participles most commonly serve one of two functions:

1. They can function as adjectives that express an action or state of being.

2. When combined with the correct form of the helping verb *have*, they form the perfect tense.

> Gerald was tired after working two full shifts.
>
> This sentence uses the past participle *tired* as an adjective linked to the subject *Gerald* by the verb *was*.

> Within three months, I had walked a total of 100 miles.
>
> In this example, the helping verb *had* joins the past participle of the verb *walk* to create a main verb.

Regular vs. Irregular Past Participles

A regular past participle is formed by adding *–ed* (or just *–d* if the verb ends in *e*) to the end of a regular verb. Irregular verbs change completely to form their past participles.

Helpful Hint

Sometimes, the past participle is formed differently than the simple past-tense version of a verb. Always look up the past participle of the verb if you are unsure what it should be.

Take a look at these irregular verbs and their past participles:

INFINITIVE	PAST	PAST PARTICIPLE
to be	was/were	been
to become	became	become
to begin	began	begun
to break	broke	broken
to catch	caught	caught
to choose	chose	chosen
to do	did	done
to deal	dealt	dealt
to drink	drank	drunk
to eat	ate	eaten
to give	gave	given
to go	went	gone/been
to keep	kept	kept
to lose	lost	lost
to say	said	said
to see	saw	seen
to speak	spoke	spoken
to take	took	taken
to think	thought	thought

On Your Own

Read the following paragraph and identify any past participles.

Throughout my education, I have learned that grammar is a very important concept to understand. I never believed my teachers when they said I would need to know these things after I had graduated. I was shocked when in my career, I was nervous about sending emails to my boss because I was worried my grammar was incorrect. Now, I know how important it is to be able to read and write at a professional level.

Present Participles

A **present participle** is formed by adding *–ing* to the end of the base form of a verb. In sentences, they can function in two ways:

1. They can function as adjectives that express an action or state of being.
2. When combined with the correct form of the helping verb *be*, they form the progressive tense.

That confusing lecture lasted way too long.

The present participle *confusing* is used here to describe the subject of the sentence, *lecture*.

We were cleaning the house when the dog came in covered in mud.

In this sentence, the present participle *cleaning* is combined with the helping verb *were* to show the action of cleaning was already in progress when the muddy dog came in.

> In talking to my friend, I realized I had been wrong to yell at the barista.
>
> Here, the present participle *talking* is used in a phrase to introduce the rest of the sentence.

On Your Own

Practice forming present participles with the following verbs:

Base Form	Present Participle
cook	
smell	
write	
break	
sing	

Perfect & Progressive Tenses

Perfect Tenses

Past-Perfect Tense

The **past-perfect tense** is used to describe a past action that was completed before another past-completed action. It is formed by combining *had* (the past-tense form of *have*) with the past participle of a verb.

Let's take a look at some examples:

> I had called my mother ten times before she picked up the phone.
>
> This example shows that the speaker had called his or her mother ten times before she picked up, an action that also happened in the past.

> After she had practiced for four hours, Kara could finally play through the whole song.
>
> This example references two past events. Kara could play the whole song in the past, but before she could do that, she had to practice for four hours.

Present-Perfect Tense

The **present-perfect tense** is used to describe an action that happened in the past and continues into the present. It is formed by combining the correct form of the helping verb *have* with a verb's past participle.

SUBJECT	HELPING VERB	REGULAR PAST PARTICIPLE	IRREGULAR PAST PARTICIPLE
I	have	added	said
you	have	compiled	gone
he/she/it	has	played	run
we	have	delivered	taught
you	have	watched	kept
they	have	exchanged	held

Note that *have* is used with first-person subjects, second-person subjects, and third-person plural subjects. *Has* is used with third-person singular subjects.

Here are some examples:

> I **have worked** hard on this project all semester, and I am still not done.

This example shows that the subject started working on the project in the past and is still working on it in the present.

> We **have recorded** Shark Week every year since it started.

In this sentence, the verb *have recorded* indicates that the subject *we* began recording Shark Week when it started and continues to record it to this day.

> The rain **has not stopped** coming down since yesterday.

Even though this sentence is written in the negative, it works the same way as the other examples. This sentence states that it began raining in the past and continues to rain into the present.

Helpful Hint

To form the negative of perfect and progressive tenses, add the adverb *not* after the helping verb and before the participle.

> Stacy has not cleaned the kitchen yet.

Future-Perfect Tense

The **future-perfect tense** indicates an action that will be completed before another future event. It is formed by combining *will have* with the past participle of a verb.

> She **will have washed** three loads of laundry by the time we eat dinner.

In this example, the main verb *will have washed* indicates that at dinner time, three loads of laundry will be finished.

> When I cross the finish line, I **will have completed** five marathons.

The **subject pronoun** *I* will cross the finish line in the future. In that future moment, the subject will have finished five marathons.

On Your Own

Read the following sentences and check the box to indicate whether the sentence is in past-perfect tense, present-perfect tense, or future-perfect tense. Additionally, identify the past participle in the sentence.

> Shelia has worked hard over the past fifteen years.
>
> ☐ Past-perfect tense
> ☐ Present-perfect tense
> ☐ Future-perfect tense

> Alyssa had tried to talk to Marion several times before.
>
> ☐ Past-perfect tense
> ☐ Present-perfect tense
> ☐ Future-perfect tense

> I will have watched ten movies by the end of spring break.
>
> ☐ Past-perfect tense
> ☐ Present-perfect tense
> ☐ Future-perfect tense

Progressive Tenses

Past-Progressive Tense

The **past-progressive tense** is used to describe actions that were already in progress in the past, actions that happened at the same time in the past, or actions that have taken place over time in the past.

Past-progressive tense is formed by using the past-tense form of the verb *be* with the present participle of a verb:

Past Tense of *be* + Present Participle

> When the man rang the doorbell, we were watching a movie.
>
> The main verb *were watching* indicates a continuous action that was completed in the past.

> While I was trying to sleep, my dog was barking at the wind.
>
> This sentence describes two past-completed actions that were continuously occurring at the same time. The subject tried to get to sleep over a period of time; likewise, the dog barked over a period of time.

> Caitlin was visiting her grandmother over summer break.
>
> In this example, the past-progressive tense is used to show that Caitlin visited her grandmother over an extended period of time.

Present-Progressive Tense

The **present-progressive tense** is used to describe a recurring action, discuss an on-going action happening in the present, or describe an event that will happen in the near future. It is formed using the present-tense form of the verb *be* and the present participle of a verb.

> Right now, they are rewriting the script for *The Immeasurable Measure.*
>
> This example shows that the subject *they* is now rewriting and will continue to do so. The action of *rewriting* is not done yet.

> It is going to be warm tomorrow.
>
> This sentence describes a near-future event.

> I am always working from 9 a.m. to 5 p.m. every weekday.
>
> The subject *I* is doing the recurring action, *working*, every day of the work week.

> **Helpful Hint**
> Sometimes, in progressive tenses, the helping verb and the present participle will be split up by adverbs like *always* and *constantly*.

Future-Progressive Tense

The **future-progressive tense** is used to describe events that will happen in the future. It is formed by combining the verb phrase *will be* and the present participle of the verb.

Sharon will be joining the army after graduation.

This example shows what the subject *Sharon* will be doing in the future after graduation.

> **Helpful Hint**
> The future-progressive tense and the simple-future tense can be used interchangeably. For example, it is correct to say "I will be mailing the package tomorrow" and "I will mail the package tomorrow."

On Your Own

Identify the present participle in each of the following sentences. Then, use the checkboxes to identify the tense of each sentence.

The storm is going to be intense this weekend.
- ☐ Past-progressive tense
- ☐ Present-progressive tense
- ☐ Future-progressive tense

She was eating her dinner when the call came in.
- ☐ Past-progressive tense
- ☐ Present-progressive tense
- ☐ Future-progressive tense

I will be studying that chapter tonight.
- ☐ Past-progressive tense
- ☐ Present-progressive tense
- ☐ Future-progressive tense

Lesson Wrap-up

Key Terms

Action Verb: a verb that indicates a physical or mental action

Adjective: a word that describes a noun or a pronoun

Adverb: a word that describes a verb, adjective, or another adverb

Base Form: the simplest form of a verb, free of alterations for tense, number, and point of view

Direct Object: a word that receives the action of a verb

Future Tense: a verb tense used to describe an action that has not yet taken place or to describe plans or instructions

Future-perfect Tense: a verb tense used to describe an action that started in the past and will be completed in the future

Future-progressive Tense: a verb tense used to describe a continuous action that will take place in the future

Gerund: a verbal that functions as a noun in a sentence and is formed by adding *–ing* to the end of the verb

Helping Verb: a verb that is added to a main verb to create a new verb that grammatically fits the sentence

Indirect Object: a word that receives the direct object of a sentence

Infinitive: a verbal that can function as a noun, adjective, or adverb in a sentence

Linking Verb: a verb that connects the subject to a description

Main Verb: the verb that expresses the primary action or state of being of a subject in a complete sentence

Participle Phrase: a phrase that uses a present or a past participle to introduce the rest of the sentence

Past Participle: a verb form that can function as an adjective or as part of a perfect-tense verb to show completed mental or physical action

Past Tense: a verb tense used to report on an event or reflect on a past experience

Past-perfect Tense: a verb tense used to describe an action that was completed before another past-completed action

Past-progressive Tense: a verb tense used to describe a continuous action that occurred at a certain time in the past

Prepositional Phrase: a group of related words that starts with a preposition and ends with a noun or pronoun

Present Participle: a verb form that can function as an adjective as part of a progressive-tense verb to express a continuous action

Present Tense: a verb tense used to describe an event or action that is happening now

Present-perfect Tense: a verb tense used to describe an action that was started in the past and has not yet been completed

Present-progressive Tense: a verb tense used to describe a continuous action that is happening in the present or will happen in the near future

Subject: the person, place, thing, event, or idea a sentence is about

Subject Pronoun: a pronoun used as the subject of a sentence

Verb: a word that represents an action, relationship, or state of being

Verbal: verb forms that function as other parts of speech (adjectives, adverbs, nouns) in a sentence

Lesson 4.4
Understanding Adjectives and Adverbs

Imagine that you are the sole witness of a hit-and-run car accident. The driver was rushed to the hospital with a concussion, so the police are relying on you to provide a detailed description of what happened.

Adjectives and adverbs are especially useful for descriptions.

To help the police investigate, you have to explain how the accident happened and what the other car looked like.

In this situation, you need adjectives and adverbs to help you describe the events. These two parts of speech are used to add detail and description to a sentence.

In this lesson, you will learn about:

Forms and Functions of Adjectives
Forms and Functions of Adverbs

Forms and Functions of Adjectives

Adjectives are used to describe **nouns** or **pronouns**. They answer the following questions:

- Which one?
- What kind?
- How many?
- How much?
- Whose?

To determine if a word is an adjective, find any words that seem to be describing, or modifying, nouns or pronouns and ask yourself the questions above. Take a look at the following example:

> Henry received a heartfelt card from his mother thanking him for the two dozen flowers.

> **What kind** of card did Henry receive? A *heartfelt* card. **How many** flowers did he send? *Two dozen*.

Here's another example:

> Once he started packing, David realized that he had bought oversized boxes.

> **What kind** of boxes did he buy? *Oversized* boxes.

Usually, adjectives appear right before or after the word they describe.

> That is a beautiful dress in the closet.

However, adjectives can also appear later in the sentence:

> Several children in the class were sick today.

> In this sentence, the **linking verb** *were* links the **subject** *children* to the adjective *sick*.

Helpful Hint

The words *a*, *an*, and *the* are special types of adjectives known as **articles**. These three words are used to modify or describe nouns and pronouns.

> Narcolepsy is a disease that can cause an inconvenient disruption to daily life.

In this sentence, the words *a* and *an* are articles describing *disease* and *disruption*.

When adjectives are used to compare two or more items, the form of the adjective changes. The following example shows the different forms of the adjective *delicious*:

> This sandwich is delicious.

> This sandwich is more delicious than the one I ate yesterday.

> This sandwich is the most delicious one I've ever tasted.

When you are comparing two items, add the word *more* before the word or the suffix *-er* to the end of the word.

> I'm kinder than any of my siblings.

> The hotel survey found that this year's customers were more satisfied than last year's.

When you are comparing more than two items, add the word *most* before the word or the suffix *-est* to the end of the word.

> Out of the three cross-country runners, Hernando is the fastest.

> Joshua Bell is one of the most talented violinists in the world.

Comparisons using two of the most common adjectives, *good* and *bad*, are formed in a slightly different way.

GOOD	BAD
good	bad
better	worse
best	worst

Further Resources
Schoolhouse Rock is a series of educational videos made in the 1970s. To watch a short explanation of adjectives, check out this video (https://youtu.be/NkuuZEey_bs).

On Your Own

Identify the adjectives (excluding articles) in the following sentences:

> The play expertly portrays the complicated and intricate web of family relationships.

> We have just received your letter concerning the upcoming publication of your new novel.

> This article thoroughly examines the role of technology in strong reading and writing skills.

Forms and Functions of Adverbs

While adjectives describe nouns and pronouns, **adverbs** describe verbs, adjectives, and other adverbs. Adverbs answer the following questions:

- When?
- Where?
- Why?
- How?
- How often?

The most common type of adverb describes a verb. These adverbs usually end in *-ly*.

> The nurse walked slowly down the hallway.

> With a shout, the tennis player angrily threw down her racket.

> How did the nurse walk? *Slowly*. How did the tennis player throw down her racket? *Angrily*.

Not all adverbs, however, end in *-ly*.

> I went to the grocery store yesterday.

> The groundhog looked down and saw its own shadow.

> You can put your assignment here.

In addition to describing verbs, adverbs can also describe adjectives and other adverbs. Here is an example:

> The new book by Meredith Lyons looked really interesting.

> This sentence uses the adjective *interesting* to describe the book by Meredith Lyons. How interesting did it look? Really interesting. The word *really* in this sentence is an adverb describing the adjective *interesting*.

The following example sentences use adverbs to describe adjectives and other adverbs:

Adjectives

> According to the press release, the new engine is more powerful than last year's.

> My kids think this is a really funny cartoon.

Adverbs

> Andrea's nine-year-old niece can sing very well.

> The radio host spoke unusually quickly.

Helpful Hint

Negative words like *never* and *not* are always considered adverbs. These words sometimes appear in the middle of a verb.

> The choir had never performed in front of so many people.
> Once a house is 75% done, the builder will not make any changes to the floorplan.

Just like adjectives, adverbs can be used to make comparisons. Use the word *more* or the suffix *-er* to compare two actions.

> The drunk driver drove more dangerously than ever before.

> To make the varsity swim team, Hunter had to train harder than last year.

To compare more than two actions, add the word *most* or the suffix *–est*.

> The administrative assistant was considered by her manager to be the most diligent employee.

> Out of all fifty people at the open house, the Coopers stayed the longest.

Comparisons using the adverbs *well* or *badly* are formed in a slightly different way:

WELL	BADLY
well	badly
better	worse
best	worst

On Your Own

Read the following sentences and identify adverbs.

> The play expertly portrays the complicated and intricate web of family relationships.

> We have just received your letter concerning the upcoming publication of your new novel.

> This article thoroughly examines the role of technology in strong reading and writing skills.

Lesson Wrap-up

Key Terms

Adjective: a word that describes a noun or pronoun
Adverb: a word that describes a verb, adjective, or another adverb
Article: a type of adjective (*a*, *an*, or *the*) that describes a noun or pronoun
Linking Verb: a verb that links the subject to a description
Noun: a word that represents a person, place, thing, event, or idea
Pronoun: a word that takes the place of a noun in a sentence

Lesson 4.5
Understanding Prepositions

Prepositions are words that show relationships among people, places, things, events, and ideas. Take a look at these examples of common prepositions:

The circle is **on** the square.
The circle is **under** the square.
The circle is **by** the square.
The circle is **near** the square.
The circle is **over** the square.
The circle is **next to** the square.
The circle is **in** the square.
The circle is **outside of** the square.
The circle is **behind** the square.

These statements use prepositions to show relationships between two shapes.

In this lesson, you will learn about:

Purposes and Functions of Common Prepositions
Purposes and Functions of Prepositional Phrases

Purposes and Functions of Common Prepositions

Prepositions are words that show relationships among the words in a sentence. Sometimes, these relationships are physical locations:

> The research team met in Harvard's genetic laboratory.

> I accidentally left my phone on that park bench.

> Marcy and Yumi met their friends at the movie theater.

However, prepositions also show relationships such as time:

> The search party began sweeping the area at noon.

> Twelve years have passed since the team's last Final Four appearance.

> The party will begin after the fireworks show.

COMMON PREPOSITIONS					
about	at	but	inside	outside	under
above	before	by	into	over	underneath
across	behind	down	like	past	until
after	below	during	near	since	up
against	beneath	except	off	through	upon
along	beside	for	of	throughout	with
among	between	from	on	to	within
around	beyond	in	onto	toward	without

Further Resources
In the past, someone may have told you not to end a sentence with a preposition. This rule goes back hundreds of years in the history of the English language. However, most people today agree that using a preposition at the end of a sentence is perfectly acceptable.
To learn a little more about the history behind preposition rules, listen to this podcast (http://www.slate.com/articles/podcasts/lexicon_valley/2012/02/lexicon_valley_why_we_think_we_can_t_end_a_sentence_with_a_preposition_.html) from *Slate*.

Purposes and Functions of Prepositional Phrases

In a sentence, prepositions are always used to introduce a prepositional phrase. **Prepositional phrases** are groups of related words that begin with a preposition and end with a **noun** or **pronoun**. The noun or pronoun that ends a prepositional phrase is known as the **object of the preposition**.

Here is an example:

> Kiely Robinson is the author [of two best-selling novels] [about her experiences] [in Peru].

> There are three prepositional phrases in this sentence. All of the phrases begin with a preposition and end with a noun or pronoun acting as the object of the preposition.

Here are a few more examples:

Child development experts [at Stanford] are studying the negative effects [of excessive television time].

I found a bag [of oranges] [under the backseat] [of my car].

> **Helpful Hint**
> The **subject** and **verb** of a sentence will never appear inside a prepositional phrase. If you are trying to locate the subject or verb, try marking any prepositional phrases first. This will help you narrow down the choices in the sentence.

In a sentence, prepositional phrases usually function as either **adjectives** or **adverbs**.

Prepositional Phrases as Adjectives

If a prepositional phrase is an adjective, it describes a noun or pronoun and answers the following questions:

- Which one?
- What kind?
- How many?
- How much?
- Whose?

Here is an example:

A young lawyer [from Albuquerque] disappeared last night.

In this sentence, the prepositional phrase *from Albuquerque* is describing the subject, *lawyer*. Which lawyer? The one from Albuquerque.

Here is another example:

I would like two vanilla cupcakes [with chocolate frosting].

The prepositional phrase in this sentence is describing the type of cupcakes. What kind of cupcakes? The ones *with chocolate frosting*.

On Your Own

Read the sentence and identify the prepositional phrase acting as an adjective.

I went to the office so I could borrow that important file of Jimmy's.

Prepositional Phrases as Adverbs

A prepositional phrase that is acting as an adverb will describe a verb and answer one of the following questions:

- When?
- Where?
- Why?
- How?
- How often?

Look at the following example:

> Flynn went [to the Kia dealership] [for a replacement part].

> In this sentence, there are two prepositional phrases acting as adverbs. The first one, *to the Kia dealership*, describes where Flynn went. The second one, *for a replacement part*, shows why Flynn went.

Here's another example:

> [In the morning], I take a thirty-minute walk [around my apartment complex].

> *In the morning* is a prepositional phrase describing how often the speaker walks, and *around my apartment complex* is a prepositional phrase describing where the speaker walks.

Helpful Hint

Remember that prepositions are *always* part of a prepositional phrase. A word that looks like a preposition but does not appear inside a prepositional phrase is probably a regular adverb.

Prepositional Phrase
The hikers were found over twenty miles into the forest.

Adverb
Do you want to stay over?

While prepositional phrases can add useful information to a sentence, too many will confuse your readers. Look at this example:

> The summer position with your organization seems ideal for giving me real-life experience in journalism and in newspaper publication with a well-respected company.

> The summer position [with your organization] seems ideal [for giving me real-life experience] [in journalism] and [in newspaper publication] [with a well-respected company].

On Your Own

Read the following sentences and identify the prepositions.

> The Boston Tea Party sparked fierce patriotism among the colonists. During the raid, hundreds of New Englanders cheered along the shoreline. According to David M. Kennedy and Lizabeth Cohen, the tea dumped into the harbor was the "perfect symbol, as almost every colonist, rich or poor, consumed this imported, caffeinated beverage." The Boston Gazette described the perpetrators of the Boston Tea Party as "brave and resolute men saving their country from ruin." For many colonists, this act became the defining moment of colonial authority and strength.

Lesson Wrap-up

Key Terms

Adjective: a word that describes a noun or pronoun
Adverb: a word that describes a verb, adjective, or another adverb

Noun: a word that represents a person, place, thing, or idea
Object of the Preposition: a word that completes the meaning of a preposition in a prepositional phrase
Pronoun: a word that takes the place of a noun in a sentence
Preposition: a word that shows a relationship among people, places, things, events, and ideas
Prepositional Phrase: a group of related words that starts with a preposition and ends with a noun or pronoun
Subject: the person, place, thing, event, or idea a sentence is about
Verb: a word that represents an action, relationship, or state of being

Lesson 4.6
Understanding Clauses and Conjunctions

As you read the following paragraph, think about how each sentence is structured. Does the writing flow easily from one idea to the next?

> To protect your skin from sun damage, you should always wear sunscreen. Re-apply it throughout the day. You spend a lot of time in the sun. Wear a hat. Use an umbrella. These precautions will protect you from sunburns. They will prevent long-term skin damage.

You probably noticed that these sentences seem choppy because related ideas are not connected. Now, take a look at this revised paragraph:

> To protect your skin from sun damage, you should always wear sunscreen and re-apply it throughout the day. When you spend a lot of time in the sun, wear a hat or use an umbrella. These precautions will not only protect you from sunburns, but they will also prevent long-term skin damage.

The revised example uses **conjunctions** to combine related words and to create new sentence structures. These can follow one of four **sentence patterns**: simple, compound, complex, or compound-complex.

In this lesson, you will learn about forming simple, compound, complex, and compound-complex sentences with the following components:

Related Words and Clauses
Coordinating Conjunctions
Subordinating Conjunctions
Correlative Conjunctions
Conjunctive Adverbs

Related Words and Clauses

A **simple sentence** includes the following:

- a **subject:** the person, place, thing, event, or idea a sentence is about
- a **predicate:** the main verb and any associated helping verbs indicating what the subject *is* or *does*
- a **complete thought:** a logically-finished idea

Here are some examples:

> The tenants washed the beach towels.
>   S   P

Dr. Wilkes reviews the patient files.
    S   P

It was delivered yesterday.
 S   P

To strengthen writing, simple sentences can be expanded with additional, combined words:

The tenants washed and folded the beach towels.

Dr. Wilkes and his assistant review the patient files.

It was delivered today or yesterday.

Clauses

When you want to emphasize bigger ideas, the simple sentence pattern might not do the trick. You can create compound and complex sentences by combining clauses. A **clause** is a word group containing a subject and a verb. There are two types of clauses:

- An **independent clause** can stand alone as a complete sentence.

  Because your order shipped early, it was delivered yesterday.

- A **dependent clause** is a word group containing a subject and a verb that cannot stand alone as a complete sentence; it depends on an independent clause.

  Because your order shipped early, it was delivered yesterday.

Sentence Patterns

All sentence patterns—simple, compound, complex, and compound-complex—include at least one independent clause. Here's a list of the combinations in each pattern:

Simple Sentence:	Independent Clause
Compound Sentence:	Independent Clause + Independent Clause
Complex Sentence:	Independent Clause + Dependent Clause
Compound-Complex Sentence:	Independent Clause + Independent Clause + Dependent Clause

Combining words, phrases, or clauses usually requires using a **conjunction**: a part of speech that connects related words or word groups. There are three main types of conjunctions:

- Coordinating conjunctions
- Subordinating conjunctions
- Correlative conjunctions

Coordinating Conjunctions

Coordinating conjunctions join similar words or groups of words together. To remember the seven coordinating conjunctions, use the acronym **FANBOYS**:

F	A	N	B	O	Y	S
for	and	nor	but	or	yet	so

Coordinating conjunctions can connect words, phrases, or clauses that carry equal weight in the sentence.

Words

The first function of coordinating conjunctions is joining two or more words, such as **nouns**, **adjectives**, **adverbs**, or **verbs**.

Nouns	Cecilia and Bea were eager to compete against each other.
Adjectives	During the tour, we saw manatees in the clear and sparkling water.
Adverbs	The oak tree's leaves fell suddenly and unexpectedly only two weeks into autumn.
Verbs	The results of the study both surprised and worried the team of scientists.

Phrases

Coordinating conjunctions can also be used to join whole phrases, such as **prepositional phrases**.

This morning, we walked on the beach and under the pier.

The extra t-shirts are in the stock room or beneath the counter.

Clauses

Finally, coordinating conjunctions can join two or more independent clauses to form a compound sentence. A **compound sentence** is a sentence pattern in which two independent clauses are connected by a **comma** and a coordinating conjunction.

The boys tried to catch the lamp before it hit the floor, but they were too late.

In this example, the independent clause *the boys tried to catch the lamp before it hit the floor* is joined to the independent clause *they were too late* with the coordinating conjunction *but*.

Here's another example:

Narwhals are a type of whale, so they travel in groups called "pods."

Here, the independent clauses are connected with the coordinating conjunction *so*, which creates a relationship between narwhals as a type of whale and what they are called when in groups.

Helpful Hint

Remember that any time you use a coordinating conjunction to join two independent clauses, you must also use a comma. Otherwise, you create a type of sentence error called a **fused sentence**. If you only use a comma and no coordinating conjunction, you create a **comma splice**.

To learn more about comma splices, see Lesson 4.8.

On Your Own

Read the following passage and identify the coordinating conjunctions.

Every day Mary and Susan leave their houses, and they walk to school together. The neighbor's dog usually follows them, but today he was nowhere to be found. Susan wondered if the dog was sick, so before they went to school, they stopped at the neighbor's house. The dog poked his nose out when his owner answered the door, and the girls smiled as they went off in the direction of the school.

To learn more about independent clauses, see Lesson 4.7.

Subordinating Conjunctions

Subordinating conjunctions introduce dependent clauses. A dependent clause is a word group that contains a subject and a verb but does not express a complete thought. Dependent clauses cannot stand on their own. Therefore, they need to be connected by a subordinating conjunction to a complete sentence. When a dependent clause is connected to an independent clause, it is called a **complex sentence**.

Here are some of the most common subordinating conjunctions:

SUBORDINATING CONJUNCTIONS			
after	because	once	when
although	even though	since	while
as	if	until	

> **Reflection Questions**
> The word subordinate means "to lower in rank." How does this definition fit with your understanding of subordinating conjunctions?

Here are some examples of complex sentences:

Even though it rained, we had a pretty good turnout for the chili bake-off.

Sarah stayed up working on the project until she couldn't keep her eyes open any longer.

Once the auditions are finished, we'll decide on the cast of the play.

In these complex sentences, the dependent clauses are used to add meaning and clarity to the rest of the sentence.

Here is an example of a **compound-complex sentence**:

Even though I was sick, I went to the grocery store, and I stopped by my friend's house.

In this compound-complex sentence, the subordinating conjunction *even though* connects the dependent clause to the compound sentence *I went to the grocery store, and I stopped by my friend's house.*

> **Reflection Questions**
> Think about how each of the previous sentences would change without the subordinating conjunctions. How do subordinating conjunctions add sentence clarity and variety?

> **Helpful Hint**
> Remember that when using a subordinating conjunction, you will sometimes need a comma depending on where the dependent clause falls in the sentence. If the dependent clause starts the sentence, a comma is needed at the end of that clause. If the dependent clause ends the sentence, no comma is needed.

On Your Own

Read the following passage and identify the subordinating conjunctions.

> While Sara was doing the dishes, she heard a knock on her door. She went to answer it even though she wasn't expecting anyone. When she opened the door, a cat peered up at her. It looked hungry and dirty and had, apparently, learned to knock. It wasn't until Sara stepped outside that she saw the pot that the cat had been rubbing against to knock on the door.

Correlative Conjunctions

Correlative conjunctions are similar to coordinating conjunctions; they both connect two or more words or word groups of equal importance. Correlative conjunctions, however, always appear in pairs:

CORRELATIVE CONJUNCTIONS		
both/and	not only/but also	whether/or
either/or	neither/nor	

> Both Sofia Vergara and Eric Stonestreet were nominated for Golden Globe awards.

> We can ship your order to either your home or your local retailer.

> That claim is neither valid nor relevant to this debate.

> Whether traveling for work or sitting on your couch, you can access your music easily.

Learning Style Tip

If you're a **visual** learner, it may help you to imagine a sentence as a two-sided scale and correlative conjunctions as weights on the scale. When they're used together, correlative conjunctions add balance to a sentence. However, using just one correlative conjunction would make the sentence, or scale, unbalanced.

Correlative Conjunctions and Subject-Verb Agreement

It's important to keep subject-verb agreement in mind when using correlative conjunctions.

When using *both/and* to join subjects in a sentence, make sure you use a plural verb:

> Both the front yard and the back yard look wonderful.

Here, the correlative conjunctions create a compound subject that needs the plural form of the verb *look*.

When using *either/or* to join subjects in a sentence, make sure the verb agrees with the subject closest to it:

> Either my parents or my boyfriend is getting me that book for my birthday.

In this example, *boyfriend* is the subject closest to the verb, so the singular verb *is* is used.

> Either my boyfriend or my parents are getting me that book for my birthday.

In this case, *parents* is the subject closest to the verb, so the plural verb *are* is used.

Helpful Hint
When determining subject-verb agreement with correlative conjunctions, the best thing to do is look at the second conjunction in the pair. When the second conjunction includes *or* or *nor*, the verb will agree with the closest subject. When the second conjunction is *and* or *but also*, the verb will be plural.

On Your Own

Read the following passage and identify the sentence that uses correlative conjunctions.

> Seattle, Washington, is appealing because it provides access to mountains, beaches, and everything in-between. Downtown Seattle, including the famous Pike Place Market, is right on the water. Originally, Pike Place was a fish market. Today, it's a maze of both indoor and outdoor shops. These shops sell everything from spices to flower bouquets, and, of course, fresh seafood. There are also many restaurants and cafés in this area. However, if you visit Pike Place, be prepared for a crowd.

Conjunctive Adverbs

Like conjunctions, **conjunctive adverbs** are used to show comparison, contrast, sequence, and other relationships between clauses.

CONJUNCTIVE ADVERBS			
accordingly	however	meanwhile	similarly
consequently	indeed	moreover	still
finally	instead	nevertheless	then
furthermore	likewise	otherwise	therefore

Recall that a coordinating conjunction and a comma can connect two independent clauses to form a compound sentence. Alternatively, two closely-related independent clauses can be connected by a **semicolon**.

> You've worked hard for this. You should run the marathon.

> You've worked hard for this; you should run the marathon.
> Independent Clause   Independent Clause

> Stephanie hadn't eaten since breakfast. She felt very weak at soccer practice.

> Stephanie hadn't eaten since breakfast; she felt very weak at soccer practice.
> Independent Clause   Independent Clause

To emphasize the relationship between the two clauses, a conjunctive adverb can be inserted after the semicolon.

> You've worked hard for this; indeed, you should run the marathon.

> Stephanie hadn't eaten since breakfast; consequently, she felt very weak at soccer practice.

Notice that conjunctive adverbs are followed by a comma unless they interrupt the flow of the sentence.

Lesson Wrap-up

Key Terms

Adjective: a word that describes a noun or pronoun

Adverb: a word that describes a verb, adjective, or another adverb

Clause: a word group that contains a subject and a verb

Comma: a punctuation mark used to separate items in a list; join compound sentences; mark introductory words, phrases, and clauses; add extra or unnecessary details to a sentence; and separate similar adjectives

Comma Splice: a sentence error made when two independent clauses are improperly joined by only a comma and no conjunction

Complex Sentence: a sentence pattern in which an independent clause is connected to a dependent clause

Compound Sentence: a sentence pattern in which two independent clauses are connected by a comma and a coordinating conjunction

Compound-complex Sentence: a sentence pattern containing at least two independent clauses and at least one dependent clause

Conjunction: a word that makes a connection between other words or a group of words

Conjunctive Adverb: a transition word that shows contrast, comparison, sequence, and other relationships between clauses

Coordinating Conjunction: a conjunction that connects words or word groups of equal importance in a sentence

Correlative Conjunctions: conjunctions that connect two or more similar ideas and always appear in pairs

Dependent Clause: a word group that contains a subject and a verb but does not express a complete thought

FANBOYS: an acronym for the seven coordinating conjunctions

Independent Clause: a word group that contains a subject and a verb and expresses a complete thought

Main Verb: the verb that expresses the primary action or state of being of a subject in a complete sentence

Noun: a word that represents a person, place, thing, event, or idea

Predicate: the part of a sentence that indicates what a subject says or does and includes a main verb + any corresponding helping verbs

Prepositional Phrase: a group of related words that starts with a preposition and ends with a noun or pronoun

Semicolon: a punctuation mark used to combine two independent clauses and separate long list items

Sentence Patterns: a set of distinct clause combinations that can make up a sentence

Simple Sentence: a sentence made up of one independent clause

Subject: the person, place, thing, event, or idea a sentence is about

Subordinating Conjunction: a conjunction that introduces a dependent clause

Verb: a word that represents an action, relationship, or state of being

Visual Learning: learning information through pictures, shapes, and colors

Lesson 4.7

Identifying the Characteristics of Sentences

We communicate in many ways from the moment our days begin until they end. From our conversations with roommates, family, friends, and coworkers, to our written to-do lists, emails, presentations, and letters, communication shapes so much of who we are.

Regardless of how or with whom we communicate, we rely on our ability to string together a group of words in to a complete thought, or sentence.

Think about this example:

> Our study group reviewed the material for most of the meeting we spent time watching video clips online.

Consider the different ways to interpret this sentence:

> Our study group reviewed the material for most of the meeting. We also spent time watching video clips online.

> Our study group reviewed the material. For most of the meeting, we spent time watching video clips online.

As you can see, sentences are important for grouping words to communicate messages. If we don't use **complete sentences** to indicate these groupings, the meaning of the text can be unclear.

There are situations in your life when sentences aren't a big deal. In a lab report for biology class, you might use a list of phrases to communicate your meaning. In a presentation, you might purposefully use an incomplete sentence for emphasis.

Reflection Questions
In text messages, emails, and social media posts, you probably don't use complete sentences. How does this affect the writing you do for school or work?

In other situations, like academic writing or business letters, complete sentences are expected. Not only do they make your message easier to follow, but they also make your meaning clearer.

In this lesson, you will learn about the following sentence components:

Capitalization and Punctuation
Parts of Speech
Subject and Predicate
Complete Thought

Capitalization & Punctuation

Complete sentences always start with a capital letter and end with a period, a question mark, or an exclamation point.

Period

Periods are used to end sentences that make a statement or relay information.

> The bucket has always been red.

Question Mark

Question marks are used at the ends sentences that ask a question or request more information.

> Why did the teacher leave early yesterday?

Simply put, a question mark is used when you're asking your audience a direct question. It can be a little confusing when a sentence asks an indirect question or makes a statement *about* a question.

Take a look at these examples:

Direct	How many reporters will be attending the game this afternoon?
Indirect	The coach wants to know how many reporters are attending the game.

Direct questions ask the audience a question and end in a question mark. **Indirect questions** tell the audience about a question and end in a period.

Exclamation Point

Exclamation points end sentences that convey emphasis or strong feeling.

Watch out for that tree!

Types of Statements

Think about each type of punctuation mark that can be used at the end of a sentence. How do you decide which one to use? Punctuation marks should fit the purpose of the sentence.

Sentences can usually be grouped into one of four types of statements: declarative, interrogative, imperative, and exclamatory.

Declarative

Declarative sentences make general statements that inform the reader and end in a period.

Congress has been working for months to balance the budget.

Interrogative

Interrogative sentences ask questions that end with a question mark. Often, we encounter interrogative sentences on exams, applications, and questionnaires.

Has the committee made a decision yet?

Imperative

Imperative sentences make commands and often address an implied (*you*) subject. They can end with a period or an exclamation point. Sometimes, commands come in the form of instructions for a course project, work-related assignment, or assembly manual. Other commands keep citizens safe in public places and on roads.

Whatever your life's work is, do it well. (Martin Luther King, Jr.)

Don't lose your ticket!

Exclamatory

Exclamatory sentences communicate statements with emotion or surprise, and they end with exclamation points. Exclamatory sentences are used to express the emotion of our experiences or those of others.

I can't believe you just did that!

Parts of Speech

Parts of speech have unique functions in a sentence. We are going to look at the eight parts of speech and where to find them in a sentence.

Nouns and Pronouns

A **noun** is a word that represents a person, place, thing, event, or idea. Nouns are the *who* and *what* in the sentence.

Sometimes, using too many nouns in one sentence or paragraph feels awkward. An easy way to add clarity and variety to your writing is to use a pronoun instead. A **pronoun** is a part of speech used to replace a noun or another pronoun.

Classifying Nouns

There are several ways to classify nouns.

Common nouns name a *general* person, place, thing, event or idea. **Proper nouns** name a *specific* person, place, thing, event, or idea.

COMMON NOUNS	PROPER NOUNS
month	September
beach	Panama City Beach
woman	Michelle Obama

A **count noun** is a noun that can be counted, and a **non-count noun** is a noun that cannot be counted.

COUNT NOUNS	NON-COUNT NOUNS
bucket	fog
glass	courage
rock	dirt

To learn more about nouns, see Lesson 4.1.

Classifying Pronouns

There are three primary types of pronouns:

Personal pronouns rename a specific noun.

> She ran out for milk.

Relative pronouns introduce dependent clauses.

> I had no idea that you wanted to see the movie so badly.

Indefinite pronouns refer to nouns in a more general way.

> Anyone is welcome to the party!

PERSONAL PRONOUNS	RELATIVE PRONOUNS	INDEFINITE PRONOUNS
I	that	all
my	which	anybody
he	whichever	many
they	who	something

On Your Own

Identify all the nouns in the following sentences:

> Don, my boyfriend, does not want to go to dinner. He said he ate turkey right after he finished watching *Modern Family*.

On Your Own

Identify all the pronouns in the following sentences.

> I told Dr. Lovell that it was your original work. He didn't believe me and said that your homework needs to be re-done.

To learn more about pronouns, see Lesson 4.2.

Verbs

Verb Types

There are three types of **verbs**: action verbs, linking verbs, and helping verbs.

Action verbs show physical or mental action.

> Cassie played in the yard all afternoon.

Linking verbs link the subject to a description.

> That lecture was interesting.

Helping verbs change the form of the main verb to grammatically fit into a sentence.

> We have visited Italy three times.

ACTION	LINKING	HELPING
act, come, eat, go, help, make, respond, take, walk	am, are, be, being, been, is, was	am, are, be, been, being, can, could, does, have, is, must, should, was, were, will, would

Verb Tenses

There are also three types of simple verb tenses: past tense, present tense, and future tense.

The **past tense** is used to report or reflect on events that took place in the past.

> Yesterday, I walked three miles.

The **present tense** is used to describe events or actions that are happening now or to reference habitual actions.

> I drink orange juice every morning.

The **future tense** is used to reference events or actions that have not yet taken place.

> She will go to the grocery store tomorrow.

To learn more about verbs, see Lesson 4.3.

Adjectives and Adverbs

Adjectives

Adjectives are used to describe nouns or pronouns.

> Will wore the red vest to church on Sunday.

> Daniel is a lovable character.

> Ron ate four eggs for breakfast this morning.

Adverbs

Adverbs describe verbs, adjectives, and other adverbs.

> Stephanie quickly changed into her next outfit before the next scene began.

> The rain fell unceasingly for two weeks.

> The comedy show was really funny.

> To learn more about adjectives and adverbs, see Lesson 4.4.

Prepositions

Prepositions are words that show relationships among people, places, things, events, and ideas.

> Before dinner, I need to finish writing my paper.

Prepositional phrases are word groups made up of a preposition and the **object of the preposition**.

> I left the plant [on my shelf].

> My dog loves to sleep [under the bed].

> To learn more about prepositions, see Lesson 4.5.

Conjunctions

A **conjunction** is a part of speech that connects two or more words, phrases, or **clauses** in a sentence. There are three types of conjunctions: coordinating conjunctions, subordinating conjunctions, and correlative conjunctions.

Coordinating conjunctions connect two related words or phrases in a sentence. A coordinating conjunction can also be used with a comma to combine two **independent clauses**.

> I wanted to go to the party, so I skipped soccer practice.

> She loves chocolate and pickles, but she does not like them together.

Subordinating conjunctions introduce dependent clauses.

> While she was waiting for the bus, it began to rain.

> Steven is going to wash the car after he cleans out the garage.

Correlative conjunctions specify the relationship between the words or word groups they connect.

> Both Amy and I are going to the party tonight.

> For Casey, walking is neither relaxing nor invigorating.

To learn more about conjunctions, see Lesson 4.6.

Interjections

Interjections are words or short groups of words that show emphasis or emotion. They can be followed by an exclamation point or a comma. In emails and letters, interjections are used as greetings:

> Good morning, all!

> Hi Emily,

> Dear Mr. Russell,

You can also use interjections to emphasize words or feelings within a sentence or paragraph.

> Well, this is certainly a surprise.

> Wow! You must check out the new exhibit at the Museum of Modern Art.

Although interjections are rarely used in academic or professional writing, you probably use them often in personal writing.

Subject and Predicate

A complete sentence must always include a subject and a predicate. The **subject** is a noun or pronoun that indicates who or what a sentence is about. The **predicate** indicates what the subject *is* or *does* in a sentence.

> The bird ate the bread crumbs.
>   S   P
>
> The subject of this sentence is the common noun *bird*. The main verb is the action verb *ate*.

> Doug ordered the coffee.
>   S   P
>
> In this example, the proper noun *Doug* is the subject. The action verb *ordered* is the main verb.

> I went grocery shopping.
> S P
>
> The **first-person pronoun** *I* is the subject of this sentence, and the verb *went* is the main verb.

> Your order was delayed until Friday.
>   S   P
>
> In this example, the helping verb *was* joins the **main verb** *delayed* to form the predicate.

Because the above examples are **simple sentences**, their subjects and predicates are fairly easy to locate. In more complex sentence structures, it can be difficult to pinpoint the subject and main verb among other nouns, pronouns, verbs, and phrases that serve other functions.

Subjects

Nouns and pronouns can serve various functions in a sentence. It's important to recognize these functions so that you can distinguish between the subject and other sentence components.

Subject Nouns and Pronouns

Subjects are usually stated explicitly as nouns or pronouns:

> John went to the store yesterday.

> He went to the store yesterday.

Subject Placement

The subject does not always have to be the first word in the sentence:

> In the middle of the Emmy awards, I fell asleep on the couch.

In most sentences in the English language, subjects come before verbs. Some sentences, however, place the subject after or inside the verb. This is especially common in questions. Look at the subject in this example sentence:

> Will you run in tomorrow's race?

Implied Subjects

Moreover, the subject is not always stated explicitly. Sentences giving the audience a command or request contain an **implied subject**. In these sentences, the speaker is talking to the audience directly.

> (You) Get off the grass!

> (You) Please pass the salad.

Compound Subjects

Subjects can also be compound. In these instances, the subjects are linked by conjunctions:

> *Horton Hears a Who!* and *The Cat in the Hat* are two famous books by Dr. Seuss.

Subjects vs Objects

Although nouns and pronouns often function as subjects, they also often function as objects. When looking for the subject of a sentence, you can rule out the following types of objects:

A **direct object** receives the action of the verb.

> Coco ate the chicken.

> Coco ate it.

An **indirect object** is a word that receives the direct object.

> Please give your coat to Heather.

> Please give your coat to her.

An object of a preposition is a noun or pronoun that completes the meaning of a prepositional phrase.

> I directed her [toward the group].

> I directed her [toward them].

Notice that the function of a pronoun determines its **case**. There are three pronoun cases: subjective pronouns, objective pronouns, and possessive pronouns.

SUBJECTIVE	OBJECTIVE	POSSESSIVE
I, we, you, he, she, it, they	me, us, you, him, her, it, them	my, mine, your, yours, his, her, hers, its, their, theirs

If the pronoun is used as the subject of the sentence, then it will be a **subjective pronoun**. If it is used as an object of the sentence, it will be an **objective pronoun**. If the pronoun shows ownership, it will be a **possessive pronoun**.

On Your Own

Locate the subject in each of the following sentences:

> A merchant ship finally rescued the survivors after six days at sea.

> In laying the foundation of his essay, Bitzer makes a number of assumptions about rhetoric.

> Burke was the author of the popular essay "Reflections on the Revolution in France."

Predicates

Like nouns and pronouns, verbs can take on a variety of forms that serve different purposes in sentences. To find the predicate, here's what to look for:

Word Groups

Remember that predicates are often made up of a helping verb + a main verb:

> On your first day of work, you will complete the first two steps in the training manual.

> Because of the weather conditions, local families were forced to evacuate.

> The contestants are writing memoirs for this year's competition.

Compound Verbs

Like subjects, predicates can also be compound. In this sentence, the main verbs are linked by a conjunction:

> As volunteers, we prepared and packaged meals for families in need.

Verbs with Other Functions

Verbs can also be used as adjectives or nouns in a sentence.

Verbs as Adjectives

> If you're an engineering student, we'd like to hear from you!

Verbs as Nouns

> Engineering has been a passion of mine for a long time.

On Your Own

Read the following sentences and identify the main verb in each one.

> A merchant ship finally rescued the survivors after six days at sea.

> In laying the foundation of his essay, Bitzer makes a number of assumptions about rhetoric.

> Burke was the author of the popular essay "Reflections on the Revolution in France."

Steps for Locating the Subject and Predicate

If you are having a difficult time identifying the subject and predicate in a sentence, follow these steps:

1. First, put (parentheses) or [brackets] around any prepositional phrases:

   > After three minutes, the box of Girl Scout cookies was completely gone.

   > [After three minutes], the box [of Girl Scout cookies] was completely gone.

2. Next, find the predicate:

   > [After three minutes], the box [of Girl Scout cookies] was completely gone.

3. Finally, ask yourself *who* or *what* is doing the action or being described:

   > [After three minutes], the box [of Girl Scout cookies] was completely gone.

   In this example, the subject is *box* and the verb is *was gone*.

Here's another example:

> After the appointment, my mom and sister were waiting for me in the lobby.

> [After the appointment], my mom and sister were waiting [for me] [in the lobby].

In this sentence, there are three prepositional phrases.

> [After the appointment], my mom and sister were waiting [for me] [in the lobby].

The verb in this sentence is *were waiting*.

> [After the appointment], my mom and sister were waiting [for me] [in the lobby].

Who *were waiting*? The subjects in this sentence are *mom* and *sister*.

Complete Thought

In addition to containing subjects and verbs, complete sentences must always express a complete thought. A **complete thought** means that the group of words is logically finished.

If a group of words contains a subject and a verb but does not express a complete thought, it is known as a **dependent clause**.

Read the following examples:

> As Caitlin smiled at the crowd of friends and family members.

> When the pilot congratulated the crewmembers on their successful flight.

> That the florist added to the bouquet at the last minute.

These dependent clauses contain subjects and verbs. However, they sound unfinished because they are missing important details.

Dependent clauses usually begin with a word that makes the rest of the sentence sound incomplete. If this word is removed, the sentence expresses a complete thought.

> ~~As~~ Caitlin smiled at the crowd of friends and family members.

> ~~When~~ the pilot congratulated the crewmembers on their successful flight.

> ~~That~~ the florist added to the bouquet at the last minute.

These examples are now complete sentences, or independent clauses. They are independent because they are a group of words with a subject and a verb that expresses a complete thought.

To learn more about independent and dependent clauses, see Lesson 4.6.

On Your Own

Read the following paragraph and identify the incomplete sentence.

While the availability of electronic resources has opened up new opportunities for reducing the cost of education. In first-year composition classes, instructors are selecting electronic textbooks or course companion websites instead of traditional print textbooks. Educators, however, are still unsure about the advantages of either type of text. More research must be conducted to determine if certain textbook formats help students learn more effectively.

Lesson Wrap-up

Key Terms

Action Verb: a verb that indicates a physical or mental action

Adjective: a word that describe a noun or a pronoun

Adverb: a part of speech that describes a verb, adjective, or another adverb

Base Form: the simplest form of a verb, free of alterations for tense, number, and point of view

Clause: a word group that contains a subject and a verb

Common Noun: a noun that represents a non-specific person, place, thing, event, or idea

Complete Sentence: a sentence that contains at least one subject and one predicate and expresses a complete thought

Complete Thought: when a group of words is logically finished

Conjunction: a part of speech that connects two or more words, phrases, or clauses in a sentence

Coordinating Conjunction: a conjunction that connects words or word groups of equal importance in a sentence

Correlative Conjunctions: conjunctions that connect two or more similar ideas and always appear in pairs

Count Noun: a noun that can be counted

Declarative Sentence: a sentence that makes a general statement that informs the reader

Dependent Clause: a word group that contains a subject and a verb but does not express a complete thought

Direct Object: a word that receives the action of a verb

Direct Question: a sentence that asks the audience a question and usually ends with a question mark

Exclamation Point: a punctuation mark that conveys emphasis or strong feeling

Exclamatory Sentence: a sentence that communicates emotion or surprise

First-person Pronoun: a pronoun used to refer to the speaker of the sentence

Future Tense: a verb tense used to describe events or actions that have not yet taken place or to describe plans or instructions

Helping Verb: a word that changes the form of the main verb so that it grammatically fits in the sentence

Imperative Sentence: a sentence that makes commands and often addresses the implied subject

Implied Subject: the subject of a sentence when the speaker is talking directly to the audience

Indefinite Pronoun: a pronoun that does not rename a specific noun

Independent Clause: a word group that contains a subject and a verb and expresses a complete thought

Indirect Object: a word that receives the direct object

Indirect Question: a sentence that tells the audience about a question and usually ends with a period

Interjection: a word or group of words that adds emphasis or emotion

Interrogative Sentence: a sentence that asks a question

Linking Verb: a verb that links the subject to a description

Main Verb: the verb that expresses the primary action or state of being of a subject in a complete sentence

Non-count Noun: a noun that cannot be counted

Noun: a word that represents a person, place, thing, event, or idea

Object of a Preposition: a word that completes the meaning of a prepositional phrase

Objective Pronoun: a pronoun that functions as an object in a sentence

Parts of Speech: the categories that classify each type of word found in a sentence

Past Tense: a verb tense used to report on an event or reflect on a past experience

Period: a punctuation mark used to end sentences that make a statement or relay information

Personal Pronoun: a pronoun that renames a specific person, animal, object, or place

Possessive Pronoun: a pronoun that shows possession of another noun

Predicate: the part of the sentence that states what the subject is doing

Preposition: a word that shows a relationship among people, places, things, events, and ideas

Prepositional Phrase: a group of related words that starts with a preposition and ends with a noun or pronoun

Present Tense: a verb tense used to describe events or actions that are happening now

Pronoun: a word that takes the place of a noun in a sentence

Pronoun Case: the form a pronoun takes based on its function—subjective, objective, or possessive—in a sentence

Proper Noun: a capitalized noun that represents one person, place, thing, event, or idea

Question Mark: a punctuation mark used at the end of a sentence that asks a question

Relative Pronoun: a pronoun used to introduce a dependent clause

Simple Sentence: a sentence made up of one independent clause

Subject: the person, place, thing, event, or idea a sentence is about

Subjective Pronoun: the form of a pronoun that functions as the subject in a sentence

Subordinating Conjunction: a conjunction that introduces a dependent clause

Verb: a word that represents an action, relationship, or state of being

Lesson 4.8

Identifying Common Sentence Errors

Writing a basic sentence is fairly easy. All you need is a **subject**, a **verb**, and a complete thought. In some situations, however, these simple sentences aren't strong enough to communicate your ideas fully.

Imagine reading a book that contains only basic sentences. It might sound something like this:

> Mara woke up. She lay in her bed for a few minutes. She wondered about the day. What was going to happen? Worry began to pool in her stomach. Her alarm clock suddenly began ringing. She decided that she wasn't ready to wake up. She pulled a pillow over her head. She went back to sleep.

Even though all the sentences in this paragraph are grammatically correct, they do not express the ideas in the most effective way. Combining some of this information to create more complex sentences will help you demonstrate the relationships between ideas.

> Mara woke up. Lying in bed, she began to think about the day. What was going to happen? As worry began to pool in her stomach, her alarm clock suddenly began ringing. Not ready to wake up, she pulled a pillow over her head and went back to sleep.

While moving and combining information can help you write more effectively, these changes can also introduce errors into your writing. Being able to correct these mistakes will ensure that you are communicating your ideas in the best way possible.

This lesson will teach you how to recognize and fix two types of sentence errors:

Fragments
Run-on Sentences

To learn more about complete sentences, see Lesson 4.7.

Fragments

A **fragment** is a sentence error that occurs when the sentence doesn't express a complete thought.

> Under the sycamore tree.

> After the cleaning crew unlocked the building.

Phrases

Some fragments are **phrases**, which are word groups that add to the meaning of a sentence but do not express a complete thought. Phrases are usually missing a subject or a main verb. Look at the following examples:

> Hoping to get tickets to the concert.

> One of the most prestigious design schools in the country, the Morris Institute for Design.

Helpful Hint

Remember that verbs do not always function as the main verbs in a sentence. A fragment might contain a verb that instead functions as a noun, adjective, or other part of speech. Look at the forms of the verb *regret* in the following sentences:

We regret to inform you of our decision.
Here, *regret* functions as the main verb of the sentence.

Regretting their loss, the players shook their opponents' hands.
In this sentence, *regretting* is a **participle** in an **adjective phrase** modifying the noun *players*. The main verb is *shook*.

Although it was a mistake, I refuse to regret my decision since it led me to something better.
In this sentence, the **infinitive** *to regret* functions as part of a phrase. The main verb is *refuse*.

Your regret won't get you anywhere.
In this example, *regret* is a noun acting as the subject of the sentence. The main verb is *won't*.

To learn more about verb forms, see Lesson 4.3.

There are two ways to correct these types of fragments:

Add a Subject or Verb

First, you can add the missing subject and/or verb to form a complete sentence:

The students   were hoping to get tickets to the concert.
Subject   Verb

One of the most prestigious design schools in the country is the Morris Institute for Design.
Verb

Combine Clauses

You can also combine the fragment with an **independent clause**: a word group with a subject and a verb that expresses a complete thought.

Hoping to get tickets to the concert, the students eagerly waited in the long line.
Independent Clause

> **Helpful Hint**
> If you are having a hard time finding the subject and verb in a sentence, follow these steps:
> 1. First, put (parentheses) or [brackets] around any **prepositional phrases**.
> 2. Look for an **action verb** or state-of-being verb.
> 3. Finally, ask yourself who or what is doing the action or being described.

Dependent Clauses

Another type of fragment is a dependent clause. Remember that **dependent clauses** have a subject and a verb, but they do not express a complete thought.

After a terrible storm came through town.

Since I woke up two hours early.

> **Helpful Hint**
> Notice that when a dependent clause acts as an introductory clause, it is followed by a **comma**.

Remove the Subordinating Conjunction

Dependent clauses are usually preceded by a **subordinating conjunction**: a word that shows the relationship between two thoughts. Some dependent clauses can be made complete by simply removing the subordinating conjunction to form an independent clause:

~~Since~~ I woke up two hours early.
Independent Clause

~~After~~ Hurricane Matthew came through town.
Independent Clause

Combine Clauses

Another way to fix these types of fragments is to combine the dependent clause with an independent clause. The subordinating conjunction should link the clauses and clarify the relationship between them. Be sure to adjust the punctuation and wording if necessary.

There were many homes left without power after Hurricane Matthew came through town.

Independent Clause   Dependent Clause

Since I woke up two hours early, I had time to clean the house before coming to class.

Dependent Clause   Independent Clause

On Your Own

Utilize the suggested methods to fix the following fragments:

1. Fix the fragment by adding the missing subject, verb, or idea.

    Once inside the house.

2. Fix the fragment by adding an independent clause.

    Even though I could read the words just fine.

Run-on Sentences

A **run-on sentence** happens when two independent clauses are combined incorrectly.

Compound Sentences

When two independent clauses are combined, they form a **compound sentence**.

Because compound sentences are made up of two independent clauses, both halves of the sentence express a complete thought. These are different from compound subjects and verbs.

In a sentence with a compound subject or verb, both of the subjects or both of the verbs are part of the same complete thought.

    We fed and walked our neighbor's dog.

    My brother and sister rode every roller coaster in the park.

In contrast, a compound sentence is made up of two completely separate thoughts, each with its own subject and verb.

    The train would get us there faster than a car, but the train will be crowded.

    Independent Clause   Independent Clause

    Angelina's *abuela* does a crossword every day; she loves word puzzles.

    Independent Clause   Independent Clause

Compound sentences are always joined in one of three ways:

- a comma and a **coordinating conjunction**
- a semicolon
- a semicolon and a conjunctive adverb

Comma + Coordinating Conjunction

    All of the plants in Group A grew at least 5 inches, but all of the plants in Group B died.

    Independent Clause   Independent Clause

Semicolon

> My mom asked me to stop at the store; she needed tomatoes for a recipe.
>
> Independent Clause   Independent Clause

Semicolon + Conjunctive Adverb

> I didn't know if I could trust her; likewise, she didn't trust me.
>
> Independent Clause   Independent Clause

Comma Splice

One type of run-on sentence is a comma splice. A **comma splice** incorrectly joins two independent clauses with only a comma.

> My roommate baked cookies last night, we ate all of them by the next day.

> During the week before finals, the Cooper Library was silent, all eight floors were full of students who were studying and writing.

Comma splices are incorrect because they leave out an important word. There are four ways to fix comma splices:

Insert a Coordinating Conjunction

Incorrect:

> I had a student government meeting tonight, I have a sorority meeting tomorrow night.

Correct:

> I had a student government meeting tonight, and I have a sorority meeting tomorrow night.

> **Helpful Hint**
>
> Your choice of coordinating conjunctions is important because it could potentially change the meaning of your sentence. Think through the following examples. How does the choice of conjunctions affect the sentence?
>
> The president conducted the meeting, and her assistants answered the reporters' questions.
> The president conducted the meeting, but her assistants answered the reporters' questions.
> The president conducted the meeting, for her assistants answered the reporters' questions.
> The president conducted the meeting, yet her assistants answered the reporters' questions.
> The president conducted the meeting, so her assistants answered the reporters' questions.

Replace the Comma with a Semicolon

Another way to fix a comma splice is to replace the comma with a semicolon. The **semicolon** shows a close relationship between the two ideas in the sentence.

Incorrect:

> I knew it was going to rain today, I completely forgot my umbrella.

Correct:

> I knew it was going to rain today; I completely forgot my umbrella.

Replace the Comma with a Semicolon + Conjunctive Adverb

Semicolons can also be used with **conjunctive adverbs**, words that come after a semicolon and show comparison, contrast, sequence, and other relationships between independent clauses.

Incorrect:

> Sarah didn't study for her test, she failed it.

Correct:

> Sarah didn't study for her test; therefore, she failed it.

Remember, conjunctive adverbs are *always* followed by a comma.

Separate Clauses

The final way to fix a comma splice is to split the sentence into two separate sentences. This method works best for two independent clauses that aren't closely related.

Incorrect:

> Andrew and Marnie have been married for two years, they have been together for over five years.

Correct:

> Andrew and Marnie have been married for two years. They have been together for over five years.

On Your Own

Utilize the suggested methods to fix the following run-on sentences:

1. Fix the comma splice by adding a semicolon.

    > Harry Potter is my favorite book series, the characters are all so brave.

    _____

2. Fix the comma splice by adding a comma and a conjunction.

    > My mother's name is Darla, my sister's name is Lindsey.

    _____

3. Fix the comma splice by separating the independent clauses into two sentences.

    > Reading can transport you to other worlds, I have an extensive book collection.

    _____

4. Fix the comma splice by adding a semicolon and a conjunctive adverb.

    > I worked on that paper for hours, I finished it.

    _____

Fused Sentences

A **fused sentence**, another type of run-on sentence, is an incomplete sentence in which two clauses are connected without the proper punctuation.

Sherri wanted an ice cream cone her mother said it would ruin her dinner.

The gift basket cost $5.99 and the shipping cost $12.35.

The dog barked loudly someone was at the door.

The magician dropped into the tank of freezing water the audience gasped in surprise.

There are four ways to fix fused sentences:

Separate Clauses

Sherri wanted an ice cream cone. Her mother said it would ruin her dinner.

Insert a Comma

The gift basket cost $5.99, and the shipping cost $12.35.

Insert a Semicolon

The dog barked loudly; someone was at the door.

Insert a Semicolon and a Conjunctive Adverb

The magician dropped into the tank of freezing water; consequently, the audience gasped in surprise.

On Your Own

Utilize the suggested methods to fix the following run-on sentences:

1. Fix the fused sentence by adding a semicolon.

   I leave work every day as the sun is going down the traffic is always terrible.

   _____

2. Fix the fused sentence by adding a comma and a conjunction.

   The freshly squeezed orange juice is very good I drink it every morning.

   _____

3. Fix the fused sentence by separating the independent clauses into two sentences.

   The socks are in the top drawer the shirts are in the closet.

   _____

4. Fix the fused sentence by adding a semicolon and a conjunctive adverb.

   She is not speaking to me I would've helped her.

   _____

> **Helpful Hint**
> To remember the seven coordinating conjunctions, use the acronym FANBOYS:
>
> For   And   Nor   But   Or   Yet   So

On Your Own

As you read the following passage, identify the sentence that contains a sentence error.

> Post-traumatic stress disorder, known as PTSD, affects millions of people each year. Individuals develop PTSD in response to experiencing some type of traumatic event. The most common forms of trauma include enduring physical or sexual abuse or experiencing the death of a close friend, witnessing wars or acts of terrorism can also cause PTSD. Although some people react to these events in a healthy manner, many find their grief or fear overwhelming.
>
> Psychiatry first recognized post-traumatic stress disorder over one hundred years ago. At the end of the Civil War, documented a condition named "Da Costa's Syndrome," which closely resembles PTSD. In subsequent years, people called the disorder combat fatigue or shell shock. Only after the Vietnam War, however, did the medical community begin to study post-traumatic stress disorder in earnest.

Lesson Wrap-up

Key Terms

Action Verb: a verb that indicates a physical or mental action

Adjective Phrase: a word group that modifies a noun or pronoun in a sentence

Brackets: a pair of punctuation marks commonly used inside parentheses or quotation marks to add minor details to a sentence

Collective Noun: a noun that denotes a group but is treated as a singular noun

Comma: a punctuation mark used to separate items in a list; join compound sentences; mark introductory words, phrases, and clauses; add extra or unnecessary details to a sentence; and separate similar adjectives

Comma Splice: a sentence error made when two independent clauses are improperly joined by only a comma and no conjunction

Complete Sentence: a sentence that contains at least one subject and one predicate and expresses a complete thought

Compound Sentence: a sentence pattern in which two independent clauses are connected by a comma and a coordinating conjunction

Compound Subject: a subject made up of two nouns or pronouns, usually joined by a conjunction

Conjunction: a word that makes a connection between other words or a group of words

Conjunctive Adverb: a transition word used after a semicolon to show comparison, contrast, sequence, and other relationships

Coordinating Conjunction: a conjunction that connects words or word groups of equal importance in a sentence

Dependent Clause: a word group that contains a subject and a verb but does not express a complete thought

Fragment: a grammatical error that occurs when a word group is punctuated as a complete sentence but does not express a complete thought

Fused Sentence: a sentence error made when two independent clauses are combined without a comma and conjunction or with only a conjunction

Independent Clause: a word group that contains a subject and a verb and expresses a complete thought

Infinitive: a verbal that can function as a noun, adjective, or adverb in a sentence

Phrase: a word group that adds to the meaning of a sentence but does not express a complete thought and usually lacks a subject and a verb

Prepositional Phrase: a group of related words that starts with a preposition and ends with a noun or pronoun

Run-on Sentence: a sentence error in which two or more independent clauses are combined improperly to create a comma splice or a fused sentence

Semicolon: a punctuation mark used to combine two independent clauses and separate long list items

Subject: the person, place, thing, event, or idea a sentence is about

Subordinating Conjunction: a conjunction that introduces a dependent clause

Verb: a word that represents an action, relationship, or state of being

Lesson 4.9
Using Consistent Subjects and Verbs

Writing is a balancing act, and whether we want to believe it or not, grammar often plays a big role in achieving this balance. This is particularly true when writing a single sentence.

A **complete sentence** always contains at least one **subject** and one **verb**. These subjects and verbs must match each other in number. **Number** refers to a way to divide words into two groups: singular and plural. Singular subjects are always used with singular verbs; plural subjects are always used with plural verbs. This consistency is known as **subject-verb agreement**.

Using consistent subjects and verbs gives your writing balance.

This consistency helps to create stability and rhythm in your writing, allowing your readers to better understand the main point without the obstacle of awkward language.

In this lesson, you will learn about the following:
    Recognizing Subject-Verb Agreement
    Identifying Situations with Abnormal Subject-Verb Agreement

Recognizing Subject-Verb Agreement

All subjects and verbs are either singular or plural. Look at the following examples:

> Charlie walks to school every day.
>
> The subject *Charlie* and the verb *walks* are singular.
>
> The students walk to school every day.
>
> The subject *students* and the verb *walk* are plural.

Notice that the spelling of singular and plural verbs appears reversed. Singular verbs usually end in the letter -*s* while plural verbs do not. Here are some additional examples:

Singular	The store owner rents a booth at the local flea market.
Plural	We rent a booth at the local flea market.

Singular	Mom is selling the house.
Plural	They are selling the house.

Identifying Situations with Abnormal Subject-Verb Agreement

While subject-verb agreement is fairly straightforward, it can be tricky to achieve in sentences that have these features:

- Compound subjects
- Indefinite pronouns
- Collective nouns as subjects
- Distracting words and phrases
- Inverted word order

Compound Subjects

A **compound subject** is a subject made up of two nouns or pronouns, usually joined by a conjunction. When a sentence contains a compound subject, use special guidelines to decide if the subject is singular or plural.

If the sentence uses the **conjunctions** *and* or *both/and*, the subject is plural.

> Myra and John answer questions at the end of each training session.

> To learn more about conjunctions, see Lesson 4.6.

If the sentence uses any of the below conjunctions, the subject closest to the verb determines the number.

nor	or	neither/nor	either/or

> Either the bathroom or the kitchen is being remodeled this year.
>
> This sentence uses the conjunction *either/or* to join a compound subject. The subject *kitchen* is closest to the verb, so the subject is considered singular.

Amy or the twins are coming with us today.

> In this sentence, the subject *twins* is closest to the verb, so the subject is considered plural.

> If the order were reversed, the subject would be singular since *Amy* is a singular subject:

The twins or Amy is coming with us today.

Indefinite Pronouns

Subject-verb agreement can become complicated when the sentence uses an indefinite pronoun as a subject. **Indefinite pronouns** refer to pronouns that do not rename a specific noun.

Some indefinite pronouns are always singular or plural, while others change form depending on their use in the sentence.

SINGULAR		PLURAL	BOTH
anybody	nobody	both	all
anyone	no one	few	any
anything	nothing	many	most
each	somebody	several	none
everybody	someone		some
everyone	something		
everything			

To determine whether the words *all*, *any*, *most*, *none*, or *some* are plural, look at the meaning of the sentence.

Singular   All of the cake has already been eaten.
Plural   All of the orders have been filled on time.

Singular   Most of the floor is covered by carpeting.
Plural   Most of the apartments are carpeted.

Some indefinite pronouns are misleading when combined with a plural subject:

> Each of the cheerleaders has her own megaphone.

> Although the word *cheerleaders* is plural, the subject is *each*, denoting individuals. If you remove the prepositional phrase *of the cheerleaders*, the sentence is still intact and more clearly refers to individuals.

Simplifying the sentence to noun, verb, and object of the verb, as in the previous diagram, is also a good test to see whether the verb should be singular. Another clue is the singular megaphone at the end of the sentence. If the subject were plural (cheerleaders) the object of the verb would be plural (megaphones).

Collective Nouns as Subjects

Collective nouns denote a group but are treated as **singular** nouns. Look at the following examples:

class	club	team	clique
family	band	congregation	faculty
company	choir	cast	department

Each of these collective nouns refers to a single group. Of course, the group is made up of many people, but if your sentence subject contains a collective noun, it's to be treated as singular.

On Your Own

For each of the following sentences, check the box next to the correct verb.

Our football team _____ going to the state playoffs.

- ☐ is
- ☐ are

The entire cast _____ offered free season tickets at the theatre.

- ☐ were
- ☐ was

Mr. Simpson's class _____ in the library on Friday mornings.

- ☐ meet
- ☐ meets

Mount Bethel's choir _____ at nursing homes every Sunday.

- ☐ sings
- ☐ sing

> **Helpful Hint**
> Business memos often address groups of people using collective nouns such as *marketing department,* *summit planning committee,* and *focus group.* Throughout the memo, you may use *committee* (singular), *committee members* (plural), or *each member of the committee* (singular), but be consistent in your application of appropriate verb forms each time you vary the noun.

Distracting Words and Phrases

The more words and **phrases** that come between a subject and its verb, the more confusing that sentence seems.

Always make sure the verb agrees with the subject and not any other words that come between the subject and the verb. Take a look at the below sentences. Which is correct?

> The people in the elevator is stuck between the third and fourth floors.

> The people in the elevator are stuck between the third and fourth floors.

Remember that the subject of a sentence will never appear inside a **prepositional phrase:** a group of related words that starts with a preposition and ends with a noun or pronoun. Try putting all of the prepositional phrases in **brackets** to help you locate the true subject of the sentence.

> The people [in the elevator] is stuck [between the third and fourth floors].

> The people [in the elevator] are stuck [between the third and fourth floors].

> Once you've identified the true subject, you can make sure that you've used the correct type of verb. In this example, the second version of the sentence is correct. Both the subject and the verb are plural.

> The people in the elevator are stuck between the third and fourth floors.

Inverted Word Order

In a sentence with **regular word order**, the subject comes before the verb. However, sentences with **inverted word order** switch the locations of these sentence parts, so the verb comes before the subject. Look at the following example:

> Into the store walks three mysterious-looking men.

> Into the store walk three mysterious-looking men.

To decide if the subject and verb are singular or plural, you must identify the true subject of the sentence.

First, put parentheses or brackets around any prepositional phrases:

> [Into the store] walks three mysterious-looking men.

> [Into the store] walk three mysterious-looking men.

Next, identify your verb:

> [Into the store] walks three mysterious-looking men.

> [Into the store] walk three mysterious-looking men.

Finally, find your subject.

> [Into the store] walks three mysterious-looking men.

> [Into the store] walk three mysterious-looking men.

Once you've determined your subject and verb, you can decide if the verb should be singular or plural. In this case, the verb should be plural because the subject is plural.

> [Into the store] walk three mysterious-looking men.

On Your Own

Read the following paragraph and identify the sentence that does not use correct subject-verb agreement.

> Photographs and video clips from the World Trade Center attacks on September 11, 2001, recall the feelings of fear and uncertainty that gripped the entire nation. Even for those who have not personally experienced the loss of a loved one in the World Trade Center attacks, images such as *The Falling Man* symbolizes the thousands of the people killed on that day. This simple news photograph and others like it have grown to encompass meaning and significance far beyond the original intents of their creators.

Lesson Wrap-up

Brackets: a pair of punctuation marks commonly used inside parentheses or quotation marks to add minor details to a sentence

Collective Noun: a noun that denotes a group but is treated as a singular noun

Complete Sentence: a sentence that contains at least one subject and one verb and expresses a complete thought

Compound Subject: a subject made up of two nouns or pronouns, usually joined by a conjunction

Conjunction: a word that makes a connection between other words or a group of words

Indefinite Pronoun: a pronoun that does not rename a specific noun

Inverted Word Order: a sentence structure in which the main verb comes before the subject

Number: a basis for agreement between singular or plural words

Paragraph: a short piece of writing that focuses on one main idea

Phrase: a word group that adds to the meaning of a sentence but does not express a complete thought and usually lacks a subject and a verb

Prepositional Phrase: a group of related words that starts with a preposition and ends with a noun or pronoun

Regular Word Order: a sentence structure in which the subject comes before the verb

Subject: the person, place, thing, event, or idea a sentence is about

Subject-Verb Agreement: when a subject and verb used in a sentence match in number and point of view

Verb: a word that represents an action, relationship, or state of being

Lesson 4.10

Using Consistent Pronouns and Antecedents

A **pronoun** takes the place of a **noun** in a sentence. Using pronouns makes your writing smoother and less repetitive. While pronouns are easy to use, they follow a strict set of rules. A pronoun is almost always paired with an **antecedent**, the word that a pronoun renames. As a result, pronouns must agree with their antecedents in both **gender** and **number**. This is known as **pronoun-antecedent agreement**.

To learn more about pronouns, see Lesson 4.2.

In this lesson, you will learn about the following:

Reference & Antecedents

Agreement

Reference & Antecedents

When used in sentences, pronouns *refer* to nouns or other pronouns. This **reference** should be clear. Otherwise, your readers might get confused about who is doing what in a sentence.

Here's an example of <u>unclear</u> reference:

They have been graded, and they can review them online.

Who can review *what* online?

Here are some ways to edit this sentence for clearer pronoun reference:

> The papers have been graded, and students can review them online.
> Your papers have been graded, and you can review them online.
> The papers have been graded, and they can be reviewed online.

An antecedent is a referent that indicates the specific person, place, thing, event, or idea a pronoun renames. Pronouns must agree with their antecedents in person, number, and gender.

> After taking the Spanish 104 final, Killian felt like a huge weight had been lifted from his shoulders.

> In this sentence, the antecedent of the pronoun *his* is the noun *Killian*.

Clear Reference to a Clear Antecedent:

> Jennifer left the party and drove her car home.

> In this example, the antecedent is clear. We know whose car Jennifer is driving home.

Ambiguous Reference:

> Jennifer left Susan's party and drove her car home.

> This example is ambiguous, or unclear, because there are two possible antecedents: *Jennifer* and *Susan*.

Missing Antecedent:

> She gave her the present, left her party, and drove her car home.

> In this example, pronouns rename other pronouns instead of antecedents, so we can't be sure whose car or party is being discussed.

On Your Own

Read the sentences below. Then, replace they with a specific noun.

> I went to the doctor's office, but <u>they</u> told me to see a dentist.

_____

> After touring the ruins of the Roman Colosseum, <u>they</u> took a train to Florence.

_____

To learn more about pronoun reference and pronoun case, see Lesson 4.11.

Agreement

Gender

The gender of a pronoun must match the gender of its antecedent. If a sentence includes a male antecedent, use male pronouns. If the sentence includes a female antecedent, use female pronouns.

MALE	FEMALE	NEUTRAL
he, him, his	she, her, hers	I, me, my, mine, we, us, our, ours, you, your, yours, it, its, they, them, their, theirs

Male	That man mows his yard every Saturday.
Female	Kayla left her purse on the subway.
Neutral	The maple tree is losing its leaves.

If the gender of an individual person is unknown, consider using the term *he or she*.

> If a student is interested in volunteering, he or she can sign up in the school office.

> An athlete should stretch before he or she exercises.

Because using the term *he or she* can sound wordy, this isn't always the best option. Instead, you can make the **subject** plural and use the neutral pronoun *they*.

> If students are interested in volunteering, they can sign up in the school office.

> Athletes should stretch before they exercise.

Helpful Hint

In conversation, you probably use the neutral pronoun *they* for both singular and plural subjects.

> If anyone wants to ride with me to the game, they can.

However, it's best to use singular pronouns for singular subjects when writing for work and school.

Number

In addition to gender, pronouns can also be singular or plural. *Singular* refers to one thing, and *plural* refers to multiple things. Singular antecedents are always paired with singular pronouns; plural antecedents are always paired with plural pronouns.

SINGULAR	PLURAL
I, me, my, mine	we, us, our, ours
you, your, yours	you, your, yours
he, him, his, she, her, hers, it, its	they, them, their, theirs

Here is an example:

> Devynne made some life-changing plans, but she has not shared them with anyone.

> In this sentence, the word *plans* is renamed with the pronoun *them*. Both of these words are plural, so the sentence is correct.

Indefinite pronouns, pronouns that do not rename a specific noun, can be a little harder to use. These pronouns are also labeled singular or plural.

SINGULAR	PLURAL	BOTH
anybody, anyone, anything, each, everybody, everyone, everything, nobody, no one, nothing, somebody, someone, something	both, few, many, several	all, any, most, none, some

When a singular indefinite pronoun is used as an antecedent, make sure you rename it with a singular personal pronoun. Here is an example:

> Someone in the previous class left his or her backpack under the table.

> In this sentence, the indefinite pronoun *someone* is singular. Since you don't know the gender of the person, it's best to use the singular term *his or her*.

Some indefinite pronouns can be both singular and plural depending on how they're used in a sentence. To decide how the words *all, any, most, none,* or *some* are being used, look at what the indefinite pronoun is renaming.

Singular   All of the cake has already been eaten.
Plural   All of the orders have been filled on time.
Singular   Most of the floor is covered by carpeting.
Plural   Most of the apartments are carpeted.

> **Helpful Hint**
> All of the singular indefinite pronouns except *each* can be broken up into two word parts. For example, *some + one = someone.* Notice that the second part, *one*, is singular. If an indefinite pronoun fits this same pattern, it is singular.

Finally, when a sentence contains a **compound subject**, use special guidelines to decide if the subject is singular or plural. A subject that is joined by the **conjunctions** *and* or *both/and* is plural.

Anthony and Liz write screenplays.

Because *Anthony* and *Liz* are joined by the conjunction *and*, they are a plural compound subject.

If the sentence uses any of the below conjunctions, use the subject closest to the **verb** to decide if the subject is singular or plural.

nor   or   neither/nor   either/or

Either the bookcase or the dresser is being painted this weekend.

This sentence uses the conjunction *either/or* to join a compound subject. The subject *dresser* is closest to the verb, so the subject is considered singular. Notice that the highlighted verb is also singular.

Grandma or the cousins are going to watch the house while we're gone.

In this sentence, *cousins* is closest to the verb, so the subject is considered plural. Notice that the highlighted verb is also plural.

On Your Own

In the following passage, identify the sentence with a pronoun and antecedent that do not agree in gender and/or number.

Little is known about the subjective experience of breast cancer survivors after primary treatment. However, these experiences are important because it shapes their communication about their illness in everyday life. The present study investigated this topic by combining qualitative and quantitative methods.

(Excerpt courtesy of "Breast Cancer Survivors' Recollection of Their Illness and Therapy" by Patricia Lindberg, et al.)

Lesson Wrap-up

Key Terms

Antecedent: the word that a pronoun renames in a sentence

Compound Subject: a subject made up of two nouns or pronouns, usually joined by a conjunction

Conjunction: a word that makes a connection between other words or a group of words

Gender: a basis for classifying feminine, masculine, and neutral words

Indefinite Pronoun: a pronoun that does not rename a specific noun

Noun: a word that represents a person, place, thing, event, or idea

Number: a basis for agreement between singular or plural words

Pronoun: a word that takes the place of a noun in a sentence

Pronoun-Antecedent Agreement: the consistency in gender and number between a pronoun and the person, place, thing, idea, or event it renames in a sentence

Subject: the person, place, thing, event, or idea a sentence is about

Verb: a word that represents an action, relationship, or state of being

Lesson 4.11
Using Correct Pronoun Reference and Case

Pronouns are words that take the place of **nouns** in a sentence. Although they are often small in size, they can have a huge impact on your writing. Misusing them can be especially confusing for your reader. To ensure that your writing is as effective as possible, pay close attention to pronoun case.

Pronoun case refers to the form of the pronoun. Which form is correct depends on the function of the pronoun in the sentence: as a subject, an object, or to show possession. Consider these examples:

Subjective	He went to school in East Texas.
Objective	David's girlfriend gave him a new video game.
Possessive	Kyle lost his glasses again.

In this lesson, you will learn how to:

Identify Subjective, Objective, and Possessive Pronoun Case

Apply Correct Case with Difficult Wording

Use Correct Pronoun Reference

Identify Subjective, Objective, and Possessive Pronoun Case

Personal pronouns have three main functions in a sentence. They act as subjects, they act as objects, and they show possession. These functions match the three pronoun cases: subjective, objective, and possessive.

To avoid errors in your writing, make sure that the case of the pronoun matches the way the pronoun is being used in the sentence. Review the table below for examples of each case.

SUBJECTIVE	OBJECTIVE	POSSESSIVE
I	me	my/mine
you	you	your/yours
she	her	her/hers
he	him	his
they	them	their/theirs
we	us	our/ours
it	it	its

To learn more about pronoun use in sentences, see Lessons 4.2 and 4.10.

Subjective Case

Subjective-case pronouns are always used as the **subject** of the sentence.

> I am planning to write my report over the next two days.

> That evening, they walked down to the football field and buried the box deep beneath the end zone.

Objective Case

Objective-case pronouns are used in two ways. First, they function as **objects of prepositions**: words that complete the meaning of a **prepositional phrase**.

> Unexpectedly, the mail carrier delivered a package addressed (to me).

> Is that stack of forms (for her)?

The second function of objective-case pronouns is as direct and indirect objects of verbs. **Direct objects** follow a **verb** and receive some kind of action. **Indirect objects**, on the other hand, receive the direct object.

Direct Object

> Be careful not to kick him on your way out!

> When Adrian found the expired jug of milk, she threw it away.

Indirect Object

> The administrator handed them a box of donations that the fourth grade class had collected.

> The judge showed him unexpected mercy.

Maybe you've been told not to say *my brother and me* and that *my brother and I* is correct. The truth is, it depends on how you're using the word group. How can you tell which is correct? Test the pronoun case by removing one of the nouns.

The usage is correct in each of the following sentences:

Object of a Verb

> My grandmother gave (my brother and) me some great advice.

Object of a Preposition

> The ball game was exciting for (my brother and) me.

Subject

> (My brother and) I went to school in Texas.

> (My brother and) I made dinner, and it tasted better than usual.

> If you remove *my brother* from the first and second examples, you'll see that using *me* is completely correct. You would never say, "My grandmother gave presents to I."

Possessive Case

The last personal pronoun form is the possessive case. **Possessive pronouns** show possession. They can function as **adjectives** or as regular pronouns.

Adjective   Do you know how to get to their house?

The park ranger accidentally left his radio in the car.

Pronoun   Octavia felt like the promotion should have been hers.

Mine is red, but yours is blue.

Possessive-case pronouns are spelled the same way as both subjects and objects.

> I left ours on the table.

> Ours is on the table.

> Helpful Hint
> Notice that none of the possessive pronouns need **apostrophes**. In this way, possessive pronouns are the opposite of possessive nouns, which always need an apostrophe.

Apply Correct Case with Difficult Wording

Relative Pronouns

Relative pronouns are used to introduce **dependent clauses**, groups of words with a subject and a verb that do not express a complete thought.

> The woman who interviewed my brother later hired him as her executive assistant.

> The pants, which had a hole in the knee, hung in his bedroom closet.

Here are the seven relative pronouns:

RELATIVE PRONOUNS			
that	whichever	whoever	whomever
which	who	whom	

Who and Whom

Although *who* and *whom* are relative pronouns, and not personal pronouns, they do have case. *Who* is a subjective case pronoun, and *whom* is an objective case pronoun. To decide which one you should use in a sentence, try substituting *he* for *who*, and *him* for *whom*. You may need to rearrange the words in the sentence slightly.

Here are some examples:

> Who helped this customer yesterday?
> He helped this customer yesterday.

> Whom are you calling at this time of night?
> You are calling him at this time of night.

Demonstrative Pronouns

Demonstrative pronouns take the place of a noun phrase or serve as adjectives in a noun phrase.

Demonstrative pronoun

> This is much longer than that.

Demonstrative adjective

> This dress is much longer than that one.

Having so many pronouns available makes it hard to know when to use *which* and when to use *that*. But these two pronouns are not interchangeable. Here's a good rule of thumb: *which* indicates unnecessary detail.

If the sentence doesn't need the clause being connected, use *which*.

> The pants, which had a hole in the knee, were hanging in his bedroom closet.

If the clause being connected is essential for clarity, the proper pronoun is *that*.

> The pants that had a hole in the knee were hanging in his bedroom closet.

Use Correct Pronoun Reference

Every time you use a pronoun, it must refer back to a clear **antecedent**, or a word that a pronoun renames. Otherwise, your writing will become confusing and potentially misleading. Read this example:

> This morning, Callie told Davina that she had been fired. She immediately started cleaning out her desk. She is interviewing her possible replacement later today.

> These sentences contain important information. However, their meaning has been completely mixed up by incorrect pronoun reference. Who was fired? Callie or Davina?

No Clear Antecedents

One common pronoun error is using a pronoun without any antecedent at all. Look at the following examples:

> Once the flood waters withdrew, they began rebuilding their town and their lives.

> Kassie contacted the police station, but they put her on hold.
> In both of these sentences, the pronoun *they* is unclear. Who exactly is *they*?

> To fix these examples, add a more specific noun in place of the pronoun:
> Once the flood waters withdrew, the citizens began rebuilding their town and their lives.

> Kassie contacted the police station, but the receptionist put her on hold.

Another pronoun commonly used without an antecedent is *it*. Whenever possible, use a noun instead.

> Many corporations have seized control of campaigns and public opinion. John Nichols and Robert W. McChesney warn the public of this corrupt process in their article, "The Money and Media Election

Complex." They claim that "corporations are now more influential than any candidate or party" (11). Corporations now control media coverage of elections. However, instead of providing a balanced understanding of each candidate, corporations use commercials to promote their own agendas to the millions of viewers. It becomes not about the candidate, but the corporation.

The last sentence in the paragraph above is unclear because it starts with the word it. Replacing this word with a specific noun phrase, like the election, would make the meaning much clearer.

Multiple Antecedents

A pronoun can also become confusing when it has more than one possible antecedent.

Zinnia mentioned to Jamie that she had spinach in her teeth.

Who had spinach in her teeth? From the information provided in this sentence, there's no clear way to know.

The best way to correct this sentence would be to replace the pronoun with a noun and re-word the sentence as necessary:

Zinnia realized that she had spinach in her teeth and mentioned this embarrassing situation to Jamie.

Zinnia mentioned the spinach in Jamie's teeth right away.

Without clear antecedents, pronouns can quickly become quite complicated.

Antecedent Rules

Finally, the antecedent of a pronoun will always be a noun, not an adjective. This is because adjectives function differently in a sentence than nouns or pronouns. Here's an example:

I called Marcel's office all morning, but he never answered.

In this sentence, the word Marcel's is an adjective and cannot act as the antecedent for he. This sentence can be fixed by replacing the pronoun with the correct noun.

I called Marcel's office all morning, but Marcel never answered.

Using a noun instead of a pronoun may feel a bit repetitive in some cases. Keep in mind, however, that using correct pronoun reference will help your readers understand exactly what your sentence means.

On Your Own

Identify the sentence that contains an incorrect pronoun reference.

After receiving an invitation to interview for her dream job at McCollum and Associates, Brenda asked her sister for help. She suggested practicing interview questions aloud. After spending over three hours preparing, Brenda felt confident about her interview skills.

Lesson Wrap-up

Key Terms

Adjective: a word that describes a noun or pronoun

Antecedent: the word that a pronoun renames in a sentence

Apostrophe: a punctuation mark used for possessive nouns, contractions, and shortened numbers and words

Demonstrative Pronoun: a pronoun that takes the place of a noun phrase and acts as an adjective

Dependent Clause: a word group that contains a subject and a verb but does not express a complete thought

Direct Object: a word that receives the action of a verb

Indirect Object: a word that receives the direct object

Noun: a word that represents a person, place, thing, event, or idea

Object of the Preposition: a word that completes the meaning of a prepositional phrase

Objective Case: the form a word takes when used as the object of a preposition, direct object, or indirect object of a sentence

Person: the point of view—first-, second-, or third-person—indicated by the form a word takes on in a sentence

Personal Pronoun: a pronoun that renames a specific person, animal, object, or place

Possessive Case: a pronoun form that shows possession or functions as an adjective

Prepositional Phrase: a group of related words that starts with a preposition and ends with a noun or pronoun

Pronoun: a word that takes the place of a noun in a sentence

Pronoun-Antecedent Agreement: the consistency in gender and number between a pronoun and the person, place, thing, idea, or event it renames in a sentence

Pronoun Case: the form a pronoun takes based on its function—subjective, objective, or possessive—in a sentence

Pronoun Reference: the connection between a pronoun and the noun it renames

Relative Pronoun: a pronoun used to introduce a dependent clause

Subject: the person, place, thing, event, or idea a sentence is about

Subjective Case: the form a word takes when it functions as the subject of a sentence

Verb: a word that represents an action, relationship, or state of being

Lesson 4.12
Using Commas

One of the most commonly misused punctuation marks is the comma. You see it everywhere, but do you understand how it functions?

A **comma** organizes the words and ideas inside a sentence. Look at these two versions of the same paragraph:

> Last summer I spent two months in Paris France living with my cousins Anna Margaret Monica and Kate. Every morning we went to a local café for espresso and croissants. Our favorite weekend activities were walking along the Seine River browsing antique stores and picnicking under the Eiffel Tower. I couldn't believe how quickly the weeks flew by.

> Last summer, I spent two months in Paris, France, living with my cousins Anna Margaret, Monica, and Kate. Every morning, we went to a local café for espresso and croissants. Our favorite weekend activities were walking along the Seine River, browsing antique stores, and picnicking under the Eiffel Tower. I couldn't believe how quickly the weeks flew by.

Organizing the information with commas makes the meaning much easier to understand.

This lesson will explain how to use commas in the following situations:

Lists
Compound Sentences
Introductory Words, Phrases, and Clauses
Extra or Unnecessary Details
Adjectives

> **Helpful Hint**
> One common strategy for adding commas to a sentence is reading the sentence aloud and adding commas whenever your voice naturally pauses. While this works in many cases, it's not a completely error-proof strategy. When you proofread, review the rules of commas to make sure that you catch as many errors as possible.

> **Further Resources**
> Using commas might not seem like a big deal, but in situations involving contracts or legal documents, incorrect commas can be costly. In 2006, a disagreement between two Canadian companies came down to the placement of a comma, costing one of the companies over one million Canadian dollars. You can read more about the story here: (http://www.nytimes.com/2006/10/25/business/worldbusiness/25comma.html).

Lists

One of the most common uses of commas is in a list. Whenever you are listing more than two items, you need to separate each one with a comma.

> We are running a special on workout gear, camping equipment, and children's shoes.

> Tomorrow's meetings are about the budget, marketing, community outreach, and insurance.

> The reception will have simple food: cheese and crackers, homemade soup, and ready-made salads.

Some people disagree about whether or not you need to use a comma between the last two items in a list since they are already joined by a **conjunction**. Compare the following examples:

> We design packaging for cookies, cupcakes, and pies.

> We design packaging for cookies, cupcakes and pies.

In MLA style, the guidelines most commonly used in writing and literature courses, you need to use this extra comma. In formats like APA, the guidelines used for advertisements and newspaper articles, you do not. Double-check with your instructor if you're unsure which rule to follow.

> **Further Resources**
> A comma used with a conjunction before the last item in a list is commonly known as the Oxford comma. To learn more about the history of the Oxford comma and the debate about its use, watch this video (https://www.youtube.com/watch?v=ptM7FzyjtRk&feature=youtu.be) from Ted Education.

> **Helpful Hint**
> While commas can be used to organize thoughts more clearly, adding too many commas to a sentence can become confusing. Here's an example:
>
> > After cleaning the house, finishing his research paper, and getting an oil change, the man, along with his two children, decided to run to the grocery store for pickles, ketchup, and chips.
>
> The writer should break this sentence into two separate sentences.

Compound Sentences

A **compound sentence** is made up of two independent clauses joined together by a comma and a conjunction. Remember that an **independent clause** is another term for a sentence: a group of words that contains a **subject**, a **verb**, and a complete thought.

> The band was sitting on the south end of the stadium, and the dance team was sitting on the north.

> The couple invited only twenty-five guests to the wedding, but at least forty people actually came.

If you forget to add the comma, the sentence is grammatically incorrect and is consider a **fused sentence**. If you have a comma but forget to add a conjunction, it is considered a **comma splice** and is also grammatically incorrect.

Besides adding a comma and a conjunction, there are two other ways to make compound sentences. You can connect the independent clauses with a **semicolon** or with a semicolon and a **conjunctive adverb**.

> She was aware how much time it took to write a book; she had written one herself.

> He had been waiting around for hours; finally, she texted him.

Don't forget that a conjunctive adverb is always followed by a comma.

You only need to use a comma with a conjunction when you are joining two independent clauses. Words and **phrases** can be joined with just a conjunction.

> The researchers began analyzing their findings and writing their article.

> Tomorrow, I plan to sleep until noon and binge-watch *House of Cards*.

On Your Own

Read the following compound sentences and write in a comma where one should be inserted.

> The computer died after a week; consequently he was furious he had paid so much money for it.

> The sun was burning bright and hot and she needed to apply sunscreen often.

> I wanted to see Stacy and go to the movies with Sarah but my mother had other ideas.

On Your Own

Read the following sentences and identify the one that uses a comma incorrectly.

The music for the road trip music has been picked, but we still need to buy snacks.

The mechanics students are learning about repairing auto brakes, and manual transmissions.

Queen Victoria had nine children, and her descendants are still part of European royalty today.

Introductory Words, Phrases, and Clauses

Introductory words, phrases, and clauses open a sentence with extra information and help your reader make connections between ideas. The following are common types of introductions:

- **Transitions**: words, phrases, or sentences that show order and make connections between ideas
- **Prepositional Phrases**: groups of related words that start with a preposition and end with a **noun** or **pronoun**
- **Dependent Clauses**: groups of words with a subject and a verb that do not express a complete thought
- **Interjections**: words or groups of words that add emphasis or emotion

Here are some examples of each:

Transition Words

Next, gently stir the flour mixture into the prepared batter.

However, the most successful Kickstarter campaign raised over $5 million.

Prepositional Phrases

By the end of the war, over 300,000 soldiers had served overseas.

After the children's recital, we all went out for ice cream.

An introductory prepositional phrase shorter than five words does not *have* to be followed by a comma, but some writers include a comma anyway to prevent confusion. Both methods are grammatically correct.

In a few years he wants to move to Vancouver, British Columbia.

Above the window, there is a bird's nest with four eggs in it.

Dependent Clauses

Since there was only one doughnut left, no one wanted to take it.

Once he had dinner in the oven, Jack started preparing dessert.

Interjections

Well, the fence will have to be replaced.

Excuse me, where is the nearest train station?

Extra or Unnecessary Details

While extra details make your writing more interesting, some extra information is not necessary to the meaning of a sentence. Think about this example:

> Jonathan, who had only slept five hours the night before, felt exhausted.

> If you were to remove the extra details, this sentence would still have the same basic meaning.

> Jonathan felt exhausted.

However, some information is essential to the meaning of the sentence. Often, these necessary phrases or clauses start with the word *that*.

> I need clothes that are office-appropriate for spring.

> The group talked about all of the people who had influenced them as children.

> Neither of these examples uses commas because the information in each one is necessary to the meaning of the sentence. Here are the same two sentences without those details:

> I need clothes.

> The group talked about all of the people.

> As you can see, you need the details to understand the meanings of these sentences fully.

If the details are not needed, you would use *which* instead of *that* and include a comma before *which*. However, commas are only used when *which* introduces nonessential information.

> The horse had learned to jump five-foot fences, which is higher than he could jump before.

> She wore her diamond earrings to dinner, which were beautiful.

Reflection Questions

In some cases, using commas around extra information can completely change the meaning of a sentence.

> The students, who skipped class that day, fell behind on their coursework.
> The students who skipped class that day fell behind on their coursework.

What is the difference between these two sentences? How do commas affect the meaning?

Adjectives

Commas are used to separate similar coordinate adjectives of equal weight. Keep in mind that **adjectives** are words that describe nouns or pronouns. If you can insert the word *and* between them, then they are of equal weight in regards to the noun, and you should use a comma.

> The impact from the accident caused severe and irreversible damage.
> The impact from the accident caused severe, irreversible damage.

> The speech about the former principal was a genuine and heartfelt tribute.
> The speech about the former principal was a genuine, heartfelt tribute.

> Because the adjectives in these sentences are similar, they can be joined by a comma.

Here is an example of adjectives of unequal weight that do not need a comma separating them.

> **The child played with the dark red ball until sundown.**
>
> In this example, a comma is not needed between *dark* and *red* because they are not of equal weight. The adjective *dark* is describing the color *red*, not the balloon.

Group Activity

As a group, come up with ten pairs of adjectives. Discuss which ones could be joined by a comma.

Helpful Hint

Two other ways to use commas are to separate cities/states and days/years.

> My great-grandmother emigrated from Copenhagen, Denmark.
>
> James J. Braddock won the world championship for heavyweight boxing on June 13, 1935.

Lesson Wrap-up

Key Terms

Adjective: a word that describes a noun or pronoun

Conjunction: a word that makes a connection between other words or a group of words

Comma: a punctuation mark used to separate items in a list; join compound sentences; mark introductory words, phrases, and clauses; add extra or unnecessary details to a sentence; and separate similar adjectives

Comma Splice: a sentence error made when two independent clauses are improperly joined by only a comma and no conjunction

Compound Sentence: two independent clauses joined by a comma and a conjunction

Conjunctive Adverb: a transition word used after a semicolon to show comparison, contrast, sequence, and other relationships

Dependent Clause: a word group that includes a subject and verb but does not express a complete thought

Fused Sentence: a sentence error made when two independent clauses are combined without a comma and conjunction or with only a conjunction

Independent Clause: a word group that includes a subject and a verb and expresses a complete thought

Interjection: a word or group of words that adds emphasis or emotion

Noun: a word that represents a person, place, thing, event, or idea

Phrase: a word group that adds to the meaning of a sentence but does not express a complete thought and usually lacks a subject and a verb

Prepositional Phrase: a group of related words that starts with a preposition and ends with a noun or pronoun

Pronoun: a word that takes the place of a noun in a sentence

Subject: the person, place, thing, event, or idea a sentence is about

Transition: a word, phrase, or sentence that shows order and makes connections between ideas

Verb: a word that represents an action, relationship, or state of being

Lesson 4.13
Using Semicolons and Colons

Semicolons and colons are two of the most commonly confused punctuation marks in the English language. This is partly because of their appearances.

The semicolon is a period stacked on top of a **comma**, and the colon is two periods stacked together. Both semicolons and colons are used to connect or separate items and ideas. Take a look at the examples below:

> "To improve is to change; to be perfect is to change often," said Winston Churchill.

> Please remember to bring these documents to your interview: your resume, your social security card, and your references.

Despite these similarities, semicolons and colons function very differently. **Semicolons** are used to combine two related sentences or to separate a list of word groups. **Colons**, on the other hand, introduce a list or quotation, end a salutation, and join related numbers.

In this lesson, you will learn about the following:

Purposes and Functions of Semicolons
Purposes and Functions of Colons

> Reflection Questions
> Why do you think semicolons and colons are commonly confused with each other? What are some good ways to remember their different functions?

Purposes and Functions of Semicolons

Using multiple short sentences in a row can make your writing sound choppy. If two ideas make more sense together, join them with a semicolon to make your writing flow smoothly.

> Greg drives like a maniac; his girlfriend is always asking him to slow down.

To make sure you're using a semicolon correctly, try separating the two independent clauses into two different sentences.

Correct	I love milk and cookies; they remind me of my grandma's house. I love milk and cookies. They remind me of my grandma's house.
Incorrect	I love milk and cookies; because they remind me of my grandma's house. I love milk and cookies. Because they remind me of my grandma's house.

As you use semicolons, remember that the first word after the semicolon should *not* be capitalized.

Semicolons can also be used to separate long list items. Regular lists use commas to separate each item.

> I bought apples, pears, bananas, and grapes.

But what happens when you list more complicated items?

> I bought juicy, green apples, crisp, fresh pears, ripe, yellow bananas, and both green and red, seedless, firm grapes.

This is where the semicolon becomes important. The sentence makes much more sense with semicolons separating each main food item:

> I bought juicy, green apples; crisp, fresh pears; ripe, yellow bananas; and both green and red, seedless, firm grapes.

Reflection Questions
The prefix *semi-* means "half." How does this meaning fit your understanding of semicolons?

On Your Own

Read the following sentence and identify the word that should be followed by a semicolon.

> On tour last year, the band stopped in Kansas City, Missouri, Seattle, Washington; and Sacramento, California.

Purposes and Functions of Colons

Colons can be used in four main ways:

- Lists
- Salutations
- Quotations
- Related numbers

Learning Style Tip
If you're a **verbal** learner, you may want to consider what a colon communicates. Think of a colon as something that says, "Let me elaborate," or, "That is to say."

Lists

First, colons can be used after a complete sentence to introduce a list.

> The travel agency offered four destinations: Houston, Panama City, Orlando, or Portland.

> My favorite movies include the following: *The Secret Garden, Memento,* and *The Legend of Zorro.*

Remember that when using a colon to introduce a list, the introductory statement must be an **independent clause**: a group of words with a subject and a verb that expresses a complete thought.

> While Rosco was at the grocery store, he picked up: a frozen pizza, a bag of chips, and two packages of ramen.

> This sentence is incorrect because the first part of the sentence is not an independent clause. Therefore, the colon is not necessary.

Salutations

Colons can also be used in the salutation of a business letter. A **salutation** is the **phrase** that greets the person or group that is receiving the letter.

Here are some examples of salutations:

> Dear Janice Brown,

> Kelly-

> To Whom It May Concern:

When you're writing for the business world, make sure to use a colon instead of a comma.

> Dear Ms. Ladson:

> To the Human Resources Department:

Quotations

Next, colons can also be used instead of a comma to introduce quotations. Just like lists, these quotes must follow an independent clause.

> Nelson Mandela said, "I like friends who have independent minds because they tend to make you see problems from all angles."

> Nelson Mandela made the following statement: "I like friends who have independent minds because they tend to make you see problems from all angles."

On Your Own

Read the sentences below and identify which one could use a colon instead of a comma.

> My history professor once argued, "The only way to make progress is by paying attention to the actions of our ancestors."

> My history professor once argued the following belief, "The only way to make progress is by paying attention to the actions of our ancestors."

To learn more about quotation marks, see Lesson 4.15.

Related Numbers

Finally, the colon is used to join related numbers.

Purpose	Examples
Journal issues	*Field and Stream* 24:5 *Journal of American Psychology* 36:2
Religious texts	Quran 27:79 Philippians 3:20
Ratios	1:3 5:4
Times	3:05 p.m. 11:59 p.m.

Lesson Wrap-up

Key Terms

Colon: a punctuation mark used to introduce a list or quotation, end a salutation, and join related numbers

Comma: a punctuation mark used to separate items in a list; join compound sentences; mark introductory words, phrases, and clauses; add extra or unnecessary details to a sentence; and separate similar adjectives

Independent Clause: a word group that contains a subject and a verb and expresses a complete thought

Phrase: a word group that adds to the meaning of a sentence but does not express a complete thought and usually lacks a subject and a verb

Salutation: a phrase that greets the person or group receiving a letter

Semicolon: a punctuation mark used to combine two independent clauses and separate long list items

Verbal Learning: learning information through written and spoken words

Lesson 4.14
Using Apostrophes

Apostrophe errors are everywhere. You can find them on signs, presentations, flyers, and websites. Look at the following examples. What do they all have in common?

Apostrophes are used incorrectly all the time.

If you noticed that all of these examples used apostrophe errors, you are correct. Some of the problems probably stood out to you, but others may have been harder to detect.

An **apostrophe** is a punctuation mark used for possessive nouns, contractions, and shortened numbers and words. Because apostrophes are small, they're easy to overlook. However, learning how to use them correctly will make you a more effective writer and help you avoid potentially embarrassing mistakes.

In this lesson, you will learn three uses for apostrophes:

Possessive Nouns
Contractions
Shortened Numbers and Words

Further Resources
When you type on a smartphone, autocorrect does a pretty good job of inserting apostrophes for you. According to some researchers, this is one way that technology is actually preserving the English language, not destroying it. To learn more, read this article from *The Atlantic*: (http://www.theatlantic.com/magazine/archive/2014/07/punctuated-equilibrium/372291/)

Possessive Nouns

A **possessive noun** shows ownership of an item. These **nouns** always use an apostrophe.

> The jury's decision shocked everyone in the courtroom.

> In tomorrow's game, be sure to wear your ankle brace.

> Both of these sentences include possessive nouns that use an apostrophe to show ownership.

There are two rules that you need to keep in mind when punctuating possessive nouns. First, to make a **singular noun** possessive, always add an apostrophe and the letter -*s*.

> My cousin's birthday party is tomorrow night at 8:00 p.m.

> According to police reports, the suspect's car had been stolen the night before.

Some writers use this rule even when the word already ends in the letter -*s* while others only add an apostrophe.

Apostrophe with -*s*	The class's field trip was canceled because of rain.
	Dr. Deidre James's dissertation was on post-colonialism in human geography.
Apostrophe only	The class' field trip was canceled because of rain.
	Dr. Deidre James' dissertation was on post-colonialism in human geography.

Both of these options are acceptable as long as you consistently use one option throughout a piece of writing.

Second, to make a **plural noun** possessive, add an apostrophe and the letter -*s* to words that don't already end in -*s* and just an apostrophe to words that do end in -*s*.

Possessive Plural Nouns without -*s*	Possessive Plural Nouns with -*s*
children's	kids'
people's	janitors'
oxen's	horses'
alumni's	students'

Common Mistakes

When using apostrophes, people make three common mistakes. One mistake is using an apostrophe with possessive **pronouns**. This is incorrect. Pronouns that are used to show ownership never include an apostrophe.

Incorrect	I think that doughnut is her's.
Correct	I think that doughnut is hers.

The second mistake is using an apostrophe to make a noun plural. This is also incorrect. Apostrophes are only added to nouns that show possession.

Incorrect   The crew spent over six hours repairing the window's on the west side of the building.

Correct   The crew spent over six hours repairing the windows on the west side of the building.

The third mistake is adding an apostrophe and -s to both parts of a compound subject. If you are referring to something that both parts of the subject possess, only add an apostrophe and -s to the second part.

Incorrect   The wedding party decorated Mike's and Nora's car with streamers and window paint.

Correct   The wedding part decorated Mike and Nora's car with streamers and window paint.

On Your Own

Read through the following sentences and identify any words with apostrophe errors.

Andrew's family and three of his best friend's are going to help him set up the tents in the backyard.

The cabin is their's, but they rent it out during the fall.

Nicole's and Kalyn's apartment is within walking distance of some good restaurants.

Contractions

Apostrophes can also be used to form contractions. A **contraction** is a **phrase** that has been shortened into one word. Here is a list of common contractions:

Phrase	Contraction
cannot	can't
has not	hasn't
he will	he'll
it is	it's
let us	let's
she is	she's
they are	they're
who is	who's
will not	won't

> Helpful Hint
> In formal academic or professional writing, you should usually avoid using contractions.

The contractions *it's* and *who's* can be difficult to use properly.

The word *it's* is a contraction that means "it is." The word *its*, on the other hand, is a possessive pronoun that shows ownership. Similarly, the word *who's* is a contraction that means "who is" while the word *whose* is a possessive pronoun.

Look at the following examples:

Contraction	Turn this song up; it's my favorite.
Possessive	By the end of March, the research study reached its conclusion.
Contraction	After dinner, my family usually argues about who's going to do the dishes.
Possessive	Whose turn is it to wash the dishes?

Group Activity
As a group, create five memes that illustrate the differences between *its* and *it's*.

Shortened Numbers and Words

The final use for apostrophes is shortening words and numbers. The apostrophe is placed wherever letters or numbers are missing.

Long	Shortened
of the clock	o'clock
hanging out	hangin' out
madam	ma'am
1990s	'90s

Further Resources
If you need a quick review of apostrophe rules, check out this illustrated flowchart (http://theoatmeal.com/comics/apostrophe) from *The Oatmeal*.

Lesson Wrap-up

Key Terms

Apostrophe: a punctuation mark used for possessive nouns, contractions, and shortened numbers and words

Contraction: a phrase that has been shortened into one word

Noun: a word that represents a person, place, thing, event, or idea

Phrase: a word group that adds to the meaning of a sentence but does not express a complete thought and usually lacks a subject and a verb

Plural Noun: a noun that represents multiple people, places, things, events, or ideas

Possessive Case: a pronoun form that shows possession or functions as an adjective

Pronoun: a word that takes the place of a noun in a sentence

Singular Noun: a noun that represents one person, place, thing, event, or idea

Lesson 4.15
Using Quotation Marks, Parentheses, and Brackets

Sometimes, sentences contain words that are nonessential to the meaning of the text or are quoted from another source. If you don't use some type of punctuation to separate this text from the rest of the sentence, your readers may become confused. Look at the following examples:

Example #1

> The Stamford Innovations website claims that robotic surgery is the most important advancement in the last 100 years of medical innovation.
>
> In this example, it's not immediately plain to the reader where the sentence ends and the quoted information begins. To make sure that you are giving proper credit to your sources, you must use quotation marks.
>
> The Stamford Innovations website claims that robotic surgery is the "most important advancement in the last 100 years of medical innovation."

Example #2

> My great uncle Ian He's 83! is still planning to run the Boston Marathon this summer.
>
> This sentence is difficult to read because there is extra information inserted right in the middle. Adding parentheses will make this sentence much clearer.
>
> My great uncle Ian (He's 83!) is still planning to run the Boston Marathon this summer.

Example #3

> "If it works, we'll help future generations!"
>
> In this example, there is no context provided for the reader, therefore it's unclear what the word *it* refers to. To clarify your writing, use brackets to insert the meaning of unclear language.
>
> "If [the cancer research experiment] works, we'll help future generations!"

In this lesson, you will learn about the purposes of the following punctuation marks:

Quotation Marks
Parentheses
Brackets

Quotation Marks

Quotation marks are punctuation marks most commonly used to repeat someone else's words.

> "Our new location will allow us to serve twice as many customers as last year," said local business owner Greg Henderson. "We plan to hire three new servers in the next month."

> According to the U.S. Department of Education website, "Eighteen percent of all 9th graders complete four-year degrees within ten years."

> In both of these examples, the exact words of a source are being repeated. The quotation marks clearly show which words belong to the author of the sentence and which ones belong to the person or website being quoted.

Quotes aren't limited to complete sentences. In some situations, you might quote just a small group of words to emphasize an important idea. Look at this sentence:

> In a recent review, food critic Ishmael Martin called the Indigo Grill "offensive to anyone with taste buds."

Quotation marks are often used around certain types of titles, including articles, short stories, poems, songs, and book chapters.

> Nathaniel Hawthorne's "Young Goodman Brown" is a short story that reveals truths about humanity.

> In Chapter 2, "Climate Change and Controversy," the author explores arguments from different points of view.

To learn more about capitalization and italics, see Lesson 4.17.

Regardless of the purpose, quotation marks always come in pairs. This helps the reader know when a quotation or title begins and when it ends. Look at the following examples:

Incorrect   "I've been busy baking my roommate, Julie, replied with a sigh.

Correct   "I've been busy baking," my roommate, Julie, replied with a sigh.

The first sentence does not use a pair of quotation marks, which makes the sentence confusing and even alters the meaning.

In the second sentence, you can clearly see which words are part of the quote and which are part of the rest of the sentence because it uses a pair of quotation marks.

On Your Own

Read the sentence below and underline or highlight the word that should be followed by quotation marks.

> "You need to start reading more, Grandma proclaimed.

Periods, **commas**, exclamation points, and question marks that appear at the end of a quote should be placed inside the closing quotation mark.

> The author argues that people prefer fast food to homemade meals because "convenience and affordability are their highest priorities."

> Ellen asked, "How long will the remodeling project take?"

> "Changing our return policy will negatively impact our customers," argued the customer service manager.

> In the last sentence, note that a comma ends the sentence within the quotation while the period is used to end the entire sentence.

Question marks and exclamation points can sometimes be an exception to this rule. If just the quote is a question or exclamation, put the punctuation mark inside of the quotation marks.

> "How long has the engine made this sputtering noise?" the technician asked.

> "This is the scariest movie I've ever seen!" shouted Elisa.

If the entire sentence is a question or exclamation, put the punctuation mark outside of the quotation marks.

> I can't believe that you've never read "The Lottery"!

> What did you think of the article "Left-Brained, Right-Brained"?

Occasionally, you might need to include a quote inside another quote. For these situations, use **single quotation marks**. These are punctuation marks used to mark a quote or title within a quote.

> The lifeguard explained, "I heard her yelling 'Someone get help!' and ran across the beach to see what was going on."

> "As part of tonight's assignment," stated Professor Bering, "you will be writing a one-page response to 'Getting In' by Malcolm Gladwell."

Single quotations are always used inside regular quotation marks. They are never used alone.

> Reflection Questions
> Think back to a time when a friend accidentally or purposefully misquoted you. What was that experience like? How does that situation relate to the use of quotation marks?

Parentheses

Parentheses, like quotation marks, are always used in pairs. They are used to add extra information—like dates, examples, or comments—to a sentence or to introduce an abbreviation.

> Henry VIII (1491-1547) ruled England for almost forty years.

> After my ancestors emigrated from Georgia (the country, not the state), they settled in West Virginia.

> Both of these sentences could be easily read without the information inside the parentheses. However, including additional details gives the reader extra information about the topic. These details are known as **parenthetical information**.

Parentheses are also used to introduce **abbreviations**, which are shortened forms of a word or phrase.

> This drug has not been approved by the Food and Drug Administration (FDA).

To learn about parenthetical information found in MLA papers, see Lesson 8.6.

Parenthetical information inside a sentence should always be placed after related words but before any punctuation marks.

Incorrect	Once the inventory reports are submitted, (and approved) we can dedicate more of our time to planning next month's event.
Correct	Once the inventory reports are submitted (and approved), we can dedicate more of our time to planning next month's event.
Incorrect	I love going to South Beach. (in Miami, FL)
Correct	I love going to South Beach (in Miami, FL).

Keep in mind that parenthetical information breaks the natural flow of a sentence. If you give your readers too many details, they may lose track of your main point.

On Your Own

Read the sentences below and identify the sentence that correctly uses parentheses.

> The best pet I ever had (and still have) is my dog Leroy. He's a little guy who only weighs twelve pounds, but he's (very friendly and excitable.)

Brackets

Brackets are most commonly used inside parentheses or quotation marks to add minor details or explanations. They are also used to clarify writing or to provide context for a direct quote.

If you want to add parenthetical information to text that is already inside parentheses, use brackets.

> My boyfriend watches all the major league sports (except the National Basketball Association [NBA]).
>
> This example includes the abbreviation for the *National Basketball Association*. Adding one set of parentheses inside another set of parentheses would be confusing, so brackets are used instead.

Brackets can also be used to insert missing text inside a quotation. Look at this quote:

> Colbie said, "I love it."
> The readers of this sentence don't know what the word *it* means.
> To make the quote clearer, the missing information is added using brackets:
> Colbie said, "I love [my new car]."

Brackets are always used inside either quotation marks or parentheses. They are never used alone.

On Your Own

Read the sentences below and identify the sentence that correctly uses brackets.

> All local universities are involved with the experiment (other than University of North Carolina [UNC]). They've decided to remain uninvolved as they don't agree with [the morality] of the research procedure.

Lesson Wrap-up

Further Resources
Sources are misquoted on the internet all of the time. In fact, there's even a special term to describe this tendency: "Churchillian Drift." (In England, people often list Winston Churchill as the author of random political quotes.)
In 2015, author Maya Angelou was misquoted on a stamp dedicated to her legacy. To learn more about this awkward mistake, check out this article:
http://www.nytimes.com/2015/04/10/opinion/the-wise-words-of-maya-angelou-or-someone-anyway.html.

Key Terms

Abbreviation: a shortened form of a word or phrase

Brackets: a pair of punctuation marks commonly used inside parentheses or quotation marks to add minor details to a sentence or insert missing text inside a quotation

Comma: a punctuation mark used to separate items in a list; join compound sentences; mark introductory words, phrases, and clauses; add extra or unnecessary details to a sentence; and separate similar adjectives

Parentheses: a pair of punctuation marks used to add extra information to a sentence or introduce an abbreviation

Parenthetical Information: in-text details that are set off by parentheses and provide extra information

Quotation Marks: a pair of punctuation marks most commonly used to repeat someone else's words

Single Quotation Marks: punctuation marks used to mark a quote or title within a quote

Lesson 4.16

Using Ellipses, Hyphens, and Dashes

Ellipses, hyphens, and dashes are some of the most commonly used and misused punctuations marks in the English language. Look at the following examples. Have you ever seen something like this?

Ellipsis

> I don't know.....maybe we should meet at 6:00.

Hyphen

> The Great Depression began in 1928? <-- double-check this date.

Dash

> Hey—are you in the middle of something?

Each of these examples uses an ellipses, hyphen, or dash incorrectly. In everyday life, this could be perfectly acceptable. Most of your friends or family members won't think twice about an incorrect hyphen.

In school or at work, however, you need to use these punctuation marks correctly. They play an important role in connecting and emphasizing the ideas in your writing.

In this lesson, you will learn about how to correctly use the following punctuation marks:

Ellipses

Hyphens

Dashes

> **Reflection Question**
> In text messages and social media posts, punctuation is often used for non-traditional purposes such as creating faces or designs. How has the definition of punctuation changed? How might punctuation continue to change?

Ellipses

An **ellipsis** is made up of three periods in a row. Sometimes, writers use ellipses in an attempt to create suspense. However, their real purpose is to show that information has been removed from a quotation.

Original

> One of the survey participants said, "I don't think this new phone, with all of its bells and whistles, is any better than the phone I use currently."

Revised

> One of the survey participants said, "I don't think this new phone . . . is any better than the phone I use currently."
>
> In this example, a portion of the text has been removed and replaced by an ellipsis. Notice that even though information has been cut from this sentence, the overall structure and meaning still makes sense.

> Helpful Hint
> Ellipses are not required at the beginning or end of a quotation. Your readers will assume that the passage began before and continued after the particular selection included in a paper.

Always add spaces before and after an ellipsis, as well as between each of the periods. Look at the following examples:

Incorrect   "The Henkel Corporation is committed to...superior customer service."

Correct   "The Henkel Corporation is committed to . . . superior customer service."

If an ellipsis comes immediately after another punctuation mark, keep both.

Original

> "I started the Stan Lee Foundation for one main purpose: to do whatever I could to fight illiteracy in children! Any child who grows up illiterate, unable to read and write—or even semi-literate—can be considered handicapped. Competition throughout the world has grown so keen that every young person needs every possible advantage to even the competitive playing field. The ability to read well, to study, comprehend, and process information is absolutely vital for success as an adult." (Stan Lee)

Revised

> "I started the Stan Lee Foundation for one main purpose: to do whatever I could to fight illiteracy in children! . . . The ability to read well, to study, comprehend and process information is absolutely vital for success as an adult." (Stan Lee)
>
> In this example, the information right before the ellipsis ends in an exclamation point. The quote includes both punctuation marks.

Anytime you use ellipses, make sure that you don't introduce a **fragment** or confusing sentence. If necessary, use **brackets** to supply any missing words.

To learn more about fragments, see Lesson 4.8.

Incorrect

> Sonia Sotomayor stated: "In every position that I've been in, . . . who don't believe I can do the work. And I feel a special responsibility to prove them wrong."

Correct

> Sonia Sotomayor stated: "In every position that I've been in, there have been naysayers . . . who don't believe I can do the work. And I feel a special responsibility to prove them wrong."

Correct

> Sonia Sotomayor stated: "In every position that I've been in, . . . I feel a special responsibility to prove [my naysayers] wrong."

Reflection Questions

Ellipses can be dangerous if they are not used correctly. How could removing text from the following quote change its meaning?

> In yesterday's press conference, Kirby Lewis said, "I currently have no intention of leaving the University of Oregon. Any rumors that I have accepted a head coaching position in Utah are false. While Utah State has extended an offer, I am staying in Oregon for at least one more season."

On Your Own

Read the passage below and identify the sentence that correctly uses ellipses.

> "There are some people who believe that controversial books should be banned . . . without exception, from our high schools. Some folks find certain content in this literature to. . . . . . unacceptable. [John Stoe] supports my decision to stand against these individuals . . . and do what is right by our children."

Hyphens

Hyphens are short lines that link together two words or word parts. They are most commonly used in the following situations:

- Compound nouns
- Compound adjectives
- Words with prefixes
- Numbers

Compound Noun

Compound nouns are **nouns** made up of two or more words. Sometimes, these words are linked together with hyphens.

| mother-in-law | two-year-old | merry-go-round | goody-goody |

> **Further Resources**
> Unfortunately, there's no quick and easy trick for knowing whether or not you should use a hyphen for a compound noun. Always use a resource like Dictionary.com (http://www.dictionary.com) if you are unsure.

Compound Adjective

Compound adjectives are two or more words that are being used to describe a noun or pronoun.

> The tribe has a long-standing tradition of holding a festival the night before winter solstice.

To make a true compound adjective, all of the words must be essential to the meaning of the sentence.

> The star-studded cast included all of my favorite celebrities.

> Andrew felt like he was having a mid-life crisis.

> In each of these examples, both of the words that form the compound adjective are essential. If you removed one of the words, the adjective wouldn't make sense:
>
> The studded cast included all of my favorite celebrities.
> Andrew felt like he was having a mid crisis.

Regular adjectives, on the other hand, are not dependent on each other in the same way:

> The tribe has an interesting religious tradition of holding a festival the night before winter solstice.

To learn more about adjectives, see Lesson 4.4.

Prefixes

The third function of hyphens is adding prefixes like *ex-* and *self-*. **Prefixes** are word parts added to the beginning of a word in order to create a new word.

> The ex-teacher used his experiences in the classroom as the basis for his novel.

> Most cameras include a self-timer function that allow photographers to include themselves in the photo.

Hyphens are also used for prefixes when the spelling of the word is potentially confusing. Look at the following example:

> The careful re-creation of the destroyed monument took archaeologists over ten years.

> In this sentence, *re-creation* means creating something again. Without the hyphen, this word might be confused with *recreation*, which refers to an activity or hobby you do for fun.

Here are some additional examples of words that would be confusing or unclear without a hyphen:

de-ice	post-WWI	all-inclusive
re-enter	anti-American	re-sign

Numbers

Finally, hyphens can be used to spell out fractions and numbers between twenty-one and ninety-nine. You do not need hyphens between numbers like one hundred or three thousand.

thirty-five	one-half	one hundred eighty-two
seventy-one	six-tenths	two thousand fifty-five

On Your Own

Determine which of the following words use hyphens correctly. Check the box next to each answer.

- ☐ Ex-con
- ☐ Fifty-three
- ☐ Happy-friendly
- ☐ Anti-makeup

Dashes

A **dash** is a line slightly longer than a hyphen. Dashes are sometimes called "em-dashes" because they are around the same length as a lowercase letter *m*.

Never add spaces before or after a dash.

Incorrect	My two favorite professors — Dr. Martingdale and Dr. Lee — were kind enough to write me letters of recommendation.
Correct	My two favorite professors—Dr. Martingdale and Dr. Lee—were kind enough to write me letters of recommendation.

> **Helpful Hint**
> To create a dash in a typed document, type two hyphens back-to-back. Many programs will automatically turn the hyphens into a dash. Using two hyphens, however, is also acceptable.

Dashes are similar to **commas**; they can both be used to add extra details to a sentence. However, there are two main situations where using dashes is preferable.

First, dashes should be used when the information being added already contains a number of commas. Having too many commas makes sentences confusing. Here's an example:

> The Fantastic Four—Mr. Fantastic, the Invisible Girl, the Human Torch, and the Thing—first appeared in a comic book in 1961.

Dashes are also used to give greater emphasis to extra information. A dash signals a longer pause to the reader than a comma. If you want your readers to stop and think about the details you are sharing, use dashes.

> The full impact of the loss—all $100,000 of it—did not yet seem real.

> **Helpful Hint**
> Because dashes interrupt the flow of your writing, use them carefully.

On Your Own

Read the passage below and identify the sentence that correctly uses dashes.

> "My mom—who raised eight children—was still able to work her entire life. She poured her blood – sweat—and tears into that job in order to support us kids."

Reflection Questions

Commas, dashes, and **parentheses** can all be used to add extra information to a sentence. Think about the following sentence. How does changing the type of punctuation change the meaning of the sentence?

In the business world, confidence and candor, two traits that are respected in men, are not always appreciated in women.

In the business world, confidence and candor—two traits that are respected in men—are not always appreciated in women.

In the business world, confidence and candor (two traits that are respected in men) are not always appreciated in women.

Lesson Wrap-up

Key Terms

Adjective: a word that describes a noun or pronoun

Brackets: a pair of punctuation marks commonly used inside parentheses or quotation marks to add minor details to a sentence

Comma: a punctuation mark used to separate items in a list; join compound sentences; mark introductory words, phrases, and clauses; add extra or unnecessary details to a sentence; and separate similar adjectives

Compound Adjective: an adjective that is made up of two or more words that describe a noun or pronoun

Compound Noun: a noun that is made up of two or more words

Dash: a punctuation mark used to add extra information, often with emphasis, to a sentence

Ellipsis: a punctuation mark used to indicate information has been removed from a quotation

Fragment: a grammatical error that occurs when a word group is punctuated as a complete sentence but does not express a complete thought

Hyphen: a punctuation mark that links together words or word parts

Noun: a word that represents a person, place, thing, event, or idea

Prefix: a word part added to the beginning of a root in order to create a new word

Parentheses: a pair of punctuation marks used to add extra information to a sentence or introduce an abbreviation

Lesson 4.17

Using Capitalization and Italics

Capitalization and italics are both used in writing as visual markers to set apart words and **phrases**. These helpful tools remind your audience to pay close attention, as important or unique information is to come.

Both capitalization and italics should be used sparingly. Using an entire paragraph of capital letters might overwhelm your readers. They might even feel like you're shouting at them. Take a look at the following example:

MRS. SHERIDAN'S ACTIONS THROUGHOUT *THE GARDEN PARTY* REPRESENT THE FRIVOLITY THAT HER DAUGHTER LAURA REJECTS. EVEN WHEN FACED WITH A TRAGEDY SUCH AS DEATH, MRS. SHERIDAN REMAINS UNINTERESTED IN THE CONCERNS OF OTHERS.

> ALTHOUGH LAURA TEMPORARILY SHOWS THIS SAME SHALLOWNESS, SHE ULTIMATELY REJECTS HER MOTHER'S VALUES.

While some magazines and websites italicize large blocks of text, it's generally a better idea to save italics for key words. An entire paragraph of italics makes reading the text and finding important information difficult.

> *Mrs. Sheridan's actions throughout The Garden Party represent the frivolity that her daughter Laura rejects. Even when faced with a tragedy such as death, Mrs. Sheridan remains uninterested in the concerns of others. Although Laura temporarily shows this same shallowness, she ultimately rejects her mother's values.*

Reflection Questions
Do you ever use only capital letters to communicate? How and why?

In this lesson, you will learn about how to correctly use the following:

Capitalization
Italics

Capitalization

Capital letters are used in a number of different ways. Here are six of the most common:

- Sentences
- Proper Nouns
- Acronyms
- Course Titles
- Salutations
- Proper Adjectives

Sentences

First, you should always capitalize the first word in any sentence.

> Some types of pears are edible, while others are strictly ornamental.

> My shoes sank into the soft mud on the riverbank.

This rule also applies to complete sentences that are quoted in another sentence.

> Author and historian Arthur Zinn once said, "Small acts, when multiplied by millions of people, can transform the world."

If you are using an **inline quotation**, a quote that fits into a sentence without a formal introduction, you do not need to use a capital letter at the beginning. Inline quotations usually follow the word *that*.

> Author Sandra Cisneros said that "very small things can make a change in the world."

Proper Nouns

Next, capitalize **proper nouns**, which are words that name a specific person, place, thing, event, or idea.

On Your Own

Read the examples and then add your own.

Proper Nouns	Examples	Add Your Own
People	George Takei Una Thompson	
Places	Mount Kilimanjaro Brazil	
Organizations	Kraft Foods Harvard University	
Days, months, and holidays	Monday Yom Kippur	
Historical events and eras	the Civil War Prohibition	
Ethnicities and nationalities	Asian American Cherokee	
Religions and deities	Hinduism Christianity	
Titles	"The Raven" *The Scarlet Letter*	

Helpful Hint

Unless they are the first words in a title, you do not need to capitalize the following words:
- **Articles**: *a, an, the*
- **Coordinating conjunctions**: *for, and, nor, but, or, yet, so*
- **Short prepositions**: *at, by, into, of, with*

Helpful Hint

If *the* or another article comes before the title of a magazine, journal, or newspaper, it should be capitalized. For example, the name of a newspaper would be *The Star Tribune*, not the *Star Tribune*.

Other Uses

Capitalization should also be used in the following situations:

Acronyms	UCLA (University of California, Los Angeles)
	MLB (Major League Baseball)
	OSHA (Occupational Safety and Health Administration)
Course Titles	Algebra 098
	Social Media Marketing
	Kinesiology II
Salutations	Dear Mr. Kendrick:
	To Whom It May Concern:
	Best Wishes,
Proper Adjectives	Hodgkin's lymphoma
	Bengal tiger
	Xerox machine

Reflection Questions
Although specific course titles such as Reading and Writing 097 are capitalized, fields of study such as history or nursing are not. What might be the reasoning behind this rule?

Group Activity
Sometimes, authors use capital letters stylistically. As a group, consider why someone might choose to capitalize something outside of these basic rules. What might the author be trying to tell you about that particular word or phrase?

Italics

Italics are slanted letters that are used to set apart certain words or phrases. Generally, italics are used in three different ways:

- Titles of longer works
- Important words
- Foreign terms

To learn about the use of italics when citing sources in MLA format, see Lesson 8.6.

Reflection Questions
In social media posts, it's impossible to use italics. Because of this, how can you set apart important words or titles?

First, italicize the titles of longer works such as books or movies. Look at the following examples:

Books	*Harry Potter and the Sorcerer's Stone*
	Sense and Sensibility
	Animal Farm
Websites	*Vox*
	The Purdue Online Writing Lab
	Bleacher Report
Magazines and newspapers	*Rolling Stone*
	The Journal of Biological Sciences
	The Harvard Lampoon
Movies	*Food, Inc.*
	2001: A Space Odyssey
	A Few Good Men
TV Shows	*The Walking Dead*
	Arrested Development
	Mister Roger's Neighborhood
Albums	*Thriller*
	Rumors
	All Eyez on Me
Works of art	*The Scream*
	Girl with a Pearl Earring
	Cloud Gate

Second, italics are used inside a sentence to emphasize important words or set apart foreign terms. Here are a few examples of both uses:

Important Words

Never attempt to remove the radiator cap on a hot car.

The store began stocking Christmas decorations in *July*.

Foreign Terms

Déjà vu is the feeling that you've been somewhere or done something before.

During biology, Dominque presented on the social practices of *apis mellifera*, an insect commonly known as the honey bee.

On Your Own

Fill in the table below with original sentences that use important words and foreign terms.

Important Words	Foreign Terms

Lesson Wrap-up

Key Terms

Article: a type of adjective (*a*, *an*, or *the*) that indicates whether a noun is specific or general

Coordinating Conjunction: a conjunction that connects words or word groups of equal importance in a sentence

Inline Quotation: a quote that fits into a sentence without a formal introduction

Italics: slanted letters most often used to set apart titles of longer works, important words, and foreign terms

Phrase: a word group that adds to the meaning of a sentence but does not express a complete thought and usually lacks a subject and a verb

Preposition: a word that shows a relationship among people, places, things, and ideas

Proper Noun: a capitalized noun that represents a specific person, place, thing, event, or idea

Lesson 4.18
Using Abbreviations and Numbers

In writing, you sometimes come across words that are special cases. Two common examples of this are abbreviations and numbers. Different types of abbreviations and numbers follow their own sets of rules.

If you are unsure how to spell or punctuate an abbreviation or number, just do a quick online search. Your assignment may require you to use a specific format like MLA. If so, make sure that you specifically look for information that fits your guidelines.

In this lesson, you will learn how to correctly use the following:

Abbreviations

Numbers

Abbreviations

Abbreviations are shortened forms of words or **phrases**. They are often used in situations when writing out a full name or term multiple times would be awkward.

On Your Own

Add some more examples to the following table.

Types	Examples	Add Your Own
Organizations	WHO (World Health Organization) WWE (World Wrestling Entertainment) CDC (Center for Disease Control)	
Titles	Mr. Myerson Ms. Bennet Dr. Spaulding	
Initials	J. K. Rowling O. J. Simpson Susan B. Anthony	
Units	6 lbs. 56 ft. 4 tsp.	
Dates and Times	Jan. 6:00 p.m. 2459 BCE	
States	MN SC PA	

When using the title of an organization in a piece of writing, use the full name first, followed by the abbreviation in **parentheses**. Afterwards, you only need to use the abbreviation. This helps your writing to be more clear and concise. Take a look at the following example and pay close attention to how the abbreviations are used.

> The Woman's National Basketball Association (WNBA) has grown in both participant and fan base since its beginnings in 1996. Because of its growing enthusiasts, the league has continued to inspire young female athletes across the country. Many girls cite WNBA players as their role models and motivators for staying involved in athletics. The WNBA is comprised of twelve teams, and its season runs from June through September.

Helpful Hint
Metric units of measurement such as meters or kilometers do not use periods in their abbreviations.
5 m
60 km

Numbers

Different types of academic writing treat numbers differently. For example, in a math class, you will almost always use numerals, like 9 or 67, when you are talking about numbers. In an English paper, however, you would spell those same numbers out as *nine* or *sixty-seven*.

The rules in this lesson apply to academic writing in MLA format. Always double-check with your instructor to see if there are special guidelines you should follow.

Spell out any numbers made up of one or two words:

> Renting an apartment in Chicago will cost at least nine hundred dollars a month.

> The tallest building in my hometown is thirty-three stories high.

> **Helpful Hint**
> Words between twenty-one and ninety-nine always contain a **hyphen**.

You should also use words to simplify a large number:

> The investment firm lost over $3.5 million last year.

> The most populous country in the world is China, which contains over 1.3 billion people.

Finally, spell out any numbers that appear at the beginning of a sentence.

> "Four score and seven years ago, our fathers brought forth on this continent, a new nation, conceived in Liberty, and dedicated to the proposition that all men are created equal."

> **Helpful Hint**
> Spelling out complex numbers at the beginning of a sentence can be awkward. In these situations, re-word the sentence so that you can use numerals instead.
>
> Fifty-seven thousand roses were used to decorate the floats in the parade.
> The floats in the parade were decorated with 57,000 roses.

Use actual numbers, or numerals, in the following situations:

Decimals and percentages	5.7 78% 91% 12.40
Dates and times	1999 402 CE February 23, 1984 5:00 p.m.
Chapter and page numbers	(46) Chapter 7 page 93 Section 12

On Your Own

Read the paragraph below and identify the sentences that use numbers correctly.

> The 4 company headquarters owned by Liberty, Inc. house a wide variety of careers and professional opportunities. There are a total of twenty thousand employees and ninety-five management positions. Each headquarters contains roughly twenty-five departments. Their customer base is large as well; they serve a population of 1,500,000 clients.

Lesson Wrap-up

Key Terms

Abbreviation: a shortened form of a word or phrase

Hyphen: a punctuation mark that links together words or word parts

Parentheses: a pair of punctuation marks used to add extra information to a sentence or introduce an abbreviation

Phrase: a word group that adds to the meaning of a sentence but does not express a complete thought and usually lacks a subject and verb

Lesson 4.19
Using Basic Spelling Rules

Imagine that you receive the following email from a new tutor:

> Dere Stuednt: I am loking forward to werking wih you this smester. Pleez remember to bring all of ur class sylubuses to our firt meeting tonite.
> -Hannah

What would your first reaction be? Based on the spelling in this email, you would probably consider canceling your meeting and finding a different tutor.

Spelling makes a big impression. Spelling errors on your resume or application may prevent you from being hired. In a presentation, issues with spelling can make you seem careless or ignorant.

In this lesson, you will learn useful spelling rules for the following situations:

IE and *EI* Words
Plural Words
Suffixes

Helpful Hint
Spell-check and autocorrect can be helpful tools when you are writing on a computer or phone. However, these programs do not always know the word that you are trying to spell. If you want to avoid embarrassing autocorrect fails, make sure to proofread your work carefully.

IE and *EI* Words

One old spelling rule that people often remember is "*I* before *E*, except after *C* or in words like *neighbor* or *weigh*." Here are a few words that follow this rule:

ie	After *c*	Words like *weigh*
achieve	ceiling	eight
believe	deceit	their
brief	perceive	sleigh
relief	receipt	vein
retrieve	receive	weight

Exceptions

Unfortunately, a number of words are exceptions to this rule.

- Use *ie* after the *-sh* sound: *ancient, patient, species*
- Use *ei* if the vowels are pronounced like the *i* in *bit*: *forfeit, foreign*
- Use *ei* in abnormal words: *either, neither, weird*

On Your Own

Check the box next to the correctly spelled word.

- ☐ reciept
- ☐ ancient
- ☐ foriegn
- ☐ releif

Reflection Questions
Can you think of any other exceptions to the "*I* before *E*" rule?

Plural Words

When you are making a word plural, pay attention to the ending of the word. If a word ends in any of the following letters, add *-es*.

-s

-sh

-ch

-x

-z

If a word ends in any other letter, just add *-s*.

On Your Own

Read the table of plural words below and add a few of your own examples.

-es	-s
mess → messes	assignment → assignments
brush → brushes	caterpillar → caterpillars
church → churches	nap → naps
box → boxes	phone → phones
maze → mazes	scissor → scissors

Words that end in -o are a special exception to this rule. Some are spelled with -es and some are spelled with -s. If you aren't sure which one to use, be sure to check a dictionary.

On Your Own

Read the table of plural words that end in -o below and add a few of your own examples.

-es	-s
echo → echoes	combo → combos
hero → heroes	logo → logos
potato → potatoes	taco → tacos
tomato → tomatoes	typo → typos
veto → vetoes	video → videos

Finally, remember that some words change their spelling or stay the same when they are made plural.

On Your Own

Read the tables below and add a few of your own examples.

Singular	Plural (Spelling Changes)
child	children
goose	geese
mouse	mice
person	people

Singular	Plural (Spelling Stays the Same)
deer	deer
fish	fish
sheep	sheep
species	species

Suffixes

Suffixes are word parts added to the end of a root in order to change the meaning. Suffixes affect the spelling of a word in three common situations.

To learn more about suffixes, see Lesson 2.7.

Silent -e

Many words in the English language end in a silent -e. If you are adding a suffix that starts with a vowel to the word, drop the silent -e.

Advise → Advising

However, if you are adding a suffix to the word that starts with a consonant, keep the silent -e.

Home → Homeward

On Your Own

Read the table below and add a few of your own examples.

Original	Vowel Suffix	Loses *e*
dance	-ing	dancing
narrate	-ion	narration
excite	-able	excitable
file	-ed	filed

On Your Own

Read the table below and add a few of your own examples.

Original	Consonant Suffix	Keeps *e*
advertise	-ment	advertisement
hope	-ful	hopeful
safe	-ty	safety
state	-ly	stately

If dropping the silent -*e* could cause confusion between two words, keep the silent -*e* and add the suffix. For example, the word *dyeing* could potentially be confused with *dying* if they weren't spelled differently.

Final -y

Words that end in the letter -*y* follow their own set of rules. When the letter before the final -*y* is a vowel, simply add the suffix to the end of the word.

> attorney + -*s* = attorneys

When the letter before the final -*y* is a consonant, change the -*y* to an -*i* before adding the suffix.

> easy + -*ly* = easily

The suffix -*ing* is an exception to this rule. Always keep the final -*y* when adding -*ing*.

> bury + -*ing* = burying

On Your Own

Read the table below and add a few of your own examples for different final -y scenarios.

Original	Suffix	New
employ	-er	employer
enjoy	-ing	enjoying
try	-s	tries
mystery	-ous	mysterious

Final Consonants

There's one more set of rules to remember when adding suffixes. When adding a suffix to a one-syllable word that ends with a *consonant-vowel-consonant* pattern, you must double the final consonant. (A **syllable** is a basic unit of a word's pronunciation.) Here are a few examples:

beg → begging

grip → gripping

hop → hopped

hot → hotter

Do the same thing to a word with multiple syllables if the **stress** (either the written or spoken emphasis) is placed on the last syllable.

begin → beginning

forget → forgetting

control → controlling

forbid → forbidden

Further Resources
The English language is filled with irregular spellings and exceptions to rules. Some organizations (http://spellingsociety.org/) want to update the language to use a simpler spelling system.

On Your Own

Read the table below and add a few of your own examples for different final consonant scenarios.

Original	New
sit	sitting
knot	knotting
refer	referred
submit	submitting

Lesson Wrap-up

Further Resources
Plural words in Old English used to be even more complicated than they are now. For example, the plural of the word *egg* was spelled *eggru*. To learn how plural words started ending in *-s* and *-es* (usually!), watch this TED Talk (http://ed.ted.com/lessons/a-brief-history-of-plural-word-s-john-mcwhorter#review) by linguist John McWhorter.

Key Terms

Stress: emphasis, either written or spoken

Suffix: a word part added to the end of a root in order to change the meaning of a word

Syllable: the basic unit of a word's pronunciation

Lesson 4.20

Spelling Commonly Confused Words

The English language contains some words that are easy to confuse. Many of these words sound the same but have different meanings. Others look completely different but have very similar meanings.

Think about your own experiences as a writer or speaker. You can probably name a few words that you mix up on a regular basis. At some point, a teacher or a friend probably pointed out your mistake and explained the differences between the two words.

Learning the definitions and functions of confusing words will help you keep them straight. Otherwise, you will find yourself making the same mistakes over and over again.

This lesson will teach you the differences between two types of commonly misused words:

Similar Sound Words
Similar Meaning Words

Similar Sound Words

The following groups of words are commonly misused because they sound so similar:

Accept and Except

The word *accept* is a **verb** that means "to receive something." For example, you can *accept* a job offer or a promotion.

The word *except*, on the other hand, is a **preposition** that is used to exclude something. You might text all of your friends *except* Justine.

> Due to budget concerns, the committee decided not to accept the proposal.

> The flood hit all of the surrounding communities except Mount Pleasant.

Affect and Effect

Affect is a verb that means "to change or influence." You can *affect* the outcome of an election with your vote.

The word *effect* is a **noun** that means "a consequence or result," as in the special *effects* used in a movie.

> The crowd was deeply affected by the news.

> Painting the wall orange had a dramatic effect on the room's appearance.

Choose and Chose

The verb *choose* means "to select something." For example, you may *choose* to write a paper about nuclear energy.

Chose, with just one -o, is the past form of the verb. After carefully considering your options, you *chose* the graphic design program.

> It's impossible for many people to choose just one favorite book.

> At dinner yesterday, I was shocked that Raul chose ice cream instead of the cheesecake.

Its and It's

Its is the possessive form of the **pronoun** *it*, while *it's* is a **contraction** meaning "it is."

> The parrot turned its head and squawked loudly.

> If this bill is passed in the House, it's almost guaranteed to pass in the Senate.

Loose and Lose

Loose is an **adjective** that means "not tight." The handle on a door can be *loose*.

Lose, on the other hand, is a verb that means "to fail a competition" or "to misplace something." You might *lose* a bet with your friends.

> After nine weeks of working out, my clothing started to feel loose.

> If the Rockets lose tonight's game, they will not advance to the playoffs.

Past and Passed

The word *past* is a noun that refers to time that has already happened. A former criminal tries to forget the *past*.

Passed is the past tense form of the verb *pass*, which means "handing an item to someone" or "receiving an acceptable score." In high school, you may have *passed* tests or basketballs.

> In the past, she has always been polite.

> The quarterback made a split-second decision and passed the football to the running back.

Than and Then

Than is a **subordinating conjunction** used for comparisons. For example, you are taller *than* your best friend.

Then is an **adverb** that shows time or order. Once you finish one task, *then* you can move on to another.

> My little brother is taller than I am.

> Clear two more tables, and then you can take a break.

Their and They're and There

Their is a pronoun that shows possession, while *they're* is a contraction that means "they are." For example, *they're* planning to publish *their* research next month. The word *there* is an adverb that refers to a specific place. You can leave your homework over *there*.

> Their opinion on the matter is completely uninformed.

> There are over twenty-five corporations headquartered in Morrisville, Indiana.

> Do you know when they're going to put their house on the market?

Too and To and Two

The word *too* is an adverb that means "also," while the word *to* is a preposition used to show direction. You might go *to* the doctor, but you probably don't want to go to the dentist, *too*. The word *two* is only used for the number two, as in *two* boxes of chocolate.

> Brayden saw that his brother received a piece of candy and decided that he wanted one, too.

> Please send a copy of your driver's license number to the Human Resources Department.

> Two of the most well-known researchers in human genetics are professors at MIT.

Whether and Weather

Whether is a subordinating conjunction that is used to indicate two choices. For example, you may not be sure *whether* or not you want to join the dance team.

The word *weather* is a noun that represents the climate of an area. The *weather* in Minnesota is cold.

> I haven't decided whether I am going to vote for Cory Booker or Kacey Drummond.

> The National Weather Service thinks that Tropical Storm Kelly will make landfall tonight.

Whose and Who's

The word *whose* is a pronoun that shows possession. An example would be the question, "*Whose* textbook is on the floor?"

Who's is a contraction that means "who is." You might ask *who's* planning to be at practice tomorrow night.

> Whose student ID card is on the table?

> Who's going to take care of the outstanding purchase orders?

Your and You're

The pronoun *your* shows possession. You may not know who *your* instructors will be next semester.

You're is a contraction that means "you are," as in *you're* invited to a going-away party.

> Your resume and qualifications seem to be a perfect fit for this role.

> If you don't take advantage of this opportunity, you're going to regret it.

Similar Meanings Words

Words with similar meanings are called synonyms. Words with opposite meanings are called antonyms.

The following words are commonly misused because they have similar or related meanings.

Between and Among

Between and *among* are both prepositions that show relationships. *Between* should be used for groups of two while *among* should be used for groups of more than two.

> Markham requested that all communication between the defendants should be approved by him first.

> I divided the Halloween candy equally among my three children.

Borrow and Lend

The words *borrow* and *lend* are both verbs. *Borrow* means "to take temporarily." *Lend*, on the other hand, means "to give temporarily." You might lend money *to* a friend or borrow money *from* a friend.

> Could you lend me ten dollars for lunch?

> After borrowing millions of dollars from the European Union, Greek banks began to fail.

Come and Go

Come and *go* are both verbs that indicate movement. However, they are opposites. The word *come* shows movement toward the speaker, and the word *go* shows movement away from the speaker.

> Are you planning to come to my house after work?

> Many CEOs go to school for history before going into business.

Fewer and Less

The words *fewer* and *less* are used to show comparisons. *Fewer* should be used for items you *can* count, *less* for items you *can't* count.

> There are three fewer volunteers than last time.

> This year, people have been donating less than usual.

Lie and Lay

The words *lie* and *lay* are both verbs. *Lie* means "to recline." When you are tired, you *lie* down. *Lay*, on the other hand, means "to set down." A carpenter might *lay* his tools on a workbench.

> The MRI nurse asked the patient to lie still while the machine completed its scan.

> You can lay your coats over the railing in the living room.

Helpful Hint

Spell-check usually won't catch misused words if they are spelled correctly. If you know you sometimes mix up certain words, try using the Find option (or Ctrl + F) in Microsoft Word to find specific words in your document. Carefully read through the sentence and determine if you've used the word correctly.

Lesson Wrap-up

On Your Own

Read the following sentences and determine which word fits in the blank. Check the box next to your answer.

> Let's meet at _____ place to work on the group project.

☐ your
☐ you're

> The squirrel stopped in _____ tracks in the middle of the sidewalk.

☐ its
☐ it's

> When it's hot outside, wear _____ clothing and drink water regularly.

☐ loose
☐ lose

> My friend _____ pens from me in class and never gives them back.

☐ lends
☐ borrows

> The article claimed that _____ music has been illegally downloaded this year.

☐ less
☐ fewer

> Every day at three o'clock, my grandfather _____ down to take a nap.

☐ lays
☐ lies

Key Terms

Adjective: a word that describes a noun or pronoun

Adverb: a word that describes a verb, adjective, or another adverb

Antonym: a word that has the opposite meaning of another word

Contraction: a phrase that has been shortened into one word

Noun: a word that represents a person, place, thing, event, or idea

Preposition: a word that shows a relationship among people, places, things, and ideas

Pronoun: a word that takes the place of a noun in a sentence

Subordinating Conjunction: a conjunction that introduces a dependent clause

Synonym: a word whose meaning is similar to that of another word

Verb: a word that represents an action, relationship, or state of being

Lesson 4.21
Proofreading Sentences for Grammar

Once you are comfortable with the rules of grammar and spelling, you must start applying this knowledge to your writing. Being able to correct your own writing errors will help you present yourself and your ideas in a more professional and academic way.

Keep in mind that proofreading skills don't happen overnight. As you continue to practice, you will find yourself becoming more comfortable with identifying and fixing grammar and spelling mistakes. Additionally, the more you write, the more you will learn from these mistakes, which will shape you into a stronger and more effective writer.

In this lesson, you will learn about the following strategies:

Determine Your Common Mistakes

Proofread in Stages

Try Multiple Reading Techniques

Take Advantage of Technology

Take Frequent Breaks

Proofreading a text for grammar and spelling can be a time-consuming task. There are a lot of rules and guidelines to keep straight. If you don't have a strategy for proofreading, you may find yourself feeling bored or overwhelmed.

Reflection Questions
Have you ever noticed grammar or spelling errors in a book, article, or document? How did this affect your opinion of the text?

To become a more effective proofreader, use the following steps:

Determine Your Common Mistakes

Everyone struggles with certain types of grammar and spelling mistakes. Think back to the papers you've written in previous classes. What errors did your teachers mark over and over again?

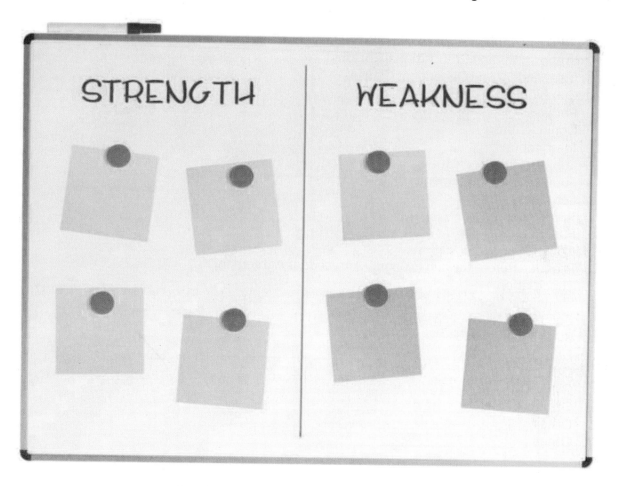

Making a list of common mistakes along with your strengths can be helpful when proofreading.

> **Helpful Hint**
> If you're not sure what grammar and spelling mistakes you commonly make, ask a friend or a Writing Center tutor to review your work and share three to five areas of weakness.

> **Helpful Hint**
> Keep a copy of your common grammar mistakes saved on your computer or in a folder. Review this list anytime you proofread your writing. Update this list every time you receive grammar feedback from an instructor.

On Your Own

Review the following list of grammar topics and check the box next to each area in which you think you need the most improvement.

- ☐ Nouns and Pronouns
- ☐ Verb Types, Forms, and Tenses
- ☐ Adjectives and Adverbs
- ☐ Prepositions and Prepositional Phrases
- ☐ Independent and Dependent Clauses
- ☐ Combining Clauses
- ☐ Phrases
- ☐ Conjunctions
- ☐ Interjections
- ☐ Subjects and Predicates
- ☐ Subject-Verb Agreement
- ☐ Sentence Fragments
- ☐ Run-on Sentences
- ☐ Fused Sentences
- ☐ Comma Splices
- ☐ Pronoun Reference and Pronoun-Antecedent Agreement
- ☐ Punctuation
- ☐ Commonly Confused Words
- ☐ Commonly Misspelled Words
- ☐ Basic Spelling Rules
- ☐ Other: _____
- ☐ Other: _____
- ☐ Other: _____
- ☐ Other: _____
- ☐ Other: _____
- ☐ Other: _____

Helpful Hint
For an expanded list of the grammar topics covered in this chapter, refer to the list of Key Terms at the end of this lesson.

Further Resources
Missing even small grammar and spelling errors can lead to big problems. In one case, a man was sentenced to 42 extra months in jail because of a typo in his paperwork. (http://www.vox.com/2014/4/15/5617676/weird-federal-math-typo-3-and-a-half-extra-years-in-prison).

Proofread in Stages

Trying to catch all of your grammar and spelling errors in just one reading is impossible. Instead, you should proofread your text in stages. During each stage, focus on correcting one type of grammar error.

To make the best use of your time, start with your most common grammar and spelling mistakes. For example, you might first proofread for comma splices, then subject-verb agreement.

Once you've worked through your list of common errors, proofread these four general areas:

Proofreading Checklist: Grammatical Sentences
☐ **Sentence Structure:** comma splices, fragments, fused sentences
☐ **Agreement:** subject-verb and pronoun-antecedent agreement
☐ **Punctuation:** commas, semicolons, colons, quotation marks
☐ **Speiling:** spelling, capitalization, numbers

Try Multiple Reading Techniques

When you proofread a text, starting at the beginning and reading all the way to the end isn't always the best strategy. It's easy to rush through your sentences without even realizing you made grammar or spelling mistakes.

- To help yourself slow down and focus, try reading your text out loud. Your brain often supplies missing words or fixes mistakes automatically when you read silently. Actually saying the words can reveal errors you would have missed otherwise.

- Another way to keep yourself focused on spelling and grammar is to read your text backwards. Read the last sentence first. Then, read the second-to-last sentence. Keep moving through your sentences in this order, looking for errors in each once. This strategy helps you focus on the contents of the sentence without getting distracted by the overall ideas in the paragraph or essay.

On Your Own

Apply the above strategies as you proofread the following passage:

So, why don't we, as a society, continue to volunteer past adolescence and into adulthood. Many argue that lack of time is the biggest factor preventing college students and young workers from giving to others. However, when a person gives of his time. He learns to see the world through the eyes of those who benefit from his volunteering. For example, a woman who helps distribute food at a food pantry sees the need in her community. She sees the value of sacrificcing a couple of hours a month; to give to others who may need some temporary help in order to survive. Because she can put a face to that need, they are willing to give up some of her down time. the activities that used to take up her off-work hours, such as television, become less engaging than the satisfaction of improving another's life.

- Finally, try printing out a paper copy of your text to proofread. Sometimes, seeing the words in a different location can help you find mistakes you previously missed. Mark any errors so that you can go back and fix them later.

Take Advantage of Technology

Most writing programs, like Microsoft Word, offer useful proofreading features. Spell-check scans your writing and identifies problems with spelling, capitalization, and punctuation. Keep in mind that a computer will not notice if you use a correctly spelled word in the wrong place. You should never rely on spell-check to do your proofreading for you.

On Your Own

Identify the misspelled word in the following sentence:

> Gaming is now headed into the new teritory of virtual reality.

Most programs also offer a handy feature that allows you to find specific words or punctuation marks in a text. If you know that you always mix up *their* and *there*, use this feature to search for these words. You can then proofread each sentence to decide if you used the words correctly. This feature is also useful for proofreading less common punctuation marks like **brackets** or **quotation marks**.

Take Frequent Breaks

As you proofread your paper, don't be afraid to take frequent breaks. Five to ten minutes should be plenty of time for you to stretch your legs or get a drink. Don't allow yourself to take too much time, however, as you might become distracted.

You should also consider breaking your proofreading across multiple days. Getting a good night's sleep will give you fresh eyes and a clear head.

Lesson Wrap-up

On Your Own

Read the following excerpt from a student essay on the prison system. Identify and mark corrections for all the errors you can find.

Most citizens do not think about the men and women behind the walls of prison systems, and they think much less about what is hapening in the prisons. Because of the lack of interest in prison policies. The system in effect in many penitentiaries today is not as effective as it could be. There are many ideas for how prisons should function, but a process needs to be enforced that is productive not only for prisoners but society. The high rate of relapses, that results in overpopulated prisons has the potential to be lower. Rehabilitating prisoners is the key to a more productive change in the prison systems because it takes into account the prisoner's background and individuality and benefits both society and prisoners. When compared with other alternatives for prisons, the rehabilitation process actually changes the lives of prisoners, thus making it the best choice.

When a prisoner is released back into society, they must learn how to thrive without reverting back to old behaviors. Violators can either change in the prison systm or remain in a career of crime. Because of the unlikelihood of changing themselves without help, inmates will most likely be put back into an overcrowded prison system in which they learn even more about breaking the law. Offenders need to be put into a situation where the ability to change is present. The best way to help prisoners change; is to make change a possibility.

On Your Own

Read the following excerpt from a student essay on the brain's role in processing depression. Identify grammatical errors and make corrections.

Many self-help gurus turn to notions of self-empowerment and willfulness to encourage depressed individuals to engage the world. However, this sort of instruction ignore what many current scientists and philosophers know: a person's ability to control his or her own thoughts is extremely limited. In his essay, Jack Burton explains that "lower-level brain modules can profoundly affect not only our ordinary sensory perceptions but also how we experience abstract symbols (65). He goes on to explain that these lower-level processes actually precede feelings of certainty when people make decisions, so unconscious thinking actually underwrites human actions Thus, it is not at all clear that positive thinking is within a person's control. While many people don't believe this to be true.

The following Key Terms include grammar topics covered throughout this chapter.

Key Terms

Action Verb: a verb that indicates a physical or mental action

Adjective: a word that describe a noun or a pronoun

Adverb: a part of speech that describes a verb, adjective, or another adverb

Antecedent: the word that a pronoun renames in a sentence

Antonym: a word that has the opposite meaning of another word

Apostrophe: a punctuation mark used for possessive nouns, contractions, and shortened numbers and words

Base Form: the simplest form of a verb, free of alterations for tense, number, and point of view

Brackets: a pair of punctuation marks commonly used inside parentheses or quotation marks to add minor details to a sentence or insert missing text inside a quotation

Clause: a word group that contains a subject and a verb

Colon: a punctuation mark used to introduce a list or quotation, end a salutation, and join related numbers

Comma: a punctuation mark used to separate items in a list; join compound sentences; mark introductory words, phrases, and clauses; add extra or unnecessary details to a sentence; and separate similar adjectives

Comma Splice: a sentence error made when two independent clauses are improperly joined by only a comma and no conjunction

Common Noun: a noun that represents a non-specific person, place, thing, event, or idea

Complete Sentence: a sentence that contains at least one subject and one predicate and expresses a complete thought

Complete Thought: when a group of words is logically finished

Complex Sentence: a sentence pattern in which an independent clause is connected to a dependent clause

Compound Noun: a noun made up of two or more words

Compound Sentence: a sentence pattern in which two independent clauses are connected by a comma and a coordinating conjunction

Compound Subject: a subject made up of two nouns or pronouns, usually joined by a conjunction

Compound-Complex Sentence: a sentence pattern containing at least two independent clauses and at least one dependent clause

Conjunction: a part of speech that connects two or more words, phrases, or clauses in a sentence

Conjunctive Adverb: a transition word that shows contrast, comparison, sequence, and other relationships between clauses

Contraction: a phrase that has been shortened into one word

Coordinating Conjunction: a conjunction that connects words or word groups of equal importance in a sentence

Correlative Conjunctions: conjunctions that connect two or more similar ideas and always appear in pairs

Count Noun: a noun that can be counted

Declarative Sentence: a sentence that makes a general statement that informs the reader

Demonstrative Pronoun: a pronoun that takes the place of a noun phrase and acts as an adjective

Dependent Clause: a word group that contains a subject and a verb but does not express a complete thought

Direct Object: a word that receives the action of a verb

Direct Question: a sentence that asks the audience a question and usually ends with a question mark

Exclamation Point: a punctuation mark that conveys emphasis or strong feeling

Exclamatory Sentence: a sentence that communicates emotion or surprise

FANBOYS: an acronym for the seven coordinating conjunctions

First-Person Pronoun: a pronoun used to refer to the speaker of the sentence

Fused Sentence: a sentence error made when two independent clauses are combined without a comma and conjunction or with only a conjunction

Future Tense: a verb tense used to describe an action that has not yet taken place or to describe plans or instructions

Future-Perfect Tense: a verb tense used to describe an action that started in the past and will be completed in the future

Future-Progressive Tense: a verb tense used to describe a continuous action that will take place in the future

Gender: a basis for classifying feminine, masculine, and neutral words

Gerund: a verbal that functions as a noun in a sentence and is formed by adding *-ing* to the end of the verb

Helping Verb: a verb that is added to a main verb to create a new verb that grammatically fits the sentence

Hyphen: a short line that links together two words or word parts

Imperative Sentence: a sentence that makes commands and often addresses the implied subject

Implied Subject: the subject of a sentence when the speaker is talking directly to the audience

Indefinite Pronoun: a pronoun that does not rename a specific noun

Independent Clause: a group of words with a subject and a verb that expresses a complete thought

Indirect Object: a word that receives the direct object of a sentence

Indirect Question: a sentence that tells the audience about a question and usually ends with a period

Infinitive: a verbal that can function as a noun, adjective, or adverb in a sentence

Interjection: a word or group of words that adds emphasis or emotion

Interrogative Sentence: a sentence that asks a question

Linking Verb: a verb that connects the subject to a description

Main Verb: the verb that expresses the primary action or state of being of a subject in a complete sentence

Non-count Noun: a noun that cannot be counted

Noun: a part of speech that represents a person, place, thing, event, or idea

Number: a basis for agreement between singular or plural words

Object of the Preposition: a word that completes the meaning of a prepositional phrase

Objective Case: the form a word takes when used as the object of a preposition, direct object, or indirect object of a sentence

Objective Pronoun: a pronoun that functions as an object in a sentence

Participle Phrase: a phrase that uses a present or a past participle to introduce the rest of the sentence

Parts of Speech: the categories that classify each type of word found in a sentence

Past Participle: a verb form that can function as an adjective or as part of a perfect-tense verb to show completed mental or physical action

Past Tense: a verb tense used to report on an event or reflect on a past experience

Past-Perfect Tense: a verb tense used to describe an action that was completed before another past-completed action

Past-Progressive Tense: a verb tense used to describe a continuous action that occurred at a certain time in the past

Period: a punctuation mark used to end sentences that make a statement or relay information

Person: the point of view—first-, second-, or third-person—indicated by the form a word takes on in a sentence

Personal Pronoun: a pronoun that renames a specific person, animal, object, or place

Plural Noun: a noun that represents multiple people, places, things, events, or ideas

Possessive Case: a pronoun form that shows possession or functions as an adjective

Possessive Pronoun: a pronoun that shows possession of another noun

Predicate: the part of a sentence that indicates what a subject says or does and includes a main verb + any corresponding helping verbs

Preposition: a word that shows a relationship among people, places, things, events, and ideas

Prepositional Phrase: a group of related words that starts with a preposition and ends with a noun or pronoun

Present Participle: a verb form that can function as an adjective as part of a progressive-tense verb to express a continuous action

Present Tense: a verb tense used to describe an event or action that is happening now

Present-Perfect Tense: a verb tense used to describe an action that was started in the past and has not yet been completed

Present-Progressive Tense: a verb tense used to describe a continuous action that is happening in the present or will happen in the near future

Pronoun Case: the form a pronoun takes based on its function—subjective, objective, or possessive—in a sentence

Pronoun Reference: the connection between a pronoun and the noun it renames

Pronoun: a word that takes the place of a noun in a sentence

Pronoun-Antecedent Agreement: the consistency in gender and number between a pronoun and the person, place, thing, idea, or event it renames in a sentence

Proper Noun: a capitalized noun that represents a specific person, place, thing, event, or idea

Question Mark: a punctuation mark used at the end of a sentence that asks a question

Quotation Marks: a pair of punctuation marks used to repeat someone else's words

Relative Pronoun: a pronoun used to introduce a dependent clause

Run-on Sentence: a sentence error in which two or more independent clauses are combined improperly to create a comma splice or a fused sentence

Semicolon: a punctuation mark used to combine two independent clauses and separate items in long lists

Sentence Patterns: a set of distinct clause combinations that can make up a sentence

Simple Sentence: a sentence made up of one independent clause

Singular Noun: a noun that represents one person, place, thing, event, or idea

Subject Pronoun: a pronoun used as the subject of a sentence

Subject: the person, place, thing, event, or idea a sentence is about

Subjective Case: the form a word takes when it functions as the subject of a sentence

Subjective Pronoun: the form of a pronoun that functions as the subject in a sentence

Subject-Verb Agreement: when a subject and verb used in a sentence match in number and point of view

Subordinating Conjunction: a conjunction that introduces a dependent clause

Synonym: a word whose meaning is similar to that of another word

Verb: a word that represents an action, relationship, or state of being

Verbal: verb forms that function as other parts of speech (adjectives, adverbs, nouns) in a sentence

Chapter 5
Style

Determining Writing Style

Everyone has a sense of style that's unique. When you wear clothing that fits your personality, you feel like yourself. If you've ever found yourself wearing an outfit that wasn't your style, you probably remember how uncomfortable and awkward you felt.

Just like your clothing choices, your writing also has a specific style that fits your personality. You sound more natural when you are comfortable with the words and structures that you use. As a writer, you must learn to adapt to your purpose or writing assignment while still being true to your own unique voice.

This lesson will discuss three factors that will help you determine style:

Purpose and Audience
Formality
Complexity

> Reflection Questions
> Think about your own writing habits and tendencies. How does your writing reflect specific aspects of your personality? What makes your writing style unique?

Purpose and Audience

The most important factors that will affect your writing style are your purpose and audience. Some of the most common **purposes**, or goals for writing, include informing, persuading, reflecting, and entertaining.

- **To inform**: sharing information about a topic
- **To persuade**: convincing the reader to adopt a belief or take an action
- **To reflect**: sharing a personal experience or belief
- **To entertain**: exploring a topic or event in a creative or humorous way

When you're writing for school or work, your purpose is often determined by instructions from your professor or supervisor. For example, if your instructor wants you to write a research paper on education reform, your purpose is probably to inform. If your boss wants you to submit a business proposal to a client, your purpose is probably two-fold: to inform and to persuade.

Once you've decided on your purpose for writing, consider your audience. Your **audience** is made up of the people who will read your writing. This might include your professor, your classmates, your coworkers, your friends, or even strangers. The **tone**, or attitude you express in your writing, should be appropriate for both your purpose and audience.

On Your Own

Imagine that you have been asked to write to a nursing class at the local college about vegetables. Take a look at the sentences below and identify the one that would be a better addition to your paper:

> Vegetables are a yummy source of protein, which gives you super strong muscles.

> Vegetables can be a good source of protein, a nutrient that promotes muscle health.

Here's another example. Which of the following sentences would best fit a paper with an informative purpose and an audience of film studies students?

> People praised the film, but I hated every minute of it.

> People praised the film, but I found it disappointing.

> The tone of the first sentence is too negative for a scholarly paper. The second sentence is more appropriate for the audience and purpose.

Reflection Questions
Who are some of the possible audiences of an email? How would the style of your writing change based on the audience?

Formality

Formality, the way a text conforms to certain standards, is another factor that affects your writing style. Some **genres**, or types of writing, require a more formal writing style than others. For example, an article for your campus newspaper would probably sound very different from an email to your best friend. Both might use a positive, enthusiastic tone; however, the email would likely sound more casual than the article. Here are some examples of texts that use different levels of formality:

Formal	Informal
Academic research paper	Personal narrative
Business proposal	Blog post
Cover letter	Text message

Informal writing usually uses first-person and second-person **pronouns** such as *I*, *me*, and *you*. For example, in an online review of a local restaurant, you would use first-person pronouns to describe your experience:

> I stopped at the Sesame Bakery this morning to pick up a doughnut. The clerk was very rude. Not only did she ignore me for over five minutes, but she also looked extremely annoyed when I asked for assistance. I will not be returning to this restaurant again.

You use informal writing in your everyday life for emails, Amazon reviews, text messages, and Facebook posts. When you communicate with your circle of friends, you can use verbal shortcuts because you know that your audience will understand.

> **Helpful Hint**
> If you are writing a more formal text, using an informal sentence will stand out as awkward. While editing, look for and remove slang terms or contractions that aren't consistent with the rest of your writing.

Formal writing is required for many professional or academic genres. In these situations, you use more complex sentence structures and technical terms and rarely use personal pronouns like *I* and *you*. Even for a formal text, however, you must write in a way that's natural to you. Don't make your writing complicated just to sound fancy.

Formal writing also follows the rules and conventions of Standard English. All of the text should be free of sentence, punctuation, and spelling errors. The following types of language may be common in informal writing, but they should be avoided in formal writing:

- **Contractions**: shortened versions of words and phrases, such as *can't* and *isn't*
- **Slang**: casual words or expressions specific to a particular group of people, like teenagers or sports fans, such as *on fleek* or *fandom*
- **Clichés**: popular phrases that have been overused, such as, "The early bird gets the worm"
- **Idioms**: phrases—unique to a certain language—that have become clichés, such as the common English saying, "It costs an arm and a leg"
- **Textspeak**: abbreviations, emoticons, and other phrases used in text messages or social media, such as *g2g* and *ttyl*

> **Helpful Hint**
> Many people use multiple end punctuation points in informal writing. Remember, multiple exclamation points, question marks, or a mixture of the two is considered inappropriate in formal writing.

Remember that your unique writer's voice can come out even in formal writing assignments. Think about the last time you dressed up for a special occasion. Even though your clothing was more formal than usual, it still reflected your individual personality. Your writing should do the same thing. Just because you can't use contractions or slang doesn't mean that you have to sound like a robot.

Complexity

Another factor in writing style is the complexity of your words and sentences. Complexity doesn't have to mean "complicated." Instead, **complexity** just means that your writing has many connected parts.

Sometimes, complicated words are unavoidable. If you're writing about a topic that involves technical or academic terms, you will probably need to use terms that are unfamiliar. However, these words are there for a purpose. Don't use complicated words just because they seem "smarter." Your writing will end up being clunky or incorrect.

> **Helpful Hint**
> Using a thesaurus while writing is a great way to add complexity to your language. However, pay attention to the meanings of the words. Just because two words are synonyms, it doesn't guarantee that their meanings and connotations are the same. For example, even if *essay* and *dictionary* are listed in a thesaurus as synonyms, most everyone would agree that they are actually very different.

Before you substitute a more complex word, ask yourself the following questions:

> Would I ever use this word in normal conversation?
> Do I understand exactly what this word means?
> Does this word seem consistent with the rest of my writing?

If the answer to any of these questions is *no*, then you should probably use a different word.

In a similar way, overly-complex sentences can make a text awkward or difficult for your reader to follow. Complicated sentences can be caused by any of the following reasons.

Prepositional Phrases

A **prepositional phrase** is a group of words that starts with a **preposition** and ends with a noun or pronoun.

To learn more about prepositions, see Lesson 4.5.

If you add too many prepositional phrases to a sentence, the reader might have a difficult time finding the **main idea**. Look at this example:

> In situations like the one that the committee of impartial voters selected, the choice between right and wrong becomes complicated by the opinions and suggestions of parties that are outside of the committee's control.

> The **subject** and **verb** in this sentence are both buried under all of the prepositional phrases. If all of this information is truly necessary, consider breaking up the sentence into two separate sentences.

Dependent Clauses

Dependent clauses are groups of related words that contain a subject and verb but do not express a complete thought. Just like prepositional phrases, too many dependent clauses can get in the way of your meaning. Think about the following example:

> Although the position seemed like a good fit, I was nervous because the job that I had before was in a completely different field that I didn't know very well.

To learn more about dependent clauses, see Lesson 4.7.

Passive Voice

In **passive voice**, the subject of the sentence is receiving the action of the verb. In **active voice**, the subject is doing the action of the verb. Sentences using active voice are more direct than sentences using passive voice. Look at these two examples:

Active	The county sheriff filed a report with the court clerk.
Passive	The report was filed with the court clerk by the county sheriff.

Both of these sentences have the same basic meaning. However, the sentence in passive voice seems to be talking around the subject rather than clearly stating its point.

To learn more about active and passive voice, see Lesson 5.7.

Remember that *complicated* doesn't necessarily equal *good*. The best writing can take a confusing topic and make it understandable to the audience.

To make sure your sentences are clear, read your text out loud and mark any areas that are difficult to read. If you find yourself running out of breath or stumbling over your words, this may be a good area to revise.

> **Helpful Hint**
> Many people tend to speak more directly than they write. If you are having a difficult time changing an overly complicated sentence, consider recording yourself explaining the information out loud.

Lesson Wrap-up

Key Terms

Active Voice: when a sentence is written so that the subject is performing an action

Audience: the people who read your writing

Cliché: a popular phrase that has been overused

Complexity: when a text has many connected parts

Contraction: a phrase that has been shortened into one word

Dependent Clause: a word group that contains a subject and a verb but does not express a complete thought

Entertaining Text: a text that explores a topic or event in a creative or humorous way

Formality: the way a text conforms to certain standards

Genre: a type of writing

Idiom: a phrase—unique to a certain language—that has become a cliché

Informative Text: a text that gives the audience information about a topic

Main Idea: the statement or argument that an author tries to communicate

Passive Voice: when a sentence is written so that the subject is receiving an action

Persuasive Text: a text that convinces its audience to adopt a belief or take an action

Preposition: a word that shows a relationship among people, places, things, events, and ideas

Prepositional Phrase: a group of related words that starts with a preposition and ends with a noun or pronoun

Pronoun: a word that takes the place of a noun in a sentence

Purpose: the goal of a text

Reflective Text: a text that shares a personal experience or belief

Slang: casual words or expressions specific to a particular group of people

Subject: the person, place, thing, event, or idea a sentence is about

Textspeak: abbreviations, emoticons, and other phrases used in text messages or social media

Tone: the positive, negative, or neutral attitude that an author expresses about a topic

Verb: a word that represents an action, relationship, or state of being

Lesson 5.2
Using an Appropriate Tone

Think of a time when you had to give a friend or family member bad news. In addition to choosing your words carefully, you probably used your voice inflections, facial expressions, and hand gestures to show your sympathy. Now imagine that you had to share that same news in a letter. How would you communicate your feelings in words only?

Because you can't use gestures or facial expressions when you write, you have to use tone. **Tone** is the positive, negative, or neutral attitude that your writing expresses about a topic.

This lesson will discuss three aspects of using tone:

Word Choice
Details
Inconsistent Tone

Helpful Hint
Remember that your tone should always fit the **purpose** and **audience** of your writing. A text message to a friend would use a very different tone from an email to a hiring manager.

To learn more about how purpose and audience affect your writing style, see Lesson 5.1.

Reflection Questions
Have you ever talked to someone whose tone didn't match what they were actually saying? How did this affect the interaction?

Word Choice

The first way to communicate tone is through word choice. All words have positive, negative, or neutral feelings attached to them. Think about these examples:

> The parents' visit was spontaneous.

> The parents' visit was uninvited.

> The parents' visit was unexpected.

> In these sentences, the word *spontaneous* sounds more positive than the word *uninvited*, although the definitions of both words are similar. The last sentence uses the word *unexpected*, which sounds neutral.

As you write, you must carefully select words that will accurately reflect the tone you want to communicate. An essay on the benefits of organic produce should use a positive and confident tone. On the other hand, a research paper on the health risks of secondhand smoke should use a more serious tone. If the purpose of your writing is to **inform**, a neutral and objective tone is usually best.

Be careful if you decide to use words that communicate extremely positive or negative feelings, as this could make your audience believe that you are a biased or overly emotional author.

On Your Own

Read the following paragraphs and circle the one that seems more reliable.

> *Looking Backward* is a misogynistic book that fails to represent women. The only time the author even discusses women's roles in modern society occurs during one miniscule chapter. Before this, no one knows anything about Edith other than her looks. Typically, the ladies are pushed out, leaving the big strong men to discuss important matters by themselves (79, 128). Conditions for the women in Bellamy's vision of the year 2000 are just as bad as in 1887.

> *Looking Backward* represents women unfairly by failing to represent them at all. The only full examination of women's roles in modern society occurs during one short

chapter. Before this, little is known about Edith beyond her physical beauty. Just as in the nineteenth century, the ladies retire early, leaving the men to discuss important matters by themselves (79, 128). Conditions for the women in Bellamy's vision of the year 2000 remain almost unchanged from those of 1887.

In the first paragraph, the author chooses words that communicate an aggressive and disapproving tone. Not only does this type of writing hurt the **credibility** of the author, it could also anger the audience. The second paragraph does a much better job of communicating its message in a specific, yet reasonable way.

> Group Activity
> As a group, discuss the tone of the following words. What similar words would convey the same meaning with a different tone?
>
> chat   quirky   walk   cautious   lengthy   nosy

On Your Own

Read the following paragraph and identify the sentence that does not the most appropriate tone.

> The leadership meeting tomorrow is mandatory. Many of the company's executives will be in attendance, so please be prompt. Also, ensure you have your laptops and up-to-date weekly reports when you arrive. The really early meeting tomorrow in the AM will be an awesome chance for us to chat about the looming lay-offs. Thank you in advance for keeping your schedule flexible.

Details

The second way to convey tone is through the details that you choose to include in or exclude from your writing. Every time you write, you make choices about what you want to communicate. Your job as an author is to select the information that will fulfill your purpose both honestly and effectively.

If you include mainly negative details about a topic, the tone of your writing will be more negative. If you include mainly positive details, the tone of your writing will be more positive. Think about these examples:

> My son-in-law Paul just became an astrophysicist at MIT, one of the most prestigious schools in the country.

> My son-in-law Paul just started an entry-level position at a school on the East Coast.

> My son-in-law Paul just became an assistant professor of astrophysics at MIT.

> The first example sentence includes a number of details that are intended to impress the audience, while the second sentence excludes details to make Paul's job seem less important. The third sentence seems to strike a good balance between the two.

Reflection Questions
How is tone expressed in an image? How is this different from or similar to the tone of a text?

Inconsistent Tone

Writing that is inconsistent in tone can come across as awkward. Think about the tone of the following example:

> Arthur Young's essay, "The Example of France, a Warning to Britain," expresses both the author's original admiration of the French Revolution and his subsequent disappointment in what the revolt became. Young remarks that by overthrowing their government, the French embraced chaos and mob rule. According to Young, the people of England need to learn from France's example in order to prevent similar tragedies. Obviously, Young is completely wrong because the citizens of a country shouldn't have to support a corrupt government that ignores the problems of common people.

> The overall tone of this paragraph could be described as neutral. However, the last sentence includes words and details that are very negative. This passage sounds awkward because the last sentence doesn't match the tone used throughout the rest of the paragraph.

To identify a shift in tone, follow these steps:

Checklist: Tone Consistency

☐ Read the text out loud to yourself.

☐ Decide if the overall tone is positive, negative, or neutral.

☐ Identify sentences that don't match the tone of the text.

☐ Look for words or details that could be altered or eliminated.

On Your Own

Read the following paragraph and use the previous steps to identify the sentence that has an inconsistent tone.

> Student teaching was a positive and rewarding experience. The students I taught were able to teach me so much more than I could teach them. Being in such a supportive school with hands-on parents made the semester move quickly. My principal critiqued me every single time she came into my room, which forced me to learn how to ignore negative leaders and press on. Student teaching showed me that I can imagine myself in no other profession, and I will be happy to one day have a classroom of my own.

Reflection Questions
Think about the sentence in the last paragraph that had a negative tone. What words and details made this sentence negative? Is there a better way to construct the sentence so it shares the same information but in a more positive way?

Lesson Wrap-up

Key Terms

Audience: the people who read your writing

Credibility: what makes someone or something believable

Informative Text: a text that gives the audience information about a topic

Purpose: the goal of a text

Tone: the positive, negative, or neutral attitude that an author expresses about a topic

Lesson 5.3
Maintaining Consistency in Tense and Person

Words can indicate the past, present, or future, as well as perspective; that's why it's important for them to be consistent. Photos courtesy of Wikimedia Commons (https://commons.wikimedia.org/wiki/Main_Page).

Have you ever read a book that jumped from one point in time to another? Maybe the first chapter was set in the future, while the second chapter was set in the past. Authors sometimes use flashbacks and flashforwards to make a dramatic story more interesting. As the reader, you must piece the story together as you observe the events from different points in time.

Similarly, some stories unfold through the different perspectives of the main characters. In the first half of the book, you might observe the events from one character's point of view; then, in the second half, you see the events from another character's point of view.

While these shifts in time and perspective can make a fictional story more interesting, the same strategies in a text for work or school would confuse your audience. This is because in academic and professional writing, time and perspective are usually the same throughout the text. Using a consistent writing style will help ensure that your main idea is as clear as possible.

This lesson will help you avoid two types of inconsistencies in your writing:

Tense

Person

Tense

Take a look at the following sentence and decide whether the action takes place in the past, present, or future:

> The experienced surfer was caught off guard when a huge wave overtook him.

> You could probably tell that the action took place in the past, but how did you know?

Group Activity

As a group, try rewriting each of the following sentences in a different tense:

She went on to become one of the most successful entrepreneurs in Silicon Valley.

Did you turn it in to your instructor?

Initially, the authorities refused to believe them.

Based on the group activity, what did you notice about changing the tense? What word determines the tense of the sentence?

Verbs use different **tenses** to tell the audience when an action took place: past, present, or future.

PAST	PRESENT	FUTURE
hated	hate	will hate
ran	run	will run
took	take	will take

Switching tenses in the middle of the same thought is awkward. Look at this example:

> The psychology experiment began by rewarding the mouse with a treat each time he successfully pressed the button. After a short time, the mouse moved directly from the treat to the button constantly; he wanted the reward. He chews the treat and looks at the button.

> Did you notice the shift? In the first two sentences, all of the action is happening in the past. Then, an awkward shift to the present interrupts the flow of the writing. To correct this mistake, the writer should change the verb tenses in the last sentence so that they match the rest of the passage.

Past, Present, and Future Tense

Sometimes, writing in the **present tense** is the best way to communicate your message. In a narrative or story, you may use present tense because you want the readers to feel as though the events are unraveling right before their eyes.

The present tense may also be used in academic writing for analyzing a piece of literature or making an argument. For example, an essay about themes in *The Crucible* might include a sentence like this:

> Arthur Miller explores humanity's selfishness and fear by describing the townspeople's unfounded accusations against their neighbors.

> This example uses present tense because the author is currently sharing his or her opinions about the play.

The **past tense** is used to report an event or reflect on a past experience. Many fictional books are also written in the past.

Here's an example of past tense from an article about voter turnout in a local election:

> Seventy-three percent of registered voters participated in last night's election; voter turnout was at an all-time high.

> The voters are not currently voting; this event took place in the past.

Helpful Hint
The present and past tenses are usually logical options for most writing.

Further Resources
Talking about the past using the present tense is sometimes called using the "historical present" tense, and it's used more frequently than you might think. Check out this podcast from Slate's "Lexicon Valley" to learn about the historical present in every type of media from Charlotte Brontë to *Seinfeld* (http://www.slate.com/articles/podcasts/lexicon_valley/2012/07/lexicon_valley_the_historical_present_in_seinfeld_and_the_novels_of_charlotte_bronte.html).

The **future tense** is used to describe plans or instructions.

> During our next meeting, we will discuss decorating ideas for our upcoming fashion show.

Regardless of the tense you use, be as consistent as possible. You don't want to confuse your readers by switching back and forth between two different points in time.

Helpful Hint
Although certain tenses are more appropriate for specific types of writing, your instructor might have guidelines for the tense that you should use in a writing assignment. Always remember to double-check the instructions.

To learn more about verb tenses, see Lesson 4.3.

Appropriate Tense Shifts

Occasionally, shifts in tense are unavoidable.

You might need to describe events that happened at two different points in time:

> We took inventory of the women's department last week, and we are working through the men's department now.

> The first part of this example happened in the past, and the second part is happening in the present. In this case, it makes sense to use two different tenses in the same sentence.

Similarly, you might need to show that a current or future action is the direct result of a past action:

> Josh left the towels out in the rain last night, so Karen is drying them in the laundry room now.

> In this example, the towels were left outside in the past, so they are now being dried in the present.

Finally, tenses can also shift within a paragraph. Consider this example:

> I just realized that my homemade cupcakes taste funny because they are missing some ingredients. Next time, I will pay closer attention to the recipe.

> Just a few moments ago, the speaker realized that the cupcakes currently taste funny because they are missing ingredients. In the future, the speaker will do a better job following the recipe.

On Your Own

Read the following passage and identify the paragraph that contains a shift in tense.

> Ralph tries to fill the role of authority figure by maintaining the signal fire and building shelters. He also assigns tasks to different groups of boys to ensure that they live in a civilized fashion. Unfortunately, since Ralph is only a young boy, his authority is not respected as much as an adult's authority would be respected.

> Piggy plays the role of the father figure, which is reflected in his appearance. He wears thick glasses, and his hair does not seem to grow. He also provides the voice of reason on the island. When the "littluns" got scared and started talking about the beast, Piggy tried to calm their fears. He maintains order by explaining that life is based on science. When Jack gets the rest of the boys frenzied about hunting, Piggy exhibits common sense by refusing to participate.

Person

In addition to consistent verb tenses, good writing also includes consistency in **person**, or point of view. There are three different points of view that you can use:

First Person	The narrator or writer is a member of the story or event.
Second Person	The reader is a member of the story or event. Questions can be directed to the reader.
Third Person	The narrator or writer is outside of the story or event. This writing strives to be unbiased.

On Your Own

Read the sentences below and identify the sentence that has a third-person point of view.

> You will want to begin the assignment by closely reading the article.

> We were able to determine that our mistake took place during phase one.

> The inmates were accused of starting the fire while the guards denied all involvement.

Personal pronouns can be first-person, second-person, or third-person. All **nouns** are considered third-person.

To determine point of view, keep an eye out for these pronouns:

POINT OF VIEW	SINGULAR	PLURAL
First Person	I, me, my, mine	we, us, our, ours
Second Person	you, your, yours	you, your, yours
Third Person	he, him, his, she, her, hers, it, its	they, them, their, theirs

To learn more about pronouns and antecedents, see Lessons 4.2 and 4.10.

On Your Own

Read the following passage and identify all the first-person pronouns in the passage.

> On the last day of my sophomore year in college, my parents told me that we were going to take a family road trip that would start the next morning. When they told me, they had already packed their suitcases and mapped out the route. I dumped the contents of my dorm room into a bag, and we piled into the car. It was the beginning of a terrible summer.

Different perspectives are appropriate for different types of writing. When writing or revising, double-check any assignment guidelines to make sure that you are using the correct one. Here are some examples of commonly used points of view in different genres:

- **First person**: Informal writing and personal reflections
- **Second person**: Instructions and advice
- **Third person**: Formal **academic writing** and professional writing

On Your Own

In the table below, rewrite each of the following sentences so that they use a different point of view:

Original	Re-written
Do you believe pets should be allowed in restaurants?	
The biker sped past us so quickly that we dropped our bags.	
It's important to check over your data before submitting your lab report.	

If your writing includes frequent shifts from one point of view to another, it can be difficult for your audience to follow.

Consider the following examples:

> After the graduates received their degrees, 80% of us went on to obtain jobs in the field of engineering.
>
> The words *graduates* and *their* are third-person, but the pronoun *us* is first-person. This sentence is incorrect.
>
> To fix this shift in person, the word *us* should be changed to *them*.
>
> After the graduates received their degrees, 80% of them went on to obtain jobs in the field of engineering.

Here's another example:

> If an employee wants a promotion, you will have to earn it.
>
> In this sentence, the **subject** *employee* is third-person. The use of the second-person pronoun *you* makes the point of view inconsistent. Unless another employee's promotion depends on your performance, you should change the word *you* to the term *he or she*.

On Your Own

Read the corrected versions of the previous sentence and decide which person (first, second, or third) is being used.

> If you want a promotion, you will have to earn it.

- ☐ First Person
- ☐ Second Person
- ☐ Third Person

> If an employee wants a promotion, he or she will have to earn it.

- ☐ First Person
- ☐ Second Person
- ☐ Third Person

> If I want a promotion, I will have to earn it.

- ☐ First Person
- ☐ Second Person
- ☐ Third Person

Point of view should also be consistent within paragraphs. Read the following example:

> I will never forget my first trip to Disney World when I was ten years old. I was so excited to try out all of the rides. You got a pass to access different rides in different parks. I also wanted to meet all the characters and get pictures with them.
>
> In this passage, the writer shifts the perspective from first-person to second-person.

To correct the error, revise the third sentence so that it uses a first-person pronoun:

I will never forget my first trip to Disney World when I was ten years old. I was so excited to try out all of the rides. I got a pass to access different rides in different parks. I also wanted to meet all the characters and get pictures with them.

Helpful Hint

Hearing your own writing is often a useful way to detect a shift in both tense and person. To check for consistent tense and person, try reading your paper aloud. You might hear issues that you missed while you were proofreading silently.

On Your Own

Read the following paragraph and identify the sentence that is inconsistent in person.

Resilience is a trait that every successful person must have. Those who become successful at something often have to first fail a number of times before they reach their goal. Taylor Swift was bullied in middle school, and Katy Perry was dropped by three record labels. Both women had to overcome obstacles before achieving their goals. There have been many times I have had to pick myself up and dust myself off while trying to reach my goals. Being resilient allows a person to make mistakes, learn from them, and eventually reach his or her goal through hard work and persistence.

Lesson Wrap-up

Key Terms

Future Tense: a verb tense used to describe an action that has not yet taken place or to describe plans or instructions

Noun: a word that represents a person, place, thing, event, or idea

Past Tense: a verb tense used to report a past event or reflect on a past experience

Person: the point of view—first-, second-, or third-person—indicated by the form a word takes on in a sentence

Personal Pronoun: a pronoun that renames a specific person, animal, object, or place

Present Tense: a verb tense used to describe an event or action that is happening now

Pronoun: a word that takes the place of a noun in a sentence

Subject: the person, place, thing, event, or idea a sentence is about

Tense: how a verb indicates when it took place: past, present, or future

Verb: a word that represents an action, relationship, or state of being

Lesson 5.4
Correcting Misplaced and Dangling Modifiers

Modifiers are words or groups of words that add extra information to a sentence. The most common types of modifiers are **adjectives** and **adverbs**. However, some **phrases** and even some clauses can also be considered modifiers.

Here is an example of each type:

Adjective	All of the varsity team students are experienced athletes.
Adverb	Seasoned Minnesotans rarely dream of living in a warmer climate.
Phrase	As she pulled out of the driveway, Bridget realized she'd forgotten something.

All the modifiers in these sentences give additional meaning and clarity. Look at those same sentences without modifiers:

> All of the students are experienced athletes.

> Seasoned Minnesotans dream of living in a warmer climate.

> Bridget realized she'd forgotten something.

> In the first and second examples, the meanings of the sentences are completely changed. The third sentence still makes sense; however, it doesn't have the same effect as the original version.

The purpose of modifiers is to add extra meaning or clarity to sentences. Using a modifier incorrectly, however, will result in a sentence that is unclear and confusing. Think about this example:

> Kate saw a mouse taking out the trash last night.

> Taking out the trash last night, Kate saw a mouse.

> Which meaning is correct? Most likely, Kate didn't see a mouse taking out a tiny mouse-sized bag of trash. By placing the modifier as close to *Kate* as possible, you can ensure that your audience understands exactly what you're trying to say.

This lesson will help you correct two types of incorrect modifiers:

Misplaced Modifiers
Dangling Modifiers

Misplaced Modifiers

A **misplaced modifier** is too far away from what it modifies. This makes the sentence potentially confusing to your audience. Here's an example:

> Daniel saw a strange-looking bird using his new binoculars.

> This modifier is misplaced because it suggests that a bird was using Daniel's new binoculars.

> To fix this sentence, move the modifier as close as possible to the word being modified.

> Using his new binoculars, Daniel saw a strange-looking bird.

> Helpful Hint
> Don't forget to add in the proper punctuation when changing the location of modifiers. If a modifying phrase is at the beginning of a sentence, it should usually be followed by a comma.

One-word modifiers should also be placed near the words they modify. Consider this sentence:

> The meerkat hid under a thick blanket of ferns, shaking.

> The meaning of this sentence would be much clearer to the audience if the modifier *shaking* were placed closer to the word it modifies.

> Shaking, the meerkat hid under a thick blanket of ferns.

Sometimes, misplaced modifiers are harder to catch because both meanings seem realistic. Consider these two versions of the same sentence:

> The books in the library cannot be purchased.

> The books cannot be purchased in the library.

> In the first version of the sentence, none of the books in the library building are for sale. In the second version, the books that are for sale can only be purchased outside of the library. The intended meaning of your sentence will determine which version is the correct choice.

Here's a slightly trickier example:

> The hiring manager nearly had to review one hundred applications.

> The hiring manager had to review nearly one hundred applications.

> The first version of the sentence implies that the hiring manager didn't have to look through any of the applications. The second version, on the other hand, states that the hiring manager did look through the applications, all ninety-nine of them.

> Reflection Questions
> Simply changing the location of a modifier can transform the meaning of a sentence. Can you think of any specific sentences where changing the location of the modifier creates a funny mistake?

Dangling Modifiers

The second type of incorrect modifier is a **dangling modifier**. In these cases, the word that is being modified is completely missing from the sentence. Look at this example:

> After reading through the police report, the mistake became abundantly clear.

> The modifier in this sentence is dangling because the sentence never identifies who is reading through the police report.

> To correct this sentence, simply add the missing information as close to the modifier as possible.

> After reading through the police report, the investigator discovered the problem.

> This sentence is now correct because the audience knows that the investigator is the one reading through the police report.

On Your Own

Read the following sentences and identify the one with correct modifiers.

> Making the bed, my sheets were untucked at the bottom.

> Since announcing his presidential campaign, the phones have been ringing all day.

> After finishing the exam, students began collecting their materials.

> **Helpful Hint**
> As you proofread your own writing, it's easy to skip over mistakes without even realizing it. Consider asking a friend to proofread your work and help you find misplaced and dangling modifiers.

Lesson Wrap-up

Key Terms

Adjective: a word that describes a noun or pronoun

Adverb: a word that describes a verb, adjective, or another adverb

Complete Sentence: a sentence that contains at least one subject and predicate and expresses a complete thought

Dangling Modifier: a word modifying another word that is missing from the sentence

Misplaced Modifier: a modifier that is too far away from the word it modifies

Modifier: a word or word group that describes or adds to another word in a sentence

Phrase: a word group that adds to the meaning of a sentence but does not express a complete thought and usually lacks a subject and a verb

Lesson 5.5
Using Word and Sentence Variety

Have you ever had trouble keeping yourself focused on reading a text? Maybe that's because it looked like the following **paragraph**:

> Alyssa had a bad night. Her work shift ran late. Alyssa came home late at night. It was very dark. The front door was locked. Alyssa could not find her keys. It started to rain. She looked for the spare. She couldn't find it anywhere. She had to bang on the door. Her parents woke up. They were angry. Alyssa had missed her curfew.

> While the paragraph tells you what happened, it probably doesn't hold your interest because every sentence is short and simple, which makes the entire paragraph boring and choppy.

Read this version of the same paragraph:

> Alyssa had a bad night after her work shift ran late. By the time she got home, it was dark outside, and the front door was locked. She was searching for her keys when it started to rain. Feeling scared and

defeated, Alyssa banged on the door. When her parents woke up, they were angry. Alyssa had missed her curfew.

Even though both examples contain essentially the same sentences, the second paragraph uses a variety of words and sentence structures to keep the reader engaged.

As a writer, your goal should always be grabbing the attention of your readers. Even if the material isn't exciting, you can still find ways to make your writing interesting and engaging.

In this lesson, you will learn how to introduce more variety into your words, phrases, and clauses.

Group Activity
As a group, discuss the effect of engaging writing. Does it make a difference whether or not a text is interesting to its readers?

Words

To avoid repetition in your writing, you should substitute words with pronouns and synonyms.

Pronouns are words that replace **nouns**. Using pronouns can help you avoid repeating the same noun over and over again. Consider this sentence:

Sally clipped the leash on Sally's dog, and then Sally walked the dog to the park.

To make this sentence more interesting and less repetitive, use pronouns as a substitute for the word *Sally*.

Sally clipped the leash on her dog, and then she walked the dog to the park.

Helpful Hint
Whenever you replace a noun with a pronoun, make sure that the relationship between the two words is clear.

To learn more about using pronouns as replacements for nouns, see Lessons 4.10 and 4.11.

Another strategy for introducing new words into your writing is using synonyms. **Synonyms** are words that share the same meaning as other words. For example, the word *vehicle* is a synonym for *automobile* or *car*. Synonyms are a useful tool for adding variety to your writing because they help you avoid repeating nouns and pronouns.

Here are some commonly used words and their synonyms.

Job
- Occupation
- Employment
- Position
- Duty

Tired
- Exhausted
- Fatigued
- Sleepy
- Worn out

Happy
- Joyful
- Blissful
- Delighted
- Pleased

Read the following passage:

Janice has always wanted to own a home of her own. When she was fifteen, her father lost his job, and her parents were unable to make payments on the family's home. As a result, Janice found herself

> staying in the homes of other relatives, moving from home to home every few weeks. To Janice, a home is more than a building: it's a symbol of security and safety.

> In this paragraph, the word *home* is repeated six times in only four sentences. This repetition makes the paragraph sound repetitive and choppy.

Here's an improved version of that same paragraph:

> Janice has always wanted to own a home of her own. When she was seven, her father lost his job, and her parents were unable to make payments on the family's house. As a result, Janice found herself staying in the apartments of other relatives, moving from residence to residence every few weeks. To Janice, a home is more than a building: it's a symbol of security and safety.

On Your Own

Look back at these paragraphs. What synonyms are used for the word home? Are there any others you can think of? Write them in the table below.

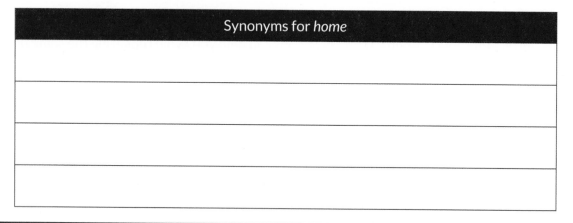

Synonyms for *home*

Helpful Hint
Although using synonyms is a quick and easy way to add variety to your writing, don't try to replace every word with a synonym. Sometimes there is no good substitute for the word. This is especially true when you are writing about a subject with technical terms and definitions.

As you search for synonyms to use in your own writing, notice how a synonym may have a slightly different meaning from one of its other synonyms. For example, you could be *hungry* but not necessarily *starving*. Be sure to choose a synonym that fits best with the meaning of your sentence.

Reflection Questions
In what situations would repeating a word be preferable to using a pronoun or synonym?

One final way to add interesting words to your sentences is to add **adjectives** that end in *-ed* or **adverbs** that end in *-ly* to the beginning of the sentence. Look at these examples:

> Unfortunately, Samantha didn't get the job.

> Exhausted, the foreman collapsed into bed after working an eighteen-hour shift.

Phrases

Another strategy for using variety in your writing is replacing single words with descriptive **phrases**. Read this example:

> The town watchman patrolled the same route every evening. At exactly 9:30 p.m., you would see the old man shuffling down Main Street. Although I never spoke to him directly, I can still picture his stooped form making its way through the streets of the town.

> In this paragraph, the noun *watchman* is replaced with the phrases *old man* and *his stooped form*. These phrases serve two purposes. First, they reduce the repetitive use of *watchman*. Second, they paint a vivid and memorable picture of what happened in the story.

Be cautious when adding phrases to your writing. Too many can be confusing and wordy. When you do use a phrase, make sure that it is adding meaning to the sentence, not just increasing the word count. Look at the following example:

> A large, cylindrical container that is filled with oil fell off of a truck and stopped traffic for five hours.

> The example uses a lot of words to say very little. In this case, it would be better to use the descriptive noun phrase *oil barrel* instead of *a large, cylindrical container that is filled with oil*.

You can also add new phrases to the beginning of a sentence to add variety and interest. Here are a few examples:

> Talking loudly, Alexis disrupted the yoga class as she walked past.

> During the drought last summer, the flower garden withered and died.

> To find the best deal on a new car, Hannah visited several dealerships.

Remember that any time you add a phrase to the beginning of a sentence, you must add a **comma**.

Clauses

A final way that you can add interest to your writing is varying the structures of your sentences.

Independent clauses are **complete sentences** that stand on their own. They are often called **simple sentences**.

> Jing was studying to be a special education teacher.

It's fine for some of your sentences to be short and simple. However, for more variety, you can join two independent clauses.

Combining two completely unrelated sentences will be confusing to your readers. When you join sentences, make sure that they are closely related.

Read these two sentences:

> Danielle wanted to go to the movies. She planned to go with her roommate.

You can combine these sentences using a comma and a **coordinating conjunction**.

> Danielle wanted to go to the movies, and she planned to go with her roommate.

> In this example, the coordinating conjunction *and* joins two simple sentences into a **compound sentence**.

Helpful Hint
To remember the seven coordinating conjunctions, use the acronym FANBOYS.

For	And	Nor	But	Or	Yet	So

Another way to combine these sentences is by using a semicolon. **Semicolons** can be used to combine two related, independent clauses.

> Danielle wanted to go to the movies; she planned to go with her roommate.

To add more variety, you can also combine two sentences by making one a dependent clause. **Dependent clauses** cannot stand alone because they do not express a complete thought. To make a dependent clause, add a **subordinating conjunction** like *although* or *because* to the beginning of a sentence.

SUBORDINATING CONJUNCTIONS			
after	because	once	when
although	even though	since	while
as	if	until	

Consider the following example:

> Shauna paid her cell phone bill late. Her service was disconnected.

> Because Shauna paid her cell phone bill late, her service was disconnected.

> Combining these sentences makes the message clearer. The subordinating conjunction *because* shows the relationship between the two ideas.

Note that when a dependent clause introduces an independent clause, a comma separates the two.

Dependent clauses can also be placed at the end of a sentence:

> Carson never liked children. Once he had a child of his own, he did like children.

> Carson never liked children until he had a child of his own.

> Notice that you won't use a comma to separate the two clauses if the dependent clause comes after the independent clause.

To learn more about coordination and subordination, see Lessons 4.6 and 5.6.

On Your Own

Read the following paragraph and look for ways to add word and sentence variety. Then, use the table below to rewrite the paragraph with your changes.

> The most significant result of the Boston Tea Party and the Intolerable Acts was the formation of the Continental Congress. In 1774, fifty-five men met in Philadelphia, PA, to discuss the Boston Tea Party and the Intolerable Acts. Some of the notable men were Samuel Adams, George Washington, and Patrick Henry. The men met for seven weeks. John Adams convinced the men of the need for a confederation. He stressed, above all, unification of purpose within the colonies. The first Continental Congress did not directly support a revolution. The Continental Congress laid the framework for a revolution by unifying the colonies. The Continental Congress also drew up documents such as the Declaration of Rights.

Lesson Wrap-up

Key Terms

Adjective: a word that describes a noun or pronoun

Adverb: a word that describes a verb, an adjective, or another adverb

Comma: a punctuation mark used to separate items in a list; join compound sentences; mark introductory words, phrases, and clauses; add extra or unnecessary details to a sentence; and separate similar adjectives

Complete Sentence: a sentence that contains at least one subject and one verb and expresses a complete thought

Compound Sentence: two independent clauses joined by a comma and a conjunction

Coordinating Conjunction: a conjunction that connects words or word groups of equal importance in a sentence

Dependent Clause: a word group that contains a subject and a verb but does not express a complete thought

Independent Clause: a group of words with a subject and a verb that expresses a complete thought

Noun: a word that represents a person, place, thing, event, or idea

Paragraph: a short piece of writing that focuses on one main idea

Phrase: a word group that adds to the meaning of a sentence but does not form a complete thought and usually lacks a subject and a verb

Pronoun: a word that takes the place of a noun in a sentence

Semicolon: a punctuation mark used to combine two independent clauses and separate long list items

Simple Sentence: a sentence made up of one independent clause

Subordinating Conjunction: a conjunction that introduces a dependent clause

Synonym: a word that has the same meaning as another word

Lesson 5.6
Using Coordination, Subordination, and Parallelism

When you write, one of your main goals should be to show connections between ideas. Some ideas are equally important to your meaning, while others are less important. The way that you structure a sentence can help establish those relationships and make your writing flow smoothly.

Read the following examples. Which **paragraph** is easier to read and understand?

> We the people of the United States, in order to form a more perfect union, because we want to establish justice, insuring domestic tranquility, provide for the common defense, to promote the general welfare, and we secure the blessings of liberty to ourselves and our posterity, do ordain and establish this Constitution for the United States of America.

> We the people of the United States, in order to form a more perfect union, establish justice, insure domestic tranquility, provide for the common defense, promote the general welfare, and secure the blessings of liberty to ourselves and our posterity, do ordain and establish this Constitution for the United States of America.

> As you can see, the structure of these paragraphs greatly affects their meaning and flow. The first example is difficult to read, and the relationship between the ideas is unclear. In the second example, it's much easier to see that all of the ideas are of equal importance.

In this lesson, you will learn three ways to add structure to your writing:

Coordination
Subordination
Parallelism

> To learn about avoiding errors when combining sentences, see Lesson 4.8.

Coordination

Coordination is used to link two related ideas. Look at the following sentences:

> Marco is a football fanatic.

> He likes baseball even better.

Because these sentences are so closely related, they can be combined to form a **compound sentence**:

> Marco is a football fanatic, but he likes baseball even better.

> In this example, two sentences have been combined using a **comma** and a **coordinating conjunction**, which is a specific type of conjunction used to link ideas of equal importance.

> **Helpful Hint**
> To remember the seven coordinating conjunctions, use the acronym FANBOYS.
> For   And   Nor   But   Or   Yet   So

To learn more about conjunctions, see Lesson 4.6.

Sometimes, the relationship between two ideas is so clear, you don't need to use a **conjunction**. Think about the following examples:

> Ask not what your country can do for you, but ask what you can do for your country.

> Ask not what your country can do for you; ask what you can do for your country.

If you read these sentences aloud, you may notice that the second sentence sounds better. Because the relationship between both sentences is so obvious, you can simply join them with a **semicolon**. Using a comma and a coordinating conjunction in this case is both unnecessary and awkward.

> **Helpful Hint**
> Whenever you combine two sentences, you must join them with either a semicolon or a comma with a coordinating conjunction. If you use just a comma or just a conjunction, your sentence is grammatically incorrect.

Subordination

While coordination is used to connect related ideas of *equal* importance, **subordination** is used to connect related ideas of *unequal* importance. For example, consider how you might combine the following sentences:

> The children couldn't finish their puzzle. Some of the pieces were missing.

Using coordination to combine these sentences doesn't work because the ideas are unequal. In this case, you need to subordinate one of the sentences by adding a subordinating conjunction:

> The children couldn't finish their puzzle because some of the pieces were missing.

OR:

> Because some of the pieces were missing, the children couldn't finish their puzzle.

> In this sentence, the **subordinating conjunction** *because* combines two clauses.

SUBORDINATING CONJUNCTIONS			
after	because	once	when
although	even though	since	while
as	if	until	

Parallelism

You might already be familiar with the term *parallel* from geometry class, where you learned that parallel lines share certain mathematical characteristics. As a result, they run side-by-side without ever intersecting.

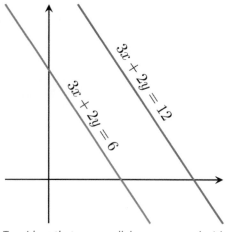

*Two ideas that are parallel are expressed with
similar words, phrases, or clauses.*

In writing, **parallelism** is used to create balance between two or more related ideas by using similarly-structured words, **phrases**, or clauses. Consider this sentence:

> My sister dyes her hair bright purple; a mohawk is how my brother wears his hair.

The two halves of this example are **independent clauses** that express related information. In each, the speaker describes a sibling's hairstyle. However, the clauses are structured differently, making it difficult to see the connection between the two ideas.

Changing the second half of the sentence will make it easier to read.

> My sister dyes her hair bright purple; my brother wears his in a mohawk.

> Both halves of this sentence are now parallel because they follow the same basic pattern:

Sibling	Action	Hairstyle
My sister	dyes her hair	bright purple
my brother	wears his	in a mohawk

You should also use parallelism for lists.

Not Parallel   Before she could go to the beach, Beth had to eat breakfast, pass a math test, and running errands.

Parallel   Before she could go to the beach, Beth had to eat breakfast, pass a math test, and run errands.

Not Parallel   My neighbor's parakeet, the cat belonging to my grandmother, and my best friend's hamster came to my dog's birthday party.

Parallel   My neighbor's parakeet, my grandmother's cat, and my best friend's hamster came to my dog's birthday party.

These sentences are easier to read when each item in the list follows the same structure.

Reflection Questions
Because parallelism adds rhythm and flow to your writing, it is often used in poems or song lyrics. Can you think of any specific examples of this?

On Your Own

Use the items below to write a complete sentence with a parallel list. You may need to change the wording.

seeing new movies
music recommendations
watch old TV shows

On Your Own

Take a look at the following examples and identify the list item that doesn't seem to fit with the others.

My favorite hobbies include playing the guitar, watching action movies, and anything with basketball.

The committee resolved to cut funding for after-school programs, decided to hold nominations for a new chairperson, and interviewing the recently hired police chief.

Learning Style Tip
If you're a **visual** learner, try highlighting or underlining each item in a list. This will help you decide if you have used parallel language to show how the items are related.

Lesson Wrap-up

Key Terms

Comma: a punctuation mark used to separate items in a list; join compound sentences; mark introductory words, phrases, and clauses; add extra or unnecessary details to a sentence; and separate similar adjectives

Compound Sentence: two independent clauses joined by a comma and a conjunction

Coordinating Conjunction: a conjunction that connects words or word groups of equal importance in a sentence

Coordination: a method for combining ideas of equal importance in a sentence

Conjunction: a part of speech that connects two or more words or word groups

Independent Clause: a group of words that includes a subject and a verb and expresses a complete thought

Paragraph: a short piece of writing that focuses on one main idea

Parallelism: a method for showing a relationship between ideas by using similarly structured words, phrases, or clauses

Phrase: a word group that adds to the meaning of a sentence but does not express a complete thought and usually lacks a subject and verb

Semicolon: a punctuation mark used to combine two independent clauses and separate long list items

Subordinating Conjunction: a conjunction that introduces a dependent clause

Subordination: a stylistic method for de-emphasizing an idea in a combined sentence

Visual Learning: learning information through pictures, shapes, and colors

Lesson 5.7

Using Active and Passive Voice

When you think of the words *active* and *passive*, what comes to mind?

The word *active* probably reminds you of outdoor activities or exercise. An active person is energetic and involved. The word *passive*, on the other hand, probably reminds you of someone who is quiet or timid. This person often avoids conflict and is less likely to be the center of attention.

In writing, active voice keeps your sentences energetic and exciting while passive voice slows them down. Too many passive sentences make a text slow and boring. Look at this example:

> In contrast, Antigone's actions are interpreted by Mary Dietz as an affirmation of the importance of politics over family. Antigone is established by Dietz's argument as a model for "citizenship with a feminist face" and an advocate for religious and civil customs (1112). In Dietz's opinion, political reform rather than maternal awareness must be devoted to by modern feminists.
>
> This **paragraph** is written almost entirely in passive voice. As you read, you probably noticed that the sentences were tedious. Using active voice would make the paragraph more interesting and engaging.

> Read the revised version below:

> In contrast, Mary Dietz interprets Antigone's actions as an affirmation of the importance of politics over family. Dietz's argument establishes Antigone as a model for "citizenship with a feminist face" and an advocate for religious and civil customs (1112). In Dietz's opinion, modern feminists must devote themselves to political reform rather than maternal awareness.

While active voice can improve your writing, using *only* active voice would sound repetitive and aggressive. Learning to find a good balance of active and passive voice will help you refine your writing skills and communicate your ideas better.

This lesson will teach you how to use both active and passive voice.

Active Voice

When a sentence uses **active voice**, the **subject** is performing an action.

> The basset hound relaxed next to her owner on the couch.

> In this sentence, the subject, *basset hound*, is doing the relaxing. Therefore, this sentence is considered active.

Active voice makes your writing more energetic.

Look at the following examples. Which sentence seems more exciting?

> After thirty-two long miles, a life-long goal was accomplished by Harmon and Whitney.

> After thirty-two long miles, Harmon and Whitney accomplished a life-long goal.

> The second sentence uses active voice to show the subjects performing an action. This sentence has more energy than the first sentence, which is written in passive voice.

On Your Own

Read the following sentences and identify the one using active voice.

> Our entire road was paved by the crew last week.

> The kitchen will be cleaned by your brother every Wednesday.

> The mischievous puppy ate three socks in one day.

When you use active voice, your writing is often more direct and clear than when you use passive voice. Think about these sentences:

> I was told by the contractors that the renovations are moving ahead of schedule.

> The contractors told me that the renovations are moving ahead of schedule.

> Both of these examples express the same basic idea. However, the sentence in active voice communicates its meaning in a much more direct way.

To turn a passive sentence into an active sentence, make sure the action is being performed by the subject. Sometimes, this information is already included in the sentence. Other times, however, you need to supply the new subject. Here are a few examples:

Passive   The runaway girls were found by the police this morning.
Active   The police found the runaway girls this morning.

Passive   During the meeting, the agenda was discussed first.
Active   During the meeting, the board members discussed the agenda first.

Passive Voice

When a sentence is in **passive voice**, the subject is receiving an action.

> The former soybean farm was turned into a new housing development by the Turner Group.

> In this example, the subject, *farm*, is not doing anything. Something else, *the Turner Group*, is doing the action to the subject.

Sentences in passive voice contain a **helping verb** in addition to a main **verb**. In the previous example, *was* is the helping verb and *turned* is the main verb.

To learn more about types of verbs, see Lesson 4.3.

In your writing, passive voice can sound both wordy and vague. Look at this example:

> The agreement will be signed by Casey after reviewing the terms with her lawyer.
>
> This sentence is confusing. A much better version would sound like this:
>
> Casey will sign the agreement after reviewing the terms with her lawyer.

Passive voice can also confuse your audience when the person or object doing the action is not named in the sentence. Here are two examples:

> A ball was thrown through Mr. Wilson's window.

> It has been mentioned that more training is needed.

> These sentences never tell the audience who is doing the actions.

On Your Own

The following sentences are written in passive voice. In the table below, rewrite them so that they are in active voice.

Passive	Active
The entire yard was raked by Sarah.	
The video was posted on Facebook by an anonymous source.	
Instructions will be read to you by the teaching assistant.	
The book was written by a best-selling author.	

While active voice is usually a better choice for your writing, there are occasions when passive voice is a better choice. First, you may want to keep the emphasis of the sentence on a word other than the subject. Look at these examples:

> Baby Sophia was delivered at 3:30 a.m. yesterday.

> Dr. Susan Jones delivered baby Sophia at 3:30 a.m. yesterday.

> The first sentence would be a better choice for a birth announcement sent to family and friends because they are much more interested in the baby than in the doctor. In contrast, a hospital report of yesterday's events is more likely to focus on Dr. Jones.

Another reason to use passive voice is to keep the meaning of the sentence purposefully vague. Look at this example:

> Due to employee oversight, your recent insurance claim was unable to be processed.

> This example purposefully uses vague language to make the insurance company sound less responsible for the oversight.

> Think about what the active version of this sentence might sound like:

> An employee overlooked your recent insurance claim.

> **Further Resources**
> The passive voice is often used by politicians to avoid taking blame for mistakes or scandals. One famous phrase, "Mistakes were made," has been used so many times, it has its own Wikipedia page (http://en.wikipedia.org/wiki/Mistakes_were_made).

One final reason to use passive voice would be to add sentence variety to a text. Too many active sentences in a row can sound choppy. Adding a few passive sentences will help you keep your writing smooth.

> We will assign a project to each team. We will schedule and monitor these projects.

> We will assign a project to each team. These projects will be scheduled and monitored.

> In the second example, one sentence is active, and one is passive. Not only does the passive sentence add variety to the text, it also helps the reader make a connection between the two sentences.

Lesson Wrap-up

> **Group Activity**
> As a group, decide which of the following sentences are active and which are passive. Then, rewrite each sentence in the opposite voice.
> The candy was devoured by an unruly group of trick-or-treaters.
> We gaped at the giant sinkhole in the backyard.
> After extensive tests, doctors concluded that the new virus is not dangerous to humans.
> You should conserve energy whenever possible.
> The empty tables were covered with a thin film of dust and pollen.

Key Terms

Active Voice: when a sentence is written so that the subject is performing an action

Helping Verb: a type of verb that changes the form of the main verb so that it grammatically fits the sentence

Paragraph: a short piece of writing that focuses on one main idea

Passive Voice: when a sentence is written so that the subject is receiving an action

Subject: the person, place, thing, event, or idea a sentence is about

Verb: a word that represents an action, relationship, or state of being

Lesson 5.8
Emphasizing Words or Phrases

Think about the last time you had an important idea that you wanted someone to consider. How did you make sure that person understood all of the essential details?

When speaking, you use voice inflections and hand gestures to emphasize certain details. This helps your audience know what information is the most important. In a similar way, advertisers use bright colors in fliers to emphasize low prices. If all the information looks identical, the audience won't notice the special sale.

Instead of gestures or bright colors, you can use words and structures to emphasize details in your writing.

In your writing, it's equally crucial to draw your audience's attention to important information. However, you can't use hand gestures or inflections in a text; you have to rely on words and sentence structures to emphasize certain ideas. Read the following examples. What are the most important details?

> The ballerina twirled across the stage and captivated the audience. Though I think you would have appreciated the performance, I enjoyed it.

> Twirling gracefully across the stage, the ballerina captivated the entire audience. Though I enjoyed the performance, I think you would have appreciated it more than anyone.

> The first sentence is difficult to understand because it buries the most important information in the middle. As you can see, moving these details around makes the second sentence much clearer.

In this lesson, you will learn three ways to emphasize important words or phrases:

Subordination
Word Order
Sentence Structure

Helpful Hint
Colors, special fonts, and large text are all acceptable ways to draw readers' attention in a magazine or advertisement but not in formal writing.

Subordination

Usually, the main **subject** and **verb** are the most noticeable words in a sentence. They express the most important ideas. Less important ideas should be **subordinated**, or deemphasized, in **dependent clauses**.

> Though it lasted only minutes, the conversation made a lifelong impact on the young boy.

> In this example, the writer uses the **subordinating conjunction** *though* to deemphasize the phrase *it lasted only minutes*. The more significant idea is emphasized in the **independent clause**: *the conversation made a lifelong impact*.

Here's another example:

> After she visited friends in Australia, Amber decided to take a job in Sydney.

> The most important clause in this sentence is *Amber decided to take a job in Sydney*, so *she visited friends in Australia* is subordinated by the word *after*.

Group Activity
Subordinating conjunctions can drastically change two independent clauses by shifting the emphasis in the sentence. As a group, can you think of some examples of sentences that require subordination to show emphasis?

Be careful not to subordinate the wrong ideas. Consider how the meaning changes in the example below.

> Though it made a lifelong impact on the young boy, the conversation lasted only minutes.

> Although this sentence is grammatically correct, the more important idea is deemphasized by the word *though*.

On Your Own

Read the following passage and identify the sentence that uses subordination.

> The famous pirate Blackbeard blockaded the port of Charleston, South Carolina, in 1718. He demanded medical supplies in exchange for the safe return of a group of prisoners. After the exchange was delayed, the pirates moved several ships into the harbor. The city was alarmed by this; Blackbeard's reputation made every coastal city fear him.

Word Order

Another way to emphasize ideas is through word order. Important information shouldn't be buried in the middle of a sentence. You can make this information more prominent by placing it at the beginning or end of a sentence. Consider the following examples:

> The actor who demonstrates the most passion and skill in today's auditions will win the lead role.

> The lead role will be won by the actor who demonstrates the most passion and skill in today's auditions.

> In the sentences above, *who demonstrates the most passion and skill* is the most important information. Placing this detail at the end of the sentence makes it stand out to the reader.

Similarly, you can emphasize **phrases** by moving them to the beginning of a sentence. By delaying the subject and verb of the sentence, you can build a feeling of suspense in your audience.

> Hoping for a miracle, the boys launched their homemade rocket.

> In this example, emphasizing the phrase *hoping for a miracle* makes readers curious about what happens next.

This technique is often used in fictional narratives or personal reflections.

> Thirty years ago today, in a tiny high school in a tiny New Jersey town, while making his way through a hallway of teenagers and the smell of Sloppy Joe Wednesdays, your grandfather spotted your grandmother for the first time.

Reflection Questions
Delaying an event is often used during intense parts of books, movies, and TV shows to draw the reader in. Can you think of any specific examples?

Sentence Structure

The third way to emphasize ideas is by using a different or unexpected sentence structure. These sentences stand out to the audience because they are different from the rest of the text.

For example, read the following paragraph:

> People change. The characters in *As You Like It* are no exception, for they each experience numerous transformations. Orlando, the eager youth, becomes honest and mature; Oliver, the murderous and envious brother, becomes a gentle shepherd; and Duke Frederick, the overly ambitious usurper, becomes a devout man of faith.
>
> In this example, the author uses a short sentence to emphasize the most important idea.

Another way to emphasize an important idea is by posing a question to your audience.

> Would you ever put your child in harm's way?

Helpful Hint
Be careful when asking your audience a question because it can shift your writing into second person. Be sure that second-person point of view is appropriate for your purpose and audience.

To learn more about point of view in your writing, see Lesson 5.3.

Keep in mind that using an entire paragraph of short sentences would actually de-emphasize the information. When all of the sentences in a paragraph look and sound alike, none of the important ideas are properly emphasized.

To learn more about using word and sentence variety, see Lesson 5.5.

Lesson Wrap-up

Key Terms

Dependent Clause: a word group that contains a subject and a verb but does not express a complete thought

Independent Clause: a word group that contains a subject and a verb and expresses a complete thought

Phrase: a word group that adds meaning to a sentence but does not express a complete thought and usually lacks a subject and a verb

Subject: the person, place, thing, event, or idea a sentence is about

Subordinating Conjunction: a conjunction that introduces a dependent clause

Subordination: a stylistic method for de-emphasizing an idea in a combined sentence

Verb: a word that represents an action, relationship, or state of being

Lesson 5.9
Choosing Clear, Concise, and Vivid Words

Telling an interesting story is difficult. To make a situation as exciting as possible, you have to include vivid descriptions and fascinating details. However, language that is too flowery or complicated might distract your audience from the **main idea**. Balancing these two extremes is essential for becoming a good storyteller.

In writing, you have to find a similar balance between keeping your readers interested and expressing your ideas clearly. Read through the following examples:

> Preparing a culinary entrée such as elbow pasta noodles and melted cheddar cheese, of the boxed variation, can be an enjoyable and tranquil undertaking if one is cognizant of the most vital procedures. First, fill a pot with an abundance of temperate water and gently situate it on the cooking apparatus, or stove, the dial of which should be directed to a temperature of great warmth. The liquid will presently begin to bubble and yield steam, at which juncture the foodstuffs, or elbow noodles, should be incorporated. When they are tender and delectable, sprinkle in the cheese mixture and blend judiciously.

> To make macaroni and cheese from a box, put water in a pot. Turn on the stove to high heat and place the pot on top. Soon, the water will boil; when it does, add the noodles. When they are fully cooked, stir in the cheese.

> In the first example, the author uses descriptive, vivid language. However, the paragraph is so complicated, it's almost impossible to follow the author's train of thought. The second example has the opposite problem. While the information is straightforward, the paragraph itself is bland and boring.

To learn more about purpose and audience, see Lesson 5.1.

Thinking about your audience and purpose will help you determine how descriptive you should be. Word choice is also an important part of drafting and revising.

In this lesson, you will learn how to effectively communicate meaning with the following word choices:

Clear Words
Concise Words
Vivid Words

Clear Words

Strong writing is clear and easy to understand. Don't be tempted to use complicated language just because it sounds "smarter." While academic and professional documents may be **formal**, they should not be confusing.

To learn more about formal and informal language, see Lesson 5.1.

Think about the following sentences:

> This stratagem will advocate tandem techniques to diminish building perpetuation expenditures.

> This proposal will suggest two ways to reduce building maintenance costs.

> While both of these examples have the same basic meaning, the second sentence is much clearer than the first.

Helpful Hint
Be careful when using **synonyms** to make your writing more interesting or academic. Some of these words have slightly different definitions that will change the meaning of a sentence.

One specific type of unclear language is **jargon**, or overly technical terms. Here's an example:

> The nomenclature of the *Acer rubrum* is derived from the visual perceptual property of the principal lateral appendages of its stems during the temperate season of autumn.

Can you tell what this sentence says? It's explaining that red maples get their name from their leaves, which turn red in the fall. However, figuring this out is difficult because of scientific jargon like *Acer rubrum* and *principal lateral appendages*.

Consider your purpose and audience before you use jargon in writing.
Photo courtesy of Wikimedia Commons (https://commons.wikimedia.org/wiki/Main_Page).

Generally, you should avoid jargon unless you are specifically writing for a technical **audience**. If you need to use unfamiliar terms, always include clear definitions.

Concise Words

Concise word choice eliminates unnecessary language from your writing. Consider the following paragraph:

> I wanted to see if you would be willing to meet with me for just a couple minutes tomorrow in the afternoon at 2:15 or sometime around then. I would really appreciate being able to hear what you think about the progress I've made with the first draft of the paper that I've been writing. Due to the fact that I am having some trouble with organizing my paragraphs, I am hoping that you can help me. It would be great if I could come to your office after class tomorrow afternoon, but I can also meet at another time if it would work better for you.

This paragraph is wordy. The author circles around the meaning of each sentence, often using four or five words instead of one. Not only are these phrases difficult to read, they are also confusing.

A much more concise version of the paragraph might look like this:

> Are you available for a brief meeting around 2:15 tomorrow afternoon? I would like to hear your feedback on my first draft of Essay #3. I am having trouble organizing my paragraphs and would appreciate your help. If another time would be better, please let me know.

The basic meaning of both versions is the same; however, the revised version is easier to read.

On Your Own

In the table below, write a more concise version of the three wordy phrases from the previous passage.

WORDY	CONCISE
just a couple minutes tomorrow in the afternoon at 2:15 or sometime around then	
the first draft of the paper I've been writing	
Due to the fact that I am having some trouble with organizing my paragraphs	

Keep in mind that a concise sentence is not always short. You don't want to confuse your readers by eliminating important information from your writing. Instead, you should focus on using words that state exactly what you want to say.

Wordy	Concise
the researchers who work at Columbia University	researchers at Columbia University
owing to the fact that	because
the type of material used for fuel purposes	used for fuel
Andrew Jackson was a man who served	Andrew Jackson served
a story that is strange	a strange story
situations that could be considered exceptions	exceptions
worked as a manager	managed

Helpful Hint

One way to make your writing more concise is to use active voice whenever possible. In **active voice**, the **subject** of a sentence is *doing* the action instead of *receiving* the action. Compare these examples:

This hotel had been highly recommended by my brother.

My brother highly recommended this hotel.

Vivid Words

The final aspect of word choice is using vivid language. When you are sharing information with your audience, you want your words to be interesting and precise.

Think about the following image. How would you describe it?

Vivid words will make your descriptions more effective.

While the contents of this image could be described with the words *bear* or *animal*, using *polar bear* helps your audience picture your words better.

Nouns and Action Verbs

To make your writing more vivid, use specific **nouns** and **action verbs**.

Vague	Vivid
girl	partner-in-crime
stuff	clutter
pet	iguana
show	*How I Met Your Mother*

Vague	Vivid
walking	striding
sat	slumped
found	discovered
going	traveling

Adjectives and Adverbs

Another way to write vividly is to use unique **adjectives** and **adverbs**. Words like *nice* and *good* are often overused. Finding a more original descriptive word will keep your writing fresh and interesting.

Vague	Vivid
nice	thoughtful
very	extremely
dark	pitch black
cold	frigid
really	undoubtedly

Use adjectives and adverbs carefully. Usually, a strong noun or **verb** alone is better than a weak noun or verb with an adjective or adverb.

> After the game, Andrew ~~slowly walked~~ home.

> After the game, Andrew trudged home.

Helpful Hint
Good writers will spend time finding the right word. As you write, take note of any words that you feel can be stronger or more vivid and revise them later.

Any type of writing can benefit from vivid language. While you may not use imaginative language in a research paper or résumé, you should still choose words that are descriptive and accurate.

Vague	Vivid
a group of experts	researchers at Harvard Medical School
a source	*Forbes* magazine
quickly went	sprinted
said	accused
those affected by the flood	citizens of Lebanon Valley
people	psychologists
some	twenty-five

Group Activity
As a group, come up with a list of vivid words to replace the vague words below.

group of people   teachers   happy   hungry   fast   boring

Lesson Wrap-up

Key Terms

Action Verb: a verb that indicates a physical or mental action

Active Voice: when a sentence is written so that the subject is performing an action

Adjective: a word that describes a noun or pronoun

Adverb: a word that describes a verb, an adjective, or another adverb

Audience: the people who read your writing

Formality: the way a text conforms to certain standards

Jargon: overly technical language

Main Idea: the statement or argument that a text communicates about its topic

Noun: a word that represents a person, place, thing, event, or idea

Phrase: a word group that adds to the meaning of a sentence but does not express a complete thought and usually lacks a subject and verb

Subject: the person, place, thing, event, or idea a sentence is about

Synonym: a word that has the same meaning as another word

Verb: a word that represents an action, relationship, or state of being

Lesson 5.10
Using Inclusive Language

Think about the following sentences:

> Like a typical teenager, Jake slept through his alarm this morning.

> After class, I am meeting that Asian girl Alice to talk about our group project.

> Policemen work hard to keep our citizens safe.

> These example sentences have one thing in common: they all include disrespectful or **exclusive language**. In the first sentence, the phrase *like a typical teenager* uses a stereotype about young people. The second sentence unnecessarily uses the phrase *that Asian girl* to describe Alice. Finally, the third example uses the term *policemen* even though both men and women serve on the police force.

When you're writing for work or school, you are often sharing information, opinions, or analysis with your readers. If your language is exclusive, the points you are making will be disturbed or lost because readers are distracted by the disrespectful comments. Using exclusive language also hurts your **credibility**.

The opposite of exclusive language is inclusive language. **Inclusive language** is respectful of people's differences. This means avoiding words that exclude certain groups of people or words that call unnecessary attention to a person's personal characteristics.

Some types of exclusive language, such as stereotypes, are obvious. In other situations, however, insensitive language is much harder to spot. By becoming familiar with the differences between inclusive and exclusive language, you can ensure that your writing is respectful and sensitive to others.

In this lesson, you will learn to use language that is inclusive based on the following factors:

Gender
Ethnicity or Culture
Physical or Mental Ability
Sexual Orientation

Reflection Questions
Why do you think inclusive language matters?

Gender

In the past, society has used **gender-specific** words like *mankind* to describe both men and women. This language is considered exclusive because it refers specifically to men even though the group includes women. In these instances, it would be better to use a **gender-neutral** term like *humankind*.

Exclusive language also uses different terms to describe men and women even though the meanings of the words are the same. Look at the following examples:

Men	Women
actor	actress
doctor	lady doctor
male nurse	nurse
policeman	policewoman
waiter	waitress

In all of these examples, the men and women are doing the same exact job. Instead of referring to them by different names, use one of the following terms:

Gender-Specific	Gender-Neutral
actor, actress	actor
doctor, lady doctor	doctor
male nurse, nurse	nurse
policeman, policewoman	police officer
waiter, waitress	waiter

Reflection Questions
What are some other professions that use different terms for men and women performing the same job? What gender-neutral terms should be used instead?

One of the trickiest aspects of using gender-neutral language is choosing the correct **personal pronoun**. Look at these examples:

When a person needs to make a phone call, he excuses himself from the room.

When a student applies for a parking permit, she must bring her license and registration.

These sentences use gender-specific **pronouns** to refer to a person and a student.

Instead of defaulting to a certain gender, use the term *he or she*.

If a student needs to leave the classroom, he or she should do it quietly.

Because using the term *he or she* can sound wordy, this isn't always the best option. You can also make the subject plural so that you can use the plural, gender-neutral pronoun *they*.

If students need to leave the classroom, they should do it quietly.

Using personal pronouns in a gender-neutral way can be difficult, especially when a person does not identify with a traditional gender. In these cases, always find out which pronoun that person prefers. Until the English language adopts a new type of pronoun, this is the best way to ensure that you are being as respectful as possible.

Helpful Hint
If the text is clearly referring to a man or a woman, use whichever pronoun makes the most sense. For example, a **paragraph** about someone taking maternity leave would obviously use the female pronoun *she*. If the same paragraph were about paternity leave, you would use the male pronoun *he*.

Another type of gender-exclusive language is using stereotypes about men and women. Look at these examples:

Brian is a real man; he loves hunting, fishing, and camping.

The relief pitcher threw like a girl for the first half of the game.

Both of these sentences use disrespectful stereotypes about men and women.

Ethnicity or Culture

Inclusive language does not make assumptions about people based on their ethnicity or culture. For example, think about the following sentences:

> All black people are really good at sports.

> Since Jane is from China, I'm going to ask her to tutor me in math.

> Alan is good at saving money; it's probably because he's Jewish.

> All of these examples contain disrespectful stereotypes about people with certain ethnic backgrounds.

While the exclusive language in the previous examples might be obvious, other kinds of exclusive language can be harder to spot. For example, referring to someone's ethnicity in an unrelated comment is unnecessary. Look at this example:

> Yesterday, police arrested Greg Lopez, a Colombian man who lives in Lebanon, PA, on armed robbery charges.

> In this sentence, the suspect's ethnicity has nothing to do with his crime. Mentioning this information is pointless.

When you do need to refer to a person's ethnicity, make sure you use the correct term. If you are unsure, look up the information.

Reflection Questions
In what situations would it be necessary to identify someone's ethnicity or cultural background in your writing?

Physical or Mental Ability

People live with a variety of physical or mental conditions. However, a person's physical or mental abilities do not define them. Calling someone "a diabetic" or "a dyslexic" equates who they are as a person with their disease or disability.

Just like gender or ethnicity, a person's physical or mental abilities should only be mentioned if this information is relevant to your purpose. When these details are important, it's best to use wording like "a man with autism" as opposed to "an autistic man." By using this kind of language, you are acknowledging the person's humanity first.

One term that you should avoid is the word *disabled*. Instead of saying "disabled parking spots," refer to them as "accessible parking spots." The parking spaces themselves are not disabled; they are accessible to people who have physical limitations. This type of inclusive language emphasizes the accessibility of the parking spot, not the limitations of the person.

Further Resources
Research shows that stereotypes can affect a person's performance on tests. To learn more about the negatives of exclusive language, check out this article from *The New York Times* (http://www.nytimes.com/2012/10/07/opinion/sunday/intelligence-and-the-stereotype-threat.html?_r=0).

Sexual Orientation

Finally, don't over-emphasize a person's sexual orientation. If this information is irrelevant to the sentence, don't mention it. For example, referring to someone as "gay Brad" is completely unnecessary. Similarly, you don't need to specify that two people are a "homosexual couple"; just *couple* is fine. When you do need to reference someone's sexual orientation, always use terms that are respectful.

You should also be careful to use wording that is inclusive. The terms *husband* and *wife* can be problematic when you are referring to couples in general. It's best to use *partner* or *spouse* unless you are talking about a specific husband and wife.

> Further Resources
> The word *homosexual* can be considered offensive because this term is often used in a clinical or political way. If you're unsure how to talk about sexual orientation in an inclusive way, review this guide (http://www.glaad.org/reference/offensive) from the Gay and Lesbian Alliance Against Defamation (GLAAD).

Lesson Wrap-up

Key Terms

Credibility: the reliability of an author or source of information

Exclusive Language: disrespectful language that refers to a person's gender, ethnicity or culture, physical or mental ability, or sexual orientation

Gender-Neutral: something that applies to all genders

Gender-Specific: something reserved for only one gender

Inclusive Language: language that is respectful of people's differences

Paragraph: a short piece of writing that focuses on one main idea

Personal Pronoun: a pronoun that renames a specific person, animal, object, or place

Pronoun: a word that takes the place of a noun in a sentence

Lesson 5.11
Proofreading Sentences for Style

Sentence style is like the icing on a cake. You already have a grammatically solid sentence, but a little more style could make it even better.

Learning to proofread for sentence style will help you express your ideas in the best possible way. That extra polish might be just what you need to earn a higher grade, impress a hiring manager, or convince a skeptical audience.

In this lesson, you will learn how to proofread a text for style issues.

Sentence style is something extra to help you express your ideas even more effectively.

Proofreading is much easier when you have a strategy in place. Proof the style of your writing with the following steps:

Review Writing Style Guidelines

Review the characteristics of good style to guide your focus as you proofread. Here are some of the most important considerations:

Proofreading Checklist: Sentence Style

- ☐ **Meaning:** clear words, concise words, vivid words, appropriate tone, inclusive language
- ☐ **Delivery:** modifiers, parallelism, coordination, subordination
- ☐ **Consistency:** consistent tone, appropriate usage of active and passive voice, consistent verb tense, consistent point of view

Think back to the papers you've written in previous classes. What kind of suggestions did your teachers usually give you? If you tend to struggle in a specific area, spend extra time reviewing information about that particular style issue.

Proofread in Stages

Proofreading in stages will help you make specific, meaningful improvements to your writing. During each stage, focus on just one style issue at a time. For example, you might start by making sure all of your **verb tenses** are consistent; then, you might look for opportunities to use more **active voice.**

> Learning Style Tip
> If you're a **sequential** learner, make a checklist of each stage in the proofreading process. Use this list as a guide as you check your writing for style issues.

Try Multiple Reading Techniques

One of the best ways to proofread for style is reading your work aloud to yourself. Actually listening to your words can help you hear confusing sentences, **parallelism** problems, and inconsistent tone.

Reading aloud also forces your brain to slow down and pay attention. When you read to yourself, it's easy to scan the words instead of actually reading them.

Get a Second Opinion

When you read your own writing multiple times, you will slowly get used to the structure and sound of your sentences. Ask a friend or family member to review your text and give you feedback. This is the perfect opportunity to get the opinion of an actual **audience** member.

If your friend doesn't mind, consider making an audio recording of him or her reading your paper aloud. You can then listen for sentences that sound awkward or confusing. Anytime your friend stumbles over words or runs out of breath, double-check those sentences for possible style issues.

> Further Resources
> NaturalReader (http://www.naturalreaders.com/index.html) or another text-to-speech service could be a helpful resource when you are proofreading your sentences for style.

Take Frequent Breaks

Taking a break from your paper is essential when proofreading for style. When you read your paragraph or document multiple times, everything will start sounding the same after a while.

To make sure that you have enough time to review your work thoroughly, schedule proofreading time in your planner. You should spread these times across multiple days. Splitting up your proofreading time will give you the fresh eyes you need.

> Helpful Hint
> Some writing programs, like Microsoft Word, offer automatic writing style suggestions. Carefully review any advice before making changes. The style suggestions are generally less reliable than the spelling suggestions.

Lesson Wrap-up

Key Terms

Active Voice: when a sentence is written so that the subject is performing an action

Audience: the people who read your writing

Parallelism: a method for clarifying the relationship between ideas by presenting them in similarly-structured words, phrases, or clauses

Sequential Learning: learning information through a step-by-step process

Tense: how a verb indicates when it took place: past, present, or future

Verb: a word that represents an action, relationship, or state of being

Chapter 6
Writing Paragraphs

Lesson 6.1
The Writing Process for Paragraphs

A **paragraph** is a short piece of writing that focuses on one **main idea**. Most paragraphs have eight to ten sentences although some are much shorter or longer depending on their purpose. The sentences in a paragraph work together to support and expand its main idea. If the ideas inside a paragraph aren't focused, your readers won't be able to follow your ideas.

Think about this example:

> As smartphone cameras become better, fewer people are buying traditional cameras. According to an article by Harvey Lloyd, the average American citizen no longer has film developed at a photo-processing store. Digital images are now the norm, with millions of people using photo-sharing sites like Instagram or Snapchat every day. In fact, these sites are growing at a faster rate than Facebook, which is still the number one social media site.

> What is the author trying to say in this paragraph? This example isn't focused because not all of the sentences contribute to the main idea. The paragraph begins by stating that people are taking digital pictures rather than buying cameras that require traditional film processing. However, by the end, it is talking about photo-sharing websites.

The **academic writing process** is a useful strategy for writing a focused paragraph. This process breaks up an assignment into five stages:

1. Pre-writing
2. Drafting
3. Revising
4. Editing
5. Submitting

> **Helpful Hint**
> This process sometimes includes one more step: peer reviewing. Peer reviews are more often part of the writing process for longer essays.

To learn more about writing longer texts, see Chapter 7.

All five stages are essential to the writing process. While skipping a step might save you time in the short term, you will have to spend time fixing or even re-writing your paragraph later.

As you use the academic writing process, don't be afraid to circle back to a previous stage. Although it should include each step, the writing process is not meant to be completely linear.

Good writers move back and forth through the different steps multiple times. If you find yourself writing in a different direction than you had previously planned, you may need to do a new round of pre-writing. Similarly, you may notice holes in your argument during revising that can be fixed with more drafting.

This lesson will review the academic writing process for paragraphs.

> Learning Style Tip
>
> If you're a **global** learner, you probably *prefer* to jump around the different stages of the writing process. Be careful not to skip any of these steps, and make sure you take the time to work through the pre-writing process so that you have direction as you move forward.

Pre-Writing

Pre-writing is the first step in the academic writing process. This step involves making decisions and planning ideas before actually writing a draft. Pre-writing also helps you identify any assignment guidelines that might affect your topic and ideas.

Don't allow yourself to skip this important step. Sometimes, students rush ahead to drafting because they want to get an assignment done as quickly as possible. However, skipping the pre-writing stage will result in a disorganized paragraph. You may also find yourself wasting more time in later stages trying to decide what you want to write.

Goals of Pre-writing

During pre-writing, you will answer the following questions:

What are the assignment guidelines?

If a writing prompt asks you to write a paragraph that has between one hundred and two hundred words, it's stating an assignment guideline.

What is my **purpose** for writing?

If the writing prompt asks you to persuade a friend to buy a used car, that is the purpose.

Who is my **audience**?

If the writing prompt was provided by your marketing professor, the professor is your audience unless you're told otherwise.

> **Reflection Questions**
> Why might you be tempted to skip the pre-writing stage of the writing process? What could you do to make sure you pre-write?

Here is an example of pre-writing in action:

> Kyle's speech instructor asked the class to write a paragraph about a time they were embarrassed to talk in front of a group. Kyle started the paragraph by pre-writing. First, he set a timer for five minutes and began typing ideas. He remembered the time he was asked to pray at church. The church incident made him remember presenting his painting during his studio art class. He came up with ten different times he had spoken in front of people. He didn't worry about writing complete sentences, and he kept writing even though he had some misspelled words. When the timer went off, Kyle had a full page of ideas.

On Your Own

In the following example, is Mario pre-writing? Check the box next to your answer.

> Mario reviews the guidelines given to him by his history instructor for a major paper. He then brainstorms possible topics for his history paper on the Civil War. After that, he is going to the library to search the databases for information about the Civil War.

☐ Yes   ☐ No

Drafting

During the second step in the writing process, **drafting**, you will start writing out your ideas.

For many students, staring at a blank screen or piece of paper is the most nerve-wracking part of a writing assignment. However, if you've done careful pre-writing, you should already know what you want to write.

A blank piece of paper is less intimidating when you follow the writing process.

While you are drafting, don't worry too much about spelling or grammar. Instead, focus on the ideas that you want to cover. Just like the term suggests, this is a *draft*, not the finished product. You can always make changes and improvements later.

Drafting involves writing your **support sentences** and **concluding sentence**. These sentences should expand on the information presented in your topic sentence. Here's an example of drafting in action:

After reviewing his pre-writing ideas, Kyle chose a topic and wrote the following paragraph:

> I normally enjoy speaking in front of others. The speech I gave when I ran for President of the freshman class was a disaster. I was scheduled to speak at a school assembly. The other candidates for the position. I was the last to speak. When I stood up, I heard a tearing sound. My pants catch on a lose screw in the chair as I was standing up. I ended up with a big whole in my pants. The laughing from the audience let me know the student body was fully aware of my wardrobe problem. I gave my speech but I was totally embarrassed.

The paragraph isn't perfect. Kyle still needs to work toward a final draft, but he has a good beginning. The paragraph has a topic sentence (a beginning), support sentence (a middle), and a concluding sentence (an end). This draft allowed Kyle to capture his thoughts on paper. He will correct any problems during the revising and editing stages.

Helpful Hint
Don't worry if your draft paragraph doesn't "sound right." It will become polished as you revise.

Group Activity
What do you do if you can't get started writing? Write down your strategies on pieces of paper and put them in a pile. Then, pick a random piece of paper and discuss the strategy. Which strategies seem most effective?

Revising

Revising is the third stage in the writing process. During this stage, you can polish your draft by adding and removing content. You can also re-organize your sentences to make sure you are communicating your ideas clearly. During this stage, you may also participate in peer reviews or receive feedback from your instructor.

To learn more about peer reviews, see Lesson 7.10.

The revising stage is usually broken into two parts:

- **Revising for Content.** Re-read your paragraph several times to look for missing information. Make sure you include all the relevant details so the people reading your paragraph understand what you are telling them.

- **Revising for Organization.** Re-read your paragraph to make sure the sentences are in logical order. Add, delete, or re-write a sentence if it makes your paragraph easier to understand. Move your sentences around as needed. You can also change word order within a sentence.

Here is an example of revision in action:

Remember, after pre-writing, Kyle picked one of his ideas and wrote a first draft of his paragraph. Then, Kyle revised his paragraph by making the following changes:

> I normally enjoy speaking in front of others,. The but the speech I gave when I ran for President of the freshman class was a disaster. I was scheduled to speak at a school assembly. The with the other candidates for the position. I was the last to speak. When I stood up, I heard a tearing sound. My pants catch on a lose screw in the chair as I was standing up. I ended up with a big an enormous whole in my pants. The laughing from the audience let me know the student body was fully aware of my wardrobe malfunction problem. I gave my speech but I was totally embarrassed.

The paragraph still isn't perfect, but his ideas are now complete and organized.

Learning Style Tip

If you're a **sequential** learner, during revision you may be tempted to fix every error you find as you read your paragraph. However, this could become overwhelming and end up wasting your time. Always make changes to the major content in your paragraph before worrying about grammar or spelling. You don't want to spend too much time perfecting a sentence that you later decide to delete from the paragraph.

Further Resources

Everyone benefits from the revision process, including famous writers. This article from Mental Floss shows the eleven changes that French author Antoine de Saint-Exupéry made to the most famous line of his book, *The Little Prince* (http://mentalfloss.com/article/57198/11-drafts-most-famous-phrase-little-prince).

Editing

Editing is the fourth stage in the writing process. This stage involves fixing grammar, style, and spelling issues.

Focus on one type of error at a time. For instance, you might start by looking for grammar errors and then move on to spelling. You will probably re-read the paragraph several times, so you may want to break the editing process into more than one session.

On Your Own

In the following example, is the advice of Ingrid's friend correct? Check the box next to your answer.

> Ingrid is having trouble finding the errors in a press release for her marketing class. Her friend suggests re-reading her paragraph several times while looking for a different type of writing error each time.

☐ Yes   ☐ No

Kyle made the following changes to correct errors:

> I normally enjoy speaking in front of others, but the speech I gave when I ran for ~~P~~president of the freshman class was a disaster. I was scheduled to speak at a school assembly with the other candidates for the position. I was the last to speak. When I stood up, I heard a tearing sound. My pants ~~catch~~ caught on a ~~lose~~ loose screw in the chair as I was standing up. I ended up with an enormous ~~whole~~ hole in my pants. The laughing from the audience let me know the student body was fully aware of my wardrobe malfunction. I gave my speech, but I was totally embarrassed.

Submitting

The last stage in the writing process is **submitting** your work. This is an opportunity to share your work with its audience. Writing that you complete for school is often meant for your instructor and classmates, but the writing you do in other situations may be for customers, coworkers, friends, or even complete strangers. As you progress in your writing, your audience will continue to grow beyond the classroom.

During the submitting stage, you will format your paragraph. You might format the text in **MLA** (Modern Language Association) style. MLA style is a method for documenting and formatting academic writing.

Here is an example of submitting in action:

Kyle completed pre-writing, drafting, revising, and editing. Now he is ready to format the paragraph before turning it in. When he re-read the assignment guidelines, Kyle noticed the paragraph must use certain font and line spacing. He made the changes to his paragraph before submitting his work. The following paragraph is ready to submit.

> I normally enjoy speaking in front of others, but the speech I gave when I ran for president of the freshman class was a disaster. I was scheduled to speak at a school assembly with the other candidates for the position. I was the last to speak. When I stood up, I heard a tearing sound. My pants caught on a loose screw in the chair as I was standing up. I ended up with an enormous hole in my pants. The laughing from the audience let me know the student body was fully aware of my wardrobe malfunction. I gave my speech, but I was totally embarrassed.

After carefully working through the five stages of the writing process, you can feel confident that your paragraph is ready to be submitted. You may think the process is long, but the time and effort pays off in better writing.

> **Helpful Hint**
> Seek help and feedback throughout the writing process, even if you've barely written anything yet! Consider finding a peer tutor to help you. If your school has a **Writing Center**, find out how you can make an appointment with a tutor.

Lesson Wrap-up

Key Terms

Academic Writing Process: a strategy that breaks up a writing assignment into five stages: pre-writing, drafting, revising, editing, and submitting

Audience: the people who read your writing

Concluding Sentence: a sentence that ends a paragraph or paper by reviewing the ideas just discussed

Drafting: a stage of writing that involves writing out ideas and support/concluding sentences

Editing: a stage of writing that involves proofreading for style, grammar, and spelling errors

Global Learning: learning information through seeing the big picture

Main Idea: the statement or argument that an author tries to communicate

MLA: the Modern Language Association is a group of scholars dedicated to research in modern languages

Organizational Pattern: the structure of a written text, used to arrange the main points of a work

Paragraph: a short piece of writing that focuses on one main idea

Pre-writing: a stage of writing that involves making decisions, planning ideas, and identifying assignment guidelines

Purpose: the goal of a text

Revising: a stage of writing that involves revising for focus and development

Sequential Learning: learning information through a step-by-step process

Submitting: a stage of writing that involves formatting a text and sharing it with its audience

Support Sentence: a sentence that explains and supports your topic sentence

Topic Sentence: a sentence that states the main point of a paragraph

Writing Center: a service that provides writing assistance

Lesson 6.2
Choosing a Topic and Scope for a Paragraph

The first step in **pre-writing** a paragraph is selecting a topic. The **topic** is the subject of the paragraph. An assignment can feel overwhelming when you don't have a topic because you won't know where to start. Without a topic, the **focus** of your writing will also be unclear. You may start to ramble, making it difficult for the reader to follow your train of thought. In contrast, a well-written topic sentence will lead to a clear and focused paragraph.

Writing a paragraph without a topic is a little like going to the grocery store without a list. Without a solid idea of what you need to buy, you may wander around the aisles aimlessly or purchase a cart full of items you don't really need. Regardless of whether you're shopping or writing, working toward a clear goal will help you stay on track.

A topic guides you through writing a paragraph like a grocery list guides you through the store.

Learning Style Tip

If you are an **active** learner who likes jumping right into a project, you may feel tempted to skip the pre-writing process. This is a bad idea! Choosing a topic is an essential step to writing a clear, focused paragraph.

Once you have a general topic selected, you need to narrow it down to something more specific. A **paragraph** is a short piece of writing that focuses on one main idea. In a single paragraph, it will be difficult to cover a large topic like "minimum wage reform" or "climate change." You just don't have enough space. Instead, your paragraph should discuss a specific aspect of those topics, such as "my experience earning minimum wage" or "how to start recycling."

This lesson will teach you three useful steps in choosing a topic and narrowing your scope:

Review the Assignment Directions
Use Brainstorming Strategies
Think about Audience, Purpose, and Constraints

Reflection Questions
Think about the last time you wrote a paragraph at work or in your everyday life. What was it? How did you know what topic to choose?

Review the Assignment Directions

Before selecting a topic for a paragraph, you need to review the requirements of the assignment. Instructors will usually give you a **writing prompt** like this one:

In at least 150 words, share an event from your past that helped shape you into the person you are today. Be sure to explain the connections between the event and the specific traits you gained from it. The final typed copy will be due Friday, at the beginning of the class period.

A writing prompt will ask you to write about a specific topic and explain any special guidelines. Read through the prompt carefully to ensure that you know exactly what your instructor expects.

Here are some questions to ask yourself as you review the assignment directions:

Is there a specific length for the paragraph?
How should the paragraph be formatted?
When is the paragraph due?
What font and spacing should be used?

Here's the same prompt; this time, the special guidelines are highlighted:

In at least 150 words, share an event from your past that helped shape you into the person you are today. Be sure to explain the connections between the event and the specific traits you gained from it. The final typed copy will be due Friday, at the beginning of the class period.

Helpful Hint
Highlight important words or phrases in the guidelines provided by your instructor. This will help you refer back to them later as you write your paper.

On Your Own

Read the following prompts, paying close attention to the assignment guidelines. Then, write your own prompt for an assignment in one of your classes.

Write a well-developed paragraph about your learning style. Make sure you have a topic sentence and supporting details. The writing rubric located in the Course Information tab will be used to grade the paragraph. Turn in the typed paragraph on Monday.
Enforcing term limits is a procedure where the number of terms an individual may hold an elected office is set by law. For example, the President of the United States may not serve more than two terms. Research the issue to better understand the potential positive and negative effects of term limits. Then, write an argumentative, five-paragraph essay explaining your position and supporting it with information from scholarly articles. Use MLA style.

On Your Own

In the following example, is Juan's friend correct? Check the box next to your answer.

> Juan is having trouble understanding a writing assignment in his history class. Juan's friend suggests highlighting any special guideline as he re-reads the writing prompt.

☐ Yes   ☐ No

On some assignments, you have the freedom to select a topic of your choice. You may come up with a great idea right away. However, if you're struggling to think of topics, try asking yourself some of these questions:

- What is my favorite hobby or activity?
- Have I heard any interesting news stories lately?
- What would be my dream job?
- What was the most enjoyable thing I did last week?
- Where is my ideal vacation spot?

Writing prompts also include key words that tell you what type of paragraph to write. Here are some examples:

- **Analyze**: examine the reasons behind a topic
- **Define**: state the meaning or nature of a topic
- **Discuss**: look at different opinions or ideas about a topic
- **Evaluate**: share the positives and negatives of a topic
- **Identify**: describe the individual parts of a topic
- **Prove**: give reasons to support a topic
- **Share**: recount a personal experience with a topic
- **Summarize**: explain the overall point of a topic

> **Learning Style Tip**
> If you're a **visual** learner, you may also benefit from drawing a picture or a diagram of a topic.

On Your Own

Read the following writing prompts and identify the key words.

> Several styles of parenting have been covered in class. Write a paragraph sharing the parenting style your parents used with you.

> Write a paragraph proving two triangles are congruent.

The key words that your instructor uses should influence the type of topic you choose. For example, you may have a difficult time *analyzing* a topic like "my favorite memory." This topic would probably fit better with a prompt that asks you to *share*.

> **Helpful Hint**
> If your instructor provides a rubric, be sure to review it for additional guidelines.

Use Brainstorming Strategies

Once you have a solid idea of what your instructor expects, you can start using **brainstorming** strategies to explore what you might want to cover in your paragraph. You may even find that your topic changes based on the new ideas you develop. If you are having trouble coming up with good ideas, that may be a sign that you need a new topic. Here are some questions to think about as you brainstorm:

- Will you use listing as you think of ideas, or would a mind map be more useful?
- Do you need to do some background research for the paragraph?

Lists

One useful brainstorming strategy is **listing**. This simply involves writing down every word and phrase that comes to mind during a set period of time.

When you use the listing strategy, you write down your ideas as you think of them. For example, if you brainstorm the topic "rock climbing," you might end up with a list that looks something like this:

> Rock climbing
>
> Safety tips
>
> Rock climbing is good exercise
>
> Famous rock climbers
>
> Most beautiful places to rock climb
>
> Equipment
>
> How to tie a knot

To start listing, follow these steps:

1. Decide how much time you want to spend listing out ideas and set a timer. Three to five minutes is usually long enough. (If you need a timer, try Timer-Tab [http://www.timer-tab.com/].)
2. Write down your topic so that it stays fresh in your thoughts. If you're trying to decide between multiple topics, write them all down.
3. Start the timer and list every word or phrase that comes to mind. Don't worry about spelling or format. You can use phrases and abbreviations instead of full sentences. Just keep writing until the timer goes off.

The purpose of making a list is to make sure all your ideas are recorded on paper. Your list provides you with choices for the focus of your first draft.

On Your Own

Now, try listing on your own. Open a blank document in a word processor or notes app, or use a blank sheet of paper. Use listing to brainstorm the topic "music festivals." When you are finished, answer the review questions below with *yes* or *no*. If any of your answers are *no*, repeat the process.

- o   I set my timer for at least 3 minutes
- o   I kept writing the entire time I was making my list
- o   I did not erase
- o   I did not take time to make corrections
- o   My list has at least 10 ideas

Brainstorming takes time and energy, but it helps you create a better paragraph.

Mind Maps

Another helpful brainstorming strategy is **mind mapping**. A mind map helps you see relationships between ideas. To create one, follow these steps:

1. Write your topic in the middle of the page. If you're trying to decide between multiple topics, write them all down.
2. Add a new word or phrase to your map, connecting it to your original topic with a line.
3. Continue adding more and more words or phrases to your map, using lines to connect related ideas.

Following is an example of a mind map for a personal narrative about a disappointing event in the writer's past. Color is not a requirement for a mind map, but you may find it is easier to keep track of the connections among ideas if you use color.

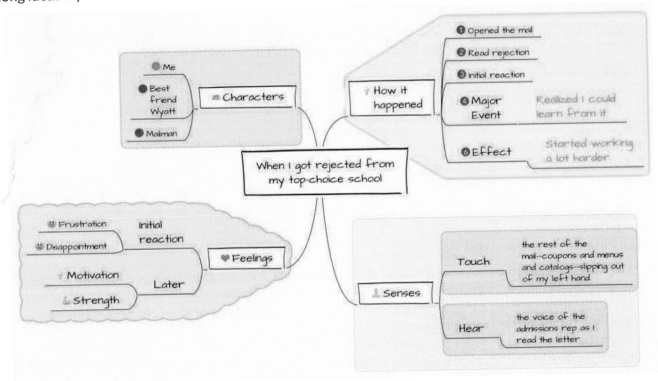

When you've finished brainstorming, read through the ideas on your mind map and highlight anything that seems interesting. This information can help you decide which aspects of your topic you want to cover in your paragraph. You may also find that you have a great idea for a new topic. If that happens, don't be afraid to complete another round of brainstorming to come up with more ideas. Remember, going back and forth in the writing process is normal and even helpful.

> Helpful Hint
> Websites like Coggle (https://coggle.it/) can be useful for creating digital mind maps. You can also use the drawing tools in PowerPoint to make something similar.

> Group Activity
> As a group, choose a broad topic and make a mind map of possible paragraph ideas. Share your mind map with the class.

On Your Own

Now, try mind mapping on your own. Open a new document in a word processor or notes app, or use a blank sheet of paper. Create a mind map on the topic "terrorism."

Does your mind map have a similar structure to the one below? Your mind map probably does not exactly match the example because you are brainstorming your own ideas. However, as long as you have brainstormed several ideas and shown the relationships among the ideas, you have a useful mind map.

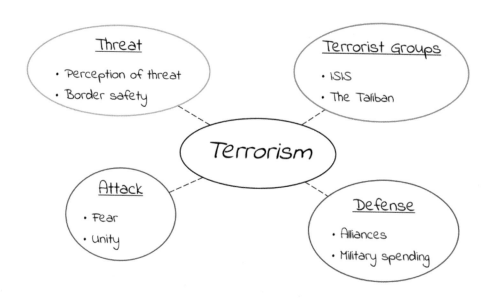

Think about Audience, Purpose, and Constraints

Once you have a list of ideas, you need to start narrowing down the scope of your paragraph. **Scope** is simply another word for *focus*. A good paragraph focuses the reader's attention on a specific topic and gives him or her a thorough understanding of that topic.

Here are some questions to think about as you consider audience, purpose, and constraints:

> Who will read the paper?
> What other rules and/or expectations must I follow?
> Is MLA format required?

First, think about the **purpose** of your paragraph. Why are you writing? While there a number of reasons for writing, some of the most common are to inform, persuade, reflect, and entertain.

- **To inform**: Informative paragraphs share information about a topic
- **To persuade**: Persuasive paragraphs persuade the reader to make an action or take a position
- **To reflect**: Reflective paragraphs reflect on a personal experience
- **To entertain**: Entertaining paragraphs explore a topic or event in a creative or humorous way

Depending on the guidelines of your assignment, you may already know your purpose. Double-check your writing prompt or assignment details to see if your instructor has asked you to write with a specific purpose in mind. Once you've decided on a purpose, you can start narrowing down the scope of your topic.

If your paragraph is about job interviews, your list of **narrowed topics** might look like this:

Purpose	Narrowed Topic
To inform	What happens in a job interview
To persuade	Why you should dress up for job interviews
To reflect	Sharing a personal experience with a job interview
To entertain	A funny story about your first job interview

Group Activity

As a group, come up with narrowed topics that inform, persuade, reflect, and entertain for each of the following general topics:

> Olympic host cities
> physical therapy
> cosmetology school
> *The Mona Lisa*
> college football

Reflection Questions
What topics do you feel most comfortable writing about? Why?

Audience is another important factor to consider when you are narrowing the scope of your topic. Your **audience** is the group of people who will read your paragraph. At school, the audience for many of your assignments will be your instructor and your classmates. Outside of school, you may have to do research to determine your potential audience.

As you think about your audience, ask yourself these questions:

- What does my audience already know?
    - Is this topic very familiar to my audience?
    - Does the topic have a lot of specialized terms the audience may not know?
    - Is my audience made up of fellow students in the same class?

- What does my audience want to know?
    - Why is my audience interested in my topic?
    - Is my topic new or unusual?
    - Will people from a variety of backgrounds be interested in my topic?

These questions will help you narrow the scope of your topic to something that your audience finds useful and interesting. Imagine that you're writing a paragraph for your welding class. All your classmates already know a lot of technical information about welding. They probably wouldn't be as interested in a paragraph about how to operate a welding torch. Instead, you might consider writing your paragraph about "the history of welding" or "best welding torches." These are topics that they may find more interesting.

Reflection Questions
How would you narrow down the topic "cars" for each of the following audiences?

fifth graders   doctors   college students   parents

On Your Own

You write for many different reasons, and your audience changes depending on your specific purpose for writing. In the following table, the left column lists several types of texts. In the right column, fill in a possible audience for each type.

Text	Audience
Report for work	
Personal blog entry	
An accident report for insurance	
Text message	
Paper for history class	

The final way to narrow the scope of a topic is to think about possible constraints or limitations. One common type of constraint is word count. If your assignment is limited to a paragraph, then you won't be able to discuss as much information as you would in an entire paper. As a general rule, the shorter the assignment, the narrower the scope.

A second constraint is time. If your paragraph is due tomorrow, you may need to write about a topic that is more familiar to you. You won't have time to do any research on a more complex subject. On the other hand, if you have a week to write your assignment, you may be able to choose an unfamiliar topic that you need to research.

The requirements of the assignment are the best place to identify possible constraints. You should have already reviewed these guidelines before selecting your topic. As you work to narrow the scope of your paragraph, read back over any requirements to make sure you are following your instructor's directions.

On Your Own

What is the best length for each of the following topics? Check the box next to your answer.

Description of the wolf in "Red Riding Hood"
- ☐ Entire book
- ☐ Four-page paper
- ☐ Three hundred-word paragraph

History of the "Red Riding Hood" fable
- ☐ Entire book
- ☐ Four-page paper
- ☐ Three hundred-word paragraph

How fables reflect changes in society
- ☐ Entire book
- ☐ Four-page paper
- ☐ Three hundred-word paragraph

> **Reflection Questions**
> Different types of writing involve different types of constraints. What are some constraints that you might face while writing for work or in your everyday life? How would those constraints affect the way you narrow the scope of a topic?

Lesson Wrap-up

Key Terms

Active Learning: learning information through participation in activities

Audience: the people who read your writing

Brainstorming: exploring and developing ideas

Constraint: a limitation that affects your writing

Entertaining Text: a text that explores a topic or event in a creative or humorous way

Focus: clear communication and support of a main idea

Informative Text: a text that gives the audience information about a topic

Listing: writing down every word or phrase that comes to mind during a set amount of time

Mind Mapping: a method for making visual connections between topics

Narrowed Topic: a topic that you have made more specific by considering your purpose, audience, and constraints

Paragraph: a short piece of writing that focuses on one main idea

Persuasive Text: a text that convinces its audience to adopt a belief or take an action

Pre-writing: a stage of writing that involves making decisions, planning ideas, and identifying assignment guidelines

Purpose: the goal of a text

Reflective Text: a text that shares a personal experience or belief

Scope: the focus of a writing assignment

Visual Learning: learning information through pictures, shapes, and colors

Writing Prompt: an assignment, with special guidelines, that asks you to write about a specific topic

Lesson 6.3

Writing a Topic Sentence

Topic sentences are the foundation of a good **paragraph**. Just as the foundation of a house keeps the floors and walls steady, a good topic sentence keeps your ideas firmly grounded.

Topic sentences are useful to you during the **writing process**. Your topic sentence should help you make decisions about your main points and **supporting details**. Anything you include in a paragraph should clearly relate back to your topic sentence. For example, if you're writing a paragraph about your favorite songs, all the sentences in that paragraph should include details about your favorite songs. You would not include a sentence about your favorite relative or your favorite dessert.

Your **audience**, however, also benefits from a clear topic sentence. Including this sentence tells readers how all the information in the paragraph is related. Without one, your audience may not understand the point of your ideas.

In this lesson, you will learn how to draft an effective topic sentence by reading about the following:

Characteristics of a Topic Sentence
Determining a Controlling Idea
Constructing the Topic Sentence

Paragraphs need a good foundation: a strong topic sentence.

Characteristics of a Topic Sentence

Before you start writing your topic sentence, you must first become familiar with what a good topic sentence looks like. Here are three guidelines to keep in mind:

- **A topic sentence should be a statement, not a question.** Topic sentences are always one-sentence statements that tell the reader exactly what to expect in a paragraph. In order to *tell*, you must use a statement. If you want to include a thought-provoking question in your writing, always place it before or after your topic sentence.

- **A topic sentence should be clear and confident.** Your topic sentence introduces your thoughts on a topic. Don't be afraid to state your opinion clearly and confidently. Using vague phrases like "kind of" or "a lot" will weaken your communication and potentially confuse your audience.

- **A topic sentence should be written in your own words.** Because a topic sentence introduces what you want to say about a topic, you should always put a topic sentence in your own words. You can still use an interesting quote or statistic in your paragraph; just put it before or after your topic sentence.

Strong	The growing popularity of mobile devices is changing the rules of web design.
	A degree in English will give you communication skills you can use in any profession.
	Although all charities claim to help people, some accomplish this goal better than others.
Weak	Mobile phones are somewhat popular with people in today's society.
	According to Martin Luther King, Jr., "Darkness cannot drive out darkness."
	A charity is an organization that gives aid to those in need.

On Your Own

Below are three possible topic sentences for a paragraph about college tuition. Identify the strongest topic sentence.

- ☐ College tuition is too high, forcing most students to take on overwhelming student loans.
- ☐ Why is college tuition so high?
- ☐ According to *The Money Tracker*, college tuition has risen at least 20% a year for the last five years.

Determining a Controlling Idea

To write a topic sentence, you need to decide on a controlling idea for your paragraph. A **controlling idea** sums up exactly what you want to say about your topic. Here are some examples:

Topic: *local food bank charities*
- have played an important role in my own life
- are experiencing a shortage of donations because of the recession
- should be able to receive state and local tax funding
- provide more than just food
- are not the best way to help the community
- helped me learn empathy and respect

Your controlling idea is always influenced by the **purpose** of your paragraph. In a **persuasive** paragraph, a good controlling idea will be an opinion or stance; in an **informative** paragraph, a good controlling idea will share interesting and specific information.

For example, imagine that you've decided to write your paragraph about "buying a used car." Depending on your purpose for writing, any of the following controlling ideas could work:

To inform	takes hours of research and planning
To persuade	is a much better idea than buying a new car
To reflect	led to a mistake that cost me over $1,000
To entertain	is what I was doing when I was abducted by aliens

On Your Own

For each purpose, fill in your own controlling ideas about the topic "rising food costs."

Topic: rising food costs	
Purpose	**Controlling Idea**
To inform	
To persuade	
To reflect	
To entertain	

Here are some additional examples:

Topic: rising food costs	
Purpose	**Controlling Idea**
To inform	can be analyzed with several online budget programs
To persuade	will be minimized if you shop with coupons
To reflect	made me a more thoughtful consumer
To entertain	are the reason I now eat at my parents' house

Constructing the Topic Sentence

To write your topic sentence, combine your **narrowed topic** with your controlling idea.

To write a specific, confident topic sentence, you must use a specific, confident controlling idea. Try writing multiple versions of the same controlling idea so that you can pick the one that works the best.

Topic: the popularity of electric cars	
Weak	they are pretty good for the environment
Stronger	they are becoming more affordable
Strongest	average citizens are interested in reducing pollution

The strongest controlling idea fits all the requirements of a good topic sentence:

- They are statements, not questions.
- They are written in the author's own words.
- They are clear and confident.

Take a look at how well-written topic sentences are composed in the following examples:

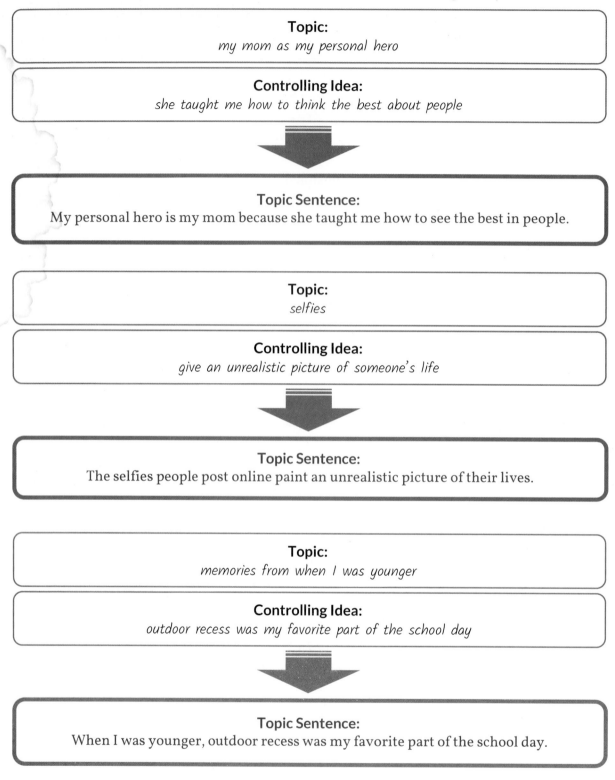

Topic:
my mom as my personal hero

Controlling Idea:
she taught me how to think the best about people

Topic Sentence:
My personal hero is my mom because she taught me how to see the best in people.

Topic:
selfies

Controlling Idea:
give an unrealistic picture of someone's life

Topic Sentence:
The selfies people post online paint an unrealistic picture of their lives.

Topic:
memories from when I was younger

Controlling Idea:
outdoor recess was my favorite part of the school day

Topic Sentence:
When I was younger, outdoor recess was my favorite part of the school day.

All of these topic sentences were created by combining a narrowed topic with a controlling idea. The wording of both parts was adjusted to make sure that they fit together smoothly, but the ideas stayed the same.

On Your Own

Use the empty organizer below to come up with a topic sentence for a paragraph of your choice.

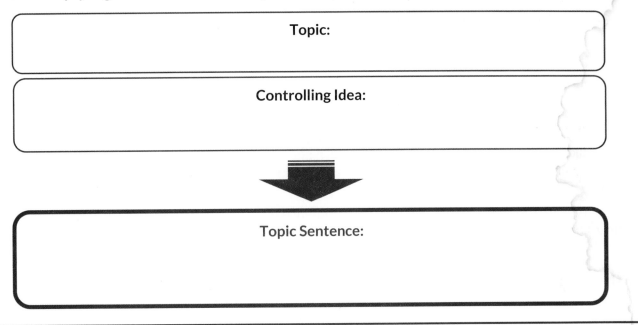

Topic:

Controlling Idea:

Topic Sentence:

Lesson Wrap-up

Group Activity
Individually, come up with persuasive controlling ideas for the following topics. Then, as a group, compare and contrast your ideas.

Bike share programs in cities
Inconsistent movie ratings
Fresh vegetables in school cafeterias

Key Terms

Academic Writing Process: a set of strategies that breaks up a writing assignment into five stages: pre-writing, drafting, revising, editing, and submitting

Audience: the people who read your writing

Controlling Idea: what an author wants to say about a topic

Entertaining Text: a text that explores a topic or event in a creative or humorous way

Informative Text: a text that gives the audience information about a topic

Narrowed Topic: a topic that you have made more specific by considering your purpose, audience, and constraints

Paragraph: a short piece of writing that focuses on one main idea

Persuasive Text: a text that convinces its audience to adopt a belief or take an action

Purpose: the goal of a text

Reflective Text: a text that shares a personal experience or belief

Supporting Detail: a piece of information, also called evidence, that is used to support a main idea

Topic Sentence: a sentence that states the main point of a paragraph

Lesson 6.4
Choosing an Organizational Pattern

Look at the pattern below. Which shape should come next?

More than likely, you were able to identify the pattern easily: square, circle, square, circle, square. This is because the human brain excels at organization. People are drawn to patterns because they are reliable and reassuring.

In your writing, **organizational patterns** help your audience understand your ideas by giving your **paragraph** structure. Organizational patterns also assist you as an author by keeping your thoughts focused and on-track.

In this lesson, you will learn the characteristics of six organizational patterns:

Cause and Effect
Chronological
Compare and Contrast
Order of Importance
Spatial
Topical

Once you are familiar with the different options, you can decide which one fits the purpose of your paragraph best.

Cause and Effect

Actions always have consequences, or results. For example, if you forget to set your alarm, you will probably oversleep and be late for class or work. The first action, not setting an alarm, is the *cause*. Oversleeping and being late is the *effect*, or result.

A **cause and effect** paragraph discusses the causes and/or effects of a topic. This organizational pattern works well for both **informative** and **persuasive** paragraphs. An informative paragraph might analyze the causes and effects, while a persuasive paragraph might use those causes and effects as evidence to support an argument.

Cause and effect paragraphs are usually structured like one of the outlines below:

Topic Sentence	Topic Sentence
Effect 1	Cause 1
Effect 2	Cause 2
Effect 3	Cause 3
Concluding Sentence	Concluding Sentence

Transitions are words, phrases, or sentences that show order and make connections between ideas. Transition words are often called "signpost words." Just like road signs guide you through city streets, transition words and phrases guide your audience through your paragraph.

You can use the following transition words and phrases to show order in a cause-and-effect paragraph:

as a result	cause	effect	since
because	due to	reason	therefore

The transitions are highlighted in the following example of a cause-and-effect paragraph:

> The events of July 10th make me refer to it as "my worst day ever." That morning, as I rushed to catch the train, one of my shoes fell off. When I turned around to pick it up, I accidentally hit a man with my heavy backpack. Because of the sudden impact, he stumbled and got stuck in the doors of the train as they closed. Everyone in the train car stared as I ran to help him, but he managed to pull himself free, spilling his entire cup of coffee on me in the process. Due to my clumsiness, it was too late to go home and change. As a result, I had to go to class in my coffee-stained clothes.
>
> Notice the cause-effect cycle in the paragraph. Additionally, a single cause can have multiple effects, and multiple causes can contribute to one effect.

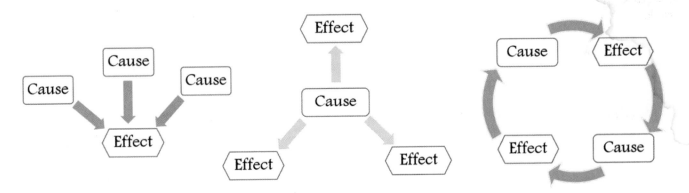

Chronological

A **chronological** paragraph shares ideas or events in the order that they occurred. This type of organizational pattern works well in paragraphs meant to inform the audience about a historical event or **entertain** the audience with an interesting story.

Chronological paragraphs can also explain a sequence of steps or a process. For example, instruction manuals are written in chronological order.

To test whether or not a paragraph should use chronological organization, try to switch the order of the events. If your topic no longer makes sense, you should probably use a chronological organizational pattern.

Chronological paragraphs are usually structured like this:

Topic Sentence
Event 1
Event 2
Event 3
Concluding Sentence

Here are some common transition words and phrases for chronological paragraphs:

after	at last	first	second	then
afterward	before	next	since	ultimately

The following passage is an example of a chronological paragraph. The transition words are highlighted.

Writing a paragraph has five steps. First, begin with pre-writing. Pre-writing allows you to brainstorm ideas so you have a place to start writing. The next stage of the writing process is drafting. Use the ideas from the pre-writing stage to write your first draft. After drafting, start revising. During the revising stage, re-write any part of the paragraph that is confusing. Also, add any missing information. The fourth stage of the writing process is editing. During this stage, read the paragraph for grammar, style, and spelling errors. The final stage of the writing process is submitting your work. Submitting allows you to share your work with an audience. If you consistently use the five stages of the writing process, you will become a better writer.

Notice how the steps are arranged in the order they must be completed. If you rearrange the sentences, the paragraph won't make sense.

On Your Own

Read the examples below and identify the passage that is written chronologically.

Last, going with the natural grain of the wood, apply the stain in an even layer. First, use sandpaper to smooth the wood and remove the existing varnish. Next, clean the surface with mineral spirits.

First, use sandpaper to smooth the wood and remove the existing varnish. Last, going with the natural grain of the wood, apply the stain in an even layer. Next, clean the surface with mineral spirits.

First, use sandpaper to smooth the wood and remove the existing varnish. Next, clean the surface with mineral spirits. Last, going with the natural grain of the wood, apply the stain in an even layer.

Compare and Contrast

The **compare and contrast** organizational pattern is used for paragraphs that discuss the similarities and differences between two topics.

For example, to write about how your dog and cat have different personalities, choose a characteristic that is relevant to both of them. After you choose the common characteristic, such as loyalty, you can describe how both your dog and your cat are loyal (compare), or how your dog is loyal while your cat is not (contrast). This structure works well for informative paragraphs.

Compare and contrast paragraphs are usually structured one of two ways:

Topic Sentence	Topic Sentence
Similarity 1	Similarity 1
Similarity 2	Difference 1
Difference 1	Similarity 2
Difference 2	Difference 2
Concluding Sentence	Concluding Sentence

Here are some common transition words and phrases in compare and contrast paragraphs:

also	differently	like	such as
as well as	however	on the other hand	too
both	in contrast	similarly	unlike
conversely			

Here is an example of a compare and contrast paragraph. The transition words and phrases are highlighted.

> My cousins are moving and have offered to sell me one of their vehicles: one is a car and the other is a truck. There are two ways the vehicles are similar. They both provide reliable transportation. Also, they are about the same price. On the other hand, the truck can haul large loads while the car can't. The other difference is fuel mileage. The car gets about thirty miles per gallon. Conversely, the truck only gets about seventeen miles per gallon. I have a week to make my decision.
>
> By using transition words and phrases, the author indicates a comparison (the transportation and price of each vehicle) and a contrast (between the hauling ability and mileage.)

Order of Importance

A paragraph arranged in **order of importance** organizes the information from most important to least important or from least important to most important.

This organizational pattern is often used to prove a point in a persuasive paragraph.

Group Activity

Together, think of three reasons why music should or should not be free. Arrange your reasons in order of importance and present them to the class.

Order of importance paragraphs are usually structured like this:

Topic Sentence
Most Important Point
Less Important Point
Least Important Point
Concluding Sentence

Here are some common transition words and phrases in order of importance paragraphs:

above all	furthermore	least/most important
equally important	key	least/most significant
first	last	second

The following passage is an example of an order of importance paragraph. The transition words and phrases are highlighted.

> There are three primary reasons why I watch basketball. The most important reason is that, while he was still alive, my grandfather took me to basketball games. Those times were the best experiences of my childhood. The second reason is that I played basketball in high school. I had to stop in order to focus on academics, but I enjoyed being on a team (and improving my jump shot). The least important reason why I watch basketball is to annoy my best friend; she loves football. We always argue about which sport is better. These are the three reasons why I watch basketball.

On Your Own

Read the following sentences and identify the transition words or phrases.

> The most important step in constructing a well-built house is using quality building materials. For contractors, hiring professional workers is an equally important consideration.

Spatial

A **spatial** paragraph describes a location or object by its physical characteristics. For example, hair color and height are physical characteristics of a person. You typically use your senses (sight, smell, taste, touch, and hearing) to describe a physical characteristic.

The description in a spatially ordered paragraph usually moves from one side to the other in an orderly way. The spatial organizational pattern works well when your purpose is to inform or entertain.

Spatial paragraphs are usually structured like this:

> Topic Sentence
> Physical Characteristic 1
> Physical Characteristic 2
> Physical Characteristic 3
> Concluding Sentence

Here are some common transition words and phrases in spatial paragraphs:

above	below	inside/outside	in the middle	opposite
across	between	in front of	next to	to the left/right

Here is an example of a spatial paragraph:

> When I saw the motorcycle parked outside of the store, I was mesmerized. The chrome headlights gleamed in the sunlight. The handle bars stretched up and over the metal-studded black leather seat. The back tire was larger than the front and had deep treads, perfect for off-roading. The combined trunk and second seat were painted a deep, shiny red. That was the beginning of my motorcycle obsession.
>
> Notice how the paragraph starts by describing the front of the motorcycle and moves all the way to the back of the bike. Although this paragraph does not use transitions, the descriptions help you mentally picture the motorcycle.

On Your Own

In the space below, use spatial organization to write a short description of your current location.

Topical

Topical paragraphs are not arranged in a particular order because all the information is of equal importance. This pattern is sometimes referred to as "listing" and is often used for informative or **reflective** writing.

Topical paragraphs are usually structured like this:

> Topic Sentence
> Topic 1
> Topic 2
> Topic 3
> Concluding Sentence

Here are some common transition words and phrases in topical paragraphs. Notice that they are very similar to the transitions used in chronological paragraphs.

also	next
finally	second
first	to begin
last	

Here is an example of a topical paragraph:

> There are several reasons why today was a great birthday. First, it's a Saturday, so I didn't have to go to work or request a day off. Also, I received texts and phone calls from most of my friends and family. Next, I got to eat dinner at my favorite restaurant. Last, my girlfriend gave me tickets to see my favorite band. Overall, I had an awesome day.

Lesson Wrap-up

On Your Own

Determine what type of organizational pattern is used in each of the following paragraphs.

> When baking a cherry pie, begin by placing a ready-made pie crust in a nine-inch pie plate. Next, add a can of cherry pie filling to the crust. After spreading out the cherries, place a second crust on the top of the filling. Finally, bake the pie at 400 degrees for about an hour.

- ☐ Cause and Effect
- ☐ Chronological
- ☐ Compare and Contrast
- ☐ Order of Importance
- ☐ Spatial
- ☐ Topical

> The kids enjoyed their trip to the zoo. It was most important that they see their favorite animals, the elephants. The antics of the otters made everyone laugh. The aviary pavilion allowed the children to see a variety of birds in their typical habitats. Least exciting was the hippopotamus. He was underwater, so we only saw a beady pair of eyes

and two small ears. The kids were exhausted and slept in the car all the way home. The trip was definitely a success.

- ☐ Cause and Effect
- ☐ Chronological
- ☐ Compare and Contrast
- ☐ Order of Importance
- ☐ Spatial
- ☐ Topical

Key Terms

Cause and Effect: an organizational pattern used to explain the causes or effects of a topic

Chronological: an organizational pattern that arranges ideas or events in the order that they occurred

Compare and Contrast: an organizational pattern used to show the similarities and differences between two topics

Entertaining Text: a text that explores a topic or event in a creative or humorous way

Informative Text: a text that gives the audience information about a topic

Order of Importance: an organizational pattern that arranges information in order of importance

Organizational Pattern: the structure of a written text, used to arrange the main points of a work

Paragraph: a short piece of writing that focuses on one main idea

Persuasive Text: a text that convinces its audience to adopt a belief or take an action

Reflective Text: a text that shares a personal experience or belief

Spatial: an organizational pattern used to describe a topic by its physical characteristics

Topical: a general organizational pattern used for equally important main points

Transition: a word, phrase, or sentence that shows order and makes connections between ideas

Lesson 6.5

Drafting a Paragraph

Once you've decided on a **topic sentence** for your paragraph, you can begin working on a first draft. Writing a first draft is just the beginning; you'll probably write two or more drafts during the **drafting** stage of the **writing process**.

A **first draft** is an opportunity for you to focus on the content of your paragraph. At this stage, you'll start putting all of your ideas together and organizing them effectively. This structure will guide the **audience** through the information in a logical, thorough way. Your focus should be on building a solid paragraph, not perfecting your grammar and spelling. You'll want to focus on grammar and spelling during the **editing** stage.

In this lesson, you will learn three important elements of a first draft:

Support Sentences

Concluding Sentences

Transitions

Writing involves several steps. Don't try to do everything at once; you'll end up missing something important. Just like with any process, you must complete each step in order to ensure the best possible outcome.

A **paragraph** is simply a short piece of writing that focuses on one **main idea**. In **academic writing**, your paragraphs have an internal structure to make them more effective. Outside of school, your paragraphs are more flexible. You may have one-sentence or even one-word paragraphs.

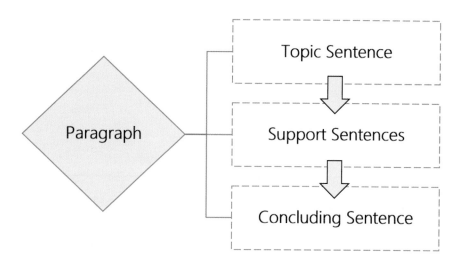

Support Sentences

Support sentences explain and support your topic sentence. Support sentences can build your argument, explain a complex topic, or tell a story. Some of these sentences will be main points that directly support your topic sentence, while others will include explanations and supporting details that expand on those main points.

Your **organizational pattern** determines the arrangement of the main points in your paragraph. For example, if you are using a **cause and effect** organizational pattern, your topic sentence is the cause, and your main points are the effects. Choose the organizational pattern that best supports your main idea and your purpose for writing.

To learn more about organizational patterns, see Lesson 6.4.

Many of your support sentences will also contain supporting details. **Supporting details** are pieces of information that make your paragraph more interesting and effective by expanding on your main points.

There are seven types of supporting details:

- **Anecdotes**: long examples told as a story
- **Descriptions**: passages that explain the appearance of someone or something using words that appeal to the senses
- **Examples**: specific instances or illustrations that demonstrate a point
- **Expert Analysis**: an opinion or statement shared by someone who is knowledgeable about a topic
- **Facts**: pieces of information that most people generally agree to be true
- **Reflections**: the thoughts and feelings of the author
- **Statistics**: numbers or percentages that represent research data

On Your Own

Read the following passage and determine the type of supporting detail it uses. Check the box next to your answer.

It's crucial that states develop better programs for providing children with adequate clothing. When I was ten, my family couldn't afford to buy me winter shoes. Instead, I wore gym shoes as I stood in a foot of snow at the bus stop in winter. Eventually, my feet became frostbitten and I missed school for a week. Worse, I almost lost some of my toes.

☐ Expert Analysis
☐ Fact
☐ Reflection
☐ Statistic
☐ Anecdote

Any supporting details that you include in your paragraph must be introduced and explained in your own words through author analysis. As you communicate your ideas, avoid creating a laundry list of facts and statistics. Facts and statistics are useful when expanding and explaining your thoughts and opinions, but they should not take the place of your own words.

> **Helpful Hint**
> Remember, to copy someone else's work without giving the author credit for their words and/or ideas is to commit plagiarism.

To learn more about plagiarism and how to avoid it, see Lesson 8.6.

Read the following paragraphs. Which one communicates its message more effectively?

The rising amount of student loan debt is a problem that affects all Americans. In an article for Bloomberg, Jeanna Smialek reported that private and federal student loans had reached over $1 trillion by the end of 2014. People who are struggling to repay student loans are much less likely to start small businesses or purchase houses (Korkki). Without consumer spending, unemployment rates will continue to drop.

The rising amount of student loan debt is a problem that affects all Americans. In an article for Bloomberg, Jeanna Smialek reported that private and federal student loans had reached over $1 trillion by the end of 2014. The burden of this debt has a large impact on the economy. People who are struggling to repay student loans are much less likely to start small businesses or purchase houses (Korkki). Without consumer spending, unemployment rates will continue to drop. Reducing student loan debt is a necessary step toward strengthening the American economy.

Both paragraphs start with the main idea that student loan debt is a problem. However, the second paragraph does a much better job of using author analysis. It includes sentences that share the author's position on how the statistics and expert analysis of the economy support the idea in the topic sentence: student loan debt affects all Americans.

Concluding Sentences

At the end of your paragraph, a **concluding sentence** ties all your ideas together. Your concluding sentence is the opposite of your topic sentence. While the topic sentence starts the paragraph by introducing a new idea, your concluding sentence ends the paragraph by reviewing the ideas you just discussed. Often, the concluding sentence also restates the topic sentence using different words.

Take a look at the following example:

> Learning to play an instrument is difficult, but it's worth it. According to research, one positive effect of playing an instrument is improved memory function. Additionally, playing an instrument can strengthen the player's mathematical skills because music has many mathematical factors like time signatures. Finally, playing music allows an individual to express themselves in a unique way. Although playing an instrument requires dedication, the benefits make it a worthwhile activity.

> Notice how the concluding sentence is not an exact copy of the topic sentence. Instead, it restates the main idea with slightly different words.

On Your Own

Read the following topic sentence.

> The libraries of today use digital technologies to provide many services that were traditionally completed by hand.

Identify the concluding sentence that best restates the topic sentence.

> Libraries provide a variety of services.

> Modern libraries use electronic resources rather than traditional paper and pencils for many of their services.

> Computer labs can be found at most modern libraries.

Your **purpose** for writing will also influence the type of concluding sentence that fits your paragraph best. In an **informative** paragraph, your concluding sentences may be a straightforward summary. In a **persuasive** paragraph, however, your concluding sentence is more likely to challenge the reader to make a decision or take action. For example, if your topic sentence states that voting in local, state, and national elections is important, then your concluding statement will likely challenge readers to vote whenever possible.

To think of ideas for your concluding sentence, ask yourself the following questions:

> How do I want my reader to respond?
> Why should my reader care?

Transitions

Transitions are words, phrases, or sentences that show order and make connections between ideas. Transitions help your audience understand the organization of your paragraph. You don't want your readers to feel lost in your writing. Transitions give your audience landmarks that they can use to follow the progression of your ideas.

Transition words are sometimes called "signpost words" because they provide direction for the audience. There are two main types of transition words: those that show order and those that make connections. Here are a few examples of each:

Order	Connections
finally	also
first	because
in conclusion	further
next	likewise
second	similarly
then	therefore

Make sure you understand the meaning of the transition word you want to use. If your transition does not accurately indicate the relationship between two ideas, your reader might not understand your writing. Look at the following example:

> Today's shipment has been delayed because of weather problems; similarly, we cannot restock the shelves.

The signpost word *similarly* does not show an accurate relationship between the two sentences. In this example, an appropriate transition would indicate that the second idea is a result of the first idea.

Here is a better way to write the sentence:

> Today's shipment has been delayed because of weather problems; ~~similarly~~ therefore, we cannot restock the shelves.

You should also consider your organizational pattern when choosing transitions. For example, a **compare and contrast** paragraph would use signpost words such as *in a similar way* or *in contrast*.

To learn more about how organizational patterns use transitions, see Lesson 6.4.

On Your Own

Read the following sentences and identify the one that uses a stronger transition word.

> I need to deposit my check; likewise, the bank is closed.

> I need to deposit my check; however, the bank is closed.

Lesson Wrap-up

Key Terms

Academic Writing: texts intended for instructors or students

Academic Writing Process: a strategy that breaks up a writing assignment into five stages: pre-writing, drafting, revising, editing, and submitting

Anecdote: a long example told as a story

Audience: the people who read your writing

Cause and Effect: an organizational pattern used to explain the causes or effects of a topic

Compare and Contrast: an organizational pattern used to show the similarities and differences between two topics

Concluding Sentence: a sentence that ends a paragraph or paper by reviewing the ideas just discussed

Description: a passage that explains the appearance of someone or something using words that appeal to the senses

Drafting: a stage of writing that involves writing out ideas and support/concluding sentences

Editing: a stage of writing that involves proofreading for style, grammar, and spelling errors

Example: a specific instance or illustration that demonstrates a point

Expert Analysis: an opinion or statement shared by someone who is knowledgeable about a topic

Fact: a piece of information that most people generally agree to be true

First Draft: the first version of a text

Informative Text: a text that gives the audience information about a topic

Main Idea: the statement or argument that an author tries to communicate

Organizational Pattern: the structure of a written text, used to arrange the main points of a work

Paragraph: a short piece of writing that focuses on one main idea

Persuasive Text: a text that convinces its audience to adopt a belief or take an action

Purpose: the goal of a text

Reflection: the thoughts or feelings of the author

Statistic: a number or percentage that represents research data

Support Sentence: a sentence that explains and supports the topic sentence

Supporting Detail: a piece of information, also called evidence, that is used to support a main idea

Topic Sentence: a sentence that states the main point of a paragraph

Transition: a word, phrase, or sentence that shows order and makes connections between ideas

Lesson 6.6
Revising and Editing a Paragraph

Once you have **drafted** your **paragraph**, you can begin the revision and editing stages of the **writing process**. A good piece of writing is revised and edited multiple times. Each time, your paragraph gets closer to becoming a final draft.

The **revision** stage of the writing process involves revising for focus and development. The **editing** stage of the writing process involves proofreading for style, grammar, and spelling errors. In other words, revising is the time to improve your ideas; editing is the time to improve your words and sentences.

Revising helps you keep your focus on content, not grammar. You don't want to spend time fixing the subject-verb agreement in a sentence only to delete the whole sentence later. Once you have revised the ideas in your paragraph, you can start editing.

In this lesson, you will learn about the third and fourth stages of the writing process:

Revising Ideas
Editing Words and Sentences

> Helpful Hint
> If your instructor provides a grading rubric, now is a good time to review it.

Revising Ideas

Focus

A **focused** paragraph clearly communicates its **main idea** and uses every sentence to support and expand that idea. For example, a paragraph about military leaders of the American Revolution will probably not include a sentence about the causes of the Civil War. Instead, all the sentences will provide **supporting details** directly related to the American Revolution.

> To learn more about supporting details, see Lesson 6.5.

As you revise for focus, you may need to change or delete information to stay on topic. Don't worry if you change an idea more than once. Keep revising. Even experienced writers make multiple revisions.

On Your Own

Read the following paragraph and identify the sentence that should be deleted to make the paragraph more focused.

> When I was growing up, my brother was the most important person in my life. My brother was important to me for three reasons. First, he was my best friend. We did everything together; we even went to summer camp together. Second, he could already drive. I wouldn't have been able to go anywhere if he wasn't willing to take me. I couldn't wait to get my own license. The third reason my brother was important is that he was the drummer in my band. I could sing, but he was the one who kept us on-beat. My brother played a vital role in my childhood.

As you revise for focus, ask yourself the following questions:

> Does my paragraph clearly accomplish my **purpose** for writing?
> Have I stated the main idea of my paragraph in a clear **topic sentence**?
> Do all of the sentences in my paragraph relate to my topic sentence?
> Does my **concluding sentence** tie together all the ideas in my paragraph?

Development

A well-developed paragraph presents information in an effective way and includes plenty of details to support its main idea. While revising for **development**, you may need to expand or add information to strengthen your ideas.

For example, imagine you've written that paragraph about military leaders of the American Revolution, and it lists George Washington without any other information. When you revise the paragraph, you add a sentence explaining that Washington, a delegate from Virginia to the Second Continental Congress, was elected commander-in-chief of the Continental Army. The extra information develops your man idea.

> Helpful Hint
> Revision is too important to rush through or skip. You may need to make extra time in your schedule or re-prioritize some of your other tasks.

On Your Own

Take a look at this paragraph from earlier in the lesson. The highlighted sentence has been added; does it strengthen the paragraph's development?

> When I was growing up, my brother was the most important person in my life. My brother was important to me for three reasons. First, he was my best friend. We did everything together; we even went to summer camp together. Second, he could already drive. My brother took me to school every morning and band practice every afternoon. I wouldn't have been able to go anywhere if he wasn't willing to take me. I couldn't wait to get my own license. The third reason my brother was important is that he was the drummer in my band. I could sing, but he was the one who kept us on-beat. My brother played a vital role in my childhood.

☐ Yes   ☐ No

As you revise for development, ask yourself the following questions:

> Is my topic narrow enough to discuss in a specific, in-depth way?
> Does my organizational pattern present the information logically?
> Do I use plenty of transitions to help the reader follow the ideas?
> Are all of my points strengthened by plenty of supporting details?
> Have I explained all my main points?

Revision Strategies

Revising for focus and development takes a significant amount of time and effort. You are not just reading the words on a page; you are actively evaluating the thoughts behind those words. To help yourself work more effectively, use these strategies:

- **Revise your work in stages.** As you move between drafting and revising, making changes in small steps is much easier than changing everything at once. Begin by revising for focus. Think through each question carefully and make any necessary changes after each one. Then, revise for development in the same way.

- **Keep copies of your previous drafts.** Use the Save As option on your computer to save each version of your paragraph. If you are writing your paragraph by hand, save hard copies in a folder or notebook. Revisions don't always go exactly as planned. You may need to return to an earlier version of your paragraph to undo or redo certain changes. Saving multiple drafts also allows you to see the way your writing improved throughout the process.

- **Get a second opinion.** If possible, ask a friend, peer, or **Writing Center** tutor to read your paragraph and share feedback or suggestions. Someone who hasn't read the paragraph multiple times will have a different perspective than you.

- **Take frequent breaks.** Giving yourself a short break between revisions is always a good idea. If you have been revising for an hour, take five minutes to stretch or to get something to eat. It's much easier to see potential problems when you've had a chance to clear your mind.

Editing Words and Sentences

Editing involves proofreading your work to make sure the writing is completely free of spelling, grammar, and style errors. Editing can be tedious, but it's important. You don't want the **audience** to focus on a spelling error instead of on your ideas. Here are some strategies to help you become an effective editor.

- **Start at the end.** After reading something multiple times, you're less likely to see errors. By reading backwards (from the last sentence to the first sentence), your eyes will be less likely to skip over or miss an error. Starting from the end gives your brain a new perspective.
- **Know your common errors.** Be aware of your strengths and weaknesses. For example, do you often have comma splices in your writing? Look carefully at each sentence to make sure you don't have any comma splices. You can also keep a record of your common errors and check the list whenever you're editing.
- **Look for one error at a time.** You can't effectively find every kind of error at once. Pick an error type (such as commonly misspelled words) and read slowly through the entire piece looking for that specific type of error. Repeat the process until you have addressed spelling, grammar, and style.

> To learn more about proofreading for grammar and style, see Lessons 4.21 and 5.11.

Helpful Hint
A word processor's spelling and grammar checkers are helpful, but they rarely catch every error. Use electronic resources and your own knowledge to thoroughly edit your paragraphs.

On Your Own

Now it is your turn to practice editing. Read the following paragraph and identify the words and phrases that need to be edited. (There are five errors total.)

> In mathematics, knowing weather to calculate the area or perimeter of a shape is essential. Calculate the area of a shape. When you want to determine the number of square units the shape occupies. In real life, area was used in situations such as calculating the amount of flooring needed for a new home. Perimeter, on the other hand, is used to calculate the length of the boundary of a shape. For example, perimeter is used too calculate the amount of fencing needed to enclose a playground. Consider the context of the situation before making the choice between area or perimeter.

Group Activity
Which strategies do you find easiest? Which strategies are more challenging? Discuss with your group any additional strategies you know for revising and editing your writing.

Lesson Wrap-up

Key Terms

Academic Writing Process: a strategy that breaks up a writing assignment into five stages: pre-writing, drafting, revising, editing, and submitting

Audience: the people who read your writing

Concluding Sentence: a sentence that ends a paragraph or paper by reviewing the ideas just discussed

Development: effective presentation of information and inclusion of supporting details

Drafting: a stage of writing that involves writing out ideas and support/concluding sentences

Editing: a stage of writing that involves proofreading for style, grammar, and spelling errors

Focus: clear communication and support of a main idea

Main Idea: the statement or argument that an author tries to communicate

Organizational Pattern: the structure of a written text, used to arrange the main points of a work

Paragraph: a short piece of writing that focuses on one main idea

Purpose: the goal of a text

Revising: a stage of writing that involves revising for focus and development

Supporting Detail: a piece of information, also called evidence, that is used to support a main idea

Topic Sentence: a sentence that states the main point of a paragraph

Transition: a word, phrase, or sentence that shows order and makes connections between ideas

Writing Center: a service that provides writing assistance

Lesson 6.7

Submitting a Paragraph

Submitting your work is the fifth stage of the **writing process**. This is an opportunity to share your ideas with your readers and reflect on all the hard work that went into your writing.

Although submitting is the shortest stage in the writing process, you must still make thoughtful choices about how you are communicating with your **audience**. You will not be able to accomplish your writing goals if you don't share your work.

Keep in mind that submitting your work is not always the end of the writing process. In some situations, you may continue to **revise**, **edit**, and improve a text even after you've submitted it.

In this lesson, you will learn two steps for submitting a paragraph:

Choose a Format
Print or Upload Your Work

> **Reflection Questions**
> Musicians expect people to listen to their music, and athletes expect fans to cheer them on. As a writer, do you expect your words to be read? Why or why not? How does this affect your writing?

Choose a Format

When you reach the submitting stage of the writing process, you need to decide on the format of your finished work. **Format** can involve any of the following details:

- **Font**
- Line spacing
- **Page margins**
- Page size
- Colors
- Image

If you are working on an assignment for school, check the guidelines in your **writing prompt**. Your instructor may have specific requirements for the format of your **paragraph**. Similarly, a paragraph being submitted to a magazine or organization may need to follow specific formatting rules.

On Your Own

Read the following writing prompt and identify the sentences that describe formatting requirements.

> A term limit is a law that sets the maximum number of times an individual may hold an elected office. For example, the president of the United States cannot serve more than two four-year terms. People hold varying opinions on term limits; some believe that term limits prevent political corruption while others think they prevent politicians from thinking about long-term issues. Research the history of term limits to better understand the potential positive and negative effects. Then, write an essay explaining your position on the topic. Your paragraph should be double-spaced and in 12-point Times New Roman font. Remember to set page margins at one inch on all sides.

If you are free to choose your own format, consider the **purpose** and audience of your paragraph. The way you would format a report for adults would be different from the format of a story for children.

Look at the following examples. How well does the purpose and audience of the paragraph fit the format of the document?

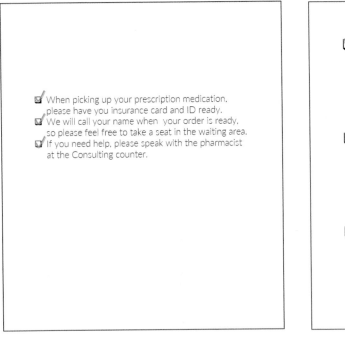

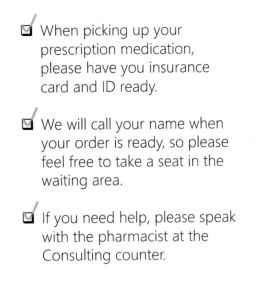

In the first example, the font and line spacing are very small. This could make the text difficult for people who have poor eyesight. The second example is formatted in a way that is much easier to understand.

> **Reflection Questions**
> Think about the formatting of books, websites, newspapers, and magazines. How does the formatting affect the way you understand and interpret the information?

Print or Upload Your Work

Next, you must prepare to print or upload your work. If you intend to print your paragraph, make sure you print it at least one day before the due date. You don't want to wait until the last minute only to discover that your printer is out of ink. Printing ahead of time also gives you a chance to look over your copy one last time before submitting it to your instructor or supervisor. Be sure to keep your document clean and unrumpled.

If you are writing a paragraph to be sent through email, double check any guidelines to make sure you are using the correct file format. In most cases, a Microsoft Word file (.docx) or PDF (.pdf) is acceptable. Before sending your document, email it to yourself so that you can test the file and make sure it opens without any issues.

Once you've emailed your official copy, you should check your Sent folder to verify that the email was delivered without any problems. Save this copy so that you have a record of your submission. If your instructor accidentally overlooks your email, you will be able to prove that you sent the file on time.

When you are uploading a paragraph to be posted online, you probably need to input the text into a website. In most cases, it's easiest to copy and paste a plain, unformatted copy and use the font and color tools on the website to make final changes before publishing.

On Your Own

Why is it important to print, submit, and/or email an assignment at least one day before it is due? Choose the correct answer.

- ☐ It gives the instructor extra time to read the assignment.
- ☐ Students who turn work in early receive higher grades.
- ☐ It gives you extra time in case you have technology issues.

> **Further Resources**
> If you are writing a paragraph for a school assignment, consider publishing it online as well. You can set up a personal blog on sites like Wordpress or Tumblr and share your thoughts with people in your immediate circles or even around the world.

Lesson Wrap-up

Key Terms

Academic Writing Process: a set of strategies in five stages: pre-writing, drafting, revising, editing, and submitting

Audience: the people who read your writing

Editing: a stage of writing that involves proofreading for style, grammar, and spelling errors

Font: the size and style of letters

Format: the style and arrangement of a text

Page Margin: the amount of space between the words and the edge of the paper

Paragraph: a short piece of writing that focuses on one main idea

Purpose: the goal of a text

Revising: a stage of writing that involves revising for focus and development

Submitting: a stage of writing that involves formatting a text and sharing it with its audience

Writing Prompt: an assignment, with special guidelines, that asks you to write about a specific topic

Chapter 7
Writing Longer Texts

Lesson 7.1
Preparing to Write a Longer Text

Simple tasks like turning on a light or opening a door can be accomplished through a single action. More complicated tasks, however, require you to perform multiple steps in a specific order. When you make a cake, you can't dump all of the ingredients in a pan and pop them into a cold oven. You have to preheat the oven, mix the ingredients in a specific order, and then bake the cake.

Many tasks need to be accomplished step by step.

Writing a long essay or a research paper is similar to baking a cake. You can't sit down to write the entire paper without any preparation or planning. Not only will this approach leave you feeling frustrated and overwhelmed, but it will also result in a lumpy mess of a paper.

The **academic writing process** is used not only for **paragraphs**, but also for writing research papers or long essays. This process breaks up a large assignment into five smaller, more manageable stages:

- Pre-writing
- Drafting
- Revising
- Editing
- Submitting

To learn more about each step of the writing process for longer texts, see Lessons 7.2-7.11.

Reflection Questions
Think about a task that requires multiple steps to perform. How is each step important?

Writing is a circular process. Good writers might move back and forth between each stage multiple times. For example, if you find yourself drafting in an unplanned direction, you may need to do additional pre-writing to find new ideas. Then, if you notice problems with the organization of your work, you may need to return to the drafting stage.

This lesson will give you an overview of the academic writing process and teach you how to use a writing schedule to keep your writing on track.

Helpful Hint
The lessons in this chapter emphasize assignments like long essays and research papers. However, you can also use this process for longer texts outside of school like résumés and cover letters, personal narratives, short stories, or presentations. Any type of writing will benefit from the additional planning and structure that the writing process provides.

Pre-Writing and Drafting

The first stage of the writing process is **pre-writing**. During this stage, you will generate ideas and plan the **purpose** and organization of your work. Don't allow yourself to skip this essential step in the writing process. Not only will pre-writing keep your paper clear and **focused**, but it will also save you time during drafting and revising.

Step-by-Step Checklist: Pre-writing

☐ | 1. Determine the **genre** and purpose.

☐ | 2. Choose a topic and narrow the **scope** of the paper.

☐ | 3. Write a **thesis statement** or **purpose statement**.

☐ | 4. Organize and outline the paper.

Drafting is the second stage in the writing process. This step involves organizing your ideas into strong paragraphs. You don't have to worry too much about grammar or spelling because those issues will be fixed later. The most important part of drafting is actually getting your words down on paper.

The drafting stage of the writing process includes the following steps:

Step-by-Step Checklist: Drafting
☐   1. Write a first draft.
☐   2. Use strong paragraph organization.
☐   3. Write an **introduction** and a **conclusion**.

Revising and Editing

Revision is the third stage of the writing process. During this stage, you will make improvements to the organization and content of the paper, moving back and forth between drafting and revising multiple times.

Once you are satisfied with your work, you can move on to the fourth stage of the writing process. **Editing** involves proofreading for style, grammar, and spelling errors. While revision is the time to improve your ideas, editing is the time to improve your words and sentences.

> Learning Style Tip
>
> If you're a **global** learner, you may find yourself focusing more on expressing the big idea of your paper and less on organizing your paragraphs. Revision is the perfect time to check your paragraph structure.

> Learning Style Tip
>
> If you're a **sequential** learner, take time during revision to make sure your individual paragraphs clearly support the main point of your paper.

Submitting

The last step in the writing process is submitting your work. **Submitting** involves adjusting the layout, design, and **format** of the paper. For a school assignment, your instructor may require a specific set of guidelines. Outside of school, you have more control over how and where your work is submitted.

Writing Schedules

A **writing schedule** is designed to keep you on track when writing a research paper or long essay. Because the academic writing process takes time and preparation, waiting until the last minute can be disastrous. Even if you manage to draft the paper, you won't have time to revise the content or correct grammar and style errors. Writing schedules help you avoid these problems by giving you a clear plan of action.

To create a writing schedule, first update your **planner**, the place where you keep your schedule and assignments. Mark the date your paper is due. If you have separate dates to turn in **outlines** or first drafts, mark all of those as well.

Next, add dedicated writing time to your schedule. If your instructor requires different parts of the paper on different days, use these due dates as a guide. If not, set your own deadlines for pre-writing, drafting, revising, editing, and submitting. Write these goals in your planner like real due dates and schedule plenty of writing time before each one.

April 13-19

MONDAY

13 Mom's B-Day

Algebra Homework:
sections 6.1 - 7.10

French Homework: Write journal

7-10 Writing

TUESDAY

14

Lit Homework: Read Chap. 1-10

6pm Algebra Study Group   7-10 Writing

Schedule your writing times just like you would plan class or work commitments.

When planning your schedule, try to spread your writing times across multiple days. Taking breaks between writing sessions helps you generate new ideas and prevents writer's block. If you push yourself too hard, the quality of your writing will decrease.

Helpful Hint
Schedule yourself an extra day for submitting your work just in case you run into technology issues. When the library printer is out of ink or your USB drive stops working, you'll be glad that you didn't wait until the very last minute to print your paper.

Lesson Wrap-up

Reflection Questions
What do you think is the most important step in the writing process?

Key Terms

Academic Writing Process: a strategy that breaks up a writing assignment into five stages: pre-writing, drafting, revising, editing, and submitting

Conclusion: a paragraph that ties together the main ideas in a paper and summarizes the main points, also called a concluding paragraph

Drafting: a stage of writing that involves writing out ideas and support/concluding sentences

Editing: a stage of writing that involves proofreading for style, grammar, and spelling errors

Focus: clear communication and support of a main idea

Format: the style and arrangement of a text

Global Learning: learning information through seeing the big picture

Introduction: the paragraph used to introduce the main idea at the beginning of a paper, also called an introductory paragraph

Outline: a tool developed during pre-writing that provides a visual of a paper's organization and ideas

Paragraph: a short piece of writing that focuses on one main idea

Planner: a place for you to organize your schedule and record any important tasks or responsibilities

Pre-writing: a stage of writing that involves making decisions, planning ideas, and identifying assignment guidelines

Purpose: the goal of a text

Purpose Statement: a sentence that tells the audience exactly what points will be covered in a longer text

Revising: a stage of writing that involves revising for focus and development

Scope: the focus of a writing assignment

Sequential Learning: learning information through a step-by-step process

Submitting: a stage of writing that involves formatting a text and sharing it with its audience

Thesis Statement: a sentence that expresses the main idea of a longer work

Writing Schedule: a method for planning dedicated writing time

Lesson 7.2

Understanding Genre and Purpose

What would you wear for the following activities?

> Walking along the beaches of Puerto Rico
>
> Dog-sledding across Antarctica
>
> Hiking the Appalachian Trail

You probably saw yourself wearing three very different outfits. In each scenario, your clothing had to adapt to the different purposes and environments of your activities.

In a similar way, you must learn to adapt your writing to different purposes and environments. For example, the papers you write in history class are very different from the emails you write in your personal life. These two types of texts fall into different **genres**, or types of writing.

Writing can adapt to fit many different environments.

Knowing how to select the best possible genre for a text will help you accomplish your goals and meet the needs of your **audience**.

In this lesson, you will learn three steps:

Determine Your Purpose for Writing
Choose an Appropriate Genre
Think about Expectations and Conventions

Determine Your Purpose for Writing

The first step in choosing a genre is determining your purpose for writing. There are four common **purposes**:

- **To inform**: Informative texts give the audience information about a topic.
- **To persuade**: Persuasive texts convince the audience to adopt a belief or take an action.
- **To reflect**: Reflective texts share a personal experience or belief.
- **To entertain**: Entertaining texts explore a topic or event in a creative or humorous way.

When writing for school, you will often find your purpose in the assignment details or writing prompt. As you read through your instructor's directions, look for verbs that indicate purpose:

Inform	Persuade	Reflect	Entertain
demonstrate	defend	narrate	illustrate
identify	evaluate	reflect	share
discuss	justify	share	tell

When writing at work or in everyday life, you may not know your purpose right away. In these situations, keep your audience in mind. The goal of your writing should be to give them the type of information that they need and expect.

Choose an Appropriate Genre

Once you've thought about your purpose for writing, you can decide on an appropriate genre. The type of writing you do should match both your audience and your occasion for writing. For example, if you are putting together a presentation for work, you probably won't write your presentation as a poem. This genre of writing wouldn't fit the audience (your coworkers) or the occasion (a work meeting).

Genres of writing can be divided into three main groups: academic writing, professional writing, and personal writing. In **academic writing**, you are writing for an audience of instructors or classmates. **Professional writing**, on the other hand, is intended for an audience of managers, coworkers, and customers. The audience for **personal writing** could be anyone.

Here are some of the genres that belong to each of the three groups:

Academic Writing	Professional Writing	Personal Writing
research papers reflection essays literature analyses research articles presentations	cover letters business proposals brochures presentations résumés	emails letters product reviews journal entries social media posts

When you are selecting a genre, you must first decide what type of audience you are trying to reach with your writing. Certain types of audiences will have expectations about the type of text they want to see. For example, your English instructor may expect a long essay or research paper while your business professor may expect a memo or a presentation.

Next, think about the occasion for writing. If your company is looking for a way to interest customers, you might choose a brochure or a poster as your genre.

Finally, consider your purpose. If the purpose of your writing is to inform the audience about a highly technical process, a manual or video would be a better choice than a brochure or an email.

Group Activity
As a group, discuss the following list of genres. What audiences, occasions, and purposes would make these genres appropriate choices? Be prepared to share your conclusions with the class.

research paper   newspaper article   infographic   financial report   parody

Reflection Questions
Genre is commonly used to categorize books, movies, and music. How does your **prior knowledge** of genre fit your understanding of writing genres?

Think about Expectations and Conventions

After you select a genre, your work isn't quite done. You must also consider the expectations and conventions that are part of that genre.

All genres have certain features that an audience expects to see. Think about romantic comedies. What do you expect to see in this type of movie? Usually, the storyline involves attractive people who fall in love despite misunderstandings and complications.

Genres of writing have their own expectations.

Here are a few examples:

Long Essay	Résumé	Blog Post
clear thesis statement well-structured paragraphs plain font	bullet points education details chronological organization	links to other websites photos short paragraphs

Once you've determined the expectations of your audience, you can adapt your writing to better meet those expectations.

In addition to expectations, all genres also have specific conventions that affect the way you write a text. Conventions can include tone, style, and grammar.

Tone

Tone is the positive, negative, or neutral attitude that an author expresses about a topic. You establish tone through the words you use and the details you include.

In some genres, such as newspaper articles or informative essays, you are expected to use a more neutral tone. In other situations, however, you may use a more positive or negative tone to express your feelings about a topic. Here are a few examples of genres that use different tones:

Commercial	Lab Report	Instructor Evaluation
excited positive happy	objective unbiased straightforward	enthusiastic honest disappointed

To learn more about identifying and using tone, see Lessons 3.1 and 5.2.

Style

Writing style affects your word choice, **formality**, and sentence **complexity**. In certain genres, you have more freedom to write in an informal style. Because this type of writing is conversational or humorous, you might include **contractions**, **slang**, and **simple sentences**.

To learn more about writing style, see Lesson 5.1.

When you are using a more formal style, however, you are expected to sound professional or academic. In these situations, you use more complex sentence structure and technical terms. Of course, this doesn't mean that your writing should sound robotic or confusing. Even in a formal style, you should make your writing clear and easy for your audience to understand.

Read the following paragraphs. Which would be a better example of a formal style of writing?

> Selfishness taints the relationships among King Lear's three daughters: Goneril, Regan, and Cordelia. Goneril and Regan are jealous of Cordelia's hold on their father's affections, and the text seems to indicate that this jealousy is motivated not by a desire for Lear's love but for wealth and power. One example of Goneril and Regan's self-centeredness is their relationship with Edmund. Initially, Goneril becomes Edmund's mistress but believes Edmund is also pursuing Regan. At one point, Goneril proclaims that she would "rather lose the battle than that sister / Should loosen him and me" (5.1.18-19). Regan, who also becomes romantically entangled with Edmund, expresses that same paranoia and questions Edmund regarding his relationship with her sister. Their jealousy finally culminates in Goneril poisoning Regan and committing suicide.

> I think there should be a greater separation between the economy and government than there is now. Corporations make billions of dollars annually, so it's natural that they will have influence in the country. However, having enough influence to basically buy government officials is wrong. It might help the corporation, but over time, the country will suffer. Instead of protecting our government from economic corruption, the Supreme Court has passed rulings that allow corporations to spend tons of money on campaigns through Super PACs. The loopholes that corporations have found to protect themselves and invade the government shows that when someone (or something) has enough money, everything, even the United States government, is for sale.

Grammar

Genre also changes the type of grammar you use. In academic and professional writing, you are generally expected to follow standard grammar and spelling rules. Even small errors, like using *your* instead of *you're*, could make you seem sloppy or unprofessional.

When you write in personal genres like emails or text messages, your grammar can be more flexible. Some of these situations may even expect non-standard grammar. For example, tweets have a length limit, so it's normal to use abbreviations and hashtags in order to save space. By adapting your writing to the conventions of your genre, you can communicate your ideas more effectively.

> ### Reflection Questions
> What are some of the non-standard grammar rules in the following genres? How are these rules established?
>
> Memes   Emails   Text messages   Tumblr posts

Lesson Wrap-up

Key Terms

Academic Writing: a text intended for instructors or students

Audience: the people who read your writing

Complexity: when a text has many connected parts

Contraction: a phrase that has been shortened into one word

Entertaining Text: a text that explores a topic or event in a creative or humorous way

Formality: the way a text conforms to certain standards

Genre: a type of writing

Informative Text: a text that gives the audience information about a topic

Personal Writing: a text intended for anyone

Persuasive Text: a text that convinces its audience to adopt a belief or take an action

Prior Knowledge: what you already know about a topic

Professional Writing: a text intended for managers, coworkers, or customers

Purpose: the goal of a text

Reflective Text: a text that shares a personal experience or belief

Simple Sentence: a sentence made up of only one independent clause

Slang: casual words or expressions specific to a particular group of people

Tone: the positive, negative, or neutral attitude that an author expresses about a topic

Lesson 7.3

Choosing a Topic and Scope for a Longer Text

Even though a research paper or essay is significantly longer than a **paragraph**, the scope of the topic must still be appropriate for the length. **Scope** is simply another word for focus.

For example, it's physically impossible for a five-page paper to cover the same amount of text as a five hundred-page book. While both of these texts might discuss the same topic, the scope of their discussion will be different.

In this lesson you will learn three useful steps in choosing a topic and narrowing your scope:

Review Instructor Guidelines
Use Brainstorming Strategies
Think about Purpose, Audience, and Constraints

Review Instructor Guidelines

When you are writing a longer text in school, you may be required to select from a list of approved topics. As you read through the possible choices, take into account your **prior knowledge** (what you already know about a topic) and your personal interests. Completing the assignment is much easier when you are interested in what you are writing.

If you are having trouble deciding between two or three topics, don't worry. You can always narrow them down later in the **pre-writing** process.

In other situations, you may have the freedom to select a topic of your choice. Try asking yourself some of these questions to come up with ideas:

What topics would be interesting to my audience?
What is the purpose and **genre** of my text?
What are some of my personal interests?
What has been happening at my college lately?
What has been happening in the news lately?
What causes am I passionate about?

You can also try searching for topics online.

Group Activity
As a group, come up with a list of 10 interesting essay or research paper topics.

Use Brainstorming Strategies

Once you've decided on a general topic, you can use **brainstorming** strategies to start developing your ideas.

Free-writing

One useful brainstorming strategy is free-writing. **Free-writing** allows you to start getting your ideas down on paper without worrying about grammar or spelling. You can use paragraphs, bulleted lists, and phrases. To start free-writing, follow these steps:

- Decide how much time you want to spend free-writing and set a timer. Five to ten minutes is usually long enough. (If you need a timer, try Timer-Tab [http://www.timer-tab.com/].)
- Write down your topic so that it stays fresh in your thoughts. If you're trying to decide between multiple topics, write them all down.
- Start the timer and start writing. Don't worry about spelling or **format**. Just keep writing until the timer goes off.

When you're finished, you might have a text that looks like this:

> Last week I read an article about the effects of mandatory minimum sentences on first-time offenders. These people are usually caught selling drugs. Even if it's their first offense, they can receive 10-15 years in prison or even life, depending on the severity of their crime. Even violent crimes like rape are not punished this severely. A lot of lawyers and judges have been arguing against these laws, which were started in the 1980s (?). There was also a story about a young man who had been arrested for armed robbery when he was 16. Even though he was a minor, he was tried as an adult. In both of these cases, the punishment seemed too harsh for the crime.

On Your Own

Practice free-writing using the following space. Add your topic at the top; then, start a timer. Keep writing down ideas until the timer goes off.

Once you've finished free-writing, you can use a second brainstorming strategy called grouping.

Grouping

Grouping helps you start organizing your thoughts and identify areas that you might want to explore further.

To practice grouping, follow these steps:

- Read through the ideas that you wrote down during free-writing and identify four or five categories of information. Write these categories at the top of the page.
- Add portions of your free-write under the appropriate category.
- Review your grouped ideas, looking for areas that you might want to explore further.

Your grouped ideas might look like this:

- mandatory minimums for drug crimes
- length of sentence
- severity of types of crimes

- movements to change sentencing laws
- some senators proposing prison reform bills
- judges think sentences are too harsh

- minors tried as adults
- harsh punishments for first-time offenders

When you're finished with brainstorming, you should have a better idea of the topic you want to discuss in your paper. Keep in mind that the writing process is circular; you may need to complete additional rounds of brainstorming later.

Think about Audience, Purpose, and Constraints

Once you've selected a topic and started generating ideas, you need to narrow the scope of your paper. Keeping your topic **focused** allows you to discuss the material in a more purposeful, in-depth way.

On longer assignments, students sometimes keep their scope broad because they don't want to run out of ideas. This strategy is dangerous. Cramming too much information into one paper will overwhelm your audience. Additionally, you may have a hard time staying organized and on-topic.

To start narrowing the scope of your text, you must first consider your purpose for writing. Four of the most common **purposes** for writing are to inform, to persuade, to reflect, and to entertain.

- **To inform:** Informative texts give the audience information about a topic.
- **To persuade:** Persuasive texts convince the audience to adopt a belief or take an action.
- **To reflect:** Reflective texts share a personal experience or belief.
- **To entertain:** Entertaining texts explore a topic in a creative or humorous way.

The purpose of your paper will affect the way you narrow down your topic. For example, narrowing down the general topic "women in filmmaking" for different purposes might look like this:

Purpose	Narrowed Topic
To inform	Katherine Bigelow's career
To persuade	Hollywood needs more films made by women
To reflect	Your personal career goals
To entertain	A humorous account of Nora Ephron's life

Group Activity
As a group, come up with **narrowed topics** that inform, persuade, reflect, and entertain for each of the following general topics:

Technology in schools   Famous musicians   Car maintenance

Hip hop fashion   The United Nations

The next step in narrowing down a topic is considering your **audience**, the people who read your writing. At school, the audience for many of your assignments will be your instructor and/or classmates. Outside of school, you may have to do research to determine your potential audience.

Once you've determined your audience, think about what they already know and what they want to know. This will help you narrow down your topic to something that your readers will find interesting and useful. For example, your instructor and classmates probably already know that smoking is bad for your health. A more appropriate topic for this audience might be "cigarette advertisements in other countries" or "the effect of public smoking bans."

One final way to narrow down the scope of a topic is to consider possible constraints. **Constraints** are the limitations of your paper. One of the most common constraints that you face in school is assignment length. A one-page paper will have a much narrower scope than a ten-page paper.

Another constraint is access to research. If you are not allowed to use outside sources in your assignment, you should choose a topic that you can discuss without outside statistics or quotes.

Be sure to review any assignment guidelines for possible constraints. You should have already reviewed these guidelines before selecting your topic. As you work to narrow the scope of your paper, read back over any requirements to make sure you are following your instructor's directions.

> **Reflection Questions**
> What are some of the other constraints that might affect your choice of topic?

Lesson Wrap-up

Key Terms

Audience: the people who read your writing

Brainstorming: exploring and developing ideas

Constraint: a limitation that affects your writing

Entertaining Text: a text that explores a topic or event in a creative or humorous way

Focus: clear communication and support of a main idea

Format: the style and arrangement of a text

Free-writing: a brainstorming strategy for getting your ideas down on paper

Genre: a type of writing

Grouping: a brainstorming strategy that helps you organize your thoughts

Informative Text: a text that gives the audience information about a topic

Narrowed Topic: a topic that you have made more specific by considering your purpose, audience, and constraints

Paragraph: a short piece of writing that focuses on one main idea

Persuasive Text: a text that convinces its audience to adopt a belief or take an action

Pre-writing: a stage of writing that involves making decisions, planning ideas, and identifying assignment guidelines

Prior Knowledge: what you already know about a topic

Purpose: the goal of a text

Reflective Text: a text that shares a personal experience or belief

Scope: the focus of a writing assignment

Lesson 7.4
Writing a Thesis or Purpose Statement

"You can't judge a book by its cover." Generally, this saying is true. If you think about it literally, however, you *can* judge a book by its cover.

Thesis and purpose statements, like book covers, help readers know what to expect.

Think about the last time you passed a rack of romance novels at the grocery store. With just a quick glance, you instantly recognized these books as romances. Now picture the types of covers you would expect to see on other genres of books: young adult novels, crime thrillers, or even textbooks. Book publishers use certain types of covers to give readers clues about the book. They don't want people to feel disappointed by a science fiction novel when they were expecting a biography.

> **Reflection Questions**
> Can you think of a time when a book or movie was completely different from what you originally expected?

Sometimes, surprising or misleading an **audience** can make fictional stories more entertaining. However, the writing you do for work or school shouldn't confuse your audience. Early in the paper, you should state the **main idea** of your writing. Just like a good cover previews what to expect in a book, a good thesis statement or purpose statement previews what to expect in a paper.

This lesson will discuss three steps in creating a thesis statement:

Decide Between a Thesis and Purpose Statement
Combine a Narrowed Topic and Controlling Idea
Strengthen Your Thesis Statement

> **Helpful Hint**
> Thesis statements are similar to topic sentences because they both preview the main idea of your writing. A thesis, however, introduces the main idea of an entire paper while **topic sentences** introduce the main idea of an individual **paragraph.**

To learn more about topic sentences, see Lesson 6.3.

Decide Between a Thesis and Purpose Statement

During the **pre-writing** phase, you need to decide whether you should use a thesis statement or a purpose statement. Both are short, concise previews of longer pieces of writing. Although they function similarly, they are used for different purposes.

The main idea of a longer text is often expressed in a thesis statement. This is especially common in **persuasive** writing. A **thesis statement** is one sentence that sums up the entire **argument** of a paper, generally without listing each of the main points. A thesis statement almost always appears near the end of the **introduction**.

The main idea of a longer work can also be stated as a purpose statement. **Purpose statements** announce the author's **purpose** and preview the main points or sections of a document. Like thesis statements, they appear in the introduction. Purpose statements are most commonly found in business and research reports.

If you're writing for school, a thesis statement is usually the better option. Thesis statements are used in **academic writing** like research papers or persuasive essays. Purpose statements are most often used for college applications, business proposals, and scientific reports.

Here some examples of both thesis statements and purpose statements:

Thesis Statements	If the income gap in America continues to grow, the economy will become increasingly unstable.
	Charles Dickens uses irony to critique the treatment of the poor in 19th century England.
	The field of sociology has developed rapidly in the past fifty years.
Purpose Statements	This report will share the results of this year's customer appreciation survey and discuss changes in customer satisfaction over the last five years.
	The purpose of this presentation is to teach you three practical ways to improve your public speaking skills.
	I would like to apply for the Educational Publishing internship posted on your careers page.

Your instructor may have specific guidelines about whether you should use a thesis statement or a purpose statement. If not, use whichever option makes the most sense for your writing.

Combine a Narrowed Topic and Controlling Idea

The first step in creating a thesis statement is reviewing your topic so that you can choose a **controlling idea**. This is the angle that you will take in discussing your topic.

One topic can be discussed in a number of ways. For example, imagine that you've narrowed down the topic of your essay to "free-range farming." Your controlling idea could be one of the following ideas:

- should not be subsidized by the government
- is a reason to support local farms
- raises meat prices
- is becoming more popular in cities
- ensures humane treatment of animals

When choosing a controlling idea, consider the purpose of your paper. If your purpose is to **persuade**, your controlling idea should share an opinion or argue a point. If your purpose is to **inform**, your controlling idea should share interesting or thought-provoking information.

On Your Own

Read the following controlling ideas for the topic "student loan debt" and determine the purpose. Check the box next to your answer.

Student loan debt should be regulated by the government.
- ☐ Persuade
- ☐ Inform

Student loan debt is the subject of numerous proposed government reforms.
- ☐ Persuade
- ☐ Inform

Reflection Questions
A controlling idea is also known as an *angle* or a *stance*. Where have you heard these terms used? How does this relate to your understanding of thesis statements?

Good controlling ideas sound confident. Avoid using **hedging words** like *sometimes* or *kind of*, as they make your meaning seem weak.

Here are some examples of weak and confident controlling ideas:

Cooking at home	
Weak	can sometimes save certain families money
Strong	will help families save money

Duties of a certified nurse's assistant	
Weak	might be rewarding for some people
Strong	are challenging and rewarding

A controlling idea should also be specific and interesting. Look at this example:

Hubble Space Telescope	
Weak	was a great invention
Weak	produces images that prove the earth is round

The first controlling idea is weak because it uses vague language. You could say that anything is a "great invention." The second controlling idea shares useless information. Almost everyone agrees that the earth is round, so there's no need to write a paper about it.

The following would be a much better controlling idea for this topic:

Hubble Space Telescope	
Strong	has been instrumental in our understanding of the universe

To review strategies for choosing and narrowing a topic, see Lesson 7.3.

Group Activity
As a group, create good and bad controlling ideas for each of the following topics:
  Using public tax money for sports stadiums
  The popularity of internet TV
  Parking on campus

To create a thesis statement, simply combine your **narrowed topic** and your controlling idea. You may have to re-word both parts to fit them into a smooth sentence, but the basic ideas should stay the same.

Topic + Controlling Idea = Thesis Statement

Narrowed Topic	Controlling Idea
the Amazon rainforest	is rapidly shrinking because of deforestation

Thesis Statement: The Amazon rainforest is rapidly shrinking because of deforestation.

Narrowed Topic	Controlling Idea
sleeping for at least eight hours a night	will improve your mental and physical health

Thesis Statement: Sleeping for at least eight hours a night will improve your mental and physical health.

On Your Own

Practice creating your own thesis statements by adding a narrowed topic and a controlling idea into the text boxes below.

Narrowed Topic	+	Controlling Idea
	+	
	+	

Once you combine your topic and controlling idea, make sure that your thesis statement accurately reflects the purpose of your paper.

Think about this example. What purpose does this thesis statement fulfill?

> Student loan debt is the subject of several proposed government reforms.
>
> If your purpose is to inform the audience about recently proposed student loan reforms, then this thesis statement passes the test. However, if your purpose is to argue for a particular reform, this thesis statement fails.

Strengthen Your Thesis Statement

To make your thesis statement stronger, consider adding additional details.

Think about the example below:

> Dachshunds + are excellent pets for people who live in apartments.
>
> Based on this thesis statement, the essay will discuss what makes dachshunds excellent pets for people with apartments.

One way to strengthen this thesis would be to include the reason for your stance. To create this type of thesis, add a **subordinating conjunction** like *because* or *including*; then insert a brief summary of your reasoning.

> Seeing a Shakespeare play in person + is better than reading it on paper + because + the actors bring the story alive.

> A term limit for Senate seats + should be introduced by Congress + in order to + prevent the corruption of elected officials.

Another type of thesis statement uses a subordinating conjunction like *although* or *despite* to recognize an opposing viewpoint or to show contrast.

> Although + smoking is becoming less common in the US, + it + is becoming more common in third-world countries.

> Despite + the recent popularity of the World Cup, + international football + has not become popular in the United States.

When you are done strengthening your thesis statement, read it out loud. If the sentence is confusing or hard to read, you may have added too much information.

> **Helpful Hint**
> As you begin **drafting** your paper, you might find that your ideas no longer match your thesis. You may need to **revise** your thesis statement or rewrite part of your draft.

Lesson Wrap-up

Key Terms

Academic Writing: a text intended for instructors or students

Argument: a reason why you should think or act a certain way

Audience: the people who read your writing

Controlling Idea: what an author wants to say about a topic

Drafting: a stage of writing that involves writing out ideas and support/concluding sentences

Hedging Word: a vague, indecisive word or term

Informative Text: a text that gives the audience information about a topic

Introduction: the paragraph used to introduce the main idea at the beginning of a paper, also called an introductory paragraph

Main Idea: the statement or argument that an author tries to communicate

Narrowed Topic: a topic that you have made more specific by considering your purpose, audience, and constraints

Paragraph: a short piece of writing that focuses on one main idea

Persuasive Text: a text that convinces its audience to adopt a belief or take an action

Pre-writing: a stage of writing that involves making decisions, planning ideas, and identifying assignment guidelines

Purpose: the goal of a text

Purpose Statement: a sentence that tells the audience exactly what points will be covered in a longer text

Revising: a stage of writing that involves revising for focus and development

Subordinating Conjunction: a conjunction that introduces a dependent clause

Thesis Statement: a sentence that expresses the main idea of a longer work

Topic Sentence: a sentence that states the main point of a paragraph

Lesson 7.5
Organizing and Outlining a Paper

When you are taking a road trip, you probably rely on GPS for directions. If the GPS malfunctions, however, you may find yourself lost in an unfamiliar location. Your only choice is to drive around until you find someone with directions. Not only does this situation feel frustrating, but it can also delay your trip by several hours.

Writing a long text is a little bit like a road trip. Without a reliable map to keep you moving in the right direction, you may get lost.

During **pre-writing**, you should develop an **outline** to keep your thoughts organized. This tool gives you a visual of the organization and ideas of your paper. In many ways, an outline is like a road map for your ideas. It will show you exactly where your writing is headed and how to get there.

In this lesson, you will learn how to use three different types of outlines:

Working Outline
Topic Outline
Sentence Outline

Helpful Hint
Consider bringing your outline to an appointment with a **Writing Center** tutor. This is a good way to get feedback on your ideas before actually writing your first draft.

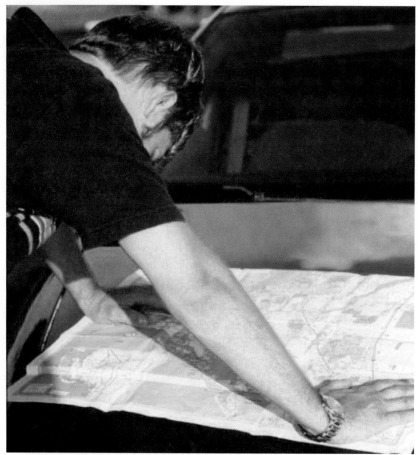

Organizing your writing will keep you from getting lost during the writing process.

Working Outline

While you are generating ideas for your paper, you should keep them organized in a working outline. **Working outlines** are informal. You don't have to use any special formatting or structure. The important functions of a working outline are to show you how your ideas are coming together and to reveal areas that need additional thought or research.

During the **brainstorming** step of pre-writing, you probably used **free-writing** and **grouping** to generate ideas about a topic. Once you've selected your topic and created a **thesis statement**, do another round of brainstorming to come up with ideas about the specific topic of your paper.

To learn more about brainstorming strategies, see Lesson 7.3.

This information is an excellent place to start when you are creating a working outline. Once you have your initial ideas grouped together into categories, you can start deciding which ones you want to include in the final paper.

If your longer text involves research, keep the working outline with you as you look up information. You can make notes about where **supporting details** or **evidence** would fit into the paper and look for areas that need additional research.

Don't be afraid to change your working outline. As you brainstorm ideas and conduct research, you may find yourself moving in a slightly different direction than you originally planned. If this happens, update your thesis statement and use your working outline to continue organizing your thoughts.

Here's an example of a completed working outline:

> **Thesis Statement**: In Katherine Boo's *Behind the Beautiful Forevers*, India's weak justice system contributes to many of the issues faced by the characters.
>
> **Support**:
>
> Mumbai's corrupt local government destroys the slums, where thousands of people live, in order to build hotels and airports.
>
> Something about access to food/healthcare; a lack of justice leads to/creates/fosters(?) an environment with no access to proper food/healthcare
>
> **Sources**:
>
> *Behind the Beautiful Forevers* → written like investigative journalism/based on real events and people
>
> United Nations reports
>
> Records of court cases on forced evictions

Topic Outline

Once you have a fairly solid idea of what you want to cover in your paper, you should begin creating a more formal outline. **Topic outlines** use short **phrases** to represent the structure of your paper.

Organizational Patterns

To begin creating a topic outline, review the information you have in your working outline. You should already have your raw material grouped into general categories. Think about how that information would fit into one of the following **organizational patterns**:

Cause and Effect

A cause and effect paper discusses either the causes or effects of a topic. This organizational pattern works well for both informative and persuasive papers. A text that is organized by cause and effect will most likely discuss one cause with multiple effects or one effect with multiple causes.

Chronological

A chronological paper shares ideas or events in the order that they occurred. This type of organizational pattern works well for informative pieces of writing about historical events.

Compare and Contrast

The compare and contrast organizational pattern is used for papers that discuss the similarities and differences between two topics. This structure works well when your purpose is to **inform**. You can choose to discuss all of the similarities first and all of the differences last, or you can alternate between similarities and differences.

Order of Importance

A paper arranged in order of importance organizes the information from most important to least important or from least important to most important. This organizational pattern is one of the most common structures for a **persuasive text**.

Spatial

A spatial text describes a location or object by its physical characteristics. This description usually moves from one side to the other in an orderly way. The spatial organizational pattern works well when your purpose is to inform or entertain.

Topical

Topical papers are not arranged in a particular order because all the information is of equal importance. This organizational pattern is often used for informative or **reflective** writing. When you are arranging the structure of a topical paper, you should consider putting your smallest or weakest point in the middle.

Building the Outline

Once you've selected an organizational pattern, you can start forming your topic outline. First, decide on **headings.** These are the main points of your paper. Usually, a main point represents one **paragraph** in a short essay and multiple paragraphs in a longer text. As you decide on headings, try to use phrases that clearly state exactly what the main point will cover. Here are a few examples of weak and strong headings:

Weak	Unrest rises
	Background information
Strong	Continental Congress formed
	America declares independence

Once you've decided on your headings, you can begin adding subheadings underneath them. **Subheadings** are the individual sub-points you want to discuss under each main point.

For example, if the first main point of your paper is "growing student loan debt," you might have some of the following sub-points:

Impact of for-profit colleges

Influence of overall economy

Increase in tuition

Rising textbook prices

Subheadings always come in groups of at least two. If you don't have enough information to add two sub-points, you should consider coming up with new ideas or eliminating that main point.

The more detailed you make your outline, the more guidance it will give you as you draft your paper. However, don't feel like your topic outline is completely set in stone. You can always make changes to your ideas later in the **drafting** and **revising** stages.

Take a look at the following example of a completed topical outline. Notice that the main headings are numbered with roman numerals. The subheadings, which are indented under the main headings, are numbered with capital letters. Finally, any minor subheadings are indented and numbered with regular numbers.

I.   Growing student loan debt
    A. Impact of for-profit colleges
        1. Financial aid
        2. Tuition
    B. Influence of overall economy
    C. Increase in tuition
        1. Public universities
        2. Private universities
    D. Rising textbook prices
II. High unemployment rates
    A. Struggling industries
    B. Globalization of the workforce
        1. Outsourcing labor
        2. Foreign parts
    C. Weak economic growth

Sentence Outline

One final type of outline is a **sentence outline**. These are very similar to topic outlines. They both follow an organizational pattern and list the main points and sub-points of the paper. Sentence outlines, however, use full sentences instead of short phrases.

Sentence outlines tend to be more complex and specific than topic outlines. These types of outlines are best used for long essays or research papers. Although a sentence outline takes more work during the pre-writing stage, it will save you time during the drafting stage because you can reuse the sentences that you used in your outline in the paper itself.

Here's an example of a completed sentence outline:

Thesis Statement: The best treatment for those diagnosed with anxiety and depression is a combination of cognitive behavioral therapy and anti-depressant medication.

I. Cognitive behavioral therapy is highly effective for forming new thought patterns conducive to overpowering the negative mental and physical effects of anxiety and depression.
    A. A trained therapist can assist patients in forming more productive thought patterns that break negative cycles of thoughts and tendencies.
    B. Strategies used by therapists can complement the use of medication.
    C. Behavioral therapy does not have the risk of physical side effects that medication poses.
II. There are both positive and negative effects of using anti-depressant medication.
    A. Medications like selective serotonin reuptake inhibitors (SSRIs) have shown positive effects on some users, including decreased depressive thoughts and increased motivation.
    B. However, SSRI medications can be very difficult to adjust to. Many users struggle with uncomfortable side effects when starting and ceasing medication.
    C. Medicine alone cannot solve the complex challenges associated with mental health conditions like depression and anxiety.

> **Helpful Hint**
> To help yourself stay organized, consider adding labels to each sentence in your outline.

> **Helpful Hint**
> Some instructors require you to submit an outline during pre-writing. Always check the assignment guidelines to see if your instructor prefers a sentence or topic outline.

Lesson Wrap-up

Key Terms

Brainstorming: exploring and developing ideas

Cause and Effect: an organizational pattern used to explain the causes or effects of a topic

Chronological: an organizational pattern that arranges ideas or events in the order that they occurred

Compare and Contrast: an organizational pattern used to show the similarities and differences between two topics

Drafting: a stage of writing that involves writing out ideas and support/concluding sentences

Entertaining Text: a text that explores a topic or event in a creative or humorous way

Evidence: a piece of information, also called a supporting detail, that is used to support a main idea

Free-writing: a brainstorming strategy for getting your ideas down on paper

Grouping: a brainstorming strategy that helps you organize your thoughts

Heading: in an outline, it is a clear statement of one of the main points of a paper

Informative Text: a text that gives the audience information about a topic

Order of Importance: an organizational pattern that arranges information in order of importance

Organizational Pattern: the structure of a written text, used to arrange the main points of a work

Outline: a tool developed during pre-writing that provides a visual of a paper's organization and ideas

Paragraph: a short piece of writing that focuses on one main idea

Persuasive Text: a text that convinces its audience to adopt a belief or take an action

Phrase: a word group that adds to the meaning of a sentence but does not express a complete thought and usually lacks a subject and a verb

Pre-writing: a stage of writing that involves making decisions, planning ideas, and identifying assignment guidelines

Reflective Text: a text that shares a personal experience or belief

Revising: a stage of writing that involves revising for focus and development

Sentence Outline: an outline that uses full sentences to represent a paper's structure

Spatial: an organizational pattern used to describe a topic by its physical characteristics

Subheadings: in an outline, they are at least two sub-points that come under a main point

Supporting Detail: a piece of information, also called evidence, that is used to support a main idea

Thesis Statement: a sentence that expresses the main idea of a longer work

Topic Outline: an outline that uses short phrases to represent a paper's structure

Topical: a general organizational pattern used for equally important main ideas

Working Outline: an informal outline with no special formatting or structure

Writing Center: a service that provides writing assistance

Lesson 7.6
Writing with Technology

What types of technology do you use every day?

The first item you probably pictured was a phone or a computer, but your interactions with technology don't stop there. Every time you swipe a credit card or ID badge, drive a car, or turn on the TV, you are using devices that your ancestors couldn't have even imagined.

While technology has made life incredibly easier, it has also introduced new challenges. Almost everyone has tried to submit an assignment only to find that the file isn't saved or the printer isn't working.

When you write on a computer, you may experience some of these same frustrations. However, learning a few basic tactics can help you avoid unexpected stress and save valuable time and energy.

This lesson will discuss four important aspects of writing with technology:

Saving Your Work
Using Grammar and Spell-Check
Formatting the Page
Using Keyboard Shortcuts

Although technology has made life easier in many ways, it comes with its own set of problems.

Reflection Questions
Have you ever had a problem with technology? How did you handle it?

Saving Your Work

One of the worst feelings in the world is losing your work when your computer unexpectedly freezes or shuts down. While these situations are often unavoidable, there are a few steps you can take to decrease your frustration and save as much work as possible.

Don't wait until the end of your writing to save your document. The longer you wait to save, the more work you could potentially lose. Instead, make a habit of saving your work every ten to fifteen minutes. If you have a hard time remembering, put a sticky note on the corner of your screen to remind yourself or set a reminder on your phone. Saving your progress as often as possible will ensure that if something unexpected happens, you'll still have most of your work saved.

You should also consider saving your work in two places. If your computer is damaged or stolen, you don't want to lose all of your documents. Even if you aren't in the middle of a project, your previous work may be important for your portfolio or résumé. Think about purchasing an external hard drive or signing up for a cloud service like Dropbox (http://dropbox.com) so that you can periodically save your important documents.

Helpful Hint
If you are using a school computer in the library or a lab, always save your work to a portable USB drive or a cloud service. Usually, campus computers are automatically wiped each night so that files don't start cluttering up the machines.

Keeping all of your files organized will ensure that you can find important documents later. Here are a few guidelines for organization:

- Create separate folders for each class. You can also consider creating subfolders for items like homework, projects, and readings.
- Use the Save As option to save a second version of a document. This will make a copy so that you can edit the new document without affecting the original one.

- Name all files with the title of the text and the date of your last edit. If you ever need to keep multiple versions of the same document, you will be able to find the most recent version quickly.

Using Grammar and Spell-Check

Most writing programs offer a function that scans your text for basic grammar and spelling errors. As you type, the computer marks incorrectly spelled words or grammar errors and offers suggestions for correcting them.

While grammar and spell-check are useful in helping you find basic errors, they are not foolproof. For example, these tools may not consistently recognize when words are out of place, when the wrong word is being used, or when proper nouns are misspelled. Because of these limitations, spell-check should never replace careful **editing**.

To enable grammar and spell-check in Microsoft Word, open the File tab and select Options in the left-hand side of the window. In the pop-up box, select Proofing and check the boxes that say "Check spelling as you type" and "Check grammar with spelling." You can also run a manual check by opening the Review tab and clicking the Spelling & Grammar button.

> Further Resources
> Most computers and phones use autocorrect to replace typing mistakes instantly. To learn more about the history of spell-check and autocorrect, read this short article (http://www.nytimes.com/2014/06/08/magazine/who-made-that-autocorrect.html?_r=1) from *The New York Times*.

Formatting the Page

When you are writing in a specific **format**, like MLA or APA style, your document must follow specific rules about page formatting. Here are a few of the common formatting options you should know:

- **Page Margins**: the amount of space between the edge of the paper and the actual words. For many formats, this margin should be one inch wide on all sides. To set page margins in Microsoft Word, open the Page Layout tab and click the Margins button on the left. If the correct margin size isn't listed as an option, select the "Custom Margins" option to create your own.
- **Headers**: a special type of page number that includes additional information such as your last name. To add a header in Microsoft Word, open the Insert tab and click the Header button. Choose the layout you want and type in the information. You can always edit this header later by double-clicking on it.
- **Page Numbers**: help your **audience** find the information that they need inside your text. In some cases, you will include a page number inside your header. Other times, you just need a page number. To add a page number in Microsoft Word, open the Insert tab and click the Page Number button. Then, choose the location and layout of your page numbers. Word will automatically mark your pages with the right number.

Using Keyboard Shortcuts

To save time while you are writing a longer text, you can use keyboard shortcuts to perform basic tasks without using your mouse. Keep a list of these shortcuts handy until you get the hang of them.

Command	Windows	Mac
Save your work	Ctrl + S	Cmd + S
Undo your last action	Ctrl + Z	Cmd + Z

Highlight all text	Ctrl + A	Cmd + A
Cut highlighted text	Ctrl + X	Cmd + X
Copy highlighted text	Ctrl + C	Cmd + C
Paste cut/copied text	Ctrl + V	Cmd + V
Bold highlighted text	Ctrl + B	Cmd + B

Lesson Wrap-up

Key Terms

Audience: the people who read your writing

Editing: a stage of writing that involves proofreading for style, grammar, and spelling errors

Format: the style and arrangement of a text

Header: information, including a page number, that goes at the top of a page

Page Margin: the amount of space between the words and the edge of the paper

Page Number: a way to help the audience find information in a text

Lesson 7.7
Writing a First Draft

Read through the following statements. Have you ever said or thought something similar?

> When I sit down to write, my mind goes completely blank. I usually end up staring at the computer screen, feeling more and more overwhelmed by the minute.

> Writing the beginning of a paper is easy for me. Toward the middle, though, I usually get stuck on a sentence that just doesn't sound right. After that, it's hard for me to finish the paper.

> It's difficult for me to keep my thoughts organized when I write. Sometimes, I start looking up research and forget what I was going to say.

For many students, **drafting** is the most difficult step in the writing process. Starting any kind of writing can be intimidating, but a longer text like a research paper can be especially daunting.

Remember that you completed much of your work during the **pre-writing** stage. You've narrowed down your topic and crafted a **thesis statement**. Additionally, you have mapped out the content of the text with an outline. With all of this preparation done, you are already halfway there.

The first step in drafting is writing a first draft of your paper. Your draft won't be perfect the first time around. During the drafting stage, you should focus on connections between your ideas. There's no pressure to produce an error-free paper. You can always **revise** and **edit** it later.

This lesson will teach you strategies for writing your first draft.

> **Reflection Questions**
> In the past, what has been your process for drafting a longer text? Was this strategy successful?

Preparation

To make sure that your writing time is productive, gather all of your supplies and materials ahead of time. You don't want to interrupt your workflow later. You will need any lists or mind-maps you made during the pre-writing process as well as your finished outline and research notes.

Pay attention to the time of day that you write. Some people are more alert in the evening while others have more energy in the morning.

Your **workspace** can also play a big role in your ability to focus. If you prefer working with background noise, try writing in the library or a coffee shop. If you work better with complete silence, find a quiet study room or buy a pair of earplugs.

Finally, avoid distractions by turning your phone on silent. If necessary, you can stash it in your backpack or purse until you're done writing.

> To review the guidelines for choosing a workspace, see Lesson 1.4.

Writing

When you are ready to write, start by reviewing your **outline**. This document is the map that will guide your writing. The basic ideas are there; you just have to help your **audience** see how they're connected.

Keep the following recommendations in mind as you write:

- **Write in any order you want.** Some people prefer to save the **introduction** and **conclusion** for last, while others like to write all of the **paragraphs** in order. Use whichever strategy you prefer.
- **Try thinking out loud.** Sometimes, saying what you mean is easier than writing what you mean. Talk out loud to yourself; then, copy those words into your paper.
- **Push yourself to keep moving.** If you get stuck on one particular word or sentence, underline or highlight that section and move forward. You can also add some brief notes about your ideas or concerns.
- **Don't worry about your grammar or spelling.** The focus of your first draft is expressing your thoughts as clearly as possible. You'll go back and fix any mistakes later.

Once you've completed a section or paragraph, stop to read back through your work. You should be clearly supporting your thesis in every paragraph. If you don't see how that section relates to the main idea, add more information or make a note to come back later.

Keep working through your entire paper in this same way, writing and reviewing in sections. This will also give you an opportunity to generate new ideas and include additional **supporting details**.

> To learn more about supporting details, see Lessons 2.4 and 2.9.

Lesson Wrap-up

Key Terms

Audience: the people who read your writing

Conclusion: a paragraph that ties together the ideas in a paper and summarizes the main points, also called a concluding paragraph

Drafting: a stage of writing that involves writing out ideas and support/concluding sentences

Editing: a stage of writing that involves proofreading for style, grammar, and spelling errors

Introduction: the paragraph used to introduce the main idea at the beginning of a paper, also called an introductory paragraph

Outline: a tool developed during pre-writing that provides a visual of a paper's organization and ideas

Paragraph: a short piece of writing that focuses on one main idea

Pre-writing: a stage of writing that involves making decisions, planning ideas, and identifying assignment guidelines

Revising: a stage of writing that involves revising for focus and development

Supporting Detail: a piece of information, also called evidence, that is used to support a main idea

Thesis Statement: a sentence that expresses the main idea of a longer work

Workspace: a location free from distractions and clutter for working and studying

Lesson 7.8
Using Paragraphs Effectively

Writing a longer text like a research paper or essay can feel like an enormous task, especially if you've never written anything this long before. To help yourself feel less overwhelmed, remember that all pieces of writing are made up of smaller parts. Just like a **paragraph** is made up of individual sentences, a longer text is made up of individual paragraphs. As you write, you only have to worry about one paragraph at a time.

A good paragraph always includes a **topic sentence** that previews the **main idea** of the paragraph. This idea is expanded by the information in the **support sentences**. Finally, the **concluding sentence** ties all of the information together.

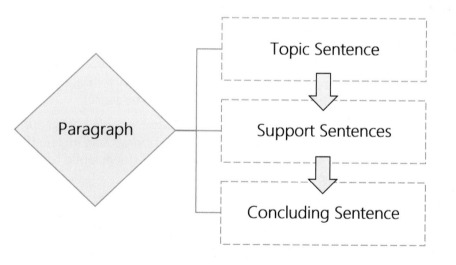

When you are writing a research paper, the basic structure of your writing is very similar to the structure of a paragraph. The **introduction** gives your **audience** a preview of the paper and announces the **thesis statement** of the paper. Then, the body paragraphs share main points that support your thesis. Finally, the **conclusion** helps your readers tie everything together by restating the thesis and summing up the main points.

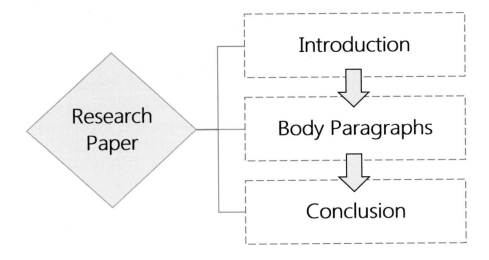

In this lesson, you will learn how to use three different types of paragraphs to build a longer text:

Introductory Paragraphs
Body Paragraphs
Concluding Paragraphs

> **Helpful Hint**
> When you are writing at work or in your personal life, the types of text you are writing might require different kinds of paragraphs or sections. For example, business reports often start with a summary, and scientific papers often start with an abstract. Be sure to research the type of structure that fits your purpose and genre before you start writing.

Introductory Paragraphs

Introductory paragraphs, or introductions, appear at the very beginning of your paper. They grab your audience's attention and introduce the main idea of your writing. In a shorter paper, you may only need one introductory paragraph. Longer papers, however, will probably require several.

Introductions start with general information about a topic. This might include background information or important terms and definitions. Often, authors begin the introduction with an interesting **fact** or **example** to get the audience interested in the topic. All of this information should slowly build toward the main idea of your paper, which is stated in your thesis.

Use the following steps to help you build a solid introduction:

Step-by-Step Checklist: Introductions

☐ | 1. Start by introducing your audience to the topic of the paper.

☐ | 2. Grab your audience's attention by sharing an interesting fact, quote, or example.

☐ | 3. Give background information about the topic, including important terms or ideas.

☐ | 4. Help your audience make connections between the topic and the main idea of the paper.

☐ | 5. End the introduction with your thesis statement.

Be careful not to get too general in your introduction. You should share background information or terms that relate to your topic, not random information about the history of the world. Look at these examples:

Weak	Throughout history, many people have enjoyed outdoor activities.
Strong	The popularity of outdoor running competitions has exploded over the last five years.

Both sentences use general information to introduce the audience to the topic of the essay. However, the first example is too vague. The second example is a much better example of general information that still relates to the topic.

Here's an example of an introductory paragraph for a short paper on post-traumatic stress disorder in children:

> Although the medical community studies post-traumatic stress disorder (PTSD) extensively in adults, psychiatrists conduct much less research on the way the disorder affects children. In fact, only during the last twenty years have psychiatrists noticed the growing occurrences of PTSD in individuals under the age of eighteen. On the Anxiety Disorders Association of America website, Stephanie Sampson notes that children develop PTSD much more easily than adults because of children's "limited coping and communication skills, the powerful influence of media exposure such as television, and the often insufficient attention focused on early identification and intervention." Additionally, many parents are unaware of the effects of trauma on their children. The ignorance surrounding post-traumatic stress disorder demonstrates how much more research and awareness is needed by psychiatrists.

Body Paragraphs

Body paragraphs contain the main points of your paper. They point back to your thesis statement by sharing supporting details, or **evidence**.

In each body paragraph, you might include any of the following **supporting details** to make your point:

- **Anecdotes:** long examples told as a story
- **Descriptions:** passages that explain the appearance of someone or something using words that appeal to the senses
- **Examples:** specific instances or illustrations that demonstrate a point
- **Expert Analysis:** an opinion or statement shared by someone who is knowledgeable about a topic
- **Facts:** pieces of information that most people generally agree to be true
- **Reflections:** the thoughts and feelings of the author
- **Statistics:** numbers or percentages that represent research data

Some body paragraphs focus on one type of evidence while others use multiple types.

Make sure to include your own analysis throughout the body. You need to tell the reader how each supporting detail relates to your current point. Don't assume that the audience knows why you included a specific piece of information.

The order of your body paragraphs depends on the **organizational pattern** of your paper. Follow your **outline** to make sure that your paragraphs are organized in a logical, meaningful way.

To review organizing and outlining a paper, see Lesson 7.5.

Throughout the body of the paper, you should use transitions to guide your audience through the information. **Transitions** unify all of your paragraphs into one smooth text by showing how ideas are related.

Transitions can be words, phrases, sentences, and even paragraphs.

Transition paragraphs

Transition paragraphs, also called "bridge paragraphs," reflect on previous ideas and make connections to upcoming ones. These paragraphs give the reader an opportunity to digest information that has been presented. Transition paragraphs are very useful in a long and complex text.

Transition sentences

Transition sentences often appear at the beginning or end of a paragraph. Like bridge paragraphs, transition sentences help the audience understand the flow of your ideas. Transition sentences work well when you don't need an entire paragraph or explanation to move from one idea to the next.

Transition words

Finally, transition words, sometimes called "signpost words," show order or relationships. Words that show *order* are like road signs, guiding your audience through the information. Words that show *relationships* help your audience see how your ideas are connected.

Here are some examples of common transition words:

Order	Relationships
finally	also
first	because
in conclusion	further
next	likewise
second	similarly
then	therefore

Concluding Paragraphs

Concluding paragraphs, or conclusions, help your audience reflect on the information you presented in your body paragraphs. In addition to summarizing all of your main points, conclusions tie your ideas to the thesis of the paper.

Conclusions are the opposite of introductions. Instead of moving toward more specific information, the conclusion moves from specific information to a more broad application of the topic. A conclusion usually begins by restating the thesis of your paper, and then sums up your main points. At the end, you may want to leave your audience with a thought-provoking question or real-world application.

To write a strong conclusion, follow these steps:

Step-by-Step Checklist: Conclusions

☐ | 1. Begin the conclusion by restating your thesis.

☐ | 2. Sum up the ideas of your main points.

☐ | 3. Explain how your main points support your thesis.

☐ | 4. Show how your thesis relates to the broader topic.

☐ | 5. Finally, challenge your audience to reflect further or take action.

The following is an example of a concluding paragraph from a short paper on post-traumatic stress disorder in children:

> Psychiatrists need more knowledge about childhood post-traumatic stress disorder. Every day, thousands of children suffer in silence due to undiagnosed PTSD. Recently, psychiatrists have begun to study in depth the disorder as it relates to children, but much more research is still needed about this confusing and little-known condition. The ignorance of parents and doctors about the symptoms and causes of the disorder demonstrates the intense need for more research. Giving physicians and parents better access to documentation and research about PTSD would improve the lives of thousands of children suffering from this disorder.

Lesson Wrap-up

Key Terms

Anecdote: a long example told as a story

Audience: the people who read your writing

Body Paragraphs: the paragraphs that contain the main points of a paper and use supporting details

Concluding Paragraph: a paragraph that ties together the ideas in a paper and summarizes the main points

Concluding Sentence: a sentence that ends a paragraph or paper by reviewing the ideas just discussed

Conclusion: a paragraph that ties together the ideas in a paper and summarizes the main points, also called a concluding paragraph

Description: a passage that explains the appearance of someone or something using words that appeal to the senses

Evidence: a piece of information, also called a supporting detail, that is used to support a main idea

Example: a specific instance or illustration that demonstrates a point

Expert Analysis: an opinion or statement shared by someone who is knowledgeable about a topic

Fact: a piece of information that most people generally agree to be true

Introduction: the paragraph used to introduce the main idea at the beginning of a paper, also called an introductory paragraph

Introductory Paragraph: the paragraph used to introduce the main idea at the beginning of a paper

Main Idea: the statement or argument that an author tries to communicate

Organizational Pattern: the structure of a written text, used to arrange the main points of a work

Outline: a tool developed during pre-writing that provides a visual of a paper's organization and ideas

Paragraph: a short piece of writing that focuses on one main idea

Reflection: the thoughts or feelings of the author

Statistic: a number or percentage that represents research data

Support Sentence: a sentence that explains and supports the topic sentence

Supporting Detail: a piece of information, also called evidence, that is used to support a main idea

Thesis Statement: a sentence that expresses the main idea of a longer work

Topic Sentence: a sentence that states the main point of a paragraph

Transition: a word, phrase, sentence, or paragraph that shows order and makes connections between ideas

Lesson 7.9
Revising a Longer Text

Drafting a long essay or research paper is challenging. Once you're finally done, you might feel ready to submit your work and be done with it. Keep in mind, however, that a first draft is still rough around the edges. Your work needs careful revision before it's ready for your **audience**.

Revising is the time to improve your ideas. In a long text like an essay or research paper, you must focus on content before grammar. You don't want to spend time fixing sentences that may be changed or deleted later. Once you have finished revising the ideas in the text, you can think about **editing** your sentences for spelling, grammar, and style errors.

In this lesson, you will learn how to revise the ideas in a longer text.

> To learn more about editing for grammar and style, see Lessons 4.21, 5.11, and 6.6.

Revising Ideas

Revising the ideas in your work involves two main areas: focus and development. A **focused** text clearly communicates its **thesis statement** and uses every **paragraph** to support and expand that thesis. As you revise for focus, you may need to change or delete information to stay on-topic. As you revise for focus, ask yourself the following questions:

> Does my text clearly accomplish my **purpose** for writing?
> Have I stated the **main idea** of my text in a clear thesis statement?
> Do all of my main points support my thesis statement?
> Do all of my paragraphs include clear **topic sentences**?
> Does my **introduction** point the audience to my thesis statement?
> Does my **conclusion** tie together all of the ideas in my text?

A **developed** text also presents information in an effective way and includes plenty of details to support its thesis statement. While revising for development, you may need to expand or add information to strengthen your ideas. As you revise for development, ask yourself the following questions:

> Is my topic narrow enough to discuss in a specific, in-depth way?
> Does my **outline** present the information logically?
> Do I use plenty of transitions to help the reader follow the ideas?
> Are all of my main points strengthened by plenty of **supporting details**?
> Have I included my own analysis to explain all of my main points?

Revising for focus and development takes a significant amount of time and effort. You are not just reading the words on a page; you are actively evaluating the thoughts behind those words. To help yourself work more effectively, use these guidelines:

Revise Your Work in Stages

As you move between drafting and revising, making changes in small steps is much easier than changing everything at once. To prevent yourself from feeling overwhelmed, try breaking a longer text into three or four sections. Revise each section in multiple stages, thinking about each question carefully and making necessary changes after each one.

Keep Copies of Your Previous Drafts

Revisions don't always go exactly as planned. You may need to return to an earlier version of your text to undo or redo certain changes. Saving multiple drafts also allows you to see the way your writing improved throughout the **writing process**.

Get a Second Opinion

If possible, ask a friend or a **Writing Center** tutor to read your work and share feedback or suggestions. Someone who hasn't read the information multiple times will have a different perspective than you.

Take Frequent Breaks

Revising a longer text is a lengthy process. If you try to cram all of this work into one night, you will not have the time to make significant changes. To ensure that your writing is as polished as possible, schedule yourself multiple revision sessions over the course of a few days.

Taking breaks will also help you clear your head between revisions. After working too long, your thoughts may start to feel muddled. Getting plenty of rest will keep your mind sharp and focused.

> **Reflection Questions**
> Have you ever re-read something that you wrote when you were younger? Usually, this experience is a little embarrassing. How does your writing change as you get older? How will it continue to improve over the next few years?

Lesson Wrap-up

Key Terms

Academic Writing Process: a strategy that breaks up a writing assignment into five stages: pre-writing, drafting, revising, editing, and submitting

Audience: the people who read your writing

Conclusion: a paragraph that ties together the ideas in a paper and summarizes the main points, also called a concluding paragraph

Development: effective presentation of information and inclusion of supporting details

Drafting: a stage of writing that involves writing out ideas and support/concluding sentences

Editing: a stage of writing that involves proofreading for style, grammar, and spelling errors

Focus: clear communication and support of a main idea

Introduction: the paragraph used to introduce the main idea at the beginning of a paper, also called an introductory paragraph

Main Idea: the statement or argument that an author tries to communicate

Outline: a tool developed during pre-writing that provides a visual of a paper's organization and ideas

Paragraph: a short piece of writing that focuses on one main idea

Purpose: the goal of a text

Revising: a stage of writing that involves revising for focus and development

Supporting Detail: a piece of information, also called evidence, that is used to support a main idea

Thesis Statement: a sentence that expresses the main idea of a longer work

Topic Sentence: a sentence that states the main point of a paragraph

Writing Center: a service that provides writing assistance

Lesson 7.10

Participating in Peer Review

By the time you reach the end of a longer draft, you've read through your ideas so many times you could probably recite certain parts by heart. You've **drafted**, **revised**, **edited**, and then drafted some more.

Sometimes, you spend so much time with your own thoughts that you have a hard time seeing any weak areas in your writing. After all, you know exactly what you were trying to communicate. Your **audience**, however, is unfamiliar with the content. They won't understand your ideas unless you've done a good job explaining your thoughts and making connections between ideas.

Participating in a peer review is one way to get a fresh set of eyes on your paper. **Peer-reviewing** is working with a classmate to give feedback on each other's papers. Sharing your ideas and receiving advice helps you both improve your draft and broaden your perspective.

The most obvious benefit of a peer review is getting feedback on your work. However, reviewing a classmate's paper also strengthens your writing skills. You have the opportunity to see how another author structures ideas, organizes support, and engages the reader. You may learn techniques that you can add to your own paper.

In this lesson, you will learn how to get the most out of a peer review as both the author and the reviewer.

> **Helpful Hint**
> Even if your class does not involve peer reviews, ask a friend or roommate to review your paper. Consider creating a checklist of items that you want them to evaluate.

Author

As an author, there are steps you should take both before and after the peer review to benefit your writing. Think about these four guidelines:

Come prepared

The more material you are able to bring to a peer review, the more feedback you will receive. If your draft is missing key points or pieces of **evidence**, your reviewer may not understand important aspects of your **main idea**. You should also consider preparing a brief list of problem areas. This will help your reviewer stay focused on the items that are most important to you.

Keep an open mind

Be open to your reviewer's feedback since that person represents your intended audience. The feedback you receive is not intended to be a personal attack. Your reviewer has invested time into helping you become a better writer, so resist the urge to become defensive or argumentative.

Ask for clarification

If you don't understand a comment, follow up with the reviewer for more clarification. Talking through an issue will give you a better understanding of how to fix it.

Filter the feedback

You should thoughtfully consider all of the feedback you receive from your reviewer. Remember, however, that the final decision rests with you. Once you've determined which suggestions you want to take, start revising and editing your draft.

Reviewer

All peer reviews are not created equal. To give your peer the best possible feedback, you must actively read the text and keep your suggestions clear and organized. Keep the following characteristics in mind as you work:

Be focused

As you peer review, stay focused on the most important issues in the text. This means giving suggestions about the **thesis statement**, organization, main points, and **supporting details**, not getting side-tracked by grammar and spelling issues. If the author has asked you to evaluate certain areas of the text, make sure that you take the time to do so.

Staying focused also means keeping your feedback manageable. Leaving comments on every single problem might be overwhelming to the author. Instead, try to keep your suggestions focused on the most critical areas of weakness.

Be honest

The whole purpose of reviewing a text is helping the author see areas of weakness that he or she previously overlooked. Sharing only positive feedback will actually hurt the author in the long run. Remember that no one is a perfect writer; everyone can benefit from a second opinion.

Be specific

The more specific information you can give, the easier it will be for the author to make changes later. Take a look at these examples of a helpful and unhelpful comment:

Unhelpful	This paragraph is confusing.
Helpful	You should consider making your **topic sentence** more specific. The evidence you include in the paragraph focuses on the benefits of social media, but your topic sentence focuses on the benefits of the internet in general.

Another aspect of making your comments more specific is adding suggestions for improvement. Instead of focusing on just the negative, share specific ways that the author can make changes. This is known as **constructive criticism** because it helps the author build on your feedback.

Be professional

As you review, keep your comments respectful and straightforward. You should avoid using any language that might hurt or offend the author. When possible, share positive comments in addition to your constructive criticism.

Be thorough

Being thorough means reading the paper carefully so that you can leave clear, thoughtful feedback. Simply skimming the text is not enough. You will not be able to evaluate the most important issues in the text if you don't read and reflect on the information.

As you read through the text, try asking yourself questions to stay focused on the most important issues. Here are a few examples:

Introduction
- Is the thesis statement of the paper clear and interesting?
- Does the organization of the main points make sense?
- Does the **introduction** grab your attention?

Body Paragraphs
- Does each body paragraph start with a clear topic sentence?
- Are all of the main points well supported with evidence?
- Do all of the main points support the main point of the paper?
- Which main point is the strongest?
- Which main point is the weakest?

Conclusion
- Does the author restate the thesis at the beginning of the conclusion?
- Does the conclusion tie together the entire paper?

Lesson Wrap-up

Key Terms

Audience: the people who read your writing

Body Paragraphs: the paragraphs that contain the main points of a paper and use supporting details

Conclusion: a paragraph that ties together the ideas in a paper and summarizes the main points, also called a concluding paragraph

Constructive Criticism: suggestions of specific ways that an author can improve his or her work

Drafting: a stage of writing that involves writing out ideas and support/concluding sentences

Editing: a stage of writing that involves proofreading for style, grammar, and spelling errors

Evidence: a piece of information, also called a supporting detail, that is used to support a main idea

Introduction: the paragraph used to introduce the main idea at the beginning of a paper, also called an introductory paragraph

Main Idea: the statement or argument that an author tries to communicate

Peer Review: working with a classmate to give feedback on each other's papers

Revising: a stage of writing that involves revising for focus and development

Supporting Detail: a piece of information, also called evidence, that is used to support a main idea

Thesis Statement: a sentence that expresses the main idea of a longer work

Topic Sentence: a sentence that states the main point of a paragraph

Lesson 7.11
Submitting a Longer Text

Submitting a longer text is a great feeling. You've worked hard throughout the entire **writing process**, and now, you finally have the opportunity to share your ideas with your **audience**.

The final version of your text might be a paper, a blog post, a book, a video, or a presentation. Regardless of the **format** you choose, your work isn't quite done. You must make a few important decisions before submitting the finished version of your work.

In this lesson, you will learn three steps in submitting a longer text:

Choose a Layout and Design
Add Visuals
Print or Upload Your Work

> Helpful Hint
> Before submitting a text for school or work, be sure to review any specific guidelines from your instructor or supervisor.

Choose a Layout and Design

The first step in submitting a longer text is choosing a layout and design. **Layout** refers to the way your writing is arranged on the page or the screen, while **design** refers to the colors, **fonts**, and images that you select.

Genre often determines the layout and design of your finished work. For example, an academic text like a research paper will probably be plainer than a personal text like a blog post. **Academic writing** may also require the use of a specific format such as MLA style, which contains a set of layout and design rules.

Here are some basic rules and guidelines for MLA formatting:

- Research papers using MLA style should include a **running head** half an inch from the top of the page, on the right-side corner of each page. In your running head, include your last name followed by the page number.
- Except for the running head, all sides of your paper should have one-inch margins. The first line of each paragraph should be indented by half an inch, and all of the text should be double-spaced.

To learn more about using MLA style, see Lesson 8.6.

> Reflection Questions
> The format of your work can affect your design choices. What are some of the differences between print and electronic formats? Why do you think these differences exist?

> Group Activity
> As a group, find five examples of well-designed texts. Create a presentation that discusses how each one uses good layout and design to communicate its message. Share your presentation with the class. (Be sure to follow the layout and design guidelines for your work!)

An MLA research paper does not require a title page. Instead, the first page of the paper includes a list of four items: your name, your professor's name, the course name and number, and the date. This list should be double-spaced and left-aligned. Then, center the title of your paper on the line preceding the first paragraph.

O'Dell 1

Kevin O'Dell

Dr. Van Vlack

FILM 302

7 January 2015

A History of Video Editing Technology

You will begin writing your paper here. There is no need for a full title page. A properly formatted header will suffice. Always be sure to check your professor's title (Dr., Ms., Professor) before placing it on your paper. Left-justify your text and follow the formatting guidelines throughout your entire paper.

An MLA title page simply lists your name, professor's name, class, and date.

In other projects, you may have more control over the final format of your writing. If so, use this as an opportunity to strengthen your writing through good layout and design choices. A well-designed document is more interesting, more readable, and more meaningful to the audience.

Imagine a science textbook filled only with tiny black and white text. You would probably struggle to read the pages or understand complex topics. This is because textbooks are designed to make the information as clear as possible. The images, fonts, and colors in textbooks aren't chosen just to look good. They are there to explain confusing concepts and highlight important ideas.

As you think about the layout and design of your finished text, consider the acronym **ACE**:

A: Are the layout and design **appealing**?

C: Are the layout and design **consistent**?

E: Are the layout and design **easy to read**?

First, your design should be *appealing* to your audience. For a paper, this may simply mean that your pages are free of stains or marks. You might also decide to include a neat cover page or to place the finished document in a plastic folder. When submitting a more creative work, you should use colors and fonts that are attractive to your audience.

You work should also have a consistent *appearance*. If you use certain fonts or colors at the beginning, continue using these so that the entire work looks neat and unified. Using consistent design and layout not only makes your work more attractive, but consistency also helps your audience understand the information better.

For example, if you have centered headings at the beginning of each section, you audience will always know when a new section starts. If you switch to left-aligned headings halfway through, your audience may think these sections are somehow different.

Finally, make sure that your work is *easy to read*. If your audience can't read the message of your text, then you haven't truly accomplished your **purpose**. An easy-to-read text uses clear fonts with a reasonable amount of spacing between lines and paragraphs. Your page or screen should also be free from clutter or distractions.

Add Visuals

Using visuals in a text helps you engage your audience better and communicate your ideas more clearly. Think about the advertisements, documents, books, and posters you encounter in your everyday life. Most likely, those texts include images.

To ensure that you are using the best possible visuals for your writing, think through the following guidelines:

Think about your purpose

Before you add an image, think about your purpose for using visuals in the text. For example, advertisements often use images to show the design and features of a product, while presentations use images to catch the audience's attention and emphasize important points. Once you've determined your purpose for using visuals, you should evaluate any potential images against that purpose. If an image doesn't help you meet your goals, think twice before including it.

Think about your genre

The **genre** of your published work will determine the type of images that you are able to include. If you are submitting an article to a magazine, that publication will have specific rules about the types of images that can be used. If you are giving a speech, you may not have access to a projector or computer.

Think about your design

Always think about the layout and design of your text before adding visuals. Images should follow the same design guidelines as the rest of the text. A visual should be appealing to your audience, consistent with the overall design, and easy to see or understand. You may need to adjust the position or size of the image to ensure that it fits into your work properly.

Print or Upload

The last step in submitting a text is actually printing or uploading the final copy. Even though this step is small, it's important. Always schedule yourself extra time in case of printer or computer problems. You don't want to realize that your printer is out of ink right before class.

You should also double-check your work once it's been printed or published. For example, if you accidentally left the last page of your document in the printer tray, you want to notice this before submitting your work to your instructor or manager.

In some situations, submitting doesn't mean the end of your work as a writer. You may be turning in your work for instructor or **peer review**. Afterward, you will use this feedback to continue improving and polishing your work. In other cases, however, this is the final step in the writing process. Either way, take a moment to congratulate yourself for a wonderful accomplishment.

Lesson Wrap-up

Key Terms

Academic Writing: a text intended for instructors or students

Academic Writing Process: a strategy that breaks up a writing assignment into five stages: pre-writing, drafting, revising, editing, and submitting

ACE: an acronym (Appealing, Consistent, Easy to read) for thinking about the layout and design of a text

Audience: the people who read your writing

Design: colors, fonts, and images included in a text

Font: the size and style of letters

Format: the style and arrangement of a text

Genre: a type of writing

Layout: the way text and images are arranged on a page or screen

Peer Review: working with another person in order to give feedback on each other's papers

Purpose: the goal of an image

Running Head: in an MLA paper, the page number and author's last name, which appear in the top-right corner of the document

Submitting: a stage of writing that involves formatting a text and sharing it with its audience

Chapter 8
Research

Lesson 8.1
Researching and Writing Responsibly

Research is required for many academic and professional tasks, but it is also something we do regularly in our daily lives. Have you ever been with a group of people and started debating about a particular topic? Maybe you felt differently than someone else did. How did you support your argument?

Researching is all about finding information to explore ideas and ultimately make arguments. You can use research to find sources of information that support your **claim**. However, you must be careful when you use these research sources in **research writing**.

Most importantly, whenever you borrow ideas to use in your own text, it's vital that you give proper credit to the authors of those ideas. If you pass off borrowed information as your own, you are committing **plagiarism**.

Additionally, many research assignments have very specific requirements. In academic settings, you will likely be asked to write a research paper using a particular **research style**. Some of the most common research styles include MLA, APA, and Chicago style. Although many of the concepts in this chapter apply to all styles, the examples you'll encounter are formatted in MLA style.

In this lesson, you will learn about the following:

The Role of Sources in Research Writing
Avoiding Plagiarism with Proper Documentation
The Basics of Research Styles

The Role of Sources in Research Writing

Research is primarily concerned with finding the right sources. **Sources** can include many forms of texts— artwork, speeches, recordings, movies, articles, etc.—that provide information relevant to your particular goal.

Some sources are more formal than others. For example, if you're using a Yelp! review as a basis for finding a good doctor in your neighborhood, you're consulting an informal source of information. However, if you've found a doctor credited in a scholarly article, you have located a formal, academic source.

Depending on your task, you may be required to use certain types of sources.

To learn more about identifying types of sources, see Lesson 8.4.

On Your Own

Think about the common categories listed in the left column. For each, provide an example of a strong, trustworthy source. The first has been completed for you.

Source	Example
A website	The U.S. Department of Education
A newspaper	
A magazine	
A book	
An interview	
A documentary	

In academic writing, citing reliable sources is not only required, it's necessary if you want to establish yourself as a reliable writer. For example, you can use **expert analysis** and **statistics** to show your audience that your argument is well-informed and supported by current research.

Often, the goal of research is to locate credible information that supports your claim. Using research to explore the right sources has multiple advantages:

- Strengthens your opinion about a topic by supporting it with fact, details, and evidence
- Offers powerful **anecdotes**, or long examples told as stories, to highlight your main arguments
- Adds validity to your writing by linking your own claims to experts within your field of study
- Provides timely and relevant information that will advance the education of your audience
- Informs your audience where they can find further information regarding your topic

On Your Own

Read and evaluate the following paragraphs. Which sounds more convincing? If you were trying to make the case against eating celery, which paragraph would you use in your own writing? Why?

Paragraph 1:

Perhaps one of humankind's most valued senses is the sense of taste. This sense helps to weed out those foods that humans don't enjoy. At the top of this list is the celery stalk. Celery is disliked by many people, in many parts of the country. So, it shouldn't be of any real surprise to hear someone complain about the taste.

Paragraph 2:

According to a recent study conducted at Yale University, "The most valued human sense is the sense of taste." This sense helps to weed out those foods that humans don't enjoy. At the top of this list is the celery stalk. According to esteemed researcher Kenneth Braymer, celery has the "lowest success rate in initial taste tests of any food" (96). So, it shouldn't be of any real surprise to hear someone say that "celery tastes like dirt." According to Dr. Kane of the Harvard University Research Team, tree bark actually has more nutritional benefit than the celery stalk (34).

Integrating Source Information

Once you've selected your research, you need to decide how to utilize each source in your writing. There are three main ways to integrate sources into your writing:

- Summarizing
- Paraphrasing
- Quoting

Summarizing

A **summary** is a few sentences that explain a large amount of information. Using summaries makes the most sense when your readers need a broad overview of a topic but not specific details. Because summaries are general, they should only be used when you need to inform your **audience** about important background information on a topic.

Take a look at the example below:

> In his novel, *Things Fall Apart*, on the rise of colonialism in Nigeria, author Chinua Achebe follows the story of Okonkwo, a tribal leader who has risen from very little and has maintained power and dominance amongst his clan and his family. As colonists begin to invade Okonkwo's land, culture, and traditions, he struggles against the forces that threaten all he knows.

In this brief summary, the author highlights important components of the story in his own words, conveying broad ideas and major conflict.

Paraphrasing

When you **paraphrase**, you explain someone's words or sentences using your own words. Paraphrases can explain a text's purpose or add clarity to the author's argument. You can paraphrase anything from a single sentence to a complex idea. Consider the example below.

Original sentence:

> "Female elephants are pregnant for a longer period of time than any other mammal, keeping their child with them for an average of twenty-two months" (Johnson 63).

Paraphrase:

> Shockingly, elephants carry their babies for close to two years; this is longer than any other mammal (Johnson 63).

Quoting

Quotations are the direct words of a source. Quotes should be reserved for instances when the author's language is powerful or unique. Otherwise, you should paraphrase the borrowed language.

Here's an example:

> Eleanor Roosevelt famously said, "You must do the things you think you cannot do."

To learn more about summarizing, paraphrasing, and quoting in MLA style, see Lesson 8.6.

Avoiding Plagiarism with Proper Documentation

Imagine that you've been working on a marketing idea that you want to propose to your boss. You show your notes and outline to your coworker for feedback. The next thing you know, that coworker is presenting your idea to your supervisor. His words are his own, but the *ideas* are yours.

> **Further Resources**
>
> To read about high-profile plagiarism cases that have happened in recent years, check out this article: https://unplag.com/blog/plagiarism-scandals-2015/

Clearly, your coworker was wrong to present your ideas as his own. For the same reason, when you use words or ideas from an outside source without crediting the author, you commit plagiarism. Most colleges take this issue seriously; one major offense is often grounds for serious punishment.

Some forms of plagiarism are much more obvious than others. For example, you probably know that it's wrong to purchase an essay online and pass it off as your own. Similarly, you know not to copy and paste text from an outside source and turn it in as if you wrote it.

However, other common forms of plagiarism are not as obvious, and students often plagiarize unintentionally. For example, if you've conducted a lot of research on a topic, you may end up writing about someone else's ideas without even realizing it. If you don't cite the source, or cite it incorrectly, you are committing plagiarism.

> **Helpful Hint**
>
> Many schools define their policies and procedures for plagiarism in a course syllabus, college handbook, and/or library website.

Track your sources as you conduct your research.

As you gather source material, it's important to keep track of where the information came from. Otherwise, you might end up citing a source incorrectly or forgetting to cite it at all.

To avoid accidental plagiarism, use a notebook or digital file to keep track of your research. The key is to immediately catalog material you think you might use in your paper. As you read a text, take note of any facts or ideas that interest you.

Some students like taking notes on index cards while others prefer copying and pasting the text into a Word document. Either method is fine as long as you carefully record the following source details:

- Type of source
- Title
- Author
- Year of publication

Whenever you copy ideas from your research, place quotation marks around direct quotes. This will help you remember that the information is not your own.

Note-taking will also help you focus on reading the text closely and ensure that you understand the ideas and words that you borrow. A common mistake students make in the research process is to get impatient and skim through texts instead of reading them. If you paraphrase a text that you don't understand, you'll likely mislead the reader.

To learn more about organizing the research process, see Lesson 8.3.

Use proper in-text citations.

Your reader should be able to distinguish between your original work and that of your sources. To avoid plagiarism, you must use correct in-text citations and signal phrases for any content that is summarized, paraphrased, or directly quoted. **In-text citations** are notes in a paragraph that tell the reader which words and ideas come from a source. **Signal phrases** are phrases used to identify source information—like the title and author—within a sentence.

Here are some examples of signal phrases:

According to [Author]...

> According to NFL commissioner Roger Goodell, "I don't expect to try to get people to like everything I do. I want them to respect what I do."

In his/her book, [*Title of Book*], [Author] discusses...

> In her article, "The High Price of Diamonds," Jenny Reed argues that the majority of people who wear diamond jewelry are unaware of the consequences of mining for this rock.

If you do not identify the author's name in the paragraph, remember to include it in an in-text citation at the end. This citation will let your readers know exactly what information you've borrowed from the source.

Don't forget to include every source you use on the **works-cited page** or in the references list even if your summarized source is the only source you've used.

Direct quotes use the exact words of outside sources. These might be individual words, sentences, or groups of sentences. You must put *all* direct quotes in **quotation marks**.

In MLA style, direct quotes require an in-text citation that includes the **page number** where the quote was originally found. If you are unable to fit the author's name in the sentence itself, add the author's last name to the citation.

> In *Jesse James: American Antihero*, professor Lawrence Bruce explains that the American public "imagined Jesse James as Robin Hood of the Wild West" (20).

> The imagery that Matthew Arnold uses in this poem "represents the author's longing for a literal and emotional home" (Edahl 33).

By including the author and title of the source, you are clearly signaling to the reader that the words in quotation marks are not your own.

Use the following questions to double-check for possible plagiarism:

Checklist: Avoiding Plagiarism

☐ Do all the direct quotes have quotation marks and citation information?

☐ Do all the paraphrases and summaries have citation information?

☐ Is it clear where the paraphrases and summaries end and where my words begin?

☐ Are all my sources listed in a works-cited page?

The Basics of Research Styles

Depending on your task and your audience, you may be asked to work with multiple formatting styles. These styles have basic formatting rules as well as requirements for citations and works-cited/reference pages. Let's review four of the most common styles:

- MLA (Modern Language Association)
- APA (American Psychological Association)
- CMS (Chicago Manual of Style)
- CSE (Council of Science Editors)

MLA

MLA style was created by a group of scholars dedicated to research in modern languages. It is used most frequently in English and foreign languages. However, it can also be used in communications, religion, and philosophy.

MLA recommends utilizing the "Think, Select, Organize" process, which requires you to *think* about what types of sources are relevant to your research, *select* appropriate sources and source information, and *organize* your citations in a clear manner.

Additionally, when drafting your works-cited page, you must use the nine MLA Core Elements to form thorough and organized citations:

- Author
- Title of source
- Title of container
- Other contributors
- Version
- Number
- Publisher
- Publication date
- Location

To learn more about applying MLA standards, see Lesson 8.6.

APA

APA style was created by psychologists to be used for academic documents like journal articles and books. It is used in many academic disciplines, so learning its general rules is a good idea for just about every student. In particular, the social sciences (like psychology and sociology), nursing, journalism, and business typically use APA style.

As a general rule, APA papers strive to sound as objective or unbiased as possible. For this reason, writers using APA style are expected to avoid first-person pronouns (like *I* and *me*), second-person pronouns (like *you* and *your*), contractions, and slang.

Since APA style is often used for writing about research and experiments, writers are asked to use the following guidelines when choosing their language:

- Be as specific as possible
- Be sensitive to labeling and unintentional prejudice
- When writing about people, write about them as active participants, not passive components

CMS

CMS is a formatting style guide published by the University of Chicago Press. Often preferred by publishers, CMS is the most comprehensive option for citing books, magazines, and journals.

Some disciplines that commonly use CMS are the arts, computer science, criminology, and history.

Unlike previously mentioned styles, CMS offers two ways of citing research sources:

- Notes-and-Bibliography Method
- Parentheses-and-Reference-List Method

The Notes-and-Bibliography Method is preferred by the humanities because it allows for easily referencing sources and inserting additional information.

Because science and technology change rapidly, the Parentheses-and-Reference-List Method is often preferred for these subjects because it prioritizes the publication dates of sources.

CSE

CSE is the formatting style guide created by the Council of Science Editors. As the name suggests, this format is most commonly used for the sciences, particularly the natural and physical sciences.

CSE has three different methods for documenting sources. Each method includes a series of in-text markers that show when a source has been used and a corresponding list of sources, typically titled "References," that appears at the end of the document. Here are the three methods:

- Citation-Sequence
- Citation-Name
- Name-Year

The citation-sequence system organizes sources at the end of the paper according to the order that they appear in the text.

In the citation-name system, each source used in the paper is assigned a number, which is used to refer to that source throughout the document. However, the list of sources at the end of the paper is arranged and numbered according to alphabetical order rather than the order that the sources appear in the document.

The name-year system uses in-text citations that include the last name of the author(s) as well as the source's publication date.

Further Resources

The Online Writing Lab (OWL) developed by Purdue University provides ample information about how to cite sources and format papers in different styles. Visit this page (https://owl.english.purdue.edu/owl/section/2/) for an in-depth explanation of each.

Lesson Wrap-up

Key Terms

Anecdote: a long example told as a story

APA (American Psychological Association) Style: the research style guide created by psychologists used for academic documents such as journal articles and books

Audience: the people who read your writing

Claim: an argument or statement, usually supported by evidence

CMS (Chicago Manual of Style): a research style guide published by the University of Chicago Press

CSE (Council of Science Editors) Style: a research style created by the Council of Science Editors

Expert Analysis: an opinion or statement shared by someone who is knowledgeable about a topic

In-text Citation: a note in a paragraph that tells the reader which words and ideas come from a source

MLA (Modern Language Association) Style: the research style guide created by a group of scholars dedicated to research in modern languages

Page Number: a way to help the audience find information in a text

Paraphrase: rewording the words of another person in order to explain the text's purpose or to add clarity to the author's argument

Plagiarism: the act of using borrowed words or ideas without giving credit to the author

Quotation Marks: a pair of punctuation marks used to repeat someone else's words

Quotation: the direct words of a source

Research Style: a set of standards used for research writing within a particular discipline

Research Writing: the process of conducting research and using sources to compose arguments

Signal Phrase: a phrase used to identify source information—like the title and author—within a sentence

Source: an original document or first-hand account that a writer consults for research

Statistic: a number or percentage that represents research data

Summary: a few sentences that explain a large amount of information

Works Cited: a list of sources at the end of an MLA-styled text

Lesson 8.2
Making a Research Plan

Think about the last time you Googled something. Every day, you conduct research by looking up information ranging from weather conditions to restaurant reviews to relationship advice. You find answers to your questions by consulting the ideas and opinions of others.

Creating an organized plan for carrying out research can help you to meet deadlines.

You do the same thing when you complete research assignments. As a writing tool, research enables you to explore your topic, support your ideas, and establish your **credibility** as an author.

Your research should play a meaningful role in the content and organization of your writing. This means that you should plan and begin your research before you sit down to write your paper. Making a research plan will give you the direction and preparation you need to use research effectively.

In this lesson, you will learn to create a research plan in four steps:

Consider Your Purpose and Guidelines
Conduct Preliminary Research
Think about Different Research Methods
Schedule a Research Timeline

Reflection Questions

What sorts of information have you looked for recently? How do you think using technology to find information has prepared you for formal research?

Consider Your Purpose and Guidelines

The first step of creating a research plan is identifying your **purpose**. This determines what role your research should play in your writing. For example, if your purpose is to persuade your audience to stop drinking soda, you'll probably use medical research or **statistics** from health organizations as **evidence**. If your purpose is to analyze three landmark Supreme Court cases, your evidence will include **examples** from each case and **expert analysis** from historians or law experts.

Here are some examples of how research might fit with different purposes:

Purpose	Evidence
To **inform** the audience about the mission of the Peace Corps	• **Facts** from the Peace Corps organization • **Anecdotes** and examples from people who have served in the Peace Corps
To **persuade** the audience that all cell phone use while driving should be banned	• Facts from law enforcement and government agencies • Statistics and expert analysis from researchers • Examples from distracted driving organizations
To **reflect** on why you want to become a doctor	• Anecdotes and **descriptions** from your personal experiences • **Reflections** on your own feelings and motivations

When writing for work or school, you'll follow guidelines determined by your instructor or supervisor. You'll need to carefully review their instructions before deciding on the types of evidence to include. For example, an instructor might require that you include information from specific types of sources, such as books or **academic journals**.

On Your Own

Complete the table with a list of purposes and appropriate types of evidence for each.

Purpose	Research
To inform the audience of the impacts of excessive after-school involvement of an athlete	

Conduct Preliminary Research

Before you get too far in the **pre-writing** process, you should conduct preliminary research on your topic. This research will help you ensure that there is enough material to support your **main idea**. If you are having a difficult time finding information, you may want to rethink your topic or **controlling idea**.

One of the easiest ways to start researching is simply to use a search engine like Google or Bing. Glance through the top five or ten sites that pop up in the search results. These will give you a quick idea of the type of source material you can expect to find during your research.

You should also do a quick search of your library's catalog to see the sources that they have available. Consider discussing your paper ideas with a librarian to get additional research ideas.

> Helpful Hint
>
> When conducting preliminary research, use search terms that are specific to your **thesis statement**. If your search is too broad, you won't get a realistic idea of the source material that's available.

Preliminary research is an excellent way to narrow down the main ideas in your paper. As you refine your **working outline**, use your research to **brainstorm** new ideas and decide which ideas are the best.

Think about Different Research Methods

The next step in planning your research is deciding on the best research methods. Here are the three most common sources:

Library Catalogs and Databases

Visiting the library is the best way to find books and academic journals. Academic journals contain articles written by researchers or other experts in a particular field. Most libraries have an online system that you can use to search available materials. You should also consider meeting with a librarian in person for assistance with your research.

Internet Searches

On the internet, you can find websites, news articles, videos, and images. Conducting online research is an excellent way to find source material on rapidly changing topics like technology and pop culture. Because of the large amount of information available online, you must carefully evaluate each source to be sure the information is credible.

Helpful Hint
Google Scholar (http://scholar.google.com) is a special search engine that helps you find articles from academic journals. Keep in mind that you probably won't get as many results as you would from an online library database.

Helpful Hint
When conducting a Google search in order to find sources for a research paper, it may be a good idea to look for websites that have a *.edu* URL. Websites with *.edu* URLs are typically associated with academic institutions and have a better chance of containing reliable source material.

To learn more about evaluating online sources, see Lesson 8.3.

Field Research

Field research involves personally collecting information through interviews and surveys. Your experience in a topic and your access to participants may limit your opportunities for field research. However, this can be an excellent way to gain information about issues that affect your campus or fellow students.

Some types of research will fit certain topics better than others. For example, if you are writing a research paper on the causes of cerebral palsy, the library will contain books and articles written by experts. However, if you are writing an essay on the lack of healthy food choices on campus, interviews with students and faculty members might make more sense.

Based on your purpose and guidelines, brainstorm the types of research that will make the most sense for your text. Double-check your assignment guidelines to see if you need to include specific types of sources in your text. It's important to consider these requirements early just in case you need to schedule extra time to gather your research.

On Your Own

Identify different types of sources that could be used for each research purpose provided.

Purpose of Research	Types of Sources
To investigate the effects of a particular medicine on lung cancer	
To persuade the audience that chemical testing on animals should be stopped	
To inform the audience of a typical student's perspective on a U.S. presidential race	

Helpful Hint
If you're conducting research on a particular subject, such as anthropology or physics, and don't know where to start, try reaching out to instructors and professors at your school who are experienced in that field. They may be able to suggest particular databases or sources that you can research.

Schedule a Research Timeline

Once you have a general idea of the research you need to conduct, you can create a timeline to keep yourself on track. Add scheduled research times to your **planner** so that you don't **procrastinate** or fall behind. Also, you should add any research deadlines that your instructor has required as part of a paper or project.

Your research may involve special situations that require extra planning. For example, if you want to meet with a librarian, you need to visit the library during open hours. Any field research will also need to be planned around the schedules of your participants.

Finally, many universities offer students the service of a **Writing Center** where you can make an appointment and receive assistance on completing your research assignment. Getting a second opinion can help you find ideas you may have otherwise missed.

Lesson Wrap-up

Key Terms

Academic Journal: a collection of articles written by researchers and peer-reviewed by other experts in a particular field

Anecdote: a long example told as a story

Brainstorming: exploring and developing ideas

Controlling Idea: what an author wants to say about a topic

Credibility: what makes someone or something believable

Description: a passage that explains the appearance of someone or something using words that appeal to the senses

Evidence: a piece of information, also called a supporting detail, that is used to support a main idea

Example: a specific instance or illustration that demonstrates a point

Expert Analysis: an opinion or statement shared by someone who is knowledgeable about a topic

Fact: a piece of information that most people generally agree to be true

Field Research: research that involves personally collecting information through interviews and surveys

Informative Text: a text that gives the audience information about a topic

Main Idea: the statement or argument that an author tries to communicate

Persuasive Text: a text that convinces its audience to adopt a belief or take an action

Planner: a place for you to organize your schedule and record any important tasks or responsibilities

Pre-writing: a stage of writing that involves making decisions, planning ideas, and identifying assignment guidelines

Procrastination: putting off work until the last minute

Purpose: the goal of a text

Reflection: the thoughts or feelings of the author

Reflective Text: a text that shares a personal experience or belief

Statistic: a number or percentage that represents research data

Thesis Statement: a sentence that expresses the main idea of a longer work

Working Outline: an informal outline with no special formatting or structure

Writing Center: a service that provides writing assistance

Lesson 8.3
Organizing the Research Process

When you are conducting research for a paper, you might find yourself struggling to keep everything straight. Maybe you remember reading a really great statistic the other day but you can't remember where you found it. After spending 45 minutes looking it up online, you realize that it doesn't fit into your paragraph the way you thought it would.

Using a system to organize your research helps you keep track of important source material. You don't want to lose an important **fact** or **example**. Organization also saves time during the **drafting** process because it helps you easily find the information you want to use. Last, organizing your research will keep you from accidentally committing plagiarism by using someone's words or ideas without giving them credit.

In this lesson, you will learn how to organize your research using three helpful tools:

Research Notes
Research Journal
Working Bibliography

> Reflection Questions
>
> Have you ever encountered plagiarism personally or seen it play out in a news story? How did it affect your opinion of plagiarism?

Research Notes

Research notes are detailed records of the source information that you find during your research. As you read through your sources, look for pieces of evidence that you think you could use in your paper. Record this information in your notes so that it's easy to find later.

Taking notes keeps your research manageable. In a typical source, you might find three to five pieces of information that you want to include in your project. Instead of scanning through the entire text every time you need to use a fact or statistic, you can use your research notes to find the exact information you need.

Research notes also prevent you from losing important information. As you conduct your research, you will read a large amount of information. You can't assume that you will remember everything. Nothing is more frustrating than realizing the **quotation** you were planning to include doesn't actually say what you thought it did.

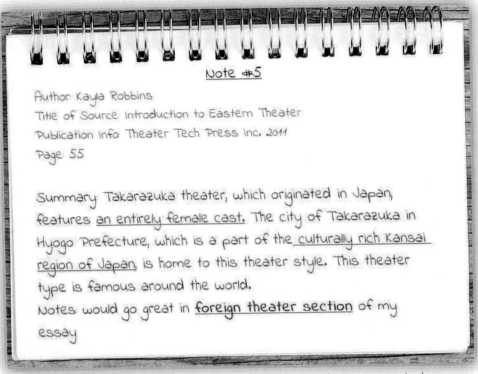

Note #5

Author: Kayla Robbins
Title of Source: Introduction to Eastern Theater
Publication Info: Theater Tech Press Inc. 2011
Page: 55

Summary: Takarazuka theater, which originated in Japan, features <u>an entirely female cast</u>. The city of Takarazuka in Hyogo Prefecture, which is a part of the <u>culturally rich Kansai region of Japan</u>, is home to this theater style. This theater type is famous around the world.
Notes: would go great in <u>**foreign theater section**</u> of my essay

Research notes are a helpful tool for keeping your research process organized.

Finally, research notes help you organize your thoughts during the **writing process**. As you **outline** your paper, start adding research under each main point. You will be able to see which main points need additional support. Once you start writing, you will know exactly how your research fits into your **main idea**.

Research notes should include the following information:

Checklist: Research Notes

- ☐ Source information, including the author, title, and publication information
- ☐ Date that you accessed or read the material
- ☐ Important information clearly labeled as **summary**, **paraphrase**, or quote
- ☐ Additional notes or ideas about using the material in your paper

Some people prefer to keep electronic research notes so that they can easily copy and paste the information into their documents. If you use this method, it's even more important to mark if the information is a summary, paraphrase, or quote so that you do not accidentally copy and paste someone else's words into your paper.

To learn more about integrating source information into your writing, see Lesson 8.6.

Other people prefer to take hand-written notes on index cards. This method is useful because you can easily move them around or spread them out on a desk as you write. If you like using index cards but don't want to write everything by hand, consider printing out all of your information and taping each note to a card.

On Your Own

Read the example paragraph below. Assume the text comes from a magazine for jobseekers. After you read the source text, read a paragraph that a student has written about the job search process. In the student's paragraph, identify the paraphrase that should have an in-text citation.

Source text:

> When searching for a job, it is vital to maintain a professional presence across all social media platforms. In other words, when you are in the midst of the job application process, any information you have put online could potentially be seen by a prospective employer. As such, you will want to refrain from posting inappropriate content on your social media profiles to avoid giving off an unprofessional and impolite image of yourself. This is not to say you should limit your own expression and creativity, but you should always be mindful of who might be looking at your posts when you are attempting to secure your dream job.

Student writing:

> If you are a college graduate looking for a job, it can feel overwhelming at times; however, there are a few tips and tricks that can help you secure a job if you are motivated. First, always carry a copy of your résumé on you if you think you might be introduced to a potential employer. Second, it is a good idea to clean up your social media presence as hiring managers and recruiters may visit your social media profiles to get an idea of what kind of candidate you are. Finally, dress to impress! Having a clean and professional appearance can go a long way when looking for a job.

Research Journal

A **research journal** is a record of your overall research process. Writing down your thoughts as you work helps you keep track of good ideas or questions.

Here's what a typical entry might look like:

> ## Food Advertisements and Eating Habits
>
> *April 9th*
>
> > Food advertisements targeting children and adolescents
> > Strategies for appealing to this age group?
> > How much influence do the ads have on this age group? Studies?
>
> *April 10th*
>
> > Laws or policies?

There's no set format for a research journal. You might keep your notes in an electronic document or write them in a notebook. Either way, feel free to include any notes or ideas that you think could be helpful later.

Research journals can help you find information about your research process. If you remember a good statistic that you forgot to write down in your notes, you can retrace your steps and find the source you need.

> **Helpful Hint**
>
> No matter what method you use to create a research journal, be sure to keep your entries organized so that they're easier to reference during the writing process.

> **Learning Style Tip**
>
> If you are a **visual** learner, consider color-coding your research journal. For example, red could indicate any notes or citations that belong in your introduction, and blue could indicate supporting details that belong in the body paragraphs.

Working Bibliography

The final tool for keeping your research organized is a working bibliography. A **working bibliography** is a running list of sources that you plan to use in your paper. Once you reach the last stage of the writing process, you will turn this bibliography into the **works-cited** page of your paper. Take a look at the examples below.

Working Bibliography Entry:

> "Promoting Public Health Through Public Art in the Digital Age"
> Authors: Kilaru, Ash, Sellers, and Merchant
> Publication Info: American Journal of Public Health, Volume 104, Issue 9, 2014, p. 1633-1635
> Useful ideas: health information in social media sites; need for "innovative approaches"

Formal Works-Cited Entry:

> Kilaru, Austin S., et al. "Promoting Public Health Through Public Art in the Digital Age." *American*
>
> *Journal of Public Health,* vol. 104, no. 9, 2014, pp. 1633-1635.

In your working bibliography, you can arrange your sources in any order you find helpful. Consider arranging them according to relevance to your topic. This will make it easier to remove, replace, and add new sources as you continue your preliminary research. The formal Works-Cited entries, however, should be in alphabetical order.

> **Helpful Hint**
>
> Often, authors number the entries in their working bibliography and record those numbers on their research notecards. This helps them record source information for each note without having to write the same thing multiple times.

Lesson Wrap-up

Key Terms

Drafting: a stage of writing that involves writing out ideas and support/concluding sentences

Example: a specific instance or illustration that demonstrates a point

Fact: a piece of information that most people generally agree to be true

Main Idea: the statement or argument that an author tries to communicate

Outline: a tool developed during pre-writing that provides a visual of a paper's organization and ideas

Paraphrase: rewording the words of another person in order to explain the text's purpose or to add clarity to the author's argument

Quotation: the direct words of a source

Research Journal: a record of the overall research process

Research Notes: a detailed record of source information you find during your research

Summary: a few sentences that explain a large amount of information

Visual Learning: learning information through pictures, shapes, and colors

Working Bibliography: a running list of sources you plan to use in your paper

Works Cited: a page at the end of your research paper that includes full bibliographic citations of each source in your essay

Writing Process: a strategy that breaks up a writing assignment into five stages: pre-writing, drafting, revising, editing, and submitting

Lesson 8.4

Identifying Types of Sources

In any research assignment, your writing is better when you've used sources to explain and support your ideas. However, some sources fit better than others in certain situations.

Imagine that you notice your car making a weird sound when you step on the brakes. You are not an expert in brake repair, so you need to find someone who can help you determine the problem.

You could ask any of the following sources for advice:

- An online forum about classic car restoration
- Your cousin who is an auto mechanic
- A book about the history of car manufacturing
- A friend who had her brakes fixed last month

How do you know which one would be the best choice in this situation? While all of these sources might be able to share interesting and useful information, your cousin who is an auto mechanic is best because he or she probably has first-hand experience repairing brakes.

When you are writing, your **purpose** and **audience** should influence the sources you choose. For example, a book about the history of car manufacturing would be an excellent source for a paper about Henry Ford. An article about local auto repair shops, however, would benefit more from an interview with your friend.

In this lesson, you will learn to group sources into two main categories:

Primary vs. Secondary

Popular vs. Scholarly

You can then use this information to help you choose the best possible sources for your writing.

Helpful Hint

Your instructor usually has specific instructions about the types of sources you should use in a paper. If these details are not included in the assignment guidelines, be sure to double-check with your instructor directly.

Primary vs. Secondary

Primary sources include original documents, first-hand accounts, speeches, research findings, and works of art. All of these items are considered primary if they were authored or created by the original source. Here are some examples:

Primary Source	Examples
Original documents	• The Declaration of Independence • *The Giver* by Lois Lowry • A letter written by Abraham Lincoln
First-hand accounts	• Video footage of a robbery • An interview with an eyewitness • A Yelp! review of a restaurant
Speeches	• The Gettysburg Address by Abraham Lincoln • "I Have a Dream" by Martin Luther King • "The Luckiest Man" by Lou Gehrig
Research findings	• Average SAT scores in 2014 • The results of an experiment • Responses from a survey
Works of art	• The *Mona Lisa* by Leonardo da Vinci • "Hey Jude" by the Beatles • *Gone with the Wind* directed by Victor Fleming

Primary sources are useful because they allow you to get as close as possible to the source of information. You can then draw your own conclusions about how that information supports the purpose of your paper.

Secondary sources are documents that discuss information from a primary source. The following are all examples of secondary sources:

- A newspaper article about the DREAM Act
- A research paper about cheating in college athletics
- A website about Australian wildlife
- A documentary about the history of jazz

On Your Own

In the table below, fill in the missing primary and secondary sources based on the ones already entered. The first row has been completed for you.

Primary	Secondary
A commencement address by Bill Gates	An article written in a newspaper reviewing the commencement address
	A book review of *East of Eden* by John Steinbeck
A study on birth rates in Ecuador	

The Mayflower Compact	
	A biography of Oprah Winfrey
A survey of millennials who use Tinder	

Reflection Questions

Would a photograph of a famous painting be a primary or secondary source? Why or why not?

As a researcher, you should always exercise caution when using secondary sources. If a source is too far from the original, it may be inaccurate.

Think back to when you used to play "Telephone" with your friends. A phrase that started as "My favorite sport is baseball" probably sounded more like "Buy new eyes for all" once it passed through multiple people. This same issue can affect the **credibility** of sources as well.

Secondary sources are useful when you don't have access to the original documents. For example, you may not be able to find original research on the genetic causes of diabetes. However, you can still use articles written by experts about this research.

Helpful Hint

Because Wikipedia is a secondary source that can be edited by anyone, it's not always the best choice for a writing assignment. However, every Wikipedia entry includes links to all of its sources at the bottom of the page. These links can be a great way to find both primary and secondary sources on your topic.

Reflection Questions

Think about yourself as a source of information. In what situations would you be considered a primary source? In what situations would you be considered a secondary source?

Popular vs. Scholarly

In addition to primary or secondary, sources can also be categorized as popular or scholarly. A **popular source** is a document that has been written for the general public. Sometimes, the authors of these sources are experts in their fields while other times, they are not.

Group Activity

In a group, determine if the following sources would be considered popular or scholarly sources:

- A *New York Times* article discussing different viewpoints on U.S. foreign policy
- A journal article describing the results of an experiment on the effects of sleep deprivation
- A magazine article listing the top ten vacation destinations in Europe in 2015
- An op-ed to your city paper written by a professor about his/her research
- A peer reviewed book on green energy in the developing world

A blog is an example of a popular source.

Here are some examples of popular sources:

Type	Example
Books	*The Blind Side* by Michael Lewis *Dreams from My Father* by Barack Obama
Magazines	*Popular Mechanics* *Newsweek*
Movies	*An Inconvenient Truth* directed by Davis Guggenheim *Mary Poppins* directed by Robert Stevenson
Newspapers	*The New York Times* *The Chicago Sun*
Websites	*The Poetry Foundation* *Buzzfeed*

Scholarly sources, on the other hand, are usually **academic journals**. These contain articles that have been written by experts and **peer-reviewed** by other experts.

There are a few major differences between popular and scholarly sources:

- **Appearance and length**: Articles in scholarly journals are usually much longer and more complex than those in popular sources. A scholarly article might also include charts and data tables as well as a large bibliography or **works-cited** list.
- **Intended audience**: Scholarly articles are specific to a particular field of study that is usually mentioned in the name of the academic journal. They use technical terms that would not appear in a popular article. Because the information in popular sources is written for the general public, the writing style is less formal than in scholarly articles.
- **Author expertise**: The author of a scholarly text is always an expert in an industry or field of study while the author of a popular text may or may not be. Often, the information in a popular source is written by a journalist who has researched the topic.
- **Peer review**: Scholarly articles are almost always reviewed by other experts. This means that a group of respected scholars and researchers approved the content. This is not a requirement of popular magazines or websites.

An academic journal is an example of a scholarly source.

Further Resources

Many scholarly journals also have their own websites. Here are just a few examples:

Journal of the Society for Cultural Anthropology (http://www.culanth.org/pages/about-the-journal)

American Journal of Public Health (http://ajph.aphapublications.org/)

The Journal of Popular Culture (http://www.journalofpopularculture.com/)

The Journal of Nutrition (http://jn.nutrition.org/)

The most common way to find scholarly sources is to use a **research database:** a website that allows you to search articles from hundreds of academic journals. You can access these databases through your college library. If you're unsure which database or keyword to use, check with a librarian.

The purpose and audience of your writing will determine if you should use popular or scholarly sources. If you are writing for an audience of experts, you should probably use a larger number of scholarly sources; however, if you are writing for the general public, you should probably use popular sources.

You are more likely to find scholarly articles on topics in science or health than topics in pop culture. If your instructor has required you to use a certain number of scholarly articles, consider doing preliminary research to decide if you can find enough sources for your topic.

> **Reflection Questions**
> Can you think of a situation when using a popular source would better than a scholarly source?

> **Group Activity**
> Research the following topics. Find at least two popular and two scholarly sources for each.
>
>   Changes in car safety features
>   The negative effects of sitting
>   Changing opinions about eBooks

Lesson Wrap-up

Key Terms

Academic Journal: a collection of articles written by researchers and peer-reviewed by other experts in a particular field

Audience: the people who read your writing

Credibility: what makes someone or something believable

Peer Review: when scholarly articles are reviewed by other experts in a particular field

Popular Source: a document that has been written for the general public

Primary Source: an original document, such as a first-hand account, speech, research result, or work of art

Purpose: the goal of a text

Research Database: an online collection of scholarly articles and academic journals

Scholarly Source: an academic document that has been written for an expert audience

Secondary Source: a document that discusses information from a primary source

Works Cited: a page at the end of your research paper that includes full bibliographic citations of each source in your essay

Lesson 8.5
Evaluating the Credibility of Sources

One of the main reasons for using research sources is to support your conclusions. If your sources aren't **credible**, your **audience** will have no reason to believe your claims. To make your writing as effective as possible, you must use sources that are trustworthy and relevant to your purpose.

Read the following paragraphs. Which one would you be more likely to trust?

> Because of the confusion regarding the symptoms of post-traumatic stress disorder, physicians often misdiagnose PTSD in children. A few common misdiagnoses are depression, hyperactivity, or Attention Deficit Disorder (ADD). Because these conditions all share common symptoms, professionals have trouble differentiating between them. In many cases, anxiety disorders overlap, and an individual may be suffering from more than one condition at a time. The *KidsHealth* website lists physical complaints and low academic performance as potential symptoms of PTSD in children. In addition, traumatized children often develop legitimate learning disabilities and problems with

attention and memory. Many teachers at Pickens County Middle School say that children with post-traumatic stress disorder are more likely to need remedial classes.

Because of the confusion regarding the symptoms of post-traumatic stress disorder, physicians often misdiagnose PTSD in children. A few common misdiagnoses are depression, hyperactivity, or Attention Deficit Disorder (ADD). Because these conditions all share common symptoms, professionals have trouble differentiating between them. In many cases, anxiety disorders overlap, and an individual may be suffering from more than one condition at a time. An article by T. Allen Gore notes that children with PTSD may vocalize physical complaints, such as stomachaches or headaches, with no medical basis. He also observes that the child's performance in school usually lowers significantly. In addition, traumatized children often develop legitimate learning disabilities and problems with attention and memory. Research conducted by Richard Famularo indicates that children with post-traumatic stress disorder are more likely to need remedial classes.

In the first example, the author uses information from sources that seem questionable. Even though both paragraphs share similar information, the sources mentioned in the second example seem much more trustworthy.

Reflection Questions

When you are trying to make an important decision, whom do you usually ask for advice? What makes this person trustworthy?

This lesson will discuss four steps of identifying a credible research source:

Look for Potential Bias in the Information
Make Sure the Information is Relevant
Check the Credentials of the Author or Organization
Research the Credibility of Source Material

Further Resources

The Onion is a humorous website that uses outrageous fake stories to comment on current events. Occasionally, journalists and politicians cite false information from *The Onion* without truly evaluating the site's credibility. Read this article (http://www.thedailybeast.com/articles/2012/09/29/fooled-by-the-onion-8-most-embarrassing-fails.html) to learn more about these embarrassing mistakes.

Look for Potential Bias in the Information

To begin evaluating the credibility of a source, search the text for signs of bias. **Bias** is a term used to describe a person's opinions and preferences. Although all authors have some amount of bias, a credible author will work to keep his or her writing as straightforward and honest as possible.

As you check for credibility, think about the author's **purpose**. In a biased text, the author may have a stated purpose that is different from the true purpose. Imagine that you are reading an article about the health benefits of exercise. The purpose of the text is to **inform**, but the author spends most of the article promoting a particular brand of energy bar. This text is not credible as the author has hidden his or her true purpose for writing.

A research source can also contain bias if the author is associated with a particular organization or **agenda**. For example, a commercial produced by a political party will contain information that supports that party's positions. This commercial would not be considered a credible source for most papers.

One final sign of bias is extremely positive or negative language. If the author uses an angry, sarcastic tone or disrespectful language, the text almost certainly contains bias.

To learn more about different types of bias and methods for finding bias in a text, see Lesson 3.3.

Helpful Hint

Using a questionable source in an essay or research paper can be acceptable in some situations. If you are discussing the stance of an organization, for instance, you might use the organization's website as a source. However, you would not want to use this same information to support the **argument** of your paper.

Reflection Questions

Think about a time when you had to mediate a conflict. Did you have to convey different sides of a story to each party? If so, did you notice how each person's account of what may have happened differed? How did each person's bias affect the situation? Was there value in investigating each person's bias when trying to understand what actually caused the conflict?

Make Sure the Information is Relevant

The second step in evaluating the credibility of a source is checking for **relevance**. A relevant source will help you **develop** the ideas in your paper by providing specific, **focused** information about a topic. If a text is full of general information that anyone could have written, it's probably not a credible research source.

Relevant sources are also current. For most topics, you should use sources that have been published or updated in the last five years. Topics that change rapidly, such as technology or science, may require sources from the last twelve months.

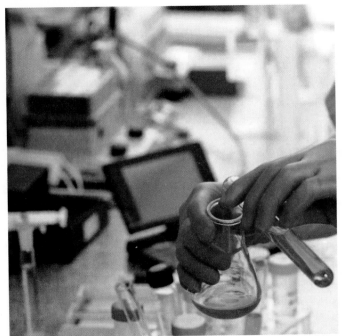

Technology develops quickly, so you must be diligent in selecting sources.

Ask yourself the following questions:

> Is the topic of the source focused or general?
> Is the information provided by the source current?
> Can it directly support one of my claims?

> **Learning Style Tip**
> If you are a **visual** learner, you can create a flowchart to help determine if a source is relevant.

Check the Credentials of the Author or Organization

The credibility of a research source can also be affected by the author's professional credentials. An expert will have extensive education and training in a topic. Think about the level of respect that this person would receive from other authors and researchers in a particular field.

Sometimes, personal experience in a topic is more important than professional credentials. For example, a famous artist would be considered an authority on art even if he or she had no formal training. In these cases, make sure that the area of experience closely matches the topic of the paper.

If you are evaluating a document or website, research the organization that published the information. A document authored by a government office or university is more likely to be credible than one authored by a for-profit company.

> **Helpful Hint**
> As you evaluate websites, pay close attention to the web addresses that end in *.gov* or *.edu* since they belong to official government or educational institutions. These sites are more likely to be credible than other websites that end in *.org* or *.com*.

As you investigate the credentials of a person or organization, be aware of potential **conflicts of interest**. For example, a pharmaceutical company would not be a good source for a paper on contaminated prescription drugs. Even though this organization is closely associated with the topic, the company's main goal is making money. This conflict of interest could lead them to omit any information that might damage the reputation of their company.

Research the Credibility of Source Material

Finally, a credible source will reference other credible sources. In research studies and articles, the authors will list their sources in the **works cited** or reference section at the end of the text. On a website, the author may include hyperlinks to sources. Skim through any source material to make sure that the information seems valid and credible.

Any time an author uses information from other persons or organizations, that material must be cited properly. If a text does not include a list of sources, the information may be plagiarized or unreliable.

A lack of sources might also indicate that the information is so general, no sources are needed. In this case, look for a better source with more specific, relevant information.

> **Helpful Hint**
>
> Sources that contain entirely original information, such as first-hand accounts, do not require sources. The author is the only source for these types of texts.

Lesson Wrap-up

Key Terms

Agenda: a person's hidden motive

Argument: a reason why you should think or act a certain way

Audience: the people who read your writing

Bias: a person's opinions and preferences

Conflict of Interest: when an author has a personal stake in a topic that affects their purpose

Credibility: what makes someone or something believable

Development: effective presentation of information and inclusion of supporting details

Focus: clear communication and support of a main idea

Informative Text: a text that gives the audience information about a topic

Paragraph: a short piece of writing that focuses on one main idea

Purpose: the goal of a text

Relevance: when information is clearly related to the text around it

Visual Learning: learning information through pictures, shapes, and colors

Works-cited Page: a page at the end of an MLA research paper that includes full bibliographic citations of each source cited in the document

Lesson 8.6
Applying MLA Styles and Formatting

Research sources support the **main idea** of your paper and give you **credibility** as an author. If you properly acknowledge your sources and format your papers consistently, your writing will be even stronger.

In English and other humanities, MLA style is what's most commonly used. The guidelines established by the **Modern Language Association (MLA)** allow readers to easily identify the sources you've used. Using MLA style also gives papers a consistent format, making them easier to read and understand.

> **Helpful Hint**
>
> Keep in mind that there are citation guidelines other than those offered by MLA. For example, disciplines like psychology may require APA citations. Always check with your professor to ensure that you are using the correct research style in your writing.

When creating your citations, MLA style recommends utilizing the "Think, Select, Organize" process, which requires you to *think* about what type of sources are relevant to your research, *select* appropriate sources and source information, and *organize* your citations in a clear manner.

In this lesson, you will learn how to:

Format Your Research Paper
Integrate Borrowed Ideas
Create a Works-Cited Page

Format Your Research Paper

When writing a research paper, it is important to use consistent formatting throughout the entire paper. Format involves things like margins, fonts, and headers. MLA style addresses two categories of formatting rules: page layout and in-text formatting.

When you set up your page layout, use these settings:

- One-inch margins
- Easy-to-read font with differentiated **italicized** and plain text options (like Times New Roman), size 12
- Left-aligned and double-spaced text
- A .5-inch indentation at the beginning of each paragraph
- Centered paper title (not italicized, underlined, in quotation marks, or bold)
- A page header .5 inches from the top right corner of each page with your last name and the page number

Additionally, you need to add a **heading** in the top left corner of the first page of your paper. It should be double-spaced and follow this template:

- Your name
- Your instructor's name
- Course name and number
- Date

Use the following guidelines for formatting in-text elements, such as numbers, names, and dates:

- Typically spell out numbers less than one hundred unless frequently used in the paper
- Choose a consistent time format for the entire paper (either 12- or 24- hour)
- When introducing the name of a person for the first time in your paper, provide the person's first and last name
- Italicize book titles and titles of longer works; put the titles of shorter or contained works in quotation marks

> Helpful Hint
>
> MLA also offers rules regarding the capitalization of words in titles and subtitles.
> **Capitalize:** nouns, pronouns, verbs, adjectives, adverbs, subordinating conjunctions
> **Do Not Capitalize:** articles, prepositions, coordinating conjunctions, *to* infinitives

Integrate Borrowed Ideas

Your reader should be able to distinguish between your original work and that of your sources. You must give credit to other authors using both in-text citations and a list of works cited. Throughout your paragraphs, **in-text citations** tell the reader which specific words and ideas come from each source. A **works-cited** page tells the reader what sources you've used in a straightforward list at the end of the paper.

To avoid **plagiarism**, you must use correct in-text citations for summarized, paraphrased, and quoted text. You can also use **signal phrases** to introduce source information, like the title and author, within a sentence.

Here are some examples:

- According to [Author's Name], ...
- In his article ["Title of Article,"] [Author's Name] argues ...
- [Author's Name] illustrates this concept in [*Title of Book*].

In-Text Citations

In-text citations provide source information in **parentheses** at the end of a sentence. These parenthetical citations allow your reader to see exactly which words and ideas you've borrowed from a particular source. In-text citations follow an author-page format. Here are a few examples of common in-text citations:

Citation with one author and single page:	(Greene 79).
Citation with one author and multiple pages:	(Brady 122-131).
Citation with two authors:	(Jackson and Brown 85).
Citation with two separate sources:	(Cleveland 55; Clark 67).
Citation with three or more authors:	(Oleksiak, et al. 155).

> **Helpful Hint**
>
> If you are citing a source in your text that is based on time instead of page numbers, like a movie or an episode in a TV series, include information on the time within the source that contains the information you are citing.
>
> (*30 Rock* 00:14:20-55)

Take a look at the following paragraph. It includes two in-text citations.

> The most effective way to learn a foreign language is frequently debated by language instructors and language learners alike. According to a 2011 study by linguist Chris Jackson, "the best way to learn a language is through early exposure; in other words, the acquisition of a foreign language is easiest at a young age" (3). In a recent documentary on language learning, scholars discuss the ease of acquiring the ability to form new sounds at a younger age, citing the challenges associated with learning tonal languages such as Chinese later in life (Thevos 01:20:20-55). Clearly, learning languages at a young age is a widely accepted method for mastering a language quickly and with ease.

The in-text citation should be as specific as possible. If you're summarizing a section of a longer text, include the page range of the borrowed information. If, however, you're summarizing an entire text, you only need to identify the author's last name.

Summaries

A **summary** explains a large amount of information in a few sentences. Using summaries makes the most sense when your readers need a broad overview of a topic but not specific details. Because summaries are general, they should only be used when you need to inform your **audience** about important background information on a topic.

Even though a summary uses completely original wording to explain the source information, you still need to credit the author using signal words and in-text citations. Keep these MLA rules in mind:

- If you're summarizing one section of a longer text, you must include an in-text citation in parentheses at the end of the final sentence. As long as you've already identified the author in a signal phrase, you can simply include the page range:

In her discussion on human rights in China, analyst Aliya Dumas suggests that there is room for improvement. In particular, Dumas notes that the treatment of women in society, policies regulating the number of children a family can have, and economic disparity between urban and rural areas are all facets of Chinese society that need to be addressed within the context of human rights. However, Dumas does note that China's economy has the potential for a more active working class and consumer rights (15-21).

- If you're summarizing the entire text, you do not need to include page numbers in the in-text citation. Instead, you can simply identify the last name(s) of the author(s) in a signal phrase or in-text citation. The following example summarizes relevant events from a novel:

Like the other protagonists in F. Scott Fitzgerald's novels, Jay Gatsby of *The Great Gatsby* is an optimist. Throughout the novel, Gatsby reaches for his dream of winning back the love of his life, Daisy Buchanan. In pursuing Daisy, however, Gatsby is unknowingly limited by his understanding of love as something that can be acquired with money. By the end of the novel, the very optimism that first enabled Gatsby to succeed is what leads him to failure.

After the summary, explain how the information relates to your argument or claim.

> Helpful Hint
> Whether or not you include an in-text citation for summaries, you will always need to include a complete and accurate bibliographic citation on the works-cited page.

Paraphrases

When you **paraphrase**, you present ideas from a source using your own words. Paraphrases are more in-depth than summaries. You should use a paraphrase when the source material contains important details or facts that support your main idea.

Paraphrases are especially important for clarifying what makes information relevant to your topic. Even though the language is yours, the ideas belong to someone else, so you still need to include an in-text citation.

Whenever you paraphrase information, make sure that the language is different from the source material. Simply changing one or two words is not enough. The following sentences are examples of good and bad paraphrasing:

Original

From early adolescence (11-12 years), children's thinking becomes more multidimensional, involving abstract as well as concrete thought. Adolescents still can be persuaded by the emotive messages of advertising, which play into their developmental concerns related to appearance, self-identity, belonging, and sexuality.

Plagiarism

Even beyond childhood, adolescents can still be persuaded by messages that play into their developmental concerns related to appearance, self-identity, sexuality, and belonging.

Correct Paraphrase

> Many food advertisements target children who do not yet understand the negative, long-term consequences of eating unhealthy foods. These advertisements also influence adolescents by playing into common developmental concerns to spark emotional responses (Story and French 3).

In the first paraphrase, the author uses the same sentence structure as the source material. Only a few words have been changed. This is not an acceptable paraphrase. The second example expresses the same ideas as the source material but uses completely different language relevant to the borrower's topic.

On Your Own

Read the passage in the "Original Text" column and paraphrase it in the space provided.

Original Text	It is widely accepted that the most efficient way to travel quickly through space is via nuclear reactor technology. In 2045, just a mere decade ago, astronaut Malea Thompson became the first human to travel to the closest star outside of our solar system, Alpha Centauri A. Scientists still debate whether or not there is other intelligent life in our galaxy, but one thing is certain: we are quickly discovering better ways to traverse the stars. An answer to this age-old question may be just a light year's reach away (Lasky and Bennett 55).
Paraphrase	

Quotations

Quotations are the direct words of a source. Quotes should be reserved for instances when the author's language is powerful or unique and when it supports your claim. Otherwise, you should paraphrase the borrowed language.

If possible, use a signal phrase to identify the original author of a quote. Place the quoted words inside **quotation marks** so that your audience knows exactly where the quotation begins and ends. When you use direct language from a source, always include an in-text citation immediately following the quote. Here's an example:

> As Alfred Mac Adam emphasizes in his introduction to *Northanger Abbey*, the "fate of women was more fixed than that of men: They could not hope for careers in trade or in the military; their educational opportunities were few ..." (xxvi).

In this example, the author's name is introduced in the signal phrase, so it does not need to be repeated in the parenthetical citation. Also notice that the page numbers are written differently because they are from the book's introduction.

Here is the corresponding works-cited entry:

Adam, Alfred Mac. Introduction. *Northanger Abbey*, by Jane Austen. Barnes & Noble Classics, 2005, pp. xiii-xxvii.

Block Quotes

If you are directly quoting prose and the quote exceeds four lines within your essay, you will need to use a block quote. A **block quote** is a special type of direct quote that indents the entirety of the quote and does not require the use of quotation marks. Place the period at the end of the quote and follow it with the in-text citation.

In a literary critique of Markus Zusak's *The Book Thief*, Dr. Alex Jones explains:

> Contrary to many other pieces of literature focusing on the Holocaust, *The Book Thief* by Markus Zusak investigates the lives of ordinary Germans while the Nazis held control over Germany. Moreover, while Zusak touches on the persecution and oppression of Jewish people in Germany, he also reinforces the fact that Jews were not the only persecuted group. For instance, Liesel, the main character, is adopted by a foster family after her mother is presumably sent to a concentration camp for belonging to the Communist Party. Zusak portrays an under-represented side of the Holocaust that prompts sincere grief and shock within the audience. (14)

The entire quote is indented by .5 inches and not placed in quotation marks. Since the signal phrase uses the source author's name, the in-text citation includes only the page number.

Keep in mind that the function of a block quote is not to simply take up space. Use block quotes only when they add support to your claim in a way that shorter quotes cannot.

Whether you are incorporating regular quotes or block quotes in your research paper, make sure you have properly explained and contextualized your quote. Simply dropping a quote into your paper without introducing or explaining it will confuse your audience. Always be sure to include your own thoughts, questions, explanations, or analyses before or after quotes.

> **Helpful Hint**
> Any time you adjust the wording of a quotation, you must take care not to distort or change the author's ideas.

Create a Works-Cited Page

The last page of your research paper should be a list of works cited. This list provides more information about each source cited in your writing. It should include every source you referenced in the body of your paper.

Generally, works-cited entries follow this structure:

[Author Name]. [Title of Source]. [Title of Container], [Other Contributors], [Version], [Number], [Publisher], [Publication Date], [Location].

The following example includes two entries:

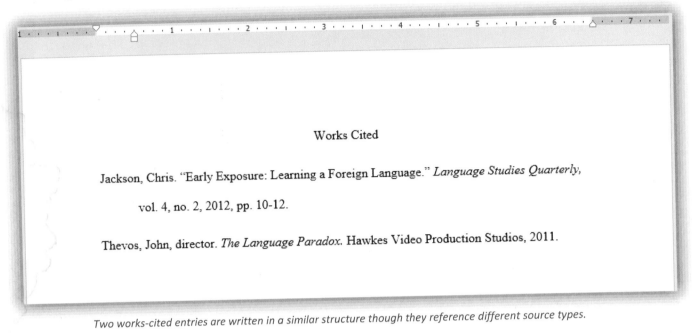

Works Cited

Jackson, Chris. "Early Exposure: Learning a Foreign Language." *Language Studies Quarterly,*

vol. 4, no. 2, 2012, pp. 10-12.

Thevos, John, director. *The Language Paradox.* Hawkes Video Production Studios, 2011.

Two works-cited entries are written in a similar structure though they reference different source types.

Notice that these entries are formatted in a similar order even though they reference two different types of sources: a journal article and a documentary.

Helpful Hint
A source may have a container. A **container** is the larger work that holds or contains your source. For example, if you are citing the chapter of a book, the container would be the book. If you are citing an episode of a television show, the television show would be the container.

Formatting the Page

Here are the key rules for formatting a works-cited page:

Header

- Maintain the page header (with your last name and page number) that appears throughout the rest of the document.

Heading

- Enter the heading, "Works Cited," on the first line of the page.
  - The heading should be centered and one inch from the top of the page.
- Add a double space between the heading and the first entry in your list.

Entries

- Double-space and alphabetize each entry in your list.
  - If a source doesn't have an author, alphabetize according to the first letter of the title.

- Left-align the first line of each entry.
  - If the entry exceeds one line, the subsequent lines should be indented. This is called a **hanging indent**.

Here's an example of a properly-formatted works-cited page:

A sample book citation

For sources with more than one author, you should only use the *Last Name, First Name* format for the first author listed. Identify all subsequent authors starting with the first name. Here's an example:

> King, Stephen, and Peter Straub. *The Talisman.* Random House, 2001.

Lesson Wrap-up

Key Terms

Audience: the people who read your writing

Block Quote: a special type of direct quote that indents the entirety of the quote and does not require the use of quotation marks

Container: the larger work that holds or contains a source

Credibility: what makes someone or something believable

Hanging Indent: a style that left-aligns the first line of an item and indents all subsequent lines

Heading: in an MLA paper, the information in the top-left corner of the first page that includes your name, your instructor's name, the course name and number, and the date

In-text Citation: a note in a paragraph that tells the reader which words and ideas come from a source

Italics: slanted letters most often used to set apart titles of longer works, important words, and foreign terms

Main Idea: the statement or argument that an author tries to communicate

MLA: the Modern Language Association is a group of scholars dedicated to research in modern languages

Page Header: in an MLA paper, the page number and author's last name, which appear in the top-right corner of the document

Paraphrase: rewording the words of another person in order to explain the text's purpose or to add clarity to the author's argument

Parentheses: a pair of punctuation marks used to add extra information to a sentence or introduce an abbreviation

Plagiarism: using the words or ideas of a source without giving credit to the author

Quotation: the direct words of a source

Quotation Marks: a pair of punctuation marks used to repeat someone else's words

Signal Phrase: used to identify source information—like the title and author—within a sentence

Summary: a few sentences that explain a large amount of information

Works-cited Page: a section at the end of an MLA-style research paper that includes full bibliographic information for each source cited in the document

Notes

Notes